English Poetry of the Romantic Period 1789–1830

Longman Literature in English Series

General Editors: David Carroll and Michael Wheeler
Lancaster University

For a complete list of titles see pages viii – ix

English Poetry of the Romantic Period 1789–1830

Second edition

J. R. Watson

 LONGMAN

London and New York

Addison Wesley Longman Limited,
Edinburgh Gate, Harlow
Essex CM20 2JE, England
and Associated Companies throughout the world.

*Published in the United States of America
by Addison Wesley Longman Inc., New York*

First published 1985
Second Edition 1992
Fourth impression 1996

ISBN 0 582 08844 5

British Library Cataloguing-in-Publication Data

A catalogue record for this book is
available from the British Library

Library of Congress Cataloging-in-Publication Data
Watson, J. R. (John Richard), 1934–
    English poetry of the romantic period, 1789–1830 / J.R. Watson. —
2nd ed.
      p.   cm. — (Longman literature in English series)
    Includes bibliographical references and index.
    ISBN 0–582–08844–5
    1. English poetry—19th century—History and criticism.
2. English poetry—18th century—History and criticism.
3. Romanticism—Great Britain. I. Title II. Series.
PR590.W33   1992
821'.709145—dc20
                                   91–36361
                                      CIP

Set in 5L in 9¹/₂/11 pt Bembo Roman
Produced through Longman Malaysia, P.

Contents

Acknowledgements

We are grateful to the following for permission to reproduce copyright
material:

Faber & Faber Ltd & Doubleday, a division of Bantam Doubleday Dell
Publishing Group, Inc for the poem 'The Lamb' from *The Collected
Poems of Theodore Roethke*, Copyright © 1961 by Theodore Roethke.

Editors' Preface

The multi-volume Longman Literature in English Series provides students of literature with a critical introduction to the major genres in their historical and cultural context. Each volume gives a coherent account of a clearly defined area, and the series, when complete, will offer a practical and comprehensive guide to literature written in English from Anglo-Saxon times to the present. The aim of the series as a whole is to show that the most valuable and stimulating approach to the study of literature is that based upon an awareness of the relations between literary forms and their historical contexts. Thus the areas covered by most of the separate volumes are defined by period and genre. Each volume offers new and informed ways of reading literary works, and provides guidance for further reading in an extensive reference section.

In recent years, the nature of English studies has been questioned in a number of increasingly radical ways. The very terms employed to define a series of this kind – period, genre, history, context, canon – have become the focus of extensive critical debate, which has necessarily influenced in varying degrees the successive volumes published since 1985. But however fierce the debate, it rages around the traditional terms and concepts.

As well as studies on all periods of English and American literature, the series includes books on criticism and literary theory, and on the intellectual and cultural context. A comprehensive series of this kind must of course include other literatures written in English, and therefore a group of volumes deals with Irish and Scottish literature, and the literatures of India, Africa, the Caribbean, Australia and Canada. The forty-seven volumes of the series cover the following areas: Pre-Renaissance English Literature, English Poetry, English Drama, English Fiction, English Prose, Criticism and Literary Theory, Intellectual and Cultural Context, American Literature, Other Literatures in English.

David Carroll
Michael Wheeler

Longman Literature in English Series

General Editors: David Carroll and Michael Wheeler
Lancaster University

Pre-Renaissance English Literature

★ English Literature before Chaucer *Michael Swanton*
English Literature in the Age of Chaucer
★ English Medieval Romance *W. R. J. Barron*

English Poetry

★ English Poetry of the Sixteenth Century (Second Edition) *Gary Waller*
★ English Poetry of the Seventeenth Century (Second Edition)
George Parfitt
English Poetry of the Eighteenth Century, 1700–1789
★ English Poetry of the Romantic Period, 1789–1830 (Second Edition)
J. R. Watson
★ English Poetry of the Victorian Period, 1830–1890 *Bernard Richards*
English Poetry of the Early Modern Period, 1890–1940
★ English Poetry since 1940 *Neil Corcoran*

English Drama

English Drama before Shakespeare
★ English Drama: Shakespeare to the Restoration, 1590–1660
Alexander Leggatt
★ English Drama: Restoration and Eighteenth Century, 1660–1789
Richard W. Bevis
English Drama: Romantic and Victorian, 1789–1890
English Drama of the Early Modern Period, 1890–1940
English Drama since 1940

English Fiction

★ English Fiction of the Eighteenth Century, 1700–1789
Clive T. Probyn
★ English Fiction of the Romantic Period, 1789–1830 *Gary Kelly*
★ English Fiction of the Victorian Period, 1830–1890 (Second Edition)
Michael Wheeler
★ English Fiction of the Early Modern Period, 1890–1940 *Douglas Hewitt*
English Fiction since 1940

English Prose

★ English Prose of the Seventeenth Century, 1590–1700 *Roger Pooley*
English Prose of the Eighteenth Century
English Prose of the Nineteenth Century

Criticism and Literary Theory

Criticism and Literary Theory from Sidney to Johnson
Criticism and Literary Theory from Wordsworth to Arnold
Criticism and Literary Theory from 1890 to the Present

The Intellectual and Cultural Context

The Sixteenth Century
★ The Seventeenth Century, 1603–1700 *Graham Parry*
★ The Eighteenth Century, 1700–1789 (Second Edition) *James Sambrook*
The Romantic Period, 1789–1830
★ The Victorian Period, 1830–1890 *Robin Gilmour*
The Twentieth Century: 1890 to the Present

American Literature

American Literature before 1880
★ American Poetry of the Twentieth Century *Richard Gray*
★ American Drama of the Twentieth Century *Gerald M. Berkowitz*
★ American Fiction 1865–1940 *Brian Lee*
★ American Fiction since 1940 *Tony Hilfer*
★ Twentieth-Century America *Douglas Tallack*

Other Literatures

Irish Literature since 1800
Scottish Literature since 1700

Australian Literature

★ Indian Literature in English *William Walsh*
African Literature in English: East and West
Southern African Literature in English
Caribbean Literature in English
★ Canadian Literature in English *W. J. Keith*

★ *Already published*

Preface to the First Edition

This book was written for the Longman Literature in English Series at the invitation of the General Editors, Professor David Carroll and Dr Michael Wheeler; I am grateful to them not only for the original suggestion but also for much kindness and encouragement during its composition.

The book's place in the series has to some extent conditioned its form. For example, I have confined myself fairly strictly within the specified dates, and have said less than I might have done in another kind of book about the development of pre-Romantic poetry; equally, I have said nothing about the Romanticism of the early Victorian period, which under different circumstances would have made a natural epilogue. And since the series will contain a book on the intellectual background of the period, I have written less than I might have done about political, social, and cultural matters: I have deliberately said nothing, for example, about the painting and sculpture of the Romantic period. Within these borderlines, I have tried to make this as useful a book for the student as possible, both in terms of general ideas and in the discussion of individual poets.

Various sections have been read by friends and colleagues, and I am deeply grateful not only to the General Editors but also to Derek Todd, David Fuller, and Michael O'Neill; and above all to Professor T. W. Craik, whose careful reading of the typescript saved me from many errors. I am also much indebted to Margaret Crane for typing the manuscript. The dedication records a long-standing debt, of another kind, to a former teacher, friend, and colleague, without whom this book might never have been written.

I have tried wherever possible to avoid repeating what I have said elsewhere about the Romantic poets, but I am conscious that in the Keats chapter there has been some inevitable recrossing of the ground which was covered in two tapes which I made in 1978 and 1982 for Norwich Tapes Ltd. I am most grateful to Norwich Tapes Ltd for permission to use this material.

Most of this book was written in the seventeenth-century splendour of Bishop Cosin's library in the University of Durham. I am most grateful to the librarians there for their help. I also wish to record my thanks to the Council of the University of Durham for allowing me sabbatical leave in the Epiphany and Easter terms of 1983.

J. R. Watson
15 June 1984

Preface to the Second Edition

I am glad that this book has been found useful, and that a second edition is now thought to be necessary: it is not often that one gets a second chance to to play an innings, or even some strokes in it, and I am grateful to all those who have made it possible. I am particularly indebted to those who reviewed the book kindly, and to those who refused to dismiss it as 'one more volume in one series too many'. Such a knee-jerk reflex must have been easy for the academic mind, and is certainly quite safe: no-one is going to condemn a reviewer for appearing to be above this kind of thing.

However, because enough undergraduates and other readers have found the book helpful, I am glad to revise the text to try to make it even more so, without destroying its principal features. In so doing, I have become aware of the extraordinary amount of quite remarkable material which has appeared during the last ten years: the number of outstanding books on Romanticism and the Romantics is astonishing – book after book breaking over the subject like waves of the sea. I have tried to find room for some of the principal insights which have emerged, although this book will, I hope, present an uncluttered view of the Romantic poets, one which will continue to be a sensible guide to students of the period who may be overwhelmed by the variety of different approaches.

The first edition of this book was written, for the most part, in 1983. Had I known then that the companion volume on the Intellectual and Cultural Context would still not have appeared eight years later, I would have been less bothered about queering the pitch for its author. As it was, I deliberately avoided the prose work of the period, both fictional and non-fictional, and also kept the study of the historical background and conditions of production to a minimum. I would also, I think, have wished to say a good deal more than I have done about Romantic Irony, bearing in mind Anne K. Mellor's important *English Romantic Irony* and the use that has been made of it, particularly by critics of Byron. If I were writing the book again from scratch – and this is a second edition, not a new book – I would, I think, acknowledge the importance of these things more clearly and uninhibitedly.

It has also become unfashionable to see the six great Romantic poets, as Harold Bloom saw them in *The Visionary Company,* as individual writers, and as major figures in their imaginative power. I happen to think that Bloom is nearer right than wrong in this, although I can perceive a wrongness as well as a rightness in his argument; I also want to acknowledge Marilyn Butler's argument about 'Revising the Canon', which criticizes the imposition of a canon of great writers and the relegation of others to the status of 'minor poets'.[1] I have accordingly moved, and partly rewritten, the last chapter in the first edition: it is now to be found before the individual chapters on the six poets, to indicate that those poets emerged from the same circumstances that gave rise to Scott and Crabbe and Southey. Professor Butler's argument seems to me on the whole to be right, and it is certainly unsatisfactory to describe these poets as 'minor'; a poet such as Clare fits into no such pattern, and Scott was a great poet in his own day. And yet I wish to preserve the chapters on the six great poets, because (in my view) Professor Butler is not entirely right; like Bloom, she is nearer right than wrong, and there is a feeling of injustice being done to certain writers, but there is also a sense that the six poets who are treated individually here are more interesting, more exciting, more sensitive to human needs, than the others, rejoicing more than others in the spirit of life that is in them.[2]

I have continued to make this an 'author-based' study: partly because I find the arrangement a useful and defining edge to a body of work, just as a book on a shelf is identified by the author's name on the spine as being different from the next book; and partly because, when intelligently read, and when seen in its proper intertextuality, the study of an individual poet can be sensitive to the particular tone, the feel, the unique experience of reading that writer and no other. So that, in addition to an understanding of the texts and their shared contexts, I am also intent on identifying something that makes Wordsworth Wordsworth, and Shelley Shelley. In so doing, however, I am concerned to see each writer in terms of the poetry, and not from a biographical point of view: I am less interested in the 'life and works' approach than in the poetry as an event, or series of events, in the history of English literature – a textual experience in that diverse history which we conveniently call 'Wordsworth' or 'Shelley'.[3]

At the same time I have become more conscious of the need to express something of the political and social history which conditioned this poetry, and I hope that the volume on the intellectual and cultural context of the period will not be too long delayed. We need to know as much as possible about the daily assumptions and cultural presuppositions of these writers, because such a knowledge helps to protect us from a subjectivity of reading; whether the assumptions are affected by spectacular events, such as the French Revolution or the fall of Napoleon, or by less obvious things such as the price of bread or the dangers of infant mortality. As Marilyn Gaull has said, 'it is on such peripheries, on the edges of great events, that most people live and where most life begins'[4]; and I have tried to recognize this in strengthening some of the historical sections of the book.

I have also added a section at the end of chapter three, entitled 'Reading the Romantic Poets', which is an attempt to say something, briefly and simply, about the impact of contemporary critical thought on the way in which the poets are read. It is important, I now think, to have some sense of what is actually involved in reading a text, and what alternatives there are; because the language of Romantic poetry, with its indeterminacies and unclosed endings, has been particularly suited to the insights of post-structuralist criticism. Those who do not wish to complicate their reading of poetry with such things may leave that section alone.

They will find the principal sections of the book largely unaltered, although I have taken the opportunity of correcting errors and making shifts of emphasis or improving the wording in places. But, as Walter Scott, perhaps the wisest and the greatest of the Romantics, wrote in the 1829 'Advertisement' to the Waverley Novels, 'where the tree falls it must lie'. This book represents a view of the Romantic poets which reflects my thinking at a particular time, and I still have much sympathy with it; as I also have with the level at which it is written. I remember, at Glasgow, early in my teaching career, an even younger colleague storming out of an encounter with some students saying angrily 'They haven't read *The Mirror and the Lamp!*' I am sure that he meant well, but I found his indignation faintly absurd, in the same way that I find somewhat absurd those who want students to know all about the current thinking of the deconstructionists on one side or the new historicists on the other; although references to their books will be found in the bibliography for those who require them.

I would like to record my thanks to my colleague at Durham, Dr Pamela Clemit, for much careful and helpful advice in the revision of this book. Its remaining shortcomings are, of course, entirely my own.

J. R. Watson
1991

Notes

1. Marilyn Butler, 'Revising the Canon', *Times Literary Supplement*, 4 December 1987.

2. The phrase is from Wordsworth, Preface to *Lyrical Ballads* (1800); in the edition by Derek Roper (Plymouth, 1987), p. 31.

3. I take the concept of 'Wordsworth' or 'Shelley' as a moment in textual history from Catherine Belsey, *John Milton: language, gender, power* (Oxford, 1988).

4. Marilyn Gaull, *English Romanticism, The Human Context* (New York, 1988), p. ix.

To John A. M. Rillie

Introduction

'My seminar on Romanticism starts tomorrow. Poor things, they
have no idea of what they have let themselves in for – . . . '
                    (W. H. Auden, letter to Ursula Niebuhr, 1943)[1]

English poetry of the Romantic period is not easy to discuss in general
terms. Nor is Romanticism, of which it is a part. Auden's wry
and compassionate humour was probably stretched to the full when
confronting his students (as he goes on to indicate in the letter) with
Kierkegaard and Reinhold Niebuhr; the present book will be more
orthodox, beginning with the suggestion that English Romantic poetry
has certain qualities which set it apart from the poetry written before it.
Such a change has been often described: subjective rather than objective,
fragmentary rather than complete, organic rather than preconceived in
form, interested in nature, the self, the wonderful, and the supernatural;
interested, too, in confusion, fluidity, indeterminacy. These matters are
easily recited, but should not be taken lightly: they are part of an
astonishing change of sensibility, under the influence of which we are
still living: our ideas about the nature of the individual, the society in
which he lives, the natural world which surrounds him, and the role
of art in society, all of these are inherited from the Romantic period.
As David Perkins has written, 'We are still living in the comet's tail of
the early nineteenth century.'[2]
    This is partly because in Western Europe the conditions for living
which still operate were being laid down at that time. There was the
awareness of radical change, of the break-up of the old stabilities of
an agricultural economy and monarchical government; there was the
drift to the cities, of which London was the first example, so that
Wordsworth, for example, could write touchingly of what was to
become a first-generation bewilderment for many:

> Above all, one thought
> Baffled my understanding, how men lived

> Even next-door neighbours, as we say, yet still
> Strangers, and knowing not each other's names.

(The Prelude, 1805, VII. 116–19)

And there was, thirdly, the dawning awareness of the coming of the machine: the machine which was made by man for his own purposes, but which has come to shape, and even in some cases to dominate, his life. The need for the individual to assert his identity against such pressures, and his intuitive turning to nature, are two of the fundamental impulses behind Romantic poetry.

We may begin with the obvious though not irrelevant observation, that English poetry of the Romantic period is dominated by six great poets. Each was conscious of the work of the others, and sometimes influenced by one or other of them; but in no sense do they ever form a 'school'. Each celebrates his own specific understanding of the world and his place in it, his insight into his own self and its relation to others, his reaction to the social and political realities of his time, and his awareness of the natural world around him. It is a poetry which is based, essentially, upon individual experience; the result is a body of work which is recognisably different from the poetry which preceded it (although signs of Romanticism can be detected earlier) but which is difficult to define without falsifying its complexity, that 'infinite complexity' of which Wordsworth wrote in the Preface to *Lyrical Ballads*:

> What then does the Poet? He considers man and the
> objects that surround him as acting and re-acting upon
> each other, so as to produce an infinite complexity of
> pain and pleasure; he considers man in his own nature and
> in his ordinary life as contemplating this with a certain
> quantity of immediate knowledge, with certain convictions,
> intuitions and deductions, which from habit acquire the
> quality of intuitions; he considers him as looking upon
> this complex scene of ideas and sensations, and finding
> everywhere objects that immediately excite in him
> sympathies which, from the necessities of his nature, are
> accompanied by an overbalance of enjoyment.[3]

Wordsworth here draws attention to two matters which are of crucial importance in the identification of Romantic poetry. The first is the almost physical sense of the poet looking about him, of the individual with his senses sharp and bright regarding the external world. The second is the accompanying sense of enjoyment. The poet 'rejoices more than other men', writes Wordsworth, 'in the spirit of life that is in him'; he delights in the world around him, and in his apprehension and understanding of it. This does not mean that his poetry ignores the evils of life: Wordsworth was one of the greatest of tragic poets, and had a deep indignation and compassion for human suffering. It does mean, however, that in his work and that of the other Romantic poets, there is an extraordinary sense of life and energy, of freshness and excitement, as they engage with the great questions raised by the self and the world. Who am I? How did I come to be as I am? What is my relationship to my fellow human beings? What are my feelings in relation to their joy and their suffering? What great moments do I wish to celebrate? What do I know of nature, or art? What is the best form of political society? What is my understanding of the past, and my hope for the future?

Each of the Romantic writers (novelists and philosophers, as well as poets) struggles to formulate answers to these questions in his own way, using the poetic technique which he has developed as an expression of his deepest self. Like the creatures in Gerard Manley Hopkins's poem, each cries 'what I do is me: for that I came'.[4] This self-expression, this authenticity, leads towards the conclusion that the main feature which the Romantic poets have in common is their individuality; this is a safe conclusion, but not entirely satisfactory, since the poets are bound to one another by intricate ties of shared ideas and responses as well. Each read the work of the others (even that of Blake, who was read by Wordsworth, certainly by 1807), and was powerfully conscious of his agreement or disagreement; an analysis of these side-glances, shared enthusiasms, and intuitive likes and dislikes will be one of the connecting threads of the present book.

The disagreements are usually concerned with the ideas which the Romantic poets had about poetry and the role of the artist, and with the reaction to great public events. It is therefore important to consider their work in relation to the features of the period which affected it, from the social and political conditions to the wider and more nebulous background of theory and practice which is called Romanticism.

Romanticism

Romanticism has many beginnings, and takes many different forms; so that in a celebrated essay, 'On the Discrimination of Romanticisms' (1924), A. O. Lovejoy argued that the word 'Romantic' should no longer be used, since it 'has come to mean so many things that, by itself, it means nothing. It has ceased to perform the function of a verbal sign.'[5] One of his solutions was to recommend the use of the word 'Romanticism' in the plural only; another was to recommend closer analysis of what Romantic ideas consist of. He gave three examples: the preference for nature over art, and for the primitive over the sophisticated; the idea that Classic art is limited, and Romantic art is infinite, Schiller's *Kunst des Unendlichen*; and the unquestionably Romantic Chateaubriand's belief in art and its rules.

Lovejoy's essay had a considerable influence, although, as he foresaw, it did not stop people talking about Romanticism. An intellectually respectable justification for doing so was provided in 1949 by René Wellek, in his essay 'The Concept of Romanticism in Literary History'.[6] Wellek discreetly defended the use of period terms, holding them to be not arbitrary labels but 'names for systems of norms'; and after a learned discussion of the use of the word 'Romantic' in its own time throughout Europe, he argued that 'on the whole there was really no misunderstanding about the meaning of "romanticism" as a new designation for poetry, opposed to the poetry of neoclassicism, and drawing its inspiration and models from the Middle Ages and the Renaissance'. In this admirable common-sense view, we can go on speaking of 'Romanticism', and be reasonably certain of what we mean. He provided a magisterial synthesis himself:

> we find throughout Europe the same conceptions of poetry
> and of the workings and nature of the poetic imagination,
> the same conception of nature and its relation to man,
> and basically the same poetic style, with a use of imagery,
> symbolism, and myth which is clearly distinct from that of
> eighteenth-century neoclassicism.[7]

This was subsequently sharpened and abbreviated to 'imagination for the view of poetry, nature for the view of the world, and symbol and myth for poetic style'.

In the chapters which follow, these unifying ideas will be found in the poetry of the major Romantic poets; although the principal purpose will not be to unearth them in each case, but rather to show how each poet makes his own discoveries about himself and the world. Wellek, after all, was concerned with an attempt to give meaning to the *concept* of Romanticism, and this is a problem in the history of ideas; the major Romantic poets were struggling with the expression, in its most authentic form, of their own individual perceptions and visions. They do not talk about Romanticism, because Romanticism did not exist as an idea for them; it is only with hindsight that we formulate their work as part of a major shift in the history of ideas in Western Europe.

I have chosen to discuss the work of each of the major poets separately. They are the six who were so memorably named by Harold Bloom as 'the visionary company'. They were those who, to paraphrase Wordsworth, rejoiced more than other men in the spirit of life that was in them; as Bloom put it, 'what allies six great poets so different in their reactions to the common theme of imagination is a quality of passion and largeness, in speech and in response to life'.[8] At the same time, these poets shared with others the conditions of the age. They write poems that are shaped by the events of the age, and whose form and substance depend on methods of production and assumptions of readership, and it could be argued that those poems are best appreciated when they are seen as emerging from the great mass of poetry written by poets who are frequently ignored.

I have tried, therefore, to relate the work of the major poets to the intellectual and emotional assumptions which helped to shape it, to see it in the context of the period, and to relate it to the work of those other poets who were writing at the same time; four chapters are intended to say something about the conditions which determined the way in which the great poets set about their work.

One of these is obviously the political and social background of the time, and the writings of those who discussed such things. Indeed, one of the ways of discussing Romanticism which has superseded Wellek's account, based as it was on the German aesthetic tradition, is to view it, as Marilyn Butler has done, in its social, intellectual, and political context. It was no accident, it would seem, that such innovative poetry flourished at a time of new political initiatives: Hazlitt said of Wordsworth's poetry that it 'partakes of, and is carried along with, the revolutionary movement of our age'.[9] Throughout his sharp and intelligent criticism, Hazlitt was keen to emphasize the relationship between the 'new' poetry of his forward-looking contemporaries and the attempts to remake society in a new and better form, most notably in the French Revolution. This is no doubt partly a matter of readiness to experiment; but it is also due to the remarkable influence of writers such as Rousseau and Godwin, so that any student of Romantic poetry should have some knowledge of what they say. It was an age, too, of sharp differences and deeply held convictions in politics. As Kelvin Everest has written, 'The Romantics worked in a cultural milieu which was powerfully charged with conflicts of political principle and party.'[10]

The second feature of importance is the development of an interest in certain subjects: in nature especially, but also in dreams and fairy-tales, the Gothic world of enchantment and magic; and, above all, in the self, that subject of endless enquiry, that absorbing, preoccupying individuality which is loved and hated, which imprisons and gives freedom, which above all is the self of multiple and bewildering and often contrary experience. Experience, social, political, personal, is shaped by the perceiving self, and in turn experience shapes that self. It is the readiness to encounter the various and compelling forms of experience which distinguishes the Romantic poets from their predecessors: they shape their poetry out of a certain daring of the mind. W. B. Yeats's poem 'A Crazed Girl' expresses this, to my mind, better than any prose summary could do:

> That crazed girl improvising her music,
> Her poetry, dancing upon the shore,
> Her soul in division from itself
> Climbing, falling she knew not where,
> Hiding amid the cargo of a steamship,
> Her knee-cap broken, that girl I declare
> A beautiful lofty thing, or a thing
> Heroically lost, heroically found.

Yeats saw the centre of the girl's experience as paradoxical, disabling yet beautiful, in division and yet dancing, lost and found, climbing and falling. It is an assertion of herself against all the pressures of ordinariness and conformity which would undermine the original self, a song against the mechanical and the soulless. Yeats perceived a gradual enveloping passiveness before 'a mechanized nature'; it was a process

> that lasted to our own day with the exception of a brief
> period between Smart's *Song of David* and the death of
> Byron, wherein imprisoned man beat upon the door.[11]

Yeats's awareness of the Romantic period as the beating on the door (as his William Blake 'beat upon the wall') suggests the third, and most important assumption that determines the outlook of the Romantic poets. This is their understanding of the poet and his function. Yeats's poem ends with the girl singing out of disaster and triumph, the singer asserting her right to sing, making a sound that is beautiful but 'no common intelligible sound':

> No matter what disaster occurred
> She stood in desperate music wound,
> Wound, wound, and she made in her triumph
> Where the bales and the baskets lay
> No common intelligible sound
> But sang, 'O sea-starved, hungry sea'.

The concept is heroic, and it is in this sense of authenticity and its preservation that I wish to see the major Romantic poets as heroic and serious. I have therefore begun with a study of the way in which they see poetry and the poet.

Some discussion of eighteenth-century poetry is inevitable, but I have stopped short of trying to plot the paths of pre-Romantic theory and practice in any detail. That would require another book, and would be covering the same ground as another book in this series. Some reference to Gray, Thomson, and Cowper will be found here, but the brief notice of their work is intended only to present them as contributors to the central preoccupations of the Romantics and not as historical predecessors in the procession of English poets. They contribute, we should understand, to the complex pattern of thought and feeling which is made up of all three divisions which follow. The poet, the context, and the subject are all one: the subject is chosen by the poet, who is influenced by the age; the subject *is* the self, *is* the age, and the age is shaped by the poet who writes about it. So, according to Shelley, poets are 'the unacknowledged legislators of the world'. In 'A Defence of Poetry' he noted that 'Poets . . . were called in the earlier epochs of the world legislators or prophets: a poet essentially comprises and unites both these characters.'[12] This conception of the poet-prophet makes an appropriate starting-place.

Notes

1. Ursula Niebuhr, 'Memories of the 1940s', in *W. H. Auden, a tribute*, edited by Stephen Spender (London, 1974), p. 112.

2. David Perkins, *The Quest for Permanence* (Cambridge, Mass., 1959), p. 3.

3. *The Poetical Works of William Wordsworth*, edited by E. de Selincourt and H. Darbishire, 5 vols (Oxford, 1940–49), II, 395–96.

4. 'As Kingfishers catch Fire, Dragonflies draw Flame', *The Poems of Gerard Manley Hopkins*, edited by W. H. Gardner and N. H. Mackenzie, fourth edition (London, 1967).

5. A. O. Lovejoy, 'On the Discrimination of Romanticisms', reprinted in *English Romantic Poets, Modern Essays in Criticism*, edited by M. H. Abrams (New York, 1960), pp. 3–24.

6. Reprinted in Wellek's *Concepts of Criticism* (New Haven and London, 1963), pp. 128–98; the essay which follows, 'Romanticism Re-examined', should also be consulted.

7. *Concepts of Criticism*, pp. 160–61.

8. Marilyn Gaull, *English Romanticism, The Human Context* (New York and London, 1988), Preface, p. vii.

9. 'Mr Wordsworth', in *The Spirit of the Age: The Complete Works of William Hazlitt*, edited by P. P. Howe, 21 vols (London, 1930–34), XI, 87.

10 Kelvin Everest, *English Romantic Poetry* (Milton Keynes and Philadelphia, 1990), p. 86.

11. W. B. Yeats, introduction to *The Oxford Book of Modern Verse* (Oxford, 1936), p. xxvii.

12. *The Complete Works of Percy Bysshe Shelley*, edited by R. Ingpen and W. E. Peck, 10 vols (London and New York, 1965), VII, 112.

Chapter 1
The Poet

Prophecy

Thomas Gray's *The Bard* was published in 1757. It was founded, according to the Advertisement,

> on a Tradition current in Wales, that EDWARD the First, when he completed the conquest of that country, ordered all the Bards, that fell into his hands, to be put to death.

Presumably this was because poets were capable of encouraging a spirit of national resistance to tyrants: the poem is a political statement of the strongest kind. In this case the Bard is portrayed in the Welsh landscape, blown by the wind, denouncing the conqueror and frightening the bravest of his soldiers:

> 'Ruin seize thee, ruthless King!
> 'Confusion on thy banners wait,
> 'Tho' fann'd by Conquest's crimson wing
> 'They mock the air with idle state . . .'
> Such were the sounds, that o'er the crested pride
> Of the first Edward scatter'd wild dismay,
> As down the steep of Snowdon's shaggy side
> He wound with toilsome march his long array.
> Stout Glo'ster stood aghast in speechless trance:
> 'To arms!' cried Mortimer, and couch'd his quiv'ring lance.
>
> (ll. 1–4, 9–14)

This is a deliberate *tour de force*, a dramatic encounter between a single poet and a vast army, between a doomed, powerless figure and the legendary medieval warrior-heroes; it is an extraordinary feat of imaginative reconstruction on Gray's part, which involved a radical rediscovery of the spectacular figure of the inspired poet and a sympathetic awareness of the sublime and savage landscape. Both Bard and landscape stand inviolable: the Bard in his integrity, the landscape in its sublimity, together defy the conqueror to do his worst, and the foretelling of history which follows makes it clear that the Welsh nation will survive, to emerge again triumphantly in the figure of Henry Tudor. This fore-knowledge makes the triumph of Edward I seem empty as well as cruel, and adds more force to the portrayal of the Bard as the poet of defiance, right, and truth. He, and the landscape in which he stands, are emblematic of inspired and justified anger:

> On a rock whose haughty brow
> Frowns o'er old Conway's foaming flood,
> Robed in the sable garb of woe,
> With haggard eyes the Poet stood;
> (Loose his beard, and hoary hair
> Stream'd, like a meteor, to the troubled air)
> And with a Master's hand, and Prophet's fire,
> Struck the deep sorrows of his lyre.
> 'Hark, how each giant-oak, and desert cave,
> 'Sighs to the torrent's awful voice beneath!
> 'O'er thee oh King! their hundred arms they wave,
> 'Revenge on thee in hoarser murmurs breathe . . .'
>
> (ll. 15–26)

According to Gray's note, this portrayal was taken from 'a well-known picture of Raphael, representing the Supreme Being in the vision of Ezekiel'. The occurrence of the Old Testament prophet Ezekiel here suggests that Gray owed a debt to a long-standing prophetic idea, to the tradition of the inspired, nationally-conscious prophet-poet: he was inspired to complete the poem by the visit to Cambridge of a blind Welsh harper, Parry who was a living example of the traditional Celtic bard. As a blind instrumentalist, Parry was the living successor of the ancient poets and prophets, in a line which went back to Homer and Teiresias; the remembrance of their greatness had been a comfort to Milton when confronting his own blindness, mindful of

> Blind *Thamyris* and blind *Maeonides*,
> And *Tiresias* and *Phineas*, prophets old:
>
> (*Paradise Lost*, III. 35–36)

and as John Dixon Hunt has pointed out, Gray called *The Bard* 'the British Ode' (British in the sense that it was concerned with the history and development of Britain, and not just of England).[1] As the many paintings of the subject indicate, it was a powerful localizing of an ancient tradition, and it became a great encouragement to the Romantic poets in the development of the bardic or prophetic strain in their poetry and of national consciousness. John Martin painted the Bard, looking down upon the tiny armies below, thus producing an image of the superior poet-figure even in defeat; and the image lingered on in Blake. According to Charles Lamb:

> he has *seen* the old Welsh bards on Snowdon . . . and has painted them from memory (I have seen his paintings), and asserts them to be as good as the figures of Raphael and Angelo but not better, as they had precisely the same retrovisions and prophetic visions. . . .[2]

Gray's image indicated that the prophetic tradition could become a British tradition, in response to the stirring times and in the figures of inspired poets, who saw their role as responding to events with the same kind of uncompromising integrity as the defiant figure on Snowdon.

Prophecy and imagination

> Now it came to pass in the thirtieth year, in the fourth month, in the fifth day of the month, as I was among the captives by the river of Chebar, that the heavens were opened, and I saw visions of God.
>
> (Ezekiel 1.1)

It may seem strange to introduce a study of the Romantic imagination with a quotation from the Old Testament, but it is not entirely random: Blake, Wordsworth, and Coleridge knew the first chapter of Ezekiel well, and quoted from it; and, as we have seen, Gray's *The Bard* contains a portrait based on Raphael's picture of Ezekiel's vision. Ezekiel was traditionally thought of as the most imaginative of the major prophets, and in his opening verse he is a prototype of the Romantic poet as visionary. He carefully records both time (the thirtieth year, the fourth month, the fifth day) and place (by the river of Chebar) and circumstance (among the captives) before announcing that 'the heavens were opened, and I saw visions of God'. The pattern is one that is common in Romantic poetry: the visionary moment is preceded by a careful note of time, and place, and circumstance. In *The Prelude*, for instance, the boat-stealing experience is preceded (in the 1805 text) by information that the young Wordsworth was at Patterdale, a schoolboy staying the night on his way home for the holidays; the so-called 'dedication' passage in Book IV comes on the way home after a dance; and the great apostrophe to imagination itself comes after a confused and disappointing moment in the Alps. Similarly, the fine sublimities of 'Tintern Abbey' are given the circumstantial and almost pedantically accurate title, 'Lines written a few miles above Tintern Abbey, on revisiting the banks of the Wye during a tour, July 13 1798'. The vision is associated with the specific moment; more important, it indicates the ever-present possibility of vision. When Blake painted his water-colour, *Ezekiel's Wheels*, he drew Ezekiel lying, not beside the river but half in it, emerging from the water which is, for Blake, the symbol for materialism; a figure totally immersed in 'the sea of time and space' is Newton, whose understanding of the world Blake deplored because it was, in his view, 'single vision' – that is, scientific and empirical, bound by material evidence. Blake, who had dined with Isaiah and Ezekiel, knew differently.

The ability of the Romantic poet to use his imagination in such a way is a fundamental feature of his art: it enables him to transform his world and to escape from it. The restrictions of his day-to-day existence can vanish as he either exercises a power over the world, or enters a world of his own: in the latter case Keats, in the 'Ode to a Nightingale', can fly away with the bird 'on the viewless wings of Poesy' into a dark, sweet-smelling world of beauty and immortality, through which he follows the nightingale's voice back in time and even beyond time, into a land where the song

> Charmed magic casements, opening on the foam
> Of perilous seas, in faery lands forlorn.
>
> (ll. 69–70)

Once this possibility is recognized, as the Romantic poets so clearly do, the imagination enjoys a creative freedom which it consciously seeks to exploit, either for the revelation of spiritual truth, or for political change, or purely for excitement and wonder, for the enriching of life by the extraordinary, the marvellous, or the sinister. This creativity of the imagination is God-like, in that its work parallels that of God in creation. 'For Blake', wrote C. M. Bowra, 'the imagination is nothing less than God as He operates in the human soul.'[3] And, as Bowra points out, Coleridge sees the parallel too: 'The primary IMAGINATION I hold to be the living Power and prime Agent of all human Perception, and as a repetition in the finite mind of the eternal act of creation in the infinite I AM.'[4] The word 'imagination' is sometimes written thus, in capitals, to emphasize its importance, as Blake, for instance, writes in a letter (to Dr Trusler, 23 August 1799): 'I know that This World Is a World of IMAGINATION & Vision.' The passage is notable for its emphasis on the importance, not just of the imagination, but of the individual use of it:

> I see Everything I paint In This World, but Every body does not see alike. To the Eyes of a Miser a Guinea is more beautiful than the Sun, & a bag worn with the use of Money has more beautiful proportions than a Vine filled with Grapes. The tree which moves some to tears of joy is in the Eyes of others only a Green thing that stands in the way. Some See Nature all Ridicule and Deformity, & by these I shall not regulate my proportions; & Some Scarce see Nature at all. But to the Eyes of the Man of Imagination, Nature is Imagination itself.[5]

By the last sentence, Blake was suggesting something which is more important to the visionary than the Keatsian escape, and that is the domination of the external world by the imagination. The discussion of the miser and of the green tree is an example of the way in which Blake saw the apprehension of the external world as shaped by the internal mind. Wordsworth saw the relationship between the mind and the external world as one of joyous harmony, in which the world influenced the poet's mind, and his mind responded to provide a reciprocal influence on his apprehension of the world. Such ideas about the mind mark a major transition from the eighteenth-century philosophies of the mind, principally those of Locke and Hartley, in which the mind was thought of as the recorder of sense impressions. In Hartley's 'Theory of Association', for instance, the impressions were placed upon the receiving mind, usually by the eye, and they remained there to combine with other impressions, building up from simple ideas to complex ones. Coleridge (who had at one stage been very impressed by this theory, and had called his son Hartley) attacked this view in *Biographia Literaria* (1817) on two grounds: that it did not allow free will (since all actions were determined by the accumulation of sense impressions), and that it could give no idea of God, since the reliance on the information of the senses precluded any speculation as to the cause of those impressions. As a counter to Hartley's theory, Coleridge proposed his own scheme of mental operation, which involved a division of the faculties into three: fancy, the primary imagination, and the secondary imagination. Some critics have questioned the validity of this,[6] but for most readers of Romantic poetry the distinction between fancy and imagination corresponds to something which is quite easily recognizable, the operation of the mind at different levels of inspiration and achievement. Indeed, Coleridge claimed that his discovery was itself based upon experience, in his case an early reading of Wordsworth's 1793 poem, *Descriptive Sketches*.[7] He describes how he became convinced

> that fancy and imagination were two distinct and widely different faculties, instead of being, according to the general belief, either two names with one meaning, or at furthest the lower and higher degree of one and the same power.[8]

As this passage indicates, fancy and imagination had been generally thought of as synonymous, in Dr Johnson's dictionary for example, and in Blake's letter to Dr Trusler quoted above, which continues: 'This World is all One continued Vision of Fancy or Imagination.'[9] The complementary quality to fancy-imagination, in earlier theories of poetry, had been judgement. Coleridge redrew the lines as follows:

> The IMAGINATION then I consider either as primary, or secondary. The primary IMAGINATION I hold to be the living Power and prime Agent of all human Perception, and as a repetition in the finite mind of the eternal act of creation in the infinite I AM. The secondary I consider as an echo of the former, co-existing with the conscious will, yet still as identical with the primary in the *kind* of its agency, and differing only in *degree*, and in the *mode* of its operation. It dissolves, diffuses, dissipates, in order to re-create; or where this process is rendered impossible, yet still, at all events, it struggles to idealize and to unify. It is essentially *vital*, even as all objects (as objects) are essentially fixed and dead.
>
> FANCY, on the contrary, has no other counters to play with but fixities and definites . . . equally with the ordinary memory it must receive all its materials ready made from the law of association.[10]

The imagination is seen as God-like in both its primary and secondary operations. The primary imagination perceives the world, and in so doing it becomes active and creative (described by Blake as seeing 'through the eye' rather than 'with the eye'); it creates the world around it, performing a function which repeats the act of Creation in the mind of God. Every act of perception, in this theory, becomes in its own way an act of creation. But it goes further than this, creating its own objects by dissolving and remaking those of the external world. Such new creation is analogous to the work of God the Creator in that it does not repeat what is already there but creates something absolutely new. The employment of the imagination in this way therefore comes to be seen as the operation of those faculties in man which are most God-like. They are mysterious and holy. This word 'holy' is one which recurs in Romantic poetry, in Blake, of course, in Wordsworth, who writes of 'the holy life of music and of verse',[11] and in Keats, who described himself certain of nothing except 'the holiness of the Heart's affections and the truth of Imagination'.[12] As C. D. Thorpe has pointed out, Keats saw the imagination as essentially connected with the heart[13]; and the heart, 'the human heart by which we live' (as Wordsworth called it) is of great importance to the Romantics because of its dual function as the seat of the affections and the impulse behind the imagination. The imagination can, and should, possess the whole of a person; the poet, in Coleridge's words, 'brings the whole soul of man into activity', and

> diffuses a tone and spirit of unity, that blends, and (as it were) *fuses*, each into each, by that synthetic and magical power, to which we have exclusively appropriated the name of imagination.[14]

A visionary so transfigured is found at the end of 'Kubla Khan'. He is recognizable by his flashing eyes and floating hair, and those who see him are frightened because he has brought with him a vision which is beyond the normal capacity of human beings to perceive:

> Weave a circle round him thrice,
> And close your eyes with holy dread,
> For he on honey-dew hath fed,
> And drunk the milk of Paradise.

Like Gray's Bard with his streaming hair, this figure is seen with wonder and dread. This fear and awe is, in Wordsworth, turned upon himself: it is his own powers that he views with astonishment, which is one reason why he has been thought of as egotistical (by Keats, and by others since); but if he is egotistical it is, paradoxically, a humble egotism, as Wordsworth contemplates with awe the powers within himself and the great possibilities of the human imagination. This is made clear in the Preface to *The Excursion*:

> Not Chaos, not
> The darkest pit of lowest Erebus,
> Nor aught of blinder vacancy, scooped out
> By help of dreams – can breed such fear and awe

As fall upon us often when we look
Into our Minds, into the Mind of Man –
My haunt, and the main region of my song.

(ll. 35–41)

And as Blake and Coleridge gave capital letters to the word 'imagination', so Wordsworth places it alone at the beginning of a line to emphasize its power and uniqueness:

Imagination! here the power so called
Through sad incompetence of human speech,
That awful Power rose from the mind's abyss
Like an unfathered vapour that enwraps,
At once, some lonely traveller.

(The Prelude, VI. 525–9)

The exclamation mark (from the 1805 text of The Prelude) is important, for it makes the word into a shout of recognition, or wonder; it is the confrontation with the other that is yet revealed within the self, man rejoicing in the God-like in himself.

This recognition of power within the individual is one reason for the intense interest in the artist's self in this period. Instead of being primarily concerned with the subject, or with the specific demands of the verse form, or with the audience, Romantic criticism was concerned with the poet; poetry became less a matter of imitation, and more preoccupied with expression. This has repercussions for the form of Romantic poetry, as we shall see; for the moment we may observe the radical shift of attention from the external properties and the audience of poetry to the poet's mind, feelings, and ideas. This complex movement has been superbly charted by M. H. Abrams in his labyrinthine study, The Mirror and the Lamp, which begins with examples of the idea that art is a mirror which reflects nature (as it appears, for example, in Dr Johnson's life of Gray in Lives of the Poets) and demonstrates the ascendancy of metaphors of the mind such as the fountain and the lamp. Abrams shows that there are various accompaniments to this movement: an interest in the passion of the artist (which can be traced back to Longinus), a belief that in primitive times poetry had been a natural expression of feeling, and a turning towards poetry as music (instead of poetry as painting, ut pictura poesis) so that the lyric becomes the poetic norm. What Abrams calls 'the criterion of intensity' becomes important in literary criticism; it is evidence that the imagination is at work, functioning in its most natural and impressive way. Its symbol is the Aeolian harp: the harp that gives out music when blown upon by the wind. And as the wind bloweth where it listeth, so the Romantic poet never knows the moment of his inspiration with any certainty. It is mysterious, natural, instinctive, and holy, the working of the human spirit inspired by something greater than itself.

Prophecy and form

When he was reading the first chapter of Ezekiel, Coleridge came to the vision of the four-faced, four-winged cherubim, and the chariot with wheels in verses 19 and 20:

> And when the living creatures went, the wheels went by them; and when the living creatures were lifted up from the earth, the wheels were lifted up.

> Whithersoever the Spirit was to go, they went, thither was their spirit to go; and the wheels were lifted up over against them: for the spirit of the living creature was in the wheels.

The sense of sympathetic movement is clear: the wheels and the spirit are one. Coleridge uses this as an emblem for certain features of Romantic poetry which are central to its mode of operation, and on two occasions he appropriates the properties of Ezekiel's vision for his own purposes: in *The Statesman's Manual* (1816) he describes the poetic qualities of the Scriptures, and contrasts them with current historical writing:

> The histories and political economy of the present and preceding century partake in the general contagion of its mechanic philosophy, and are the *product* of an unenlivened generalized Understanding. In the Scriptures they are the living *educts* of the Imagination; of that reconciling and mediatory power, which incorporating the Reason in Images of the Sense, and organizing (as it were) the flux of the Senses by the permanence and self-circling energies of the Reason, gives birth to a system of symbols, harmonious in themselves, and consubstantial with the truths, of which they are the *conductors*. These are the Wheels which Ezekiel beheld, when the hand of the

> Lord was upon him, and he saw visions of God as he sate
> among the captives by the river of Chebar. *Whithersoever*
> *the Spirit was to go, the wheels went, and thither was their*
> *spirit to go: for the spirit of the living creature was in the wheels*
> *also.*[15]

Coleridge was quoting from memory, or he altered the wording deliberately: either way, his variation on Ezekiel makes the point more clearly. He is arguing that in a living educt of the imagination, something which is issuing out from the creative mind as from a fountain or a spring, the words and their meaning cannot be separated. This is very different from the neo-Classical precepts of the eighteenth century, as P. W. K. Stone has demonstrated: he points out that language, for the rhetoricians of the period, was 'the dress of thought'. There was considerable attention to rules and principles of style, and to theories of composition. Stone quotes Alexander Gerard's *Essay on Genius* (1774), in which there is a revealing conjunction of the words 'mechanical or instinctive', suggesting that behind them both is the theory of association.[16] The process of composition is a conscious one, in which language is employed to produce certain effects. Figurative language, for instance, was a striking example of the dress of thought: it was employed deliberately and ornamentally, to contribute to 'vivacity' and to enliven the subject.[17]

For Coleridge, the process of language was completely different, and it was linked to that of the imagination itself. A poem was not the clothing for a thought but an organic and living creation, the thing itself. 'I would endeavour', he wrote to William Godwin, 'to destroy the old antithesis of *Words & Things*, elevating, as it were, Words into Things, & living Things too.'[18] So he was determined that there should not be a rhetorician's separation of the subject-matter and the expression:

> The truths and the symbols that represent them move in
> conjunction and form the living chariot that bears up (for
> *us*) the throne of the Divine Humanity.[19]

The symbol is the point at which the imagination, the divine power within man, becomes visible and defined; but the symbol is the truth of the imagination itself. It is found in all educts of the imagination, but especially in the Scriptures. There the nature and purposes of God are revealed, and in this process prophecy and history, inspiration and fact, are united: 'the Sacred History becomes prophetic, the Sacred Prophecies historical, while the power and substance of both inhere in its Laws, its Promises, and its Comminations'.[20] If the Scriptures are prototypes of the imaginative work, in which the imagination is incarnated as it were, they are also primary examples of a poetry in which disparate elements are unified. The words become 'living words', the 'living educts of the imagination', as Coleridge described them in the Preface to *Aids to Reflection*, where again he quotes Ezekiel:

> The wheels of the intellect I admit them to be: But such as Ezekiel beheld in *the visions of God* as he sate among the captives by the river of Chebar.[21]

The image from Ezekiel is a good example of Coleridge's ability to select a meaningful symbol from Scripture: as words are to meaning, so are the wheels to the chariot – inseparable, for the words are the meaning, and in the conjunction of words/wheels and meaning/chariot there is an imaginative perception of a resemblance hitherto unremarked. So Coleridge is here practising what he is preaching: the image is consubstantial with the truth of which it is the conductor, and it is alive with a new perception. It is a concrete image for an abstract idea, as metaphor is: when Coleridge describes words as 'the wheels of the intellect', he is fusing two dissimilar things into a new and living organism.

The kind of theory to which Coleridge's ideas are opposed is found, in a purposely simple form, in one of Lord Chesterfield's letters to his son. Prose, says Lord Chesterfield, is the language of common conversation, but poetry 'is a more noble and sublime way of expressing one's thoughts':

> For example, in prose, you would say very properly, 'it is twelve of the clock at noon', to mark the middle of the day; but this would be too plain and flat in poetry; and you would rather say, 'the Chariot of the Sun had already finished half its course.' In prose you would say, 'the beginning of the morning' or 'the break of day'; but that would not do in verse; and you must rather say, 'Aurora spread her rosy mantle.' Aurora, you know, is the Goddess of the morning. This is what is called poetical diction.
>
> (letter xxv, 26 April 1739)

The idea that poetry is some kind of dressing up of commonplaces with a wardrobe of figures of speech is, of course, deeply foreign to Coleridge's way of thinking. It is a deliberate separation of the subject-matter from the expression; and it may well be that Coleridge was actually thinking of such classical comparisons as Aurora spreading

her rosy mantle when he compared the poetry of the Hebrew scriptures
with that of the Greek and Latin authors:

> It must occur to every Reader that the Greeks in their
> religious poems address always the Numina Loci, the
> Genii, the Dryads, the Naiads, &c &c – All natural Objects
> were dead – mere hollow Statues – but there was a Godkin
> or Goddessling *included* in each – In the Hebrew Poetry
> you find nothing of this poor Stuff – as poor in genuine
> Imagination, as it is mean in Intellect – At best, it is
> but Fancy, or the aggregating Faculty of the mind – not
> *Imagination*, or the *modifying*, and co-adunating Faculty.
> This the Hebrew Poets appear to me to have possessed
> beyond all others – & next to them the English. In the
> Hebrew Poets each Thing has a Life of it's own, & yet
> they are all one Life. In God they move & live, & *have*
> their Being – not *had*, as the cold System of Newtonian
> Theology represents – but *have*.[22]

Aurora is imposed upon the morning, at least by modern poets (it is
possible to imagine the original conception as completely fresh and
living in Coleridge's sense); in the Hebrew poets, on the other hand,
it is impossible to think of the meaning except through the way it is
expressed. It can lay hold of an idea primarily in concrete terms, as
children do, before they can reason in abstract terms; and one important
theory of metaphor was that it was the normal speech of primitive
people. Shelley, for instance, believed that in the infancy of society all
authors were poets.[23] So did Wordsworth:

> The earliest poets of all nations generally wrote from
> passion excited by real events; they wrote naturally, and
> as men: feeling powerfully as they did, their language
> was daring, and figurative. In succeeding times, Poets,
> and Men ambitious of the fame of Poets, perceiving the
> influence of such language, and desirous of producing the
> same effect without being animated by the same passion,
> set themselves to a mechanical adoption of these figures of
> speech, and made use of them, sometimes with propriety,
> but much more frequently applied them to feelings and
> thoughts with which they had no natural connection
> whatsoever.[24]

This puts the matter very clearly: from earliest times to Lord Chesterfield
figures of speech have been employed, but in the latter case they are

mechanically adopted as a kind of embroidery. In early societies it was different. Terence Hawkes puts it as follows: '"primitive" legends and myths were not *lies*, so much as poetic, *metaphorical* responses to the world'.[25] This is what stands behind Wordsworth's Preface to *Lyrical Ballads*: he is rejecting the current habits of figurative embellishment because he wants to use 'a language arising out of repeated experience and regular feelings' which is 'a more permanent, and a far more philosophical language than that which is frequently substituted for it by Poets'. This is the 'language really used by men', a language which is *naturally* figurative: through it ordinary things are 'presented to the mind in an unusual aspect'.

> and further, and above all, to make these incidents and
> situations interesting by tracing in them, truly though not
> ostentatiously, the primary laws of our nature: chiefly, as
> far as regards the manner in which we associate ideas in a
> state of excitement.[26]

The last phrase is crucial: it indicates the concern with the power of the imagination to associate dissimilar things, to join them (as the metaphysical poets had done) in a fusion which is imaginative, illuminating, and above all passionate. Coleridge (who said that Wordsworth's Preface was half a child of his own brain) reinforces this in his definition of poetry and the poet in Chapter 14 of *Biographia Literaria*:

> The poet, described in *ideal* perfection, brings the whole
> soul of man into activity, with the subordination of its
> faculties to each other, according to their relative worth and
> dignity. He diffuses a tone and spirit of unity, that blends,
> and (as it were) *fuses*, each into each, by that synthetic and
> magical power, to which we have exclusively appropriated
> the name of imagination.[27]

As an example of this unifying power we may choose the lines from Wordsworth which Coleridge said he would have recognized anywhere. They come from 'There was a Boy', the short blank-verse passage which was published in 1800 and which later became part of Book v of *The Prelude*: at the conclusion of the section describing the call and answer, the boy hears a series of sounds in the silence:

> And, when there came a pause
> Of silence such as baffled his best skill:
> Then sometimes, in that silence, while he hung

Listening, a gentle shock of mild surprise
Has carried far into his heart the voice
Of mountain-torrents; or the visible scene
Would enter unawares into his mind
With all its solemn imagery, its rocks,
Its woods, and that uncertain heaven received
Into the bosom of the steady lake.

(ll. 16–25)

There are many things which could be said about this beautiful passage, in particular about the rhythms and delicate line-endings: the way in which the mind 'hangs', for instance, at the end of the third line, just as the boy 'hung/Listening'. But if we concentrate on the use of metaphorical language, we can see that the unobtrusive metaphors have a very important part to play in the overall effect. Surprise, for instance, comes as a 'gentle shock', an image which catches both the sharpness of shock and the contrasting softness of 'gentle'; then there are the important operative verbs, 'carried . . . into' and 'enter', both of which suggest the shock and the scene making a movement into the mind, taking it and possessing it. Towards the end there is the image of 'that uncertain heaven', uncertain because it is shifting and changing, 'received/into the bosom' of the lake; in which the sudden image of the lake as a receiving maternal figure is complemented by 'steady', where it becomes both 'reliable' and 'calm', so that the image of the sky can be seen upon its surface.

The language of this passage is continually that of a natural, visualized scene, fused (to use Coleridge's essential word) with the internally supplied values and epithets. So the scene enters into the mind 'with all its *solemn* imagery', and the sound of mountain-torrents is the 'voice' of waterfalls which speak or sing. This activating of the landscape is the work of the creative and imaginative mind, making the internal external and the external internal.

This may be seen in another way by considering the concept of organic form. This is customarily described as being essentially Romantic, because it is the opposite of 'received form' or preconceived form. In received form a poet decides before writing what kind of shape or form the poem is to be in: he pours his thoughts into a ready-made mould. Organic form, on the other hand, develops freely from the subject and the poet's treatment of it, and contains no received or preconceived elements. Herbert Read has described its working as follows:

The form of a work of art is inherent in the emotional
situation of the artist; it proceeds from his apprehension of

that situation (a situation that may involve either external objective phenomena or internal states of mind) and is the creation of a formal equivalence (i.e. a symbol) for that situation. It resists or rejects all attempts to fit the situation to a ready-made formula of expression, believing that to impose such a generalized shape on a unique emotion or intuition results in insincerity of feeling and artificiality of form.[28]

Read puts his finger on the central determining factor of organic form: the apprehension of the situation, the way in which it is created or understood, is the situation itself. As we have seen, the imagination is unique to every individual, and God-like within each; therefore every situation is itself unique. It is also impossible to describe an external, material world, a world 'out there' objectively unless the describer is a scientist and restricts his language to scientific description. That description is false to the complex interaction of the internal mind and the external world: it is what Blake called seeing 'with the eye' (Newton's way of seeing) rather than 'through the eye'. Seeing 'through the eye' is an active process, the operation of the imagination on the external world, shaping and transforming it at the moment of perception. Thus a particularly powerful imagination can transform the world, and according to Blake should do so:

> To see a world in a grain of sand
> And a heaven in a wild flower,
> Hold infinity in the palm of your hand
> And eternity in an hour.
>
> ('Auguries of Innocence', ll. 1–4)

This is an extreme example of the complex process of interaction between the internal mind and the external world. It is possible to describe the external world accurately, but even when we do so we are not certain that our sense-impressions are the same as those of others, except at the simplest level; and for the Romantics the recognition that the sense-data are transformed and understood by each individual mind is vital, because it is that transformation which declares the individual.

If the subject-matter (so called) of the poem is affected by the perceiving mind, then every apprehension of the external world is different, and therefore the form of Romantic poetry is individual too. It develops in relation to the way in which the subject-matter develops in the mind of the poet, sometimes in a way which allows the greatest originality and freedom. There is a particular sense in which the form obeys the deepest feelings of the poet, and this can lead to moments of unexpected imaginative excitement, as Wordsworth saw:

> Visionary power
> Attends upon the motions of the winds
> Embodied in the mystery of words;
> There darkness makes abode, and all the host
> Of shadowy things do work their changes there
> As in a mansion like their proper home.
> Even forms and substances are circumfused
> By that transparent veil with light divine,
> And through the turnings intricate of verse
> Present themselves as objects recognised
> In flashes, and with a glory scarce their own.
>
> (*The Prelude*, 1805, v. 619–29)

Wilson Knight thought these lines confusing,[29] and they are certainly complex: but they seem to indicate that the external world (here signified by the synecdoche 'the winds'), when it is described in the mystery of words, can take on a visionary power; that somehow, obscurely, certain magical changes happen so that forms and substances are transformed ('circumfused . . . with light divine'). They appear as objects, yet not quite as objects, for they have a glory which is scarcely their own, given through words in the mystery of imaginative poetry.

At the centre of any conception of the form of Romantic poetry, therefore, is the idea that 'the motions of the winds' are 'Embodied in the mystery of words'. The prophetic or imaginative mind transforms the sense-data into something new and individual through the power of its speech; at this point the internal and external become mutually interactive, as the spirit of the living creature is in the wheels also.

To pour such a mysterious interaction into received form is to invite the criticism that it is falsifying the individuality of each experience. Nevertheless, the Romantics do sometimes use traditional forms, as well as such free-running structures as blank-verse conversation poems: they write sonnets, odes, Spenserian stanzas, and *terza rima*. It is in the use of such forms that the individuality occurs: it is the subordination of the received form to the imaginative authenticity of each individual experience which makes the work of each poet so distinctive. As Coleridge said, 'of all we see, hear, feel and touch the substance is and must be in ourselves'.[30]

It is because of this that symbol is so important, because symbol is the external world understood, given meaning, not mechanically, but organically, that is given its meaning through the creative perception of the mind so that its inner meaning is brought out. The meaning is not imposed upon it, but drawn out from it. So Coleridge continues:

> The artist must imitate that which is within the thing, that which is active through form and figure, and discourses to us by symbols – the *Naturgeist*, or spirit of nature, as we unconsciously imitate those whom we love; for so only can we hope to produce any work truly natural in the object and truly human in the effect.[31]

Herbert Read notes that this paragraph closely follows Schelling, and at this point we must consider briefly the effect of German philosophy on Coleridge and on the theory of romantic poetry. Coleridge seems to have borrowed freely from German writers; but he regarded truth as a 'divine ventriloquist', so that it did not matter from whose mouth the sounds proceeded, provided that the words were audible and intelligible. He therefore used the work of German philosophers, of whom the most important was Immanuel Kant. Kant carried out what he himself called a 'Copernican revolution' in philosophy: Coleridge referred to him as 'the illustrious sage of Königsberg' whose work 'at once invigorated and disciplined my understanding'.[32] Kant grappled with the problem which had teased eighteenth-century philosophers, and had led Berkeley to suggest that the external world could not exist without a mind to behold it. How do we acquire knowledge, and what is the relation between the mind and the external world? Kant's answer proposed an interaction between the two: sense-impressions exist and can be perceived by the reason, but they can only be fully understood by the understanding, which applies to them the comprehension of time and space, and employs categories which enable them to be related to other sense-impressions. Kant's 'understanding', which resembles Coleridge's 'imagination' has thus a shaping power, without losing sight of the original sense-data. This was carried further by Fichte, whose *Theory of Scientific Knowledge* (1794) argued that the object was created by the subjective mind. This was a potent argument in the Romantic period, because it corresponded with a specific kind of potent individual experience, of the kind described by Wordsworth as an 'abyss of idealism', when the self is sure only of itself and begins to distrust the reality of all other things in the world:

> I was often unable to think of external things as having external existence, and I communed with all that I saw as something not apart from, but inherent in, my own immaterial nature. Many times while going to school have

> I grasped at a wall or tree to recall myself from this abyss
> of idealism to the reality.[33]

Kant saw the imagination as a mysterious power, which he called 'the understanding working blind', which allows us to be aware of the relationship between our selves and our world through the shared understanding and governance of time. But the presence of the world is vital if the imagination is not to become random, and in this sense Coleridge's idea of the imagination as repeating in the finite mind the act of God's Creation is different from Kant's, and more responsive to the external world.[34]

Kant and Fichte represent two attempts to understand the relationship of the creative mind to the external world: in the one the mind is a shaping power which recognizes the independent existence of the external world (and imagination is a blind power); in the other the mind determines the world, shaping it in accordance with an individual creative perception (when the students broke Fichte's windows. Goethe said that it was a painful way to be apprised of the non-ego). The reconciliation of the internal and external, the 'it is' and the 'I am',[35] was the work of Friedrich Schelling, who saw that in Fichte the problem was 'no object and an absolute subject'; the opposite (in Spinoza, whom Coleridge read and admired) was 'no subject and an absolute object'. The danger of the first was randomness and fantasy; the danger of the second was determinism and necessity (which was one reason, for instance, why Coleridge rejected Hartley).

Coleridge's theories were very close to those of Schelling (Coleridge himself spoke breezily of 'a genial coincidence'),[36] and there is some controversy about how much Coleridge actually took from him. Schelling assigns the highest importance to the imagination in the process of interaction between the internal and the external: it is the power which sees the relation between the self and the object as both active and passive, and sees that twofold activity as part of a simultaneous process, so that nature becomes, in the phrase which Wordsworth borrowed from Young:

> all the mighty world
> Of eye, and ear, – both what they half create,
> And what perceive –
> ('Tintern Abbey', ll. 105–7)

and from Schelling Coleridge may have gained the idea, if not the word, for his coinage 'esemplastic' (meaning 'to shape into one') as an epithet for the imagination.[37] Certainly the unifying force of the imagination is of fundamental importance to both writers: according to Coleridge, the imagination 'struggles to idealize and to unify'. It is a special power of the mind, which can transform the material world of the materialist or of the scientist. Kant's distinction between reason and understanding, therefore, leads directly towards this view of the imagination as able to unify that which is normally separate and divided. Fancy adds together the elements of the world, as perceived by Kant's reason; imagination transforms them. Coleridge then divides the imagination, as we have seen, into primary and secondary, and again he is close to Schelling, who wrote: 'Intelligence is productive in twofold wise, either blindly and unconsciously, or with freedom and consciousness; unconsciously productive in the perception of the universe, consciously in the creation of an ideal world.'[38]

Schelling's phrase 'an ideal world' points towards the tradition of Platonic thought, and Coleridge also makes it clear that he is indebted to the neo-Platonic and mystical traditions of such writers as Jacob Boehme, the seventeenth-century mystical writer. Blake and Shelley were also considerably affected by this tradition: in all of them there is a reaching towards the ideal world, and an interpretation of the actual world as an inferior copy. The contrast between the ideal and the actual is found in much Romantic poetry: it is part of the fascination which the poets have with the world of dream and vision, and it is part, too, of the idealism which leads to revolution. It can be seen in the work of certain other German Romantics. Coleridge translated Schiller's *Wallenstein* (1800), and greatly admired *The Robbers* (1781): the latter is a powerful protest against convention and corruption, in which a young man is turned into a criminal by being the victim of lies and misrepresentation. He becomes a bandit, and one of the first examples of the noble robber in the Romantic period. Linked with this type is the great myth of Prometheus, who stole fire from heaven: his defiance and integrity under punishment are qualities which make him a symbol for all those who defy tyranny. Goethe was one of the first to be attracted by the myth in this period, writing a dramatic fragment on it in 1773.

Schiller described Goethe as having an intuitive habit of mind, an eye for organic unity, and a love of Greek antiquity. And, in spite of *Werther*, there was a distinctly classical and scientific bent to Goethe's many-sided mind, which seemed unromantic to those of the school of German Romantics who established the *Athenaeum* in Berlin in 1798. They preferred to see nature as something which stimulated the imagination, and they loved the mysterious and beautiful aspects of it, such as dark forests or mountains: Goethe, on the other hand, longed to discover the laws of nature through experiment and scientific analysis. In his theories of poetry, and his ideas about the nature and purpose of life, Goethe was too reasonable and well organized for many of the other Romantics; but he himself was a great admirer of two of them, A. W. Schlegel, who translated Shakespeare into German, and Friedrich Schlegel, who studied Sanskrit and who drew attention to the orient as a source for Romantic inspiration.

For an understanding of English Romantic poetry, however, the practitioners in the German states are less important than the philosophers. Kant, Fichte, and Schelling, as we have seen, explored the relationships between the mind and the external world; on the subject of feeling, the most important writer was Lessing. His *Laocoön* (1766) uses the statue of Laocoön and his two sons being strangled by serpents to discuss what the subtitle calls 'the limits of painting and poetry'. Until this time, a phrase from Horace's *Ars Poetica*, '*ut pictura poesis*', had been held to justify the idea that poetry and painting were 'sister arts': poetry was 'a speaking picture' and painting 'a silent poem'. Lessing saw that too close an attention to the parallel between the two arts led to a love of description in poetry, and of allegory in painting; and 'the detailed description of corporeal objects . . . has always been acknowledged by the finest judges to be mere cold, insignificant work' (Ch. 17). Meanwhile, the artist of the Laocoön statue had to set limits to the expression of bodily pain, because his art was confined to a single moment; the poet, on the other hand, can set it in a context of time, understanding the character of Laocoön and thus giving his grief more feeling. The interesting development which is foreshadowed in Lessing's enquiry is the examination of each art in respect of its ability to express feeling – in this case pain and grief. Instead of aiming to be pictorial, art attempts to be expressive, to render as accurately as possible the feelings and emotions.

The dilution of the theory of *ut pictura poesis* and of the conception of poetry and painting as sister arts was followed by an equally potent theory that the art closest to poetry was music. This has important consequences for Romantic poetry: it meant a return to the lyric form, by Shelley, Byron, and Thomas Moore, in a way which had not been known since the Elizabethans. It also increased the vigour and range of metaphor. Metaphor, which joins dissimilar things, is often called into question when the reader's mind is concerned with the physical appearance of those things: in an age in which the eye is less active (and both Wordsworth and Coleridge, as we shall see, thought of the eye as despotic) the comparisons can escape question and the poet is free to invent new comparisons, to establish relations between dissimilar things, and above all, to use language to express the interlocking structures of the mind. 'Language', says Terence Hawkes, 'is utterance: it utters (or "outers") the inner reality and, by Imagination, imposes this on the world beyond.'[39] Through language, new meanings are created by figures of speech, and generated by the imagination working at full pressure. This is why the words themselves are living words, the natural expression of an imaginative mind: they are the wheels of the intellect, 'but such as Ezekiel beheld in *the visions of God* as he sate among the captives by the river of Chebar'.

Notes

1. John Dixon Hunt, *The Figure in the Landscape* (Baltimore and London, 1976). p. 149.

2. *The Letters of Charles and Mary Lamb*, edited by E. V. Lucas (London, 1935), II, 425.

3. C. M. Bowra, *The Romantic Imagination* (London, 1950), p. 3.

4. *Biographia Literaria*, edited by James Engell and W. J. Bate (London, 1983), I, 304 (Ch. XIII). References to *Biographia Literaria* will be given from this edition, which is vol. 7 of *The Collected Works of Samuel Taylor Coleridge*: chapter references will also be given, to facilitate the use of other editions.

5. *The Letters of William Blake*, edited by Geoffrey Keynes, third edition (Oxford, 1980), p. 9.

6. Notably Barbara Hardy, 'Distinction without Difference: Coleridge's Fancy and Imagination', *Essays in Criticism*, 1 (1951), pp. 336–44.

7. *Biographia Literaria*, I, 80 (Ch. IV).

8. *Biographia Literaria*, I, 80 (Ch. IV).

9. *The Letters of William Blake*, p. 9.

10. *Biographia Literaria*, I, 304–5 (Ch. XIII).

11. *The Prelude*, 1805, I, 54.

12. Keats to Benjamin Bailey, 22 November 1817; *The Letters of John Keats*, edited by H. E. Rollins, 2 vols (Cambridge, 1958), I, 184.

13. C. D. Thorpe, *The Mind of John Keats* (New York, 1926), p. 105.

14. *Biographia Literaria*, II, 15–16 (Ch. XIV).

15. *The Statesman's Manual*, in *Lay Sermons*, edited by R. J. White (London, 1972), pp. 28–29 (vol. 6 in *The Collected Works of Samuel Taylor Coleridge*).

16. P. W. K. Stone, *The Art of Poetry, 1750–1820* (London, 1967), p. 34: 'Fancy forms the plan in a sort of mechanical or instinctive manner.'

17. See Stone, Ch. 6.

18. *Collected Letters of Samuel Taylor Coleridge*, edited by E. L. Griggs (London and New York, 1956–71), I, 626; quoted by Terence Hawkes, *Metaphor* (London, 1972), p. 53.

19. *Lay Sermons*, p. 29.

20. *Lay Sermons*, pp. 29–30.

21. *Aids to Reflection*, seventh edition (London, 1854), p. xv.

22. *Collected Letters*, ii, 865–66.

23. *A Defence of Poetry* in *The Complete Works of Percy Bysshe Shelley*, edited by R. Ingpen and W. E. Peck, 10 vols (London, 1965) vii, 110–11.

24. Appendix to the Preface to *Lyrical Ballads; The Poetical Works of William Wordsworth*, edited by E. de Selincourt and H. Darbishire, 5 vols (Oxford, 1940–49), ii, 405.

25. Hawkes, *Metaphor*, p. 39.

26. Preface to *Lyrical Ballads; Poetical Works* ii, 386.

27. *Biographia Literaria* ii, 15–16 (Ch. xiv).

28. Herbert Read, *The True Voice of Feeling* (London, 1947), p. 21.

29. G. Wilson Knight, *The Starlit Dome* (London, 1941), p. 9.

30. 'On Poesy or Art', reprinted in *Biographia Literaria*, edited by J. Shawcross (Oxford, 1907), ii, 259.

31. *Biographia Literaria*, ed. Shawcross, ii, 259.

32. *Biographia Literaria*, i, 153 (Ch. IX).

33. *Poetical Works*, iv, 463.

34. See D. M. MacKinnon, 'Coleridge and Kant', in *Coleridge's Variety*, edited by John Beer (London, 1974), pp. 183–203.

35. See Thomas McFarland, *Coleridge and the Pantheist Tradition* (Oxford, 1969), Ch. 3.

36. *Biographia Literaria* i, 160 (Ch. ix).

37. *Biographia Literaria* i, 168 (Ch. x).

38. Introduction to *Einwurf eines Systems der Naturphilosophie*, quoted in *Biographia Literaria* i, 272.

39. Hawkes, *Metaphor*, p. 54.

Chapter 2
Texts and Contexts

Prophecy and history

As we have seen, Ezekiel was 'among the captives by the river of Chebar', one of the Israelites carried into captivity in Babylon by Nebuchadnezzar in 598 B.C.; as a representative of an oppressed people, Ezekiel was a poet-prophet who was keeping alive a sense of national identity and encouraging a spirit of resistance. The parallel with Gray's Bard is clear, even without the connection through the Raphael painting; and writers of the Romantic period did not hesitate to draw upon the Old Testament as source material parallel to their own experience. Tom Paine, for instance, writing during the American War of Independence, described George III as 'the hardened, sullen-tempered Pharaoh of England'.[1] If George III is Pharaoh, then the American colonists manifestly occupy the same place as the children of Israel: their struggle is as noble and just, and they are led by a second Moses in George Washington. In *America: A Prophecy* (the first of his works to be so called) Blake portrayed Washington as speaking to his friends, 'the souls of warlike men who rise in silent night'; Orc, Blake's symbol of revolution in the material world, emerges at this point in a welter of Old and New Testament images. Night turns to morning, 'The grave is burst, the spices shed, the linen wrapped up'; the slave grinding at the mill is exhorted to run out into the field; 'the bones of death' (a reference to the valley of dry bones in Ezekiel 37) 'Reviving shake, inspiring move; breathing! awakening!' (Pl.6, l.4) while 'Empire is no more' and 'now the Lion & Wolf shall cease' (from Isaiah ll). Orc, who promises these, also affirms that

> every thing that lives is holy, life delights in life;
> Because the soul of sweet delight can never be defil'd.
> Fires inwrap the earthly globe, yet man is not consum'd;
> Amidst the lustful fires he walks; his feet become like brass,
> His knees and thighs like silver, & his breast and head like gold.
> (Pl.8, ll.13–17)

The image of man walking freely through the fire (and being refined by it) is from the story of the burning fiery furnace, also the creation of Nebuchadnezzar; as an emblem of the American people, rising to their full stature as free human beings, it sets divinely inspired fortitude against tyranny, a tyranny which is powerless against right and truth. Man walking through the lustful fires with the soul of sweet delight becomes beautiful, purged by the refiner's fire (Malachi 3.2), and Blake sees Orc as encouraging this process through revolution; presumably the tyrants will perish, as the verse from Malachi suggests.

Towards the end of this war, as Sir George Otto Trevelyan wrote picturesquely, 'America hung over the Western horizon like a red ball of fire.'[2] Its presence in the early poetry of Wordsworth and in Blake would seem to confirm this. The Declaration of Independence was an inspiration:

> We hold these truths to be self-evident, that all men are
> created equal, that they are endowed by their Creator
> with certain unalienable Rights, that among these are Life,
> Liberty, and the Pursuit of Happiness.

The war thus appeared as a struggle between freedom-loving men in their natural dignity under God and the petty tyranny of an incompetent monarch; there were many supporters of the American colonists in Britain, and George III was ridiculed in the popular press. In America, the institution of monarchy was powerfully attacked by Tom Paine, in a pamphlet entitled *Common Sense*. In a brilliant image that anticipates Blake, Paine sees monarchy as a consequence of the Fall of man: 'Government, like dress, is the badge of lost innocence; the palaces of kings are built upon the ruins of the bowers of paradise.'[3]

When Paine came to apply these principles to the state of America in 1776, his position was clear. America had a chance to break away from her disadvantageous connections with Britain and make a new start, a republican one. In the same spirit Blake, writing in 1791–93, saw in *America: A Prophecy* that the idea of revolution would spread across Europe:

> France, Spain and Italy
> In terror view'd the bands of Albion and the ancient Guardians
> Fainting upon the elements, smitten with their own plagues.
> They slow advance to shut the five gates of the law-built heaven,
> Filled with blasting fancies and with mildews of despair,
> With fierce disease and lust, unable to stem the fires of Orc;

> But the five gates were consum'd, & their bolts and hinges melted,
> And the fierce flames burnt round the heavens & round the abodes
>   of men.
>   (Pl. 16, ll. 16–23)

The American Revolution has been described as 'the watershed that divided eighteenth- from nineteenth-century England'.[4] Nevertheless, its impact upon the consciousness of Europe was entirely superseded by the spectacular events of the French Revolution. Charles James Fox wrote on 30 July 1789, just after the fall of the Bastille: 'How much the greatest event it is that ever happened in the world! and how much the best!'[5] The sense of being present at some apocalyptic event of history was common at this time: hopes were high that mankind was about to see the end of the old world and the beginning of a new and better one. Wordsworth, looking back at this time over ten years later, gave expression to what must have been a widespread feeling at the outset of the French Revolution:

> O pleasant exercise of hope and joy,
> For great were the auxiliars which then stood
> Upon our side, we who were strong in love,
> Bliss was it in that dawn to be alive,
> But to be young was very heaven!
>   (*The Prelude*, 1805, x. 689–93)

Similarly Coleridge remembered how

> When France in wrath her giant-limbs upreared,
> And with that oath, which smote air, earth, and sea,
> Stamped her strong foot and said she would be free,
> Bear witness for me, how I hoped and feared!
>   ('France: an Ode', ll. 22–25)

Such approval of what was going on in France was characteristic of much British opinion, which observed the development of affairs with curiosity and sympathy, seeing in the early stages of the upheaval a repetition of the English Revolution of 1688. The great exception was Burke, who saw the Paris mob as very different. The events of October 1789 confirmed his worst suspicions: the revolutionaries broke into the royal apartments at Versailles, and compelled the King and his family to return to Paris. Burke, who had witnessed mob violence of a particularly unpleasant kind in the anti-Catholic Gordon riots of 1780, warned a French correspondent that 'the power of bad men is no indifferent thing'.[6] In *Reflections on the Revolution in France* (1790), he dwelt at some length on the unceremonious invasion of the palace at Versailles by 'a band of ruffians and assassins'[7]; in his celebrated description of Marie Antoinette, Burke describes an ideal which never really existed, but which becomes an emblem of the old order which is being destroyed:

> I thought ten thousand swords must have leaped from their scabbards to avenge even a look that threatened her with insult. But the age of chivalry is gone. That of sophisters, economists, and calculators, has succeeded; and the glory of Europe is extinguished for ever.[8]

Burke sees the French Revolution as nothing less than a plunge back into savagery, an abandoning of all the progress which has been made over the centuries; and in the spread of revolutionary sentiment to England, he sees a danger to the whole of European civilization. In this view, and in his advocacy of reform rather than revolution, Burke undoubtedly exaggerated the benefits of the social contract and the institutions of government under which he lived: his appeal to tradition and chivalry takes little account of the human misery which flourished alongside them, and which the poets were quick to apprehend. Wordsworth's early poems, for instance, contained a number of figures whose undeserved suffering is caused by the American war and by an unfair and uncaring society; Blake pointed out the miseries of the Londoners in his daily observation: Mary Wollstonecraft, in *A Vindication of the Rights of Men* (1790), attacked Burke's use of rhetoric for political purposes and pointed out that it was all very well for Burke to be moved by the plight of Marie Antoinette –

> but the distress of many industrious mothers, whose helpmates have been torn from them, and the hungry cry of helpless babes, were vulgar sorrows that could not move your commiseration.[9]

But the most powerful voice raised in reply was that of Tom Paine, whose pamphlet *Rights of Man* was published in February 1791.[10] Like Blake's unhappy chimney sweeper from *Songs of Experience*, whose parents 'are gone to praise God, & his Priest & King/Who make up a heaven of our misery', Paine saw the established figures of Burke's system as corrupt and malign. Rank and aristocracy were part of this: 'through all the vocabulary of Adam, there is not such an animal as a duke or a count'.[11] While the American and French governments will always be remembered for their honourable origins, the British government begins in usurpation and monarchical tyranny. The consequence of this is clear. America and France have shown the way: 'The iron is becoming hot all over Europe' and now is the time to strike for freedom:

> When all the governments of Europe shall be established on the representative system, nations will become acquainted, and the animosities and prejudices fomented by the intrigues and artifice of courts will cease. The oppressed soldier will become a free man; and the tortured sailor, no longer dragged through the streets like a felon, will pursue his mercantile voyage in safety. [12]

After the execution of Louis XVI on 21 January 1793 the debates in the National Convention developed into a struggle for power between the Girondins and the Jacobins: the Girondins saw themselves as the successors of the great Roman republicans, but they were mainly from the provinces and lacked the support of the Parisians. A key figure in the Jacobin hold upon the Paris sections was Marat; when he was murdered in his bath by Charlotte Corday on 13 July 1793, he became a martyr of the revolution, and his death helped to ensure the triumph of the Jacobins. The Girondins were executed in October, and the 'Reign of Terror' followed, in which not only aristocrats and clergy were guillotined but also any who were suspected of opposing the Jacobin cause. The austere and incorruptible Robespierre pressed on with the task of ridding France of those who were not wholehearted supporters of the revolution. The Committee of Public Safety dedicated itself to the task of creating a new society, purged of all doubt, self-interest, and hesitation; in the process it created a climate of fear and suspicion, as one potential victim denounced another (especially after the law of 10 June 1794, which enabled the committee to condemn suspects without proper trial). Wordsworth described it in *The Prelude*:

> Tyrants, strong before
> In devilish pleas, were ten times stronger now;
> And thus beset with foes on every side
> The goaded land waxed mad; the crimes of few
> Spread into madness of the many; blasts
> From hell came sanctified like airs from heaven.
>
> (1805, x. 309–14)

So tyrannical did the Committee of Public Safety become that the fall of Robespierre in July 1794 was regarded by many as a new liberation.

Wordsworth's own rejoicing is recorded in a memorable passage of *The Prelude*.[13]

Opinions about France were complicated by her foreign policy. The success of the battle of Valmy (described by Goethe as beginning 'a new age in the history of the world'[14]) led to French counter-offensives in 1793, following declarations of war against England, the Netherlands, and Spain. When England declared war against France in turn in 1793, Wordsworth was appalled, as *The Prelude* makes clear: he rejoiced at the news of French victories, and in the 'Letter to the Bishop of Llandaff', written in 1793, he put forward a classic argument for the use of force by the revolutionary state:

> Alas, the obstinacy and perversion of man is such that she is too often obliged to borrow the very arms of Despotism to overthrow him, and, in order to reign in peace, must establish herself by violence. She deplores such stern necessity, but the safety of the people, her supreme law, is her consolation.[15]

A. B. Grosart, the nineteenth-century editor of Wordsworth's prose, called this letter 'Apology for the French Revolution, 1793', and certainly at this stage Wordsworth saw the revolution as 'a convulsion from which is to spring a fairer order of things'. Burke is called in the letter an 'infatuated moralist', and Wordsworth confesses himself 'the advocate of Republicanism'. The events of 1794 modified his opinion, although we must be careful not to take the hindsight of *The Prelude* as an entirely correct account of his feelings at the time.

From 1792 onwards the French had aided revolutionary elements in Switzerland. Various incursions into Swiss territory took place in the following years, and in 1798 a major invasion was undertaken, when the French occupied Lausanne and Berne. This inspired Coleridge's repentant 'France: an Ode', published in the *Morning Post* on 16 April 1798, which acknowledges his enthusiasm for the French Revolution and his dismay at Britain's declaration of war in 1793. Now he hears the voice of freedom from Switzerland:

> I hear thy loud lament,
> From bleak Helvetia's icy caverns sent –
> I hear thy groans upon her blood-stained streams!
> Heroes, that for your peaceful country perished,
> And ye that, fleeing, spot your mountain-snows
> With bleeding wounds; forgive me, that I cherished
> One thought that ever blessed your cruel foes!

The *Morning Post* added a note to condemn 'the unprincipled and atrocious conduct of France', and added complacently that 'it is very satisfactory to find so zealous and steady an advocate for Freedom as Mr COLERIDGE concur with us in condemning the conduct of France towards the Swiss Cantons'.[16] Switzerland was something of a symbol, since it had a reputation for mountain-loving freedom, and had been associated with myths of an alpine golden age in former times; but, as Geoffrey Carnall has noted, the Swiss showed little inclination to rise against the occupation, and the anti-French feeling petered out. So Southey could write to Humphry Davy in the autumn of 1799:

> Massena, Buonaparte, Switzerland, Italy, Holland, Egypt,
> all at once! the very spring-tide of fortune! It was a dose
> of gaseous oxide to me, whose powerful delight still
> endures.[17]

Southey was referring to the 1798 campaigns of Bonaparte and Massena; his reaction shows how difficult it is to plot any consistent response from Romantic poets to the political situation. Matters became clearer, of course, with the rise of Napoleon, who became First Consul of France in 1799 and Emperor of France in 1804. It was possible to see him as one more example of tyrannical power, an evil like the British monarchy (Wordsworth and Southey shocked De Quincey as late as 1807 by their anti-monarchical sentiments).[18] Some of the dislike of the Duke of Wellington, too, may have been due to his individual power; it appeared in these years as if the only dominant figures were kings, emperors, and generals. Pitt and Fox, the only statesmen capable of providing strong leadership, were dead; the French Revolution was in ruins; and the Napoleonic code had been established throughout Europe. William Hazlitt summed up the reactions of many:

> For my part, I set out in life with the French Revolution,
> and that event had considerable influence on my early
> feelings, as on those of others. Youth was then doubly
> such. It was the dawn of a new era, a new impulse had
> been given to men's minds, and the sun of Liberty rose
> upon the sun of Life in the same day, and both were proud
> to run their race together. Little did I dream, while my
> first hopes and wishes went hand in hand with those of the
> human race, that long before my eyes should close, that
> dawn would be overcast, and set once more in the night of
> despotism – 'total eclipse!'[19]

It is against this background that we must see the work of the first-generation Romantic poets. But in order to understand it fully, we must go back to Rousseau, and then to the most influential philosopher of radicalism in his day, William Godwin.

Rousseau

The influence of Jean Jacques Rousseau (1712–78) on the Romantic period is pervasive: not only did his writings anticipate specific movements and ideas, but their general tone and fundamental principles were influential in determining the broad movements of feeling and thought in the second half of the eighteenth century. His work had an arresting simplicity, together with an attractive energy and passion: he gave expression with a new intensity to the love of freedom, the interest in the self, the passion of love, the state of man in society, and the admiration of nature. In all these he had an extraordinary ability to perceive matters with a fresh eye: he was in all subjects an original thinker, and his thought, like that of his Romantic successors, was based on his experience and his feeling. He lived in a state of frequent excitement: on the day when he read in the *Mercure de France* of the Dijon Academy's prize essay subject, 'Has the restoration of the arts and sciences had a purifying effect upon morals?', he said, 'The instant I read it; I saw another universe and I became another man.'[20] The new universe which he saw was a reaction against the universe into which he had been gradually assimilated: the simplicities of childhood had disappeared, to be replaced by a complex social, philosophical, and cultural environment, by the urbanities of Paris, the philosophy of Hobbes, and the pressures of religion. With the insight of genius, Rousseau saw the opening which the Dijon Academy's title provided for him: the arts and sciences, as practised in his own day, could be seen as an artificial series of distractions from a wiser and better way of life. Modern arts and sciences were part of a whole fabric of manners, society, and government, and these prevented man from understanding or feeling the truth: 'Politeness requires one thing; decorum that; ceremony has its forms, and fashion its laws, and these we must always follow, never the promptings of our own nature' (p. 6).[21] Arts and sciences can actually be deceptive, in that they distract men from the love of liberty, by the way in which they 'fling garlands of flowers over the chains which weigh them down':

> They stifle in men's breasts that sense of original liberty,
> for which they seem to have been born; cause them to love

their own slavery, and so make of them what is called a
civilized people.
Necessity raised up thrones; the arts and sciences have
made them strong. (pp. 4–5)

Rousseau advocated a virtuous simplicity in place of a civilization
of art and science: in the second part of the *Discourse* he ridicules the
idea of scientific progress and speculative philosophy, concluding with
an appeal to the human heart and to the voice of conscience. Both are
pointers towards virtue, 'sublime science of simple minds' (p. 26).

This *Discourse*, which won the prize in 1750, was followed by the
more important *Discourse* of 1754, on 'What is the origin of inequality
among men, and is it authorized by natural laws?' This celebrated
essay describes man in a state of nature, like a noble animal, free of
disease, naked, and without 'all the superfluities which we think so
necessary'. There are advantages, says Rousseau pithily, in 'carrying
one's self, as it were, perpetually whole and entire about one' (p. 48).
Man is unaggressive, indeed compassionate; against Hobbes's view of
man as naturally wicked, Rousseau sets the idea of savage man with
'natural compassion' which is 'the pure emotion of nature, prior to all
kinds of reflection' (p. 67). Opposed to this instinctive goodness are
two things: property, and the domination of one man over another.
Rousseau compresses the history of man into a very small space, passing
over 'in an instant a multitude of ages' (p. 79). But the import of what
he has to say is clear: the development of human society has led to an
inequality and slavery which are far more disadvantageous to man than
his earlier state:

from the moment one man began to stand in need
of the help of another; from the moment it appeared
advantageous to any one man to have enough provisions
for two, equality disappeared, property was introduced,
work became indispensable, and vast forests became
smiling fields, which man had to water with the sweat of
his brow, and where slavery and misery were soon seen to
germinate and grow up with the crops. (p. 83)

This takes Rousseau towards his powerful conclusion, which is that
in modern society we are no longer self-sufficient, while the savage
'breathes only peace and liberty' (p. 104).

Towards the end of the *Discourse*, Rousseau's consideration of
developing societies leads him to a condemnation of tyrannical government: government, he argues, should be by contract, in which the good

monarch should obey the laws of the state, while the subjects obey the monarch. The argument is taken up again in *The Social Contract* (1762), which begins with the celebrated and spectacular sentence; 'Man is born free; and everywhere he is in chains.' In considering the contracts between men which make up civil society, Rousseau was following a long tradition, going back to Plato's *Republic* and including such seventeenth-century theorists as Milton, who believed in the sovereignty of the people; Hobbes, who believed that people were bound to obey their ruler, whether he governed well or ill, because the worst government was preferable to anarchy; and Locke, who regarded rulers as men to be obeyed until they governed tyrannically, in which case the response was to be rebellion or emigration. Rousseau's contribution to this argument was to insist on a social contract as an expression of the 'General Will'. The General Will was a collective sense of the political course to be followed, arrived at democratically, and seen as sovereign: 'The people, being subject to the laws, ought to be their author: the conditions of society ought to be regulated solely by those who come together to form it' (p. 193). Rousseau recognizes that there has to be some form of government, but it has to represent the interests of society, and of the individual within that society. Seen in this light, many traditional institutions become suspect: a man put in authority loses his sense of proportion, justice, and reason, and so monarchy is suspect, especially hereditary monarchy:

> in a republic the public voice hardly ever raises to the
> highest positions men who are not enlightened and capable,
> and such as to fill them with honour; while in monarchies
> those who rise to the top are most often merely petty
> blunderers, petty swindlers, and petty intriguers, whose
> petty talents cause them to get into the highest positions
> at court, but, as soon as they have got there, serve only to
> make their ineptitude clear to the public. The people is far
> less often mistaken in its choice than the prince; and a man
> of real worth among the king's ministers is almost as rare
> as a fool at the head of republican government.   (p. 222)

The voice of indignation and morality which is heard here, and throughout Rousseau's political writings, is the same voice which is heard from the Jacobins of the French Revolution. The emphasis on popular support as an indication of the rightness of their policies, and the alliance of the Jacobins with the people of Paris, were over-simplifications of Rousseau's theories; but by their very simplicity they had a powerful appeal.

Similarly, among the many virtues which are displayed in *Julie* or

La Nouvelle Héloïse (1761) are a dislike of ostentation; a fair treatment of workers and domestic staff; charity towards the poor; and liberal ideas on education, which recognize that a child should be allowed to develop at its own pace and not be forced to act as an adult.[22] The last theory is found again in *Émile*, Rousseau's treatise on education: his belief in the original goodness of man and the corruption of modern society is carried over to an idea of the child as naturally able to use freedom to good effect. This is why education is so important: since morality is latent in the feelings, it is vital that natural growth and development are not twisted.

Rousseau had already anticipated the Romantic poets in his theories of the natural man and the corruptions of modern society; in the *Confessions* and in *Les Rêveries du Promeneur Solitaire*, Rousseau discovered a wealth of material in his own recollections and feelings. 'I have resolved on an enterprise which has no precedent', he wrote at the beginning of the *Confessions*,[23] insisting not only on his originality but also on his uniqueness: 'I am made unlike any one I have ever met; I will even venture to say that I am like no one in the whole world' (p. 17). The *Confessions* is an extraordinary achievement, in which Rousseau recounts the development of his life, including his wrongdoing and shameful behaviour, and protests the fundamental goodness of his nature and motives. He sends his children to an orphanage, for instance, not because he is an unnatural father, but because he wants them to become workers and peasants instead of adventurers and fortune-hunters, and because he sees himself as a member of Plato's Republic.

His peculiar and rather nauseating lack of insight is something which occurs at other points in the Romantic view of the self; somehow the actions which appear in retrospect to be wrong are not those of the best self, the true self. In Rousseau's *Confessions* the worst example is his false accusation of the servant girl Marian. Rousseau had stolen a little pink and silver ribbon, and blamed the theft on the girl, 'a good girl, sensible and absolutely trustworthy', with 'that fresh complexion that one never finds except in the mountains' (p. 87). When the philosopher reflects that he may have ruined the girl's life, he finds the memory deeply disturbing, but he also observes that 'Never was deliberate wickedness further from my intention than at that cruel moment.' So, side by side with the invitation to sit in judgement is the awareness of the complexity of moral discriminations. Is the central self our best, or our worst? The *Confessions* not only encourages the reader to ask the question, but it challenges our simple notions of morality and character. It invites the reader to question his own superiority, and to acknowledge the coexistence of good and evil simultaneously in an individual; it invites him also to admire a certain honesty in the author, and to have compassion on human frailty. Moreover, the introspection is part of a complicated enquiry into the whole nature of human behaviour: Rousseau begins the *Rêveries du Promeneur Solitaire* with the romantic question 'What am I?'

He was, said Byron, 'One, whose dust was once all fire'. Byron's salute to Rousseau in *Childe Harold's Pilgrimage* is significant of the emotions aroused by the *Confessions* and *La Nouvelle Héloïse*. Like others (Kant, for instance) Byron was enchanted by Rousseau's style, the way in which he could express emotion:

> he knew
> How to make madness beautiful, and cast
> O'er erring deeds and thoughts a heavenly hue
> Of words, like sunbeams, dazzling as they past
> The eyes, which o'er them shed tears feelingly and fast.
>
> (*Childe Harold's Pilgrimage*, III. st. 77)

Byron identified the central appeal of Rousseau as being to the feelings, which in reading the *Confessions* transform any tendency to judgement into a mixture of compassion and admiration. Byron also saw Rousseau as having a love which was 'passion's essence', not for any living person but for 'ideal beauty':

> *This* breathed itself to life in Julie, *this*
> Invested her with all that's wild and sweet;
> This hallow'd, too, the memorable kiss
> Which every morn his fever'd lip would greet,
> From hers, who but with friendship his would meet;
>
> (III. st. 81)

To the recently separated Byron there was much to be said for this kind of ideal love, pushing the feelings as far as possible without engaging in a permanent relationship. Rousseau, in other words, painted an ideal; and so, too, he painted an ideal in political terms, as Byron goes on to acknowledge. From Rousseau came

> Those oracles which set the world in flame,
> Nor ceased to burn till kingdoms were no more;
>
> (III. st. 81)

Shelley also admired Rousseau, if admired is not too weak a word. He wrote to Peacock of 'the divine beauty of Rousseau's imagination, as it reveals itself in Julie',[24] and in the *Essay on Christianity* of 1815 he compared Rousseau to Jesus Christ.[25] He was, to Shelley, both visionary and moralist, poet and thinker. It is thus Rousseau who appears in Shelley's strange phantasmagoric final poem 'The Triumph of Life'. The poem is written in *terza rima* in imitation of Dante, and as Dante is guided by Virgil, so Shelley is addressed by Rousseau; the vision of hell which it conjures up includes a nightmare picture of Rousseau himself:

> I turned, and knew
> (O Heaven have mercy on such wretchedness!)
>
> That what I thought was an old root which grew
> To strange distortion out of the hill side,
> Was indeed one of those deluded crew,
>
> And that the grass, which methought hung so wide
> And white, was but his thin discoloured hair,
> And that the holes he vainly sought to hide,
>
> Were or had been eyes:
> (ll. 180–88)

In the poem Rousseau, like all the others, has been affected by life, the triumphant, confusing, corrupting, and bewildering force which destroys the ideality of thought and the permanence of love. He speaks of his own limitations:

> 'Before thy memory,
>
> 'I feared, loved, hated, suffered, did and died,
> And if the spark with which Heaven lit my spirit
> Had been with purer nutriment supplied,
>
> 'Corruption would not now thus much inherit
> Of what was once Rousseau, – nor this disguise
> Stain that which ought to have disdained to wear it;
>
> 'If I have been extinguished, yet there rise
> A thousand beacons from the spark I bore'
> (ll. 199–207)

Rousseau has been overcome by the pressing confusion and chaos of life; the world is one in which, as the poet himself remarks

> God made irreconcilable
> Good and the means of good;
> (ll. 230–31)

and so the hopes, even of Rousseau and Shelley, disappear in the weltering confusion of life: what began in idealism and hope ends in despair.

Byron, expressing himself more simply, had doubts about the effect of Rousseau's ideas, which 'roused up to too much wrath' the people of France:

> They made themselves a fearful monument!
> The wreck of old opinions – things which grew,
> Breathed from the birth of time: the veil they rent,
> And what behind it lay, all earth shall view.
> But good with ill they also overthrew,
> Leaving but ruins, wherewith to rebuild
> Upon the same foundation, and renew
> Dungeons and thrones, which the same hour refill'd,
> As heretofore, because ambition was self-will'd.
>
> (*Childe Harold's Pilgrimage*, III. st. 82)

The extraordinary image of the thrones refilling, as if by some perverse natural process (as if, once the thrones have been re-established, they fill themselves) is an example of the way in which Rousseau's ideas became submerged in a process of returning to the old patterns of society. In this generation the distance between the ideal and the actual, between the hopes of mankind and the historical events, becomes a painful reminder of man and of the fallen world. And so the fragment of 'The Triumph of Life' ends in a terrible question: 'Then, what is life? I cried.'

In the struggle to answer this question the Romantics found many guides, and depended on their own experience and on their reading of contemporary events. To them Rousseau was an idealist and poet, who pointed out what was wrong with society and what was fundamentally good in man. The great exception to the general admiration of Rousseau was Blake, who lumped him together with Voltaire as anti-religious:

> Voltaire! Rousseau! You cannot escape my charge that
> you are Pharisees & Hypocrites, for you are constantly
> talking of the virtues of the Human Heart and particularly
> of your own, that you may accuse others, & especially the
> Religious, whose errors you, by this display of pretended
> Virtue, chiefly design to expose.[26]

To Blake, both Voltaire and Rousseau were 'mockers', denying the deep truths of religion; in his poem from the Rossetti manuscript, 'Mock on, mock on, Voltaire, Rousseau' he portrays them as throwing sand against the wind (the wind of the Holy Spirit), and the wind blows it back again, so that they are blinded by their own sand which they have raised:

> And every sand becomes a gem
> Reflected in the beams divine;
> Blown back they blind the mocking eye,
> But still in Israel's paths they shine.
>
> (ll. 5–8)

The image of the children of Israel is a reminder of how Blake saw himself and the visionaries who agreed with him as a race set apart, a remnant; they wished to have nothing to do with Rousseau's freethinking. To the other Romantics Rousseau's views on religion were part and parcel of his demonstration of the truth about man: that he was naturally good, and that modern society had ruined him. Rousseau was the first of the Romantics and revolutionaries who hoped for a new world in which man could return to his original goodness. The most important of these, for the Romantic poets, was William Godwin.

Godwin

There is plenty of evidence for the very considerable impact of William Godwin, radical and reformer, on the English Romantic poets. Southey 'read and studied and all but Worshipped' Godwin,[27] and Coleridge wrote a sonnet to him. Wordsworth, according to Hazlitt, told a student to 'throw aside your books of chemistry, and read Godwin on Necessity'.[28] 'Godwin on Necessity' is a reference to Book IV, Chapters 7 and 8 of Godwin's *Enquiry concerning Political Justice*, although the whole work was very influential, especially during what Hazlitt called 'the revolutionary tempest' of the French Revolution. In his essay on Godwin in *The Spirit of the Age* (1825), Hazlitt observed that he 'indulged in extreme opinions, and carried with him all the most sanguine and fearless understandings of the time'[29]; by 1825 he had almost disappeared from view. Hazlitt attributed this fall from popular esteem to 'too much ambition'; not, to be sure, ambition for Godwin himself but for mankind: 'He conceived too nobly of his fellows . . . – he raised the standard of morality above the reach of humanity, and by directing virtue to the most airy and romantic heights, made her path dangerous, solitary, and impracticable.'[30]

With the hindsight of 1825 this may have seemed so; in 1793 it was a different matter. The very idealism of Godwin, his impossibly high conception of the nobility of man, was a major reason for his popularity. An accidental late flowering of his influence took place in 1811, when Shelley, having discovered with 'inconceivable emotion' that Godwin was still alive (so quiet had he become) began a correspondence with him; meetings in 1812 and 1813 led to Shelley's love for Godwin's daughter Mary, and to their elopement in 1814. Godwin's influence on Shelley was considerable: H. N. Brailsford even said that 'it would be no exaggeration to say that Godwin formed Shelley's mind, and that *Prometheus Unbound* and *Hellas* were the greatest of Godwin's works'.[31] The claim seems extravagant, especially as Shelley had a poetic imagination and Godwin very clearly had not, but Shelley's idealism was certainly encouraged by his early reading of Godwin and their subsequent meetings.

The whole conduct of rational action, as Godwin perceives it, is consequent upon his theoretical position that 'to a rational being there can be but one rule of conduct, justice, and one mode of ascertaining that rule, the exercise of his understanding' (ll. vi).[32] Such an appeal to reason, issuing forth in justice, is the kind of return to first principles which recalls Rousseau, to whom Godwin acknowledges a debt in the Preface (p. ix). Like Rousseau, Godwin argues that the root of much of the evil in the world comes from property:

> with grief it must be confessed, that, however great and
> extensive are the evils that are produced by monarchies
> and courts, by the imposture of priests and the iniquity
> of criminal laws, all these are imbecile and impotent,
> compared with the evils that arise out of the established
> administration of property.   (VIII. ii)

Property leads to a love of distinction; to the exploitation of one man by another; and to the inequality of individual power and opportunity. Remove these inequalities, and all will be well.

In spite of this improbable and unfounded optimism, Godwin produces in this and other passages a heady mixture of idealism with criticism of current situations: it is not difficult to see the very considerable appeal of his book to the radicals and poets of 1793. The humanitarian instincts of the work, its attack on monarchy, aristocracy, and other inequalities, and its advocacy of public good over private needs and affections, all had a powerful compulsion for certain minds. Henry Crabb Robinson, for instance, said that *Political Justice* 'made me feel more generously . . . I had never before felt so strongly the duty of not living to one's self, but of having for one's sole object the good of the community.'[33] Similarly, Wordsworth recorded in *The Prelude* his debt to

> the philosophy
> That promised to abstract the hopes of man
> Out of his feelings, to be fixed henceforth
> For ever in a purer element, . . .
> (1805 text, x. 806–9)

The whole of this section is an eloquent tribute to Godwin, although Wordsworth's hindsight seems to give the lines something of a wry twist, as if to make it clear that he now knows better:

> What delight!
> How glorious! – in self-knowledge and self-rule
> To look through all the frailties of the world,
> And, with a resolute mastery shaking off
> The accidents of nature, time, and place,
> That make up the weak being of the past,
> Build social freedom on its only basis:
> The freedom of the individual mind,
> Which, to the blind restraint of general laws
> Superior, magisterially adopts
> One guide – the light of circumstances, flashed
> Upon an independent intellect.
> (x. 818–29)

This is surely intended to be a little too enthusiastic to be convincing; by 1804, when Wordsworth was writing this book of *The Prelude*, he had come to believe strongly that nature, time, and place cannot be shaken off, but that they have a powerful influence upon the mind and the affections. But nine years earlier matters had been different: Godwin probably first met Wordsworth in February 1795, at a meeting of radicals, and Godwin believed that he had converted Wordsworth 'from the doctrine of self-love to that of benevolence'.[34]

The conversion was symptomatic of the immediate and powerful influence of Godwin on younger minds; so was the gathering of radical friends. Godwin flourished in a particular milieu, that of the reform associations agitating for parliamentary improvement during the heady period of the French Revolution; he flourished at a particular time, perhaps by the very idealism and optimism which seemed in a few years' time to be theoretical and unfounded. To his readers at the moment of his heyday he was clearly some kind of radical lighthouse, signalling unmistakably a course towards a better world. If he seemed blind to the pressures of personal feeling (as Wordsworth came, mistakenly, to believe) and blind to the realities of economic life ('Godwin writes', said H. N. Brailsford, 'as though he had never seen a factory nor heard of capital'[35]), he nevertheless provided, in *Political Justice*, a seminal account of the aspirations of the time.

Notes

1. *The Complete Writings of Thomas Paine*, edited by Philip S. Foner, 2 vols (New York, 1945), I, 24.

2. Sir George Otto Trevelyan, *The American Revolution*, 4 vols, (London, 1917), III, 175.

3. *Complete Writings*, I, 4–5. *Common Sense* was followed by sixteen pamphlets which Paine entitled The American Crisis and signed 'Common Sense'.

4. Dorothy Marshall, *Eighteenth Century England* (London, 1962), p. 448.

5. *Memorials and Correspondence of Charles James Fox*, edited by Lord John Russell, 4 vols (London, 1853–57), II, 361.

6. Quoted in R. R. Fennessy, *Burke, Paine, and the Rights of Man* (The Hague, 1963), p. 98.

7. *The Works and Correspondence of the Right Honourable Edmund Burke*, edited by Earl Fitzwilliam and Sir R. Bourke, 8 vols (London, 1852), IV, 209.

8. *Works and Correspondence*, IV, 212–13.

9. Fennessy, p. 204.

10. *Complete Writings*, I, 258–59: Paine describes Burke as supporting 'the Quixotic age of chivalric nonsense'.

11. *Complete Writings*, I, 287.

12. *Complete Writings*, I, 449.

13. *The Prelude*, 1805, x, 466–566.

14. Quoted in J. M. Thompson, *The French Revolution* (Oxford, 1943), p. 317.

15. *The Prose Works of William Wordsworth*, edited by W. J. B. Owen and J. W. Smyser, 3 vols (Oxford, 1974), I, 33–34.

16. *The Complete Poetical Works of Samuel Taylor Coleridge*, edited by E. H. Coleridge, 2 vols (Oxford, 1912), I, 243.

17. Quoted in Geoffrey Carnall, *Robert Southey and his Age* (Oxford, 1960), p. 47.

18. Carnall, p. 82.

/ in Youth', *The Complete Works of William*
ve, 21 vols (London, 1930–34), XVII, 196–97.

Jean-Jacques Rousseau (Cambridge, 1955), p. 96.

.re to the Everyman edition of *The Social Contract*
.islated and edited by G. D. H. Cole, revised by J. H.
.nn C. Hall (London, 1973).

.oduction to *La Nouvelle Héloïse*, translated and abridged by Judith
.well (University Park, Pennsylvania, and London, 1968).

.ge references are to the Penguin edition of the *Confessions*, translated by
.I. Cohen (Harmondsworth, 1954).

24. Shelley to Peacock, 12 July 1816; *The Letters of Percy Bysshe Shelley*, edited
by Frederick L. Jones, 2 vols (Oxford, 1964), I, 480.

25. 'Essay on Christianity', *The Complete Works of Percy Bysshe Shelley*, edited
by R. Ingpen and W. E. Peck, 10 vols (London, 1965), VI, 247: Rousseau is
'the philosopher among the moderns who in the structure of his feelings and
understanding resembles most nearly the mysterious sage of Judaea'.

26. *Jerusalem*, plate 52; *The Complete Writings of William Blake*, edited by Geoffrey
Keynes (London, 1966), p. 682. For the reception of Rousseau in England,
see Edward Duffy, *Rousseau in England: The Context for Shelley's Critique of
the Enlightenment* (Berkeley and Los Angeles, 1973).

27. H. N. Brailsford, *Shelley, Godwin and their Circle* (London, 1913), p. 52.

28. *Complete Works*, XI, 17.

29. *Complete Works*, XI, 16.

30. *Complete Works*, XI, 17.

31. Brailsford, p. 174.

32. All references are to Godwin's own divisions into book and section; I have
used the edition of *Political Justice* by F. E. L. Priestley (Toronto, 1946).

33. Quoted in F. M. Todd, *Politics and the Poet* (London, 1957), p. 59.

34. Mark Reed, *Wordsworth, The Chronology of the Early Years, 1770–1779*
(Cambridge, Mass., 1967), p. 164.

35. Brailsford, p. 165.

Chapter 3
Preoccupations, and Ways of Reading Them

Nature

The Romantic poets, with the exception of Blake, have always been celebrated for their love of nature.[1] Wordsworth in particular described it with inexhaustible enthusiasm, seeing

> In nature and the language of the sense
> The anchor of my purest thoughts, the nurse,
> The guide, the guardian of my heart, and soul
> Of all my moral being.
> ('Tintern Abbey', ll. 107–11)

For all of them there was a joy to be found in the natural world which was not present in man-made institutions or practices. Byron gave expression to this most airily and simply in *Childe Harold's Pilgrimage*:

> I live not in myself, but I become
> Portion of that around me; and to me
> High mountains are a feeling, but the hum
> Of human cities torture: I can see
> Nothing to loathe in nature, save to be
> A link reluctant in a fleshly chain,
> Class'd among creatures, when the soul can flee,
> And with the sky, the peak, the heaving plain
> Of ocean, or the stars, mingle, and not in vain.
> (III. st. 72)

Such a delight in nature is not of course new. The immediate predecessors of the English Romantics were Milton and the eighteenth-century writers who followed him, and before that the classical poets, especially Theocritus, Virgil, Horace, and medieval writers such as Chaucer. Milton's description of the Garden of Eden in *Paradise Lost*

Book IV became a model for a painterly landscape of lawns, downs, hills, and valleys; while in Book IX a Miltonic simile becomes a good example of the idea that nature is refreshment after the city:

> As one who long in populous City pent,
> Where Houses thick and Sewers annoy the Aire,
> Forth issuing on a Summers Morn to breathe
> Among the pleasant Villages and Farmes
> Adjoind, from each thing met conceaves delight,
> The smell of Grain, or tedded Grass, or Kine,
> Or Dairie, each rural sight, each rural sound;
>
> (IX. 445–51)

The first line becomes a cliché of Romantic poetry, used by both Coleridge and Keats; the general sentiments of the passage are found in Coleridge's 'Reflections on having left a Place of Retirement', the opening of *The Prelude*, and elsewhere.

Wordsworth believed that nature poetry was in a poor way after Milton:

> it is remarkable that, excepting the nocturnal Reverie of
> Lady Winchilsea, and a passage or two in the 'Windsor
> Forest' of Pope, the poetry of the period intervening
> between the publication of the 'Paradise Lost' and the
> 'Seasons' does not contain a single new image of external
> nature; and scarcely presents a familiar one from which it
> can be inferred that the eye of the Poet had been steadily
> fixed upon his object, much less that his feelings had urged
> him to work upon it in the spirit of genuine imagination.[2]

The terms in which this grumble is written suggest that Wordsworth valued either new natural perceptions, or familiar ones that were accurately and imaginatively described. He found these qualities in James Thomson's *The Seasons* (*Winter*, 1726; the complete *Seasons*, 1730). *The Seasons* is significant because it was the first major poem-sequence of modern times to concentrate principally upon nature, although it also contains, besides brief narratives, elements of devotional, scientific, georgic, historical, and geographical thinking.[3] Much of the poem's sublimity comes from the apprehension of the created world as evidence for the existence of God and of His benevolence. Thomson adds to this the Virgilian descriptions of country and farming life, patriotic effusions, and stories such as the Damon and Musidora passage from 'Summer' or the Lavinia and Palemon story from 'Autumn'. *The Seasons* is a busy poem, encyclopaedic in its concern for art, religion, and science, concerned not only with the appearances of nature but also its attendant ideas, from philosophical speculation to theological problems of pain and suffering.

It anticipates the Romantics in two ways: in its very accurate, abundant, and loving attention to the external world, to the glorious variety of flowers, trees, weather, and other effects; and in its use of subjective impressions. However involved the poem may be in speculating and organizing (in a way which may be understood and shared by all), its particular observation and shaping perception is the work of an individual mind of great originality. Although Thomson is not articulate about the mysterious power of landscape in the way that Wordsworth and Coleridge are, he is certainly aware that his sense-impressions are related to his feelings. 'He is', writes James Sambrook, 'concerned less with natural objects "themselves", than with the emotional, intellectual and devotional experience of a consciousness responding to those objects.'[4]

This responding consciousness in Thomson is dominated, as might be expected from this period of Newtonian physics, by the power of the eye. There are occasional 'prospects', in the same manner as Dyer's *Grongar Hill* (published in the same year as Thomson's *Winter*, 1726): the appreciation of such views, and the structuring of them, owes a great deal to the seventeenth-century landscape painters, Claude Lorrain, Salvator Rosa, and Gaspar Poussin. Thomson celebrated their work in a famous stanza from 'The Castle of Indolence':

> Sometimes the pencil, in cool airy halls,
> Bade the gay bloom of vernal landskips rise,
> Or Autumn's varied shades imbrown the walls:
> Now the black tempest strikes the astonished eyes;
> Now down the steep the flashing torrent flies;
> The trembling sun now plays o'er ocean blue,
> And now rude mountains frown amid the skies,
> Whate'er Lorrain light-touched with softening hue
> Or savage Rosa dashed, or learned Poussin drew.
>
> (I. st. 38)

Paintings by these artists were picked up by wealthy English connoisseurs on the Grand Tour as reminders of the Italian *campagna* (rendered so peacefully and with such delicate light by Claude) or as souvenirs of the hazardous crossing of the Alps (in the rugged landscapes of Salvator Rosa). In England these painters created their own particular taste by which they were to be enjoyed – and by which other landscapes were to be appreciated also. They taught the eighteenth-century poets to 'see': that is to see nature in their way, through their eyes, as either pastoral and calm or rugged and terrifying. And since this was the great age of landscape gardening or 'improvement', they had a profound effect on the design of grounds and parks. Instead of the formal patterns of the previous century, grounds were now laid out with lakes and hills, diversified with buildings or ruins, often leading the eye to the distance in the manner of a Claude painting; while William Kent even planted dead trees at Kensington in imitation of Salvator Rosa, who often painted dead or broken trees in his landscapes.

It was Kent, according to Horace Walpole, who first 'leaped the fence, and saw that all nature was a garden'.[5] He constructed views (at Rousham in Oxfordshire, for instance) in which the eye was led from the garden close to the house into the valley and across to the further hillside, where Kent placed an 'eye-catcher'. Once the landscape that was unimproved became part of the view, it was a short step to the next stage of 'picturesque travel', in which connoisseurs of landscape went on tours to see views that resembled the paintings of Claude and Salvator Rosa. Often they took with them a 'Claude glass', a device which was essentially a tinted mirror: by standing with their backs to the landscape and using the mirror as a frame, the picturesque travellers could discover an original 'Claude'. So Thomas Gray, visiting the Lake District in 1769, wrote to his friend Wharton:

> From hence I got to the *Parsonage* a little before Sunset, & saw in my glass a picture, that, if I could transmit to you, & fix it in all the softness of its living colours, would fairly sell for a thousand pounds. This is the sweetest scene I can yet discover in point of pastoral beauty; the rest are in a sublimer style.[6]

Gray was one of the first travellers to appreciate the full beauty of the Lake District, although his criteria were usually visual, depending (as the last sentence shows) on the common distinction between the pastoral beauty of Claude and the sublime style of Salvator Rosa. This division had been given philosophical substance by Edmund Burke, whose *Philosophical Inquiry into the Origin of our Ideas of the Sublime and Beautiful* had been published in 1757. Burke was responsible for a subjective and psychological theory, which located the origins of our feelings in self-preservation: if we felt terror before a landscape, it was sublime. If we felt pleasure, it was beautiful.

Burke's *Enquiry* is an interesting forerunner of the Romantic response to landscape because it emphasizes the importance of individual feeling. Nevertheless the criteria for appreciating landscape were still rigorously visual, and picturesque travel continued to flourish with an almost comic regard for the importance of the eye. In response to popular demand, a number of guidebooks were written, commending the specific delights of certain views and the 'stations' from which they could be seen; the best known were those by William Gilpin, who wrote a series of 'Observations, relative chiefly to Picturesque Beauty' on several parts of the British Isles. His volume on the Lake District, published in 1786, contains several sections analysing the particular beauties of mountain and lake scenery. In them we discover that mountains 'rising in regular, mathematical lines, or in whimsical, grotesque shapes, are displeasing' (I. 83); that he has known 'many a good landscape injured by a bad water boundary' (I. 96); and that islands 'are either a beauty, or a deformity to the lake; as they are shaped, or stationed' (I. 97).[7] Gilpin is very perceptive about landscape, and especially about the presence of light and shade in it; but all is directed to the search for the picturesque which he defined as 'that peculiar kind of beauty, which is agreeable in a picture'.[8]

Such a definition gave rise to the question, 'how does the picturesque differ from the beautiful?', which was answered by theoreticians such as Uvedale Price (*Essay on the Picturesque*, 1794) and Richard Payne Knight (*The Landscape*, 1794). They argued that the picturesque effect involved roughness and rugged surfaces, and that wrinkled forms and asymmetrical shapes were more picturesque than smooth and regular ones. In Knight's case this was combined with an attack on Capability Brown, the greatest landscape gardener of the eighteenth-century, whose smooth lawns and clumps of trees were deplored by the enthusiasts of the picturesque.

The writings of sterile aesthetes such as Price and Knight would be of little interest if it were not for the fact that the picturesque was an important factor in the formation of Romantic nature poetry. Wordsworth's first published poem, *An Evening Walk* (1793), begins with the kind of division noted by Gray into sublime and pastoral. There are two generalized Lake District landscapes in the opening paragraph, the first after Salvator Rosa, the second after Claude (beginning at line 9):

> Far from my dearest friend, 'tis mine to rove
> Thro' bare grey dell, high wood, and pastoral cove;
> His wizard course where hoary Derwent takes
> Thro' craggs, and forest glooms, and opening lakes,
> Staying his silent waves, to hear the roar
> That stuns the tremulous cliffs of high Lodore:
> Where silver rocks the savage prospect chear
> Of giant yews that frown on Rydale's mere;

Where peace to Grasmere's lonely island leads,
To willowy hedgerows, and to emerald meads;
Leads to her bridge, rude church, and cottag'd grounds,
Her rocky sheepwalks, and her woodland bounds;
Where, bosom'd deep, the shy Winander peeps
'Mid clust'ring isles, and holly-sprinkled steeps;
Where twilight glens endear my Esthwaite's shore,
And memory of departed pleasures, more.

(ll. 1–16)

This is generalized, after the manner of Gilpin's illustrations, which were 'taken from the *general face of the country*; not from any *particular scene*' (I. xxv). In Wordsworth's case, although place-names are mentioned, they unite to form a composite landscape of lake and mountain.

There are signs of a swift reaction against the picturesque in his next poem, *Descriptive Sketches*. Its original title was 'Picturesque Sketches', but at some point Wordsworth realized that the fussy precepts of picturesque writers were inadequate as a response to Switzerland and the Alps. He wrote a peculiarly strong note which declared that the Alps were 'insulted' by the word 'picturesque' and condemned the appreciation of the scenery according to 'the cold rules of painting'. Later, when summing up this period of his life in *The Prelude*, Wordsworth described the picturesque as 'never much my habit', but remembered

giving way
To a comparison of scene with scene,
Bent overmuch on superficial things,
Pampering myself with meagre novelties
Of colour and proportion, to the moods
Of Nature, and the spirit of the place,
Less sensible.

(*The Prelude*, 1805, XI. 157–63)

He then goes on to widen the discussion in an important way, by linking the picturesque with the domination of the eye ('The most despotic of our senses') and seeing it as a tyrant whose rule is thwarted by Nature itself: that is, the true feeling for the natural world takes over from the superficial appreciation, as Nature

summons all the senses each
To counteract the other and themselves,
And makes them all, and the objects with which all
Are conversant, subservient in their turn

To the great ends of liberty and power.
But this is matter for another song;

                                              (XI. 179–84)

Wordsworth is here referring to *The Recluse*, the great philosophical
poem which he did not write; *The Excursion*, which is the only part of
it which was completed, is concerned with the way in which human
minds can be shaped and purified by nature (as the Wanderer's is) or can
be unaffected by nature, as the despondent Solitary's is. In his description
of the Wanderer, Wordsworth is giving his most explicit statement of the
power of natural landscape in childhood to give strength and stability;
we have reached a stage in which nature is no longer a background, or
a plaything for the rich landowners to alter at will, but a source of vital
and mysterious power, and an object and an inspirer of love.

    The tradition of nature poetry which derives from Thomson is
twofold: it is pictorial, and it is sublime, for nature is the great handiwork
of God, the revelation of his power and benevolence on earth. To
generate the kind of love of which Wordsworth speaks there has to be
an intimacy, even a familiarity with nature, that comes through personal
experience. The great poet of familiar nature was William Cowper. Not
only did he celebrate the gentle scenery of Buckinghamshire, but he did
so in a way which was calculatedly informal. His major poem, *The Task*,
begins 'I sing the sofa', an unpromising opening for a nature poem,
or perhaps for anything else; but after a few mock-heroic paragraphs
describing the history of sofas, Cowper turns deftly into his celebration
of the natural world:

                        The sofa suits
        The gout limb, 'tis true; but gouty limb,
        Though on a sofa, may I never feel:
        For I have lov'd the rural walk through lanes
        Of grassy swarth, close cropt by nibbling sheep,
        And skirted thick with intertexture firm
        Of thorny boughs; have lov'd the rural walk
        O'er hills, through valleys, and by rivers' brink,
        E'er since a truant boy I pass'd my bounds
        T' enjoy a ramble on the banks of Thames;

                                        (*The Task*, I. 106–14)

The plurals here (lanes, boughs, hills, valleys, rivers) indicate Cowper's
interest in the abundance and variety of nature. So do the two 'rural
walks': they are part of a sense of delightful freedom in *The Task*, a
freedom to walk now this way, now that way. While Thomson and
the picturesque writers looked for ways of interpreting landscape or

ordering it, Cowper accepts it. He believes it comes from God ('God made the country, and man made the town') but he does not use landscape as Thomson had done to make a grand gesture towards the beneficent Creator. Demands are not made upon the poet: he can like what he wishes to like, and ignore the rest. On winter afternoons, for instance, he can close the curtains, shut out nature, and settle down cosily with a cup of tea. However valetudinarian this may be (Byron thought Cowper a 'coddled poet') it has the merit of being an authentic response; and in its informality and directness it anticipates Wordsworth and Coleridge.

Cowper's informal blank verse was an example to the Romantics of a medium which could be used to express their feelings of close intimacy with nature. Coleridge used it with delightful informality:

> Low was our pretty Cot: our tallest Rose
> Peep'd at the chamber-window. We could hear
> At silent noon, and eve, and early morn,
> The Sea's faint murmur. In the open air
> Our myrtles blossom'd; and across the porch
> Thick Jasmins twined: the little landscape round
> Was green and woody, and refresh'd the eye.
>
> ('Reflections on having left a Place of Retirement', 1–7)

Wordsworth also follows Cowper in his attachment to a local landscape, but his expression is habitually more elevated and passionate. He would be destitute of all human feeling, he says,

> if I should fail with grateful voice
> To speak of you, ye mountains, and ye lakes
> And sounding cataracts, ye mists and winds
> That dwell among the hills where I was born . . .

> if, in this time
> Of dereliction and dismay, I yet
> Despair not of our nature, but retain
> A more than Roman confidence, a faith
> That fails not, in all sorrow my support,
> The blessing of my life, the gift is yours
> Ye mountains, thine O Nature. Thou hast fed
> My lofty speculations, and in thee
> For this uneasy heart of ours I find
> A never-failing principle of joy
> And purest passion.
>
> (*The Prelude*, 1805, II. 439–42, 456–66)

In passages such as this one from Wordsworth there is evidence of an entirely new relationship with nature. No longer is the external world a source of pleasure: it is a moral force, a source of inspiration, a support in time of trouble, a blessing and a joy. The transition from the nature of Thomson and Cowper can be seen with particular clarity in 'Lines composed a few miles above Tintern Abbey, on revisiting the banks of the Wye during a tour. July 13 1798': I have quoted the whole title because it is an eighteenth-century one, which would have given any reader of *Lyrical Ballads* the expectation that this was to be a poem about picturesque landscape seen on a tour. The first paragraph appears to confirm this: it is built up like a Claude painting, with a dark sycamore in the foreground framing the view, and the prospect opening up in background, middle distance, and foreground. Only in the second paragraph does the poem turn into something else:

> These beauteous forms,
> Through a long absence, have not been to me
> As is a landscape to a blind man's eye: . . .
>
> (ll. 21–23)

It is important to notice that Wordsworth celebrates the memory of sight here, and the seen landscape is still important: but what was a picture to Gilpin becomes for Wordsworth a source of joy and of the mood in which 'we are laid asleep/In body, and become a living soul' (ll. 45–46). Throughout the poem Wordsworth returns to the actual landscape, but each time the appreciation of it is deepened and profoundly altered by the intervening sections which describe its effect upon the poet's mind. So the landscape affects the mind, and the mind reciprocally affects the landscape. 'The common feat of the romantic nature poets', says W. K. Wimsatt, 'was to read meanings into the landscape.'[9]

This reciprocal action between the mind and the natural world is, of course, capable of an infinite number of variations in meaning, productive of the 'infinite complexity' which Wordsworth describes in the Preface to *Lyrical Ballads* and which has already been quoted. Consequently the reaction to nature by individual poets is better studied under each separate author's work; but some general categories of Romantic nature poetry require to be discussed at this point.

The first is the genuine pleasure at seeing, hearing, and feeling the freshness of the natural world. The association of nature with health, both physical and spiritual, comes from a love of fresh air, movement, cleanness, and freedom. The contrast between this and the life in towns and cities is a frequent one: and if such a contrast is sometimes sentimental, ignoring, for instance, the miseries of the exhausted agricultural labourer, it was none the less felt to be real, and nature to be beneficial. Even John Clare, who was himself one of the rural poor, took delight in the seasons, the weather, the birds, and the flowers. His poetry celebrates what the other Romantic poets knew only at second hand: what it was like to be a countryman, to live with all the hardships of country life as well as its beauty. Clare knew the fatigue and boredom of agricultural work, the exposure to cold and rain, and the helpless despair of the peasant who saw the land being enclosed by the rich. Other poets can write of poverty, and of beauty: but none can get as close as Clare to the experience of the two together, and to the pathetic ignorance of the ploughman who loves beauty but is unable to express his thoughts (in 'Dawnings of Genius').

Secondly, the landscape and the natural world are not just seen for their beauty, but for their ability to express some of the elusive truths and perceptions of the mind. In their search to find ways of expressing their internal feelings, the Romantic poets look outwards to nature to find emblems of the mind. They externalize their emotions in describing them through natural correspondences: the calm and steady lake, the high mountain, the stream or river. Moreover, this is more than a mechanical correspondence: it is a kind of creative relationship between the internal mind and the external world, put at its simplest by Byron:

> Are not the mountains, waves, and skies, a part
> Of me and of my soul, as I of them?
>
> (*Childe Harold's Pilgrimage*, III. st. 75)

Mountains correspond to that side of him which is aspiring, high, and proud, just as the sea is a symbol of depth, and boundlessness, and storm; in Italy he identifies with the landscape, decayed and yet beautiful in the wreck of its past glory, seeing himself as 'a ruin amidst ruins' (IV. st. 25). On an entirely different scale, Clare sees the snail and identifies it as a brother with its delicacy and timidity:

> With earnest heed and tremulous intent,
>   Frail brother of the morn,
> That from the tiny bents and misted leaves
>   Withdraws his timid horn,
>   And fearful vision weaves: . . .
>
> ('Summer Images', ll. 108–12)

The tender sympathy of this portrayal seems to add to the accuracy; it is a reminder that the process of seeing nature in correspondence with the mind does not in any way involve a falsification of nature; rather the reverse, for somehow the interaction between the mind and the external world enhances the perception of both. So Wordsworth can produce a natural analogy for the retrospective processes of his poetry in *The Prelude*:

> As one who hangs down-bending from the side
> Of a slow-moving boat upon the breast
> Of a still water, solacing himself
> With such discoveries as his eye can make
> Beneath him in the bottom of the deeps,
> Sees many beauteous sights – weeds, fishes, flowers,
> Grots, pebbles, roots of trees – and fancies more,
> Yet often is perplexed, and cannot part
> The shadow from the substance, rocks and sky,
> Mountains and clouds, from that which is indeed
> The region, and the things which there abide
> In their true dwelling; now is crossed by gleam
> Of his own image, by a sunbeam now,
> And motions that are sent he knows not whence,
> Impediments that make his task more sweet;
> Such pleasant office have we long pursued
> Incumbent o'er the surface of past time –
> With like success.
>   (*The Prelude*, 1805, IV. 247–64)

In this carefully measured and beautifully articulated passage, Wordsworth dwells carefully on each aspect of the natural world, the surface of the lake and its depths, because they represent what he wishes to say about the mind and its interpretation of the past. Similarly, Coleridge uses landscape to describe the working of the imagination, in *Biographia Literaria*: he speaks of 'the two cardinal points of poetry':

> the power of exciting the sympathy of the reader by a
> faithful adherence to the truth of nature, and the power of
> giving the interest of novelty by the modifying colors of
> imagination. The sudden charm, which accidents of light
> and shade, which moon-light or sun-set diffused over a
> known and familiar landscape, appeared to represent the
> practicability of combining both. These are the poetry of
> nature.[10]

The last sentence is crucially illuminating: by its changing appearances, the transformations of light and colour, nature is making its own poetry, a poetry which is true to itself, yet also changed into something more wonderful. It is an external image for the creative processes of the mind, as Coleridge is striving to identify them.

The third aspect of Romantic nature poetry is its association of nature with moral and physical health. In an age when the air of cities was smoky, and those with weak lungs were advised to live in the country or beside the sea (as John Constable's wife, for instance, was), it is not difficult to see why nature should have been thought of as health-giving; but there was also a widespread belief that it was good for mankind in other ways. The pleasure in nature, like laughter, is one beneficial factor; another is the belief that there is a wholesome hunger after the natural and pure. This has a philosophical basis in the work of Hartley, who contrasted 'the Offensiveness, Dangers and Corruptions of Populous Cities' with 'the Health, Tranquility and Innocence, which the actual View, or the mental Contemplation, of rural Scenes produces.'[11] So Coleridge pictures his friends on a country walk, and especially their visitor, Charles Lamb, on holiday from the India House in London:

> Now my friends emerge
> Beneath the wide wide Heaven – and view again
> The many-steepled tract magnificent
> Of hilly fields and meadows, and the sea,
> With some fair bark, perhaps, whose sails light up
> The slip of smooth clear blue betwixt two Isles
> Of purple shadow! Yes! they wander on
> In gladness all; but thou, methinks, most glad,
> My gentle-hearted Charles! for thou hast pined
> And hunger'd after Nature, many a year,
> In the great City pent, . . .
>
> ('This Lime-Tree Bower my Prison', ll. 20–30)

Even Blake, who thought that 'Natural objects always did and do now weaken, deaden & obliterate Imagination in Me' delighted to celebrate the joys of the summer morning, or spring, or the spontaneous and natural life of lambs and of children. Children were often linked with the moral and beneficent properties of nature, in two ways. First, they were believed to have the same kind of unspoiled simplicity, a simplicity which was preserved by freedom and by a lack of pressure. Thus Coleridge contrasts his own childhood with that which he promises for his child:

> For I was reared
> In the great city, pent 'mid cloisters dim,

And saw nought lovely but the sky and stars.
But *thou*, my babe! shalt wander like a breeze
By lakes and sandy shores, beneath the crags
Of ancient mountain, and beneath the clouds, . . .
('Frost at Midnight', ll. 51–56)

Secondly, as this quotation implies, there was a belief that a natural education was more beneficial than a traditionally academic kind. Blake lamented that children had to go to school on a summer day, and rejoiced that he was not sent to an art school:

Thank God, I never was sent to school
To be flogged into following the style of a fool.
(Miscellaneous Notebook Verses, *c.* 1807–9)

Wordsworth also contrasted the life of the 'boy of Winander' in Book v of *The Prelude* with the precocious book-learner; and when Wordsworth first began to compose a poem on his own life, in the winter of 1798–99, he began with a question about the influence of nature upon him:

Was it for this
That one, the fairest of all rivers, loved
To blend his murmurs with my nurse's song,
And from his alder shades and rocky falls,
And from his folds and shallows, sent a voice
That flowed along my dreams?
(*The Prelude*, 1799, i. 1–6)

The radiance which the adult remembers as part of the natural vision brings us to the fourth and final way in which nature is perceived by the Romantic poets. It is not so much moral as visionary: that is, nature possesses a power and a radiance which is quite beyond the normal encounters of the mind with the external world. At such moments, nature becomes transfigured with a numinous quality which can only be described as coming from God, or from something beyond the power of man to understand. Thus when Wordsworth returns from Cambridge to Hawkshead, he walks round the Lake of Esthwaite in the evening:

Gently did my soul
Put off her veil, and, self-transmuted, stood
Naked as in the presence of her God.
(*The Prelude*, 1805, iv. 140–42)

Nature is not God here, and Wordsworth is not a pantheist; but
nature produces in the poet's soul the same kind of feelings of
confrontation with the sacred. Nature is a power which can inspire
awe and love, and be evidence of a mysterious and wonderful power
in the universe.[12]

The encounter between the poetic mind and this magnificence in
and beyond nature is one of the most heroic features of Romantic
poetry. For from the early eighteenth-century onwards, the process
of natural appreciation involves more and more demands upon the
emotional strength of the poet. At first there was the formal garden,
tidy and mathematical; then the informal garden, le jardin anglais, after
Claude; then the picturesque; and then the final confrontation with
all the 'otherness' of nature itself – nature in all its abundance, its
imperfection, its confusion, its randomness, and its beauty. Romantic
poets go out to meet it without the armour of the picturesque, to try
to order it, to struggle for meaning and sense. Sometimes they succeed
in articulating the most impressive interaction between the mind and
the external world; at other times they are lost, as Keats is on the top
of Ben Nevis, 'blind in mist':

> mist is spread
> Before the earth, beneath me, – even such,
> Even so vague is man's sight of himself!
> ('Read me a lesson, Muse, and speak it loud', ll. 7–9)

Wordsworth too is lost, crossing the Alps; but like Yeats's crazed
girl, the poets are heroically lost and heroically found. It is at the
moment of being lost that Wordsworth discovers the full power of
the imagination rising up before him, finding his central self at the
moment of greatest confusion. It is this process of loss and gain, of
the struggle for self-definition and for understanding, which marks
out the Romantic poet from his predecessors. It is simple to see where
the self is in a formal garden, or armed with a Claude glass in a
picturesque landscape: man has his inviolable and superior place in
a world which is ordered and kept at arm's length. But if nature
is confronted, really confronted, the problem becomes deeper, more
insoluble, more pressing. Keats broods on the passing of beauty, the
heartache of the nightingale's song, the end of autumn; Wordsworth
steals a boat, and finds the mountains changing, the cliff apparently
coming after him. In both cases the great questions arise, pushing
themselves forward insistently: 'who am I?' 'what is my relationship
to the world?'. And even if the answer is sometimes incomplete, the
actual asking of the question, the vulnerability is itself heroic.

Dreams

Dreams are extraordinary examples of the private and unexpected workings of the individual mind; they have a mysterious and involuntary quality about them, an unpredictable and inconsequential mode of operation which suggests that the mind is stranger, freer, and more resourceful than any mechanical account would allow; and they operate in symbols. The symbolic operation of dreams links them with the working of the poetic imagination, which can allow one thing to stand for another, and can transform abstraction into symbol. It is not difficult to see why the Romantic poets were fascinated by dreams.

Their interest is related to the concern for the experience of childhood. According to Freud, dreams can involve a considerable degree of 'primary process thinking', the kind of mental activity found in babies, who are not sure where their own selves end and the outer world begins. As they develop into infants and change to 'secondary process thinking', small children still have regressions into primary process thinking, taking refuge in fantasy from the complexities of the world of reality. Gradually the attention to the outside world comes to dominate the conscious and waking mind, in a process of development which will be familiar to the readers of Wordsworth's 'Immortality Ode':

> Shades of the prison-house begin to close
>   Upon the growing Boy,
>   But He
> Beholds the light, and whence it flows,
>   He sees it in his joy;
> The Youth, who daily farther from the east
> Must travel, still is Nature's Priest,
>   And by the vision splendid
>   Is on his way attended;
> At length the Man perceives it die away,
> And fade into the light of common day.
>
> (ll. 67–76)

Wordsworth anticipates Freud's connection between the mental processes of infancy and the operation of dreams by describing the world of his first vision as

>   Apparelled in celestial light,
> The glory and the freshness of a dream.
>
> (ll. 3–4)

Dreams are precious evidence of an activity which is now impossible in the normal conditions of adult wakefulness. In the waking state the ego's censorship of fantasy takes over: there is a cognizance of space and time, of probability, and of cause and effect. Our whole perception of consciousness is involved with this process, as Erasmus Darwin (whom Coleridge read and met) wrote in *Zoonamia* (1794): 'we gain our idea of consciousness' by comparing ourselves with the scenery around us; and of identity by comparing our present consciousness with our past consciousness'.[13] *Zoonamia* has an important section on sleep, in which Darwin discusses dreams. He argues that the consciousness of our own existence is the result of the voluntary exertion of the mind; in dreams this voluntary exertion is suspended, and so 'we neither measure time, are surprised at the sudden changes of place, nor attend to our own existence, or identity'.[14] The opposition here is between the waking consciousness, which is associated invariably with an awareness of time and place, and the unpredictable and unbounded dream-world. Blake used the same opposition between 'the sea of time and space', which he saw as deflecting him from the path of vision or truth, and the imagination:

> I am under the direction of Messengers from Heaven, Daily
> & Nightly; but the nature of such things is not, as some
> suppose, without trouble or care. Temptations are on the
> right hand & left; behind, the sea of time & space roars and
> follows swiftly; he who keeps not right onward is lost, & if
> our footsteps slide in clay, how can we do otherwise than
> fear & tremble?[15]

So too Freud's 'primary process thinking' has been summed up as 'The direct expression of the unconscious instinctual drives' and as illogical, disregarding time and space. Secondary process thinking involves 'the processes used by the ego to deal with the demands of the real world and to modify the demands made by the instinctual drives. They are therefore based on logical thinking in contrast to the illogical pictorial thinking of the primary process.'[16] Given these parallels, it is perhaps not surprising that the Romantics saw much in common between the dream-world and the world of the imagination, and that they were in consequence extremely interested in dreams. These could be either the dreams of sleep, or waking dreams; the latter were often described as 'reveries', for instance by Erasmus Darwin:

> whilst I am thinking over the beautiful valley, through
> which I yesterday travelled, I do not perceive the
> furniture of my room: and there are some, whose waking

imaginations are so apt to run into perfect reverie, that in
their common attention to a favourite idea they do not hear
the voice of the companion, who accosts them, unless it is
repeated with unusual energy.[17]

This contrast between yesterday's landscape and today's room uncannily
anticipates Wordsworth's 'Tintern Abbey', written four years later,
in which the poet remembers the landscape when he is 'in lonely
rooms, and 'mid the din/Of towns and cities'; and it is noticeable
that Wordsworth's language for such a reverie in which he sees the
scenery of the Wye valley includes the image of sleep, so that

> we are laid asleep
> In body, and become a living soul:
> While with an eye made quiet by the power
> Of harmony, and the deep power of joy,
> We see into the life of things.
>
> (ll. 45–49)

The idea that the soul awakes during these reveries is common in
Romantic poetry. As we have seen, Blake associated them with visionary
power; Keats describes a waking dream in the 'Ode to a Nightingale',
and wonders which is real, the actual world of time and place, or the
ideal world of the imagination in which the poet flies on the wings of
poesy to a dark, sweet-smelling, and magic world of the nightingale.
  Darwin emphasizes further points about dreams: he notes, for
example the great vivacity of dreams, whether sleeping or waking,
and that this is accompanied by variety, novelty, and distinctness.
There is an amazing 'rapidity of the succession of transactions in
our dreams' (I. 205), but Darwin also believes that these have some
relation to our waking lives (which puts him closer to Freud than
to the Romantics): his observation that 'we recall the figure and the
features of a long lost friend' in dreams (I. 205) is very close to
the recorded experience of Coleridge, who frequently dreamed of
his school desk-mate C. V. Le Grice. He noted that he was never
astonished in these dreams to find himself back at Christ's Hospital,
and his notebook entry (1250) says that his dreams were 'uncommonly
illustrative of the non-existence of Surprize in sleep', another observation
which echoes Darwin. Darwin observed two remarkable properties of
dreams, their inconsistency and their total absence of surprise: he saw
these as the result of the involuntary workings of the mind. During
our conscious hours the mind can voluntarily reject inconsistencies,
but in dreams the most unusual connection of ideas and images takes
place (I. 215–16).

Coleridge also read Andrew Baxter's *An Enquiry into the Nature of the Human Soul* (1733), which contains a long essay on dreaming. Writing in an age of mechanical philosophies of mind, Baxter boldly accepts that dreams are involuntary; they are 'chimerical and wild', and Baxter rejects all mechanical explanations for them, such as illness, heat, or cold. In so doing, he emphasizes not just the non-mechanical processes, but also the living excitement of dreams, 'in which there is so much *variety, action* and *life,* nay oftentimes *speech* and *reason*' (II. 78).[18] Baxter's problem is that dreams clearly happen, but are quite inexplicable in terms of normal eighteenth-century discourse. This is made clear in a footnote near the end, in which Baxter imagines an objector saying that his theories make dreams 'mere *enchantment* and *Rosicrucian-work,* which it is absurd to admit into philosophy and among natural appearances'; but, says Baxter,

> if it be a common and constant appearance in nature, how can it be absurd to admit it into philosophy, or allow it a place among *natural phaenomena?* . . . as to the accounting for it any other way, I am not able; let any one try it who pleases.

> But, after all, do not *those* who are least willing to admit of *enchantment* and *Rosicrucian-work* among the *appearances* of *nature,* find themselves so *enchanted, deluded, imposed upon* every night? (II. 231–32)

So Baxter defends the originality and enchantment of dreams, seeing them as spontaneous and living, the product of an imagination which sounds curiously like Coleridge's:

> If imagination be taken as something belonging to the soul; it is its own active power of voluntarily joining ideas together, without objects *ab extra* to cause them. (II. 37n)

Baxter also anticipates Coleridge in an interesting association of atheism with deadness, which looks forwards to Coleridge's praise of the Hebrew poetry of the Scriptures as being alive – 'in God they live and move and *have* their being':

> Atheism is equally unentertaining to the *fancy,* and to the rational faculty; disagreeable to our nature in every respect; beginning and ending in *universal deadness*; a world of brute matter, tossed about by chance, without a governing mind, and living immaterial beings in it, affords a lonely

> unpleasant prospect to the soul. If things were thus, we
> should want scope for the imagination, and even for
> rational enquiry; and must soon come to empty chance, or
> unsupported necessity, which extinguishes ideas, and puts
> an end to all pursuit.   (II. 108–9)

So dreams, in the writings of Andrew Baxter, are evidence of a living soul, and of a marvellous and mysterious imagination. The suggestion that a world of dead matter prevents the imagination from realizing its possibilities is very close to the Romantic view that the mind cannot be bound by circumstances or by necessity. Dreams are evidence for this belief, against a mechanical world of cause and effect and against the despotism of the senses, especially the eye.

The 'marvellous poetry' of dreams (F. W. Hildebrandt's phrase)[19] is important in the Romantic period, for several reasons. In the first place, dreams make new worlds, in which the imagination produces combinations and things previously unthought of. The imagination is sovereign, untrammelled and unquestioned. Secondly, Freud recognized (belatedly) that dreams depend to a great extent on the use of symbols: two consequences of this are of considerable interest. One is the idea that things which are now symbolically related were probably united in earlier times by conceptual and linguistic identity.[20] If we remember the widespread belief (articulated by Wordsworth in his 'Appendix' to the Preface to *Lyrical Ballads*) that in primitive times figurative language was the natural speech, it is clear that Freud and the Romantic poets were thinking along the same lines. The other concerns the infinite possibilities of symbols, and the many different levels on which they can be interpreted. The multi-layered, open text of the Romantics is strikingly akin to this: it is a poetry which does not provide a text which can be read in one way only, but which is suggestive, allowing a multiplicity of readings and reverberating in different ways in the mind.[21] Finally in Freud's description we should observe the powerful distinction which he made between dream-thoughts and dream-content. Dream-thoughts can be written down and analysed, whereas dream-content is always compressed and transformed. In this condensation, the content is often differently centred from the dream-thoughts: Freud called this process 'dream-displacement', and linked it with dream-condensation as one of the determining factors of dreams. At the centre there is often something deep and obscure, what Freud called 'the dream's navel, the spot which reaches down into the unknown'.[22]

The construction of a dream, and its partial interpretation, have therefore much in common with their counterparts in art; once this is observed, or even suspected, it gives rise to a distinctive kind of poetry,

concerned with the nature and processes of dreaming. A good example
is Byron's 'The Dream', in which he philosophizes about dreams in a
nicely antithetical way:

> They leave a weight upon our waking thoughts
> They take a weight from off our waking toils,
> They do divide our being; they become
> A portion of ourselves as of our time,
> And look like heralds of eternity;
>
> (ll. 7–11)

Sleep, he argues, has its own world, which is

> A boundary between the things misnamed
> Death and existence: Sleep hath its own world,
> And a wide realm of wild reality.
>
> (ll. 2–4)

He then goes on to make the significant leap between the mind in
dream-work and the mind in its usual creative and active operations,
seeing the two things as part of the same process:

> They make us what we were not – what they will,
> And shake us with the vision that's gone by,
> The dread of vanished shadows – Are they so?
> Is not the past all shadow? – What are they?
> Creations of the mind? – The mind can make
> Substance, and people planets of its own
> With beings brighter than have been, and give
> A breath to forms which can outlive all flesh.
>
> (ll. 15–22)

Byron's poem is characteristically direct, tackling the question of the
dream head-on. Other Romantic poets experience the dream-world as
an integral part of their most important imaginative experience, and
write about it without asking questions or rationalizing. They do so in
several ways.

The first of these is the direct reporting of sleeping dreams, of which
the most conspicuous examples are Wordsworth's account of the desert
Arab in Book v of *The Prelude* and Coleridge's 'Kubla Khan'. Both
poems contain examples of the mysterious and transforming power of
dreams. In *The Prelude*, for example, the Arab upon a dromedary is also
Don Quixote on Rosinante ('Of these was neither, and was both at once',
l. 126, 1805 text). He has a stone and a shell, representing geometry and

poetry respectively; they are symbols, and the poet records his complete
surrender to the imaginative vision in which they can be both books and
stone or shell:

> Strange as it may seem
> I wondered not, although I plainly saw
> The one to be a stone, th' other a shell,
> Nor doubted once but that they both were books,
> Having a perfect faith in all that passed.
>
> (1805, v. 110–14)

The interpretation of this dream is not simple, although as editors
have pointed out[23] the description of the Arab or 'semi-Quixote' as
'an uncouth shape' associates him with the discharged soldier whom
Wordsworth had befriended (as related in *The Prelude* at the end of Book
IV, immediately before this dream). The displacement of the discharged
soldier into the Arab underlines his strangeness: his progress in the
dream suggests that he has become an embodiment of well-intentioned
humanity, trying to preserve truth (in the form of geometric certainties)
and beauty (in the form of poetry). He rides through the desert, the waste
land of dryness (as it is, for example, in Ezekiel) but in his attempts to
preserve geometry and poetry he seems likely to be overwhelmed by
the uncontrollable, the great waters, by that which is magnificent but
also totally beyond the control of mankind.

The matter is complicated by the dream's similarity to a dream of
Descartes, dating from 1619. This may have been related to Wordsworth
by Beaupuy, or possibly by Coleridge,[24] and the fact that it is second
hand may account for the 1805 text of *The Prelude's* placing of the dream
in the third person. In the revisions of 1839 Wordsworth changed it to
become his own dream, and in a sense, imaginatively, he then took
possession of it. The waters of destruction (if Beaupuy was the source)
may have been the power and violence of the French Revolution, or so
it can seem with hindsight; it is impossible to say. What remains is a
curious and fascinating blend of possible starting-points for the dream:
Beaupuy, the discharged soldier, the sufferings of the English destitute,
the energies of the French Revolution, and the relation of all or some
of these to the Quixote figure, who would preserve scientific truth
and the wonder of poetry. These provide a characteristic dream set
of possibilities, a multi-layered and elusive range of meanings, open to
interpretations that are significantly different but often complementary;
but in addition to these, what remains in the mind so remarkably is
the imagery of the dream itself, that extraordinary sharp strangeness
which the reader encounters at this point in *The Prelude*. It was, said

De Quincey (who remembered it twenty years after reading it in manuscript), 'the very *ne plus ultra* of sublimity'.[25]

There is no difficulty about the starting-point for 'Kubla Khan'. In the introductory note to the poem, Coleridge described how he had been taking opium, and fallen asleep while reading a sentence from a travel book, *Purchas his Pilgrimes*, concerning Kubla's palace and the wall around its gardens. The dream-poem which develops from this is an extraordinarily clear and sharp rendering of this into pictorial imagery, followed by the sharp contrasting section on the wild scenery outside; the two are connected by the same kind of random and chimerical association that is found in dreams. The mystery of the poem, its teasing lack of logic, is part of its fascination; although it took Coleridge a long time to pluck up courage to recognize this to the full and publish the poem. He first called it 'Of the Fragment of Kubla Khan', and published it only in 1816 (having written it in 1798) after Byron had encouraged him to do so. Even then it was sent into the world 'rather as a psychological curiosity, than on the ground of any supposed *poetic* merits.'[26] In the well-known note to the poem, Coleridge claimed that it was unfinished because he had been interrupted during the writing down of the verse which had come to him in sleep; this account may or not be substantially true, but the inability to remember dreams clearly is a common experience, unless they are written down immediately.

That Coleridge was interested in 'Kubla Khan' as a dream-poem is suggested by his note in the introduction to the poem which reminds the reader that there are other dreams of pain and disease (as Erasmus Darwin had made clear), and drawing attention to his fragment 'The Pains of Sleep', published with 'Kubla Khan' and 'Christabel' in 1816. In this poem he describes three nights in succession of horrible dreams in which he saw

> a fiendish crowd
> Of shapes and thoughts that tortured me:
> A lurid light, a trampling throng,
> Sense of intolerable wrong,
> And whom I scorned, those only strong!
>
> (ll. 16–20)

In this extract the nightmare seems to be associated with the poet's waking thoughts of fear, guilt, and shame. On the third night he wakes from the dream and weeps, and acknowledges a connection between his own sins and shortcomings and the horrors of the night.

In this way the dreams of sleep are interesting to the Romantics because they reveal something of the strange inner workings of the mind, its astonishing capacity for beauty and its fearful and dark terrors.

This is closely connected with the second way in which the romantic imagination functions in relation to dreams: its reporting of waking dreams or reveries. As we have seen, Erasmus Darwin drew attention to the mind's capacity to wander from its present circumstances, and the visionary imagination is often seen at work in this way. Keats's 'Ode to a Nightingale' is a good example, as I have suggested: it is a poem which moves from a state in which it is aware of its circumstances and problems, enjoys a free-ranging imaginative encounter with the world of the nightingale, and then returns to its waking state at the end (although it is not sure which is the more 'real'). Another example of this movement, though it is described from the point of view of a *spectator ab extra* and is therefore in the third person, is Wordsworth's 'The Reverie of Poor Susan'. In the city, Susan hears the song of a captive thrush, and she sees her own country before her eyes:

> Green pastures she views in the midst of the dale,
> Down which she so often has tripped with her pail;
> And a single small cottage, a nest like a dove's,
> The one only dwelling on earth that she loves.
>
> (ll. 9–12)

Then the vision disappears:

> She looks, and her heart is in heaven: but they fade,
> The mist and the river, the hill and the shade:
> The stream will not flow, and the hill will not rise,
> And the colours have all passed away from her eyes!
>
> (ll. 13–16)

Often the dreams or reveries are like this: not only do they disappear, but they leave the poet uncomfortably aware of the dreariness of his surroundings relative to the beautiful world of his dreams. In both sleeping and waking dreams a contrast can be made between the ideal and the actual, between the beautiful possibility and the often undesirable reality. Blake uses this technique in 'The Chimney Sweeper' from *Songs of Innocence*, in which the little boy dreams of Heaven but wakes up to work on a dark morning.

The uncontrollable nature of dreams, together with their beauty and terror, leads us to the third way in which dreams are related to the Romantic imagination. This is when the word 'dream' is used as simile or metaphor, to indicate the blissful or strange nature of an experience:

> oh, then, the calm
> And dead still water lay upon my mind

Even with a weight of pleasure, and the sky,
Never before so beautiful, sank down
Into my heart, and held me like a dream.

(The Prelude, 1805, II. 176–80)

Wordsworth's poetry often has such trance-states, and in the 'Immortality Ode' the winds come to him 'from the fields of sleep'. In the same way the word 'slumber' can be used to indicate a much longer period of time than just one night, a period in which the mind was relieved from the responsibility of considering (in this case) such things as death and ageing:

A slumber did my spirit seal;
I had no human fears:
She seemed a thing that could not feel
The touch of earthly years.

No motion has she now, no force;
She neither hears nor sees;
Rolled round in earth's diurnal course,
With rocks, and stones, and trees.

('A slumber did my spirit seal')

Here the speaker is living in a 'dream' of happiness from which he awakes in the second half of the poem. This use of dream, or sleep, or slumber, to indicate a trance-like or visionary state is indicative of a whole movement away from definiteness into something unfixed, mysterious, and unpredictable. In the passage from *The Prelude* above, Wordsworth describes the circumstantial detail of the boy playing his flute upon the rocky island, and then the verse turns away into the record of his own feelings, and so into the gradual mystery of a beautiful dream. This is no longer recording experiences, whether sleeping or waking, but seeing those experiences, and others, as dream-like. It is a short step from this to a point at which questions begin to be asked about the nature of life itself in relation to such moments, and about the kind of 'reality' that exists in it. Is the period of slumber, in the case of the 'Lucy' poem, more imaginatively and morally 'alive' than the period of awakening? Is the love for Lucy more potent and lasting than the knowledge of her death? In these ways, the enquiry into dreams produces a questioning of our waking lives themselves, as it does in *A Midsummer Night's Dream* and *The Tempest*:

we are such stuff
As dreams are made on, and our little life
Is rounded with a sleep.

(The Tempest, IV. i. 156–58)

Shelley, in particular, uses the image of a dream symbolically in pursuit of Platonic speculations about life as a semblance of reality rather than the reality itself. If life itself is a dream, we shall awake to a greater reality when the soul is freed from the body (as described by Plato in the *Phaedo*). The lovely ending of 'The Sensitive Plant' is an example. When all things in the garden go to rack and ruin, after the Lady's death, Shelley comments:

> Whether that Lady's gentle mind,
> No longer with the form combined
> Which scattered love, as stars do light,
> Found sadness, where it left delight,
>
> I dare not guess; but in this life
> Of error, ignorance, and strife,
> Where nothing is, but all things seem,
> And we the shadows of the dream,
>
> It is a modest creed, and yet
> Pleasant if one considers it,
> To own that death itself must be,
> Like all the rest, a mockery.
>
> That garden sweet, that lady fair,
> And all sweet shapes and odours there,
> In truth have never passed away:
> 'Tis we, 'tis ours, are changed; not they.
>
> For love, and beauty, and delight,
> There is no death nor change: their might
> Exceeds our organs, which endure
> No light, being themselves obscure.

If love, and beauty, and delight are the only permanent things, then human life is unreal and fleeting like a dream, and our lives are mysterious in their purpose and content.

The poet's duty is to celebrate those moments of life in which love, and beauty and delight are found. If, when they happen, it seems like a dream, or a dream come true, then that is one of the functions of the imagination, as Keats realized when he told Benjamin Bailey that 'The imagination may be compared to Adam's dream – he awoke and found it truth.'[27] In Book VIII of *Paradise Lost* Adam recounts his falling asleep and dreaming of the creation of Eve, and then waking to find her present in the flesh. Keats, characteristically, sees the imagination as making the dream become flesh, and certainly one of the functions of Romantic poetry is to do this. In its most characteristic mode, however, the process is not so simple as recording dreams or capturing the dream-like loveliness of a moment. There is often a teasing uncertainty about the nature of the experience which is being recounted, a difficulty in distinguishing the shadow from the substance; and it is in this indeterminacy that Romantic poetry often flourishes. In it strange, beautiful, and terrifying experiences occur, *as if* in dreams; and dreams take on the qualities of waking life. When Wordsworth meets the leech-gatherer, in 'Resolution and Independence', he has an abstracted period during the conversation, an example of what Erasmus Darwin would call 'reverie':

> The old Man still stood talking by my side;
> But now his voice to me was like a stream
> Scarce heard; nor word from word could I divide;
> And the whole body of the Man did seem
> Like one whom I had met with in a dream;
>
> (ll. 106–10)

The transformation of dream into reality, or of reality into dream, is a vital activity of the Romantic imagination. It transforms strangeness into truth, as Coleridge saw: when describing the plan of *Lyrical Ballads*, he observed that his efforts were going to be directed to 'persons and characters supernatural, or at least romantic':

> yet so as to transfer from our inward nature a human
> interest and a semblance of truth sufficient to procure for
> these shadows of imagination that willing suspension of
> disbelief for the moment, which constitutes poetic faith.[28]

We suspend our disbelief, and the shadows become real: the dream seems to be true. Whether it is literally or scientifically true does not matter; in fact it is better left uncertain. This is why 'The Rime of the Ancient Mariner' exercises such a spell over the reader; it is a 'poem of pure imagination', but it is told in a way which makes it seem urgently human and absolutely credible. If it is classified as a dream, its power immediately disappears, because it can be parcelled up and put away in a category. Lamb saw this clearly, when he opened the 1800 edition of *Lyrical Ballads*:

> I am sorry that Coleridge has christened his Ancient
> Marinere 'a poet's Reverie' – it is as bad as Bottom the
> Weaver's declaration that he is not a Lion but only the
> scenical representation of a Lion. What new idea is gained
> by this Title, but one subversive of all credit, which the
> Tale should force upon us, of its truth?[29]

Lamb's invocation of *A Midsummer Night's Dream* is significant, for it reminds the reader of the play in which Shakespeare brilliantly teases the spectator with ideas of illusion and reality. The action is magical and beautiful, terrifying and sinister, a very midsummer madness; and madness and dreams are closely allied, as David Simpson has pointed out.[30]

Finally, the dream-like modes of Romantic poetry have consequences for its interpretation. There is often a dark and mysterious centre to Romantic poetry, an inscrutable and magical quality that exists in image and symbol, and in the spaces between them. This is the poetic equivalent of Freud's 'the dream's navel, the spot which reaches down into the unknown': on the page there are infinite uncertainties in the gaps within the text itself, forming what Wolfgang Iser calls 'a no-man's-land of indeterminacy',[31] and in the multi-layered possibilities of the images and symbols themselves. The reader has to accept the mysterious and respect it. It is necessary to activate an imagination in order to receive the poem at all: not, of course, to try to 'understand' it, to limit it to one interpretation, or to the confined edges of the reader's own mind, but to experience its power and its mysterious magic. And this, as we shall see, affects the way in which the work of the Romantic poets is read.

The human condition

The Romantic poets' interest in nature and in dreams is balanced by an equally strong interest in the social and political state of the world around them, and in the effect of this upon themselves as human beings. The tendency to see the Romantic period as imaginative and irrational has to be modified by the need to acknowledge its powerful awareness of politics, class, and international affairs. All the poets were politically committed: one (Leigh Hunt) went to prison for his beliefs, and one (Wordsworth) witnessed part of the French Revolution at first hand. For all of them idealism conflicted with experience: the awareness that politics is the art of the possible became a source of tension, as they reluctantly came to terms with it (in the case of Wordsworth) or fiercely rejected it (as Shelley and Blake did).

In every case, the major Romantic poets allied themselves with revolutionary causes. Blake became a member of a radical circle in London; Wordsworth was a friend of Godwin and others; Coleridge was an enthusiast for Pantisocracy a scheme which he and others, including Southey, drew up for settling in a community in America.

Byron spoke in the House of Lords on behalf of framebreakers: Shelley was a political agitator in Ireland, and Keats a supporter of Leigh Hunt in his attack on the Prince Regent. Throughout, their stand was dictated by what they saw with their own eyes and judged to be true.

The England which they looked out on was divided between the progressive, forceful, energetic, and successful elements on the one hand and the discontented, neglected, and poverty-stricken on the other. During the eighteenth century certain significant material changes took place: roads became better, canals were built, and iron-smelting became a major industry. Abraham Darby's iron bridge over the Severn is dated 1779; in the same decade Richard Arkwright set up spinning mills at Cromford in Derbyshire. In London, Henry Fielding and his brother John had both worked hard as magistrates to make the city less violent and better policed; while in the villages the rural trades and the labouring poor continued to depend upon the land, at first as individual farmers and later as workers for others who had enclosed the land.

In the countryside enclosure was a major feature of the later part of the eighteenth century, although it had been going on intermittently for many years. It was given considerable encouragement after 1660, and was seen by one historian of 1682 as one of the principal benefits of 'His Majesty's most happy Restoration'. Abuses in the system under His Majesty's government's most ineffective control led to standing orders for enclosure in 1774, after which enclosure became better regulated, and hence more widely accepted. It involved (i) the laying together of scattered properties, (ii) the abolition of common rights, and (iii) the hedging and ditching of the new properties.[32]

The immediate effect of this was the cruel sense of life being brutally changed. It is found most movingly in the poetry of John Clare, the Northamptonshire peasant-poet who wrote so accurately and lovingly about his native village of Helpston and its surrounding countryside. Clare saw the fields that he loved changing year by year:

> By Langley bush I roam but the bush hath left its hill
> On cowper green I stray 'tis a desert strange & chill
> & spreading lea close oak ere decay had penned its will
> To the axe of the spoiler & self interest fell a prey
> & crossberry way & old round oaks narrow lane
> With its hollow trees like pulpits I shall never see again
> Inclosure like a Buonaparte let not a thing remain
> It levelled every bush & tree & levelled every hill . . .
>
> ('Remembrances', ll. 61–68)

Nor was it just the poor who suffered: the small landowner often had his land prised from him by force, as larger property-owners attempted to acquire neighbouring plots. In one of the 'Salisbury Plain' poems, an early and uncompromising version of 'Guilt and Sorrow', Wordsworth describes the relentless pressure put upon the weak by the strong:

> There rose a mansion proud our woods among,
> And cottage after cottage owned its sway,
> No joy to see a neighbouring house, or stray
> Through pastures not his own, the master took;
> My Father dared his greedy wish gainsay
> He loved his old hereditary nook,
> And ill could I the thought of such sad parting brook.
>
> But, when he had refused the proffered gold,
> To cruel injuries he became a prey,
> Sore travers'd in whate'er he bought and sold:
> His troubles grew upon him day by day,
> Till all his substance fell into decay . . .
>
> ('Adventures on Salisbury Plain', ll. 300–11)

The drift to the towns and to the new industries was the consequence of this: it led to the increase in the urban population which began in the eighteenth century and became a major problem in the nineteenth.

The sensitivity to the sufferings of the poor is found everywhere: 'To a Young Ass', which describes the ass's master as living 'Half famish'd in a land of luxury', is an example of the way in which Coleridge evokes compassion for others, whether poor, or city-bound, in his early poetry. Both Keats and Shelley were concerned with the destructive effects of capitalism: in *Queen Mab* Shelley describes a great spirit forced 'to mould a pin, or fabricate a nail' (v. 142), and in *Isabella* Keats describes the proud brothers as enjoying the fruits of others' labours:

> . . . for them many a weary hand did swelt
> In torched mines and noisy factories,
> And many once proud-quiver'd loins did melt
> In blood from stinging whip; – with hollow eyes
> Many all day in dazzling river stood,
> To take the rich-ored driftings of the flood.
>
> For them the Ceylon diver held his breath,
> And went all naked to the hungry shark; . . .
>
> (st. 14–15)

The dislike of capitalists and the middle classes is found also in Byron, though from a different point of view: Byron despises them for the style of their lives and for their hypocrisy (anticipating Matthew

Arnold's treatment of the Victorian middle class). They were allied with
the evangelicals, justifiably flushed with success after the abolition of
the slave trade, who were denounced by Cobbett as 'canting hypocrites'
who wanted 'to teach the poor to starve without making a noise'.[33]

All the Romantic poets are compassionate about the poor, and
sceptical about the use of political power and religious influence. In
the face of such human misery, kings and princes stand condemned,
and religion seems the pious luxury of a flaccid middle class. Indeed,
it is possible that the experience of being poor was seen as somehow
more authentic than other modes of living (much as fear and guilt are
seen as authentic in the twentieth century). To be poor is to be naked
and unaccommodated, neglected by the powerful and unsupported by
any provision apart from the poor relief and the workhouse. So we find
Wordsworth, in the Preface to 'Guilt and Sorrow', brooding in 1793 on
the 'distress and misery' that would be caused by the war with France,
and on the 'calamities, principally those consequent upon war, to which,
more than other classes of men, the poor are subject'. A major tenet
of the Preface to *Lyrical Ballads* is the belief that the *experience* (not the
language) of the poor in the countryside is more authentically human
than the experience of those classes who are protected by money or the
structures of society:

> Humble and rustic life was generally chosen, because, in
> that condition, the essential passions of the heart find a
> better soil in which they can attain their maturity, are less
> under restraint, and speak a plainer and more emphatic
> language; because in that condition of life our elementary
> feelings coexist in a state of greater simplicity, . . .[34]

The feelings speak 'a plainer and more emphatic language': the idea
is metaphorical, not literal, as it has so often been taken to be, and
Wordsworth is speaking of the inability of the poor to disguise their
suffering and their feelings – not being cushioned by money, land, or
rank. The figures of *Lyrical Ballads* are good examples: Goody Blake,
Simon Lee, Betty Foy, Martha Ray, have no support from the society
in which they live, but have to cope with their own problems using
their own resources. In the noble letter written to John Wilson about
'The Idiot Boy', for example, Wordsworth specifically identifies the
mothers and fathers of mentally defective children in 'the lower classes
of society' as demonstrating love in a particularly pure form. The
wealthy can send their children away, or pay for people to look after
them: the poor have to do it themselves, and in their case (which has
no hope of reward or return) we see 'the strength, disinterestedness and
grandeur of human love'.

There is, therefore, an existential authenticity in the lives of the poor, and this is intuitively recognized by the Romantic poets, whether or not they then go on to call for political action. Wordsworth, in particular, is interested in the way in which poverty can either be survived with fortitude (the leech-gatherer, the discharged soldier in *The Prelude* Book IV) or can lead to crime. Often good men, as William Godwin had recognized, are driven to do evil by becoming desperate: Wordsworth gives an extreme example, of a murderer, in 'Guilt and Sorrow'.

Crime, whether the result of economic and social pressure or not, is a major interest of the Romantics. Wordsworth's *The Borderers*, for instance, creates a situation which is as bad as it is possible to find: an old, blind man is left to die on a bleak waste land. The drama traces the complicated web of deception by which a good man is led to engineer this: it is an example of confusion rather than criminal psychology, but is illuminating about the way in which well-intentioned men can end up by doing evil (in this respect the drama is related to the French Revolution, which shows the same thing happening on a national scale). Not far removed from this is a figure such as Coleridge's ancient mariner, who shoots the albatross without any apparent motive. Other criminals, such as Shelley's Count Cenci, wish to push the limits of human behaviour as far as they can be extended:

> I do not feel as if I were a man,
> But like a fiend appointed to chastise
> The offences of some unremembered world . . .
>
> (*The Cenci*, IV. i. 160–62)

Mario Praz, in *The Romantic Agony*, ascribes this strain of Romanticism to the influence of the Marquis de Sade: the fascination which it exerts over the Romantic mind is found more in the novel than in poetry, but it is given a firm local base in Crabbe's *Peter Grimes*, a poem which gives a local habitation to sadism in the figure of the cruel fisherman. Grimes is a wild and lawless man,

> But no success could please his cruel soul,
> He wish'd for one to trouble and control;
> He wanted some obedient boy to stand
> And bear the blow of his outrageous hand;
>
> (ll. 53–56)

After the deaths of three boys, he is ostracized by the community, and punished by fearful visions, dying in terror and pain. He is one example of the interest in punishment, which is found in 'The Ancient Mariner' and in the renderings of the figure of Cain in Coleridge and Byron.

What drives man to crime? How is he punished, and how does his punishment affect him? These are fundamental questions for the Romantics, and the answers range on a continuum from explicable crime (of the kind found in Wordsworth) to the crime which, as in Count Cenci or the ancient mariner, is ultimately a mystery. These questions and answers are often explored in Gothic fiction, which is outside the scope of this book, but which needs to be remembered when considering the treatment of mysterious, strange, or criminal figures in poetry. Gothic literature is not just a matter of exploiting atmosphere, of manipulating stage-properties such as ruined abbeys, cellars, tunnels, castles, or suits of armour: it is concerned with the unusual or strange behaviour of individuals, with alienation, heart-searching, and frustrated hope. Sometimes, in Gothic poetry, the mystery is deepened by the presence of forces or figures who control others. Coleridge's Christabel, for instance, appears to be dominated by the mysterious Geraldine, and Keats's knight-at-arms is under a spell, like one of Spenser's knights:

> I saw pale kings, and princes too,
> Pale warriors, death-pale were they all;
> Who cry'd – 'La belle Dame sans merci
> Hath thee in thrall!'
>
> ('La Belle Dame sans Merci', ll. 37–40)

The influence of the ballad form is clear: in particular, Thomas Percy's *Reliques of Ancient English Poetry* (1765) quickened an interest in the form and subject-matter of popular ballad and ancient folk-tale. Percy's collection included ballads such as 'The Ancient Ballad of Chevy Chase', 'The Battle of Otterbourne', 'The Jew's Daughter', 'Edward, Edward', and 'Sir Patrick Spence'. Percy described them as having 'a romantic wildness', and as being 'in the true spirit of chivalry'; he noted also that they had been for the most part produced by minstrels, whose state had declined since the sixteenth century.[35] Percy's work inspired Chatterton to produce imitation medieval poems, and Scott remembered that

> The very grass sod seat to which (when a boy of twelve
> years old) I retreated from my playfellows, to devour the
> works of the ancient minstrels, is still fresh and dear to my
> memory.[36]

Wordsworth was 'proud to acknowledge his obligations to the Reliques'[37] and Coleridge admired them too, as the opening of 'Dejection, an Ode' suggests. More important than these individual examples, however, is the diffusion of the spirit of ballad literature and its transformation into the mysterious violent heroism of the Byronic figure such as Lara:

> Too high for common selfishness, he could
> At time resign his own for others' good
> But not in pity, not because he ought,
> But in some strange perversity of thought,
> That swayed him onward with a secret pride
> To do what few or none would do beside;
> And this same impulse would, in tempting time,
> Mislead his spirit equally to crime;
>
> (*Lara*, I. st. 18)

His love is frustrated because 'his early dreams of good outstripp'd the truth' and this leads to wild passions and a stormy life. But he is clearly a hero: his capacity for love and hate are greater than those of most men, and he stands out from the crowd in every way.

The Byronic hero, from Childe Harold onwards, is characteristic of an interest in the unusual and heroic figure. In the political world of the time it was an age of heroes, such as Pitt and Fox. Wordsworth, in remote Grasmere, after a stormy day, thought of the dying Fox: 'A Power is passing from the earth', he wrote. While others write about warlike heroes (Nelson, Wellington, Napoleon), Wordsworth celebrates the liberators, such as Thomas Clarkson, who wore himself out in the fight against slavery, and Toussaint l'Ouverture, leader of the insurrection at St Domingo when Napoleon re-established slavery there, who was taken to Paris and died in prison:

> Thou hast left behind
> Powers that will work for thee; air, earth, and skies;
> There's not a breathing of the common wind
> That will forget thee; thou hast great allies;
> Thy friends are expectations, agonies,
> And love, and man's unconquerable mind.
>
> ('To Toussaint l'Ouverture', ll. 9–14)

The last magnificent phrase echoes and re-echoes across the political poetry of the period. It sets an inviolable individuality against the compromise and servitude of tyrants and their vassals. It is found in Keats's admiration for Leigh Hunt, imprisoned for telling the truth, in Byron's description of Bonnivard in the Castle of Chillon, in Shelley's portrait of Ugolino in 'The Tower of Famine'. These are heroes in their suffering, as great as Pitt or Nelson in success: their greatness comes from their ability to withstand corruption, and in this respect they are projections of what the poets themselves would like to be, heroic crusaders against false thinking, illiberal policies, and unfair systems of government. They are contemporary manifestations of Gray's bard figure.

But this heroism is not confined to such matters as politics. Wordsworth saw heroism in the actual growth of the human soul, and Keats in his letters (characterized by Lionel Trilling as 'the poet as hero') describes the world in terms of self-making and self-achieving:

> The common cognomen of this world among the
> misguided and superstitious is 'a vale of tears' from which
> we are to be redeemed by a certain arbitrary interposition
> of God and taken to Heaven – what a little circumscribed
> straightened notion! Call the world if you Please 'The vale
> of Soul-making' . . .[38]

Behind the human manifestations of heroism lies the concept itself, and the great figures of myth and legend who give expression to it. The central one is Prometheus, the daring fire-stealer, the revolutionary and the benefactor of mankind, who can suffer unimaginable and unending tortures and still forgive his torturers. His superiority to Jupiter the tyrant is obvious: he embodies within himself all the aspirations of nobility, power, and generosity which the Romantic poets desired to possess.

Keats described Wordsworth as a poet of the 'egotistical sublime', and it is a curious coincidence that a few months earlier than Cowper's 'The Castaway', which views the self with so much despair, Wordsworth should have begun work on the recollections of his own early life that were to grow into The Prelude. The coincidence is instructive: Cowper is writing out of the imprisonment of his own self,[39] cast overboard in the damnation of which he was certain; Wordsworth was celebrating the survival of his central self, of the imaginative powers which had been nurtured in childhood and attained a new maturity through the experiences which followed. Nothing in The Prelude is more daring than this acceptance of the self, and nothing is more like tight-rope walking than the path which Wordsworth treads between the justified celebration of his own personality and a complacent egotism. To the Romantics the self can still be a prison: Byron, deep in the writing of his adventure tales, wrote in his journal (27 November 1813): 'To withdraw *myself* from *myself* (oh that cursed selfishness!) has ever been my sole, my entire, my sincere motive in scribbling at all.'[40] Byron attempted, or said he did, to 'lose himself' in the world of nature around him:

> I live not in myself, but I become
> Portion of that around me;
>
> (III. st. 72)

he writes in *Childe Harold's Pilgrimage*; although in the journal of the tour which inspired Canto III he decided that none of the sublime effects of alpine scenery 'enabled me to lose my own wretched identity in the majesty & the power, and the Glory-around-above-& beneath me'.[41]

It is tempting to see the Romantic poets as following this pattern, as trying to lose themselves in nature; but it would not be true. Primarily the Romantic poets are interested in themselves, in what Kathleen Coburn has called 'the self-conscious imagination';[42] this can relate to nature, but in ways which enhance its own self-awareness. As Harold Bloom has written: 'In the covenant between Wordsworth and nature, two powers that are totally separate from each other, and potentially destructive of the other, try to meet in a dialectic of love.'[43] The central image is that of the soul, no longer used in a specifically religious sense but as that which is capable of feeling and independent of the senses. The soul is an endless subject of interest, a place of struggle and heroic feats:

> O heavens, how awful is the might of souls,
> And what they do within themselves while yet
> The yoke of earth is new to them, the world
> Nothing but a wild field where they were sown.
> This is in truth heroic argument,
> And genuine prowess –
>
> (*The Prelude*, 1805, III. 178–83)

Cowper was concerned with the soul in an evangelical religious way, preoccupied with his own damnation; Wordsworth saw the soul as the first necessary gift of a poet, 'the vital soul' of a thinking and feeling person whose response to the world is somehow more exciting and alive than that of most people. In the Preface to *Lyrical Ballads*, therefore, Wordsworth described the poet as 'a man speaking to men; a man, it is true, endowed with more lively sensibility, more enthusiasm and tenderness, who has a greater knowledge of human nature, and a more comprehensive soul, than are supposed to be common among mankind';[44] and he saw a daily communication with nature as one way of encouraging this. This role is closely connected with the prophetic: the poet is given special powers, or he wins through to them. There is a powerful motive in the need to carve out a set of beliefs and codes of behaviour from individual experience. The self thus becomes important as the testing-ground of that experience and the centre of moral feeling; and the more stable and creative the self, the more it can rejoice in its relationship with the external world. The result is an interest in the individual self which leads to an endless fascination with the feelings, the gifts, the intellectual and emotional power, time and place. Self-consciousness therefore leads, paradoxically, to a greater interest in the external world, in the features of it which affect the individual. 'Who is it that can tell me what I am?' is the echoing question: who, and what, and where, and when? Where was I born, what are my lasting memories, what was my relationship with my parents, how do I respond to the world around me? – these are all questions which arise from the self-consciousness of the Romantic poet.

That self-consciousness results in Romantic Irony, which is not the simple irony of saying one thing and meaning another; it is a concept identified by Friedrich Schlegel, a philosophical irony which sees the world as 'fundamentally chaotic', and art as finding a form which responds to this. It has been definitively studied by Anne K. Mellor, in *English Romantic Irony* (1980), where she points out that Schlegel saw the artist as aware of his humanity and his limitations at the very moment when he is creating the fictions of his own mind. It involves a self-awareness that is also a sense of limitation:

> Philosophical irony, this inevitable and all-important
> consciousness of the limitations of human knowledge and
> of human language, is thus the necessary prerequisite and
> counter force to love and creative imagination. It criticizes
> and thus negates one's excessive commitment to the
> fictions of one's own mind, thereby enabling one to sustain
> contact with reality. It insists that 'The fancy cannot cheat
> so well/As she is fam'd to do.' And thus it renews one's
> direct participation in an always-becoming life.[45]

The result is a poise between assertion and negation, between commitment and detachment – 'the use of opposing voices, ideas, and even artistic structures operates both to affirm and to undermine the artist and his vision'.[46] The most obvious example of this is found in the work of Byron, with its endlessly shifting perspectives, and its changes of mood, in which one section will undercut another; but in its emphasis on the unstable relationship between the order of art and the chaos of life, and between the artist's work and his inner consciousness, Romantic Irony indicates a movement and flux at the heart of Romanticism.

Reading the Romantic Poets

One of the reasons why so much has been written about Romantic poetry during the last twenty years is that it has seemed to be particularly responsive to the kinds of questioning posed by modern critical theory. These include questions about language and meaning, and about form and content: in certain ways the poetry written during this period is exceptional in its awareness of the problems of language and the indeterminacies of meaning. Romantic poetry often ends in a question mark, as Keats's 'Ode to a Nightingale' or Shelley's 'I dream'd that as I wander'd by the way' do; even if they do not, they often conclude with a puzzling indefiniteness. Who is to say what is meant by 'My heart aches, and a drowsy numbness pains/ My sense'? or by

> 'Beauty is truth, truth beauty' – that is all
> Ye know on earth, and all ye need to know

or by the version with different punctuation:

> 'Beauty is truth, truth beauty – that is all
> Ye know on earth, and all ye need to know' . . .?

The problems involve not only the deliberate questions, but also the open-endedness of poems, and a pervasive indeterminacy of meaning, in addition to the problems introduced by what are, essentially, different texts. When Wordsworth writes in *The Prelude* Book VII of seeing the blind beggar in the streets of London, he remarks upon him as a single form standing out from the crowd:

> As the black storm upon the mountain-top
> Sets off the sunbeam in the valley, so
> That huge fermenting mass of human-kind
> Serves as a solemn background, or relief,
> To single forms and objects, whence they draw,
> For feeling and contemplative regard,
> More than inherent liveliness and power.
>
> (1850 text, VII. 619–25)

Wordsworth is speaking of a natural effect – the black cloud and the sunbeam – and the way in which faces stand out from the crowd; but he is also speaking of the way in which the human mind works, of the way in which it shapes and 'draws liveliness and power' to enable 'feeling and contemplative regard'. There is not only a complex interaction between external and internal here, between the workings of the mind and the objects of contemplation, so that it is difficult to know where one ends and the other begins; there is also a series of words which are suggestive rather than definitive – 'feeling', 'contemplative regard', 'inherent liveliness', 'power'. His choice of these words indicates a probing curiosity into the workings of the mind which is beautifully contrasted with the portrayal of the beggar. Surrounded by the 'fermenting mass', an image which suggests the seething and endless activity of yeast, the beggar stands still, with a written paper held on his chest:

> to explain
> His story, whence he came, and what he was.
>
> (VII. 641–2)

The paper is the beggar's life story, as *The Prelude* is Wordsworth's, and we may detect, perhaps, a subtle questioning here: how can a piece of paper tell you everything about a person? In contrast to it is the poet's response:

> Caught by the spectacle my mind turned round
> As with the might of waters; an apt type
> This label seemed of the utmost we can know.
> Both of ourselves and of the universe; . . .
>
> (VII. 643–6)

When the poet's mind turns 'as with the might of waters', we sense the power of the image but also the difficulty of ascribing any precise meaning to it; and the suggestion that a brief label with a name and address is a type (or emblem) of 'the utmost we can know' is a bold statement of mystery. In one sense, perhaps, it is all that we can be sure of; but in another sense, it suggests that we should contemplate the external world not as something material (and taken for granted) but as wonderful, mysterious, unfathomable – in the same way as we can only partially know and understand our own selves.

The lines are characteristic of Wordsworth in their extraordinary ability to engage intricately with the processes of the mind, to suggest and re-suggest, to be complex and simple, precise and indeterminate. And an understanding of them depends, also, on the reader. Wordsworth was (and is) describing this moment *to* somebody – to Coleridge in the first instance, but beyond him to any reader who cares to pick up the poem; and, of course, the interpretation of the passage will depend on the reader's response, not only to the obvious meaning of the beggar standing out from the crowd, but also to the syntax, the imagery, the patterning of the lines, the rhythms, the ebb and flow of defined and undefined, of thought and feeling, reason and mystery. So the understanding depends on two things: the language which is used, and the way in which that language is read.

Language

We recognize this poem, this part of the poem, the work of this author, because it is itself, and not anything else. The differences or unlikenesses may seem obvious, but they are important: they draw attention to the way in which words function in relationship to one another, as systems of signs, and how the signs differ from one another to give meaning (so that we understand a sign because our minds register that it is not another sign). Each line, each expression, is an individual use of the resources of language: there is also the abstract thing behind, which we call 'language', the resources from which the individual utterances are drawn. Saussure, from whom structuralist criticism descends, called these respectively *langue* (the language system) and *parole* (the individual speech taken from that language). The writer chooses one set of words, and thus presents his individual *parole*, selected from the possibilities of the *langue* (we recognize a poem by its form – the shape and number of the verses, and then by the differences in the lines and words).

Every poet has to make his or her choice, to accept the formal limitation which is imposed by the need to use words; each makes an individual decision, and the text which results depends for its identity on the difference between it and another text, or the text which it might have been and is not. An art such as Blake's depends on making the familiar unfamiliar, often in surprising ways, and deceptively. An examination of his language draws attention to the way in which (as with all poetry) the art is in the devices of language, and especially in those devices which set it apart from everyday communication. The Russian Formalist Viktor Shklovsky, best known for his idea of 'defamiliarization', distinguished between 'practical' language, the language of everyday use (often thought of as 'economical') and poetic language: in 'practical' language, thought becomes habitual, whereas, 'the technique of art is to make objects "unfamiliar" . . . Art removes objects from the automatism of perception.' The result is a language which we recognize, perhaps unconsciously, as different from that of everyday speech, in spite of what Wordsworth said about the 'selection of language really used by men'. The deviation from a norm is what produces style: figurative language, and unusual word order, are the rhetoric by which we encounter a 'special perception of the object'.[47]

Interpretation

The work of art is comprehended as such by the boundaries which the writer imposes upon it. So Formalist criticism would draw attention to the way in which a work *selects* from the innumerable possibilities of speech; and as Rene Girard has written, 'To examine a work of art . . . [is] to attempt to discover what the work *omits* as much as – if not more than – what it includes. That is surely the first step in any critical venture.'[48] We appreciate the individuality of a work of art not only by what it says, but also by what it does not say – so that *Kubla Khan*, for example, does not seem to be about Coleridge's changing opinions on the French Revolution, as *France: an Ode* is.

And yet it is very difficult to be *sure* that *Kubla Khan* is not about the French Revolution: the idea of a prince, such as Kubla, building a palace for his own pleasure, and enclosing it with a wall, and subsequently hearing 'ancestral voices prophesying war' may suggest that there is, somewhere, an element of the poem which would encourage a political interpretation, or at least suggest that the French experience of a popular rising against the *ancien régime* and the execution of Louis XVI is not entirely irrelevant.

There is a 'common-sense' attitude to such a theory, which would dismiss it as nonsense, or at least peripheral to the poem's meaning. But is such common sense sufficient? Are we justified in dismissing other interpretations, and if so by what authority do we do it? Romantic poetry, by its very language, its complex inclusions and exclusions, encourages the asking of such awkward questions. So does the climate of European politics: the 'authority' by which so many value judgements have been made during the years that literature has been studied in universities (since late in the nineteenth century) has been linked by some writers with the culture of nationalism, imperialism, and class. In every case we meet the danger of an individual or a collective viewpoint which presses the claims of its own interpretations and value judgements.

The debates of critics, of course, serve a purpose (however unlikely this may seem) in allowing the clash of different viewpoints. Each of those points of view is in danger of what Heidegger identified as the hermeneutical circle, in which the reader receives from a text what suits him or her, because he or she brings to it certain preconceived ideas and preferences. The reader gets from a text what he or she brings to it; and David Simpson has argued that this is something which the literature itself exists to frustrate: 'Romantic poetry', he writes, 'is organized to make us confront the question of authority, especially as it pertains to the contract between author and reader.'[49] Much of the most interesting work on Romantic poetry in recent years has focussed on this destabilizing of the author–reader relationship, in which the reader is denied a single or simple reading, and prevented from finding a simple authorial voice: in David Simpson's words, one kind of reader 'might tend to enact a synthesis of the various contraries within the poem as part of the process of reading:

> For such a reader, this synthesis would be a precondition of intelligibility; he would be looking for a voice which could speak for a coherent personality, one into which he could comfortably read himself.[50]

The meaning is unsettled: we may recognize the force of this in many places, including, very obviously, Blake's lyrics and Wordsworth's 'Lucy' poems. An example such as

> A slumber did my spirit seal;
> I had no human fears:
> She seemed a thing that could not feel
> The touch of earthly years . . .

is full of problems, ambiguities and indeterminacies.

Such criticism deconstructs the simple and surface meanings and replaces them with unstable and hidden ones, and in the process it opens up new opportunities for the understanding of Romantic poetry. It is also liberating, in a heady manner: critics such as Roland Barthes have argued that texts should just be experienced, and not interpreted – a text 'answers not to an interpretation, liberal though it may be, but to an explosion, a dissemination'.[51] Barthes even rejects the suggestion that one text influences another, because this produces what he calls the 'myth of filiation', in which one text is produced by its relationship with an earlier one; this, of course, would push the second text towards a stable entity, subject to interpretation.

But the text is, as Terry Eagleton has neatly put it, an invitation to the reader to construct signs into meaning.[52] It thus becomes a test of the reader's ability to 'read', to bring to the text as much of the necessary knowledge and sensitivity as possible. Criticism often involves the provision of that knowledge, in the understanding of history and historical conditions, or in pointing out the debt of one author to another. Yet in pointing out these things, the best criticism will clearly not be over-explicit or rigid. In the understanding of Romantic poetry, it will be poised between 'meaning' and indeterminacy, between emphasizing the specific debts of one poet to another and acknowledging the general awareness of other speech and writing.

In the recognition of specific meaning, the concept of intertextuality, in which one text is in relationship with another, is of importance to Romantic poetry. *The Prelude* is Wordsworth's attempt at an epic, written in the shadow of *Paradise Lost*; and, as we have seen, Gray's *The Bard* was a prototype of a certain kind of prophetic utterance. Yet beyond these individual debts there are obscurer ones, and Mikhail Bakhtin has described the processes of intertextuality thus:

> Any speaker is himself a respondent to a greater or lesser degree. He is not, after all, the first speaker, the one who disturbs the eternal silence of the universe. And he presupposes not only the existence of the language system he is using, but also the existence of preceding utterances – his own and others' – with which his given utterance enters into one or other kind of relation (builds on them, polemicizes with them, or simply presumes that they are already known to the listener). Any utterance is a link in a very complexly organized chain of other utterances.[53]

The most interesting study of this is Harold Bloom's *The Anxiety of Influence*, in which he argues that poets are always uneasily aware of their predecessors: weak poets will imitate, but strong poets will misread the older poets and wrestle with them. Wordsworth's attitude to Milton is one example; Blake's challenge to Isaac Watts's very successful *Divine and Moral Songs for Children* is another.

Some critics would argue that this is an artificial or conscious borrowing, rather than intertextuality proper, for they would point out that all writing is intertextual. 'The text', says Roland Barthes, 'is a tissue of quotations drawn from the innumerable centres of culture'.[54] This idea recognizes that words are, as we have seen, signs, involved in sign systems. We understand them, and the systems, not by some instant and marvellous process through which we arrive at some immediate understanding of meaning, but through a complex and patient accumulation of knowledge since childhood. 'We know our native language', writes Mikhail Bakhtin, '– its lexical composition and grammatical structure' –

> not from dictionaries and grammars but from concrete utterances which we hear and which we ourselves reproduce in live speech communication with people around us. We assimilate forms of language only in forms of utterances and in conjunction with those forms . . . If

> speech genres did not exist and we had not mastered them,
> if we had to originate them during the speech process and
> construct each utterance at will for the first time, speech
> communication would be almost impossible.[55]

Everything we say, in any given situation, is thus related to everything else that has ever been said, to the whole language system; it relates to everything we have and are, to half-remembered quotations, to the culture we are a part of, to our body and our past. In addition, however, there is a conscious level at which these things become significant and evident; with written texts, we recognize what is original by the way in which it differs from what has been written before. We know, conversely, that it is a borrowing, or an echo, or a cliché, if it echoes words that have been used previously in the same sign system. Or at other times we can recognize that one text is alluding to another, indeed, only has significance *because* it is alluding to another. Every text is written upon, or over against, previous texts, and intertextuality is a recognition of the inevitability of this process. But sometimes it sharpens the meaning with undeniable force: as in Wordsworth's 'Simon Lee', which alludes at the end to previous poetic statements about ingratitude, and stands them on their heads.

Reading and Writing, the Interpretive Community

If Romantic poetry is often characterized by an indeterminacy or elusiveness of meaning, more responsibility is placed on the shoulders of the reader. In one sense, the reader takes the signs on the page and interprets them in such a way that he is reading creatively, writing his own poem from the indications which are given. He is supplied with what Roland Barthes would call a 'writerly' text, one with which the reader can experiment, and even 'play'. This idea of 'play' is important to Barthes, who uses it in at least two senses: that of 'playing' the text, or with the text, as a pianist might play a piece; and as a image for the flexibility of the text, which Barthes likens to the 'play' of a door, or of any construction in which there is some 'play', or movement. The mind 'plays' the text, and gets pleasure from doing so – what Barthes calls 'le plaisir du texte'.[56]

The relevance of this to Romantic poetry is, I hope, obvious: one principal delight of the work of Blake, Wordsworth, Coleridge and the others is the way in which their poems encourage a creative reading which is also a 'playing' of the texts and a playing with the texts. But if this is the case, is there any point in writing a book on Romantic poetry at all? Does the reading of romantic poetry – or rather the 'writing' of it in the reading activity – become an individual activity in which all meanings can be made to seem valid? In the multiple voices, the plural texts, and the endless play of indeterminate signifiers, are we to find any common ground that enables us to write meaningfully about Romantic poetry?

Perhaps the most useful answer is that given by Stanley Fish, in his concept of the 'interpretive community'. In his book *Is there a Text in this Class?*, Fish describes a student asking the question 'Is there a text in this class? . . . I mean in this class do we believe in poems and things, or is it just us?'.[57] Fish's answer is that human beings form interpretive communities, and that these

> are made up of those who share interpretive strategies
> not for reading (in the conventional sense) but for writing
> texts, for constituting their properties and assigning their
> intentions. In other words, these strategies exist prior to the
> act of reading and therefore determine the shape of what
> is read rather than, as is usually assumed, the other way
> around.[58]

The implications of this are that the reading of Romantic poetry may change, as the assumptions of the readers change: indeed, the reading of all great literature is a dialogue between the past and the present, so that the perceptions of it are perpetually changing. Good critics make us see the work of the past in a different way, more clearly or more definitively – or they can make us acknowledge that the literature of the past is more elusive and polysemic than we had thought.

If the literature of the Romantic period is subject to such variable readings and re-readings, it is all the more necessary to understand the historical context in which the poetry was written and produced. This is one way out of the hermeneutical circle, in which our responses would be conditioned by the presuppositions of our own age. The other is to perceive the mode of operation of Romantic poetry, and here we can use the concept of the poets as prophet-figures, producing a kind of secularized religion, as I have done in much of the present book; or the concept of Romantic Irony, which emphasizes the fertility of the chaos which is the world, and the way in which the artist responds to it with what Anne K. Mellor calls 'an aesthetic mode that sustains this ontological reality, this never-ending becoming'.[59]

Reading the Romantic poets, therefore, is a matter of being sensitive to their stated aims, but also to their necessary fluctuations of meaning and their indeterminacies of stance. It requires a knowledge of the historical, social, and intellectual circumstances in which they worked, but also an awareness of their self-awareness, and of their state of becoming as well as being. The poets find themselves, as Wordsworth did, fascinated by the actual business of writing, in which the label on the blind beggar seems 'an apt type' or emblem –

> of the utmost we can know,
> Both of ourselves and of the universe;

With its implication that Schlegel would have recognized – that there is far more of the universe, of its wonders and its chaos, than we can ever know.

Notes

1. See Alfred North Whitehead, *Science and the Modern World* (Cambridge, 1933), p. 101: Whitehead contrasts *Paradise Lost* and Pope's *Essay on Man* with the opening of *The Excursion*, which begins out of doors.

2. Essay, supplementary to the Preface, *The Poetical Works of William Wordsworth*, edited by E. de Selincourt and H. Darbishire, 5 vols (Oxford, 1940–49) II, 419–20.

3. See the introduction to *The Seasons*, edited by James Sambrook (Oxford, 1981), especially pp. xcii–xxxiv.

4. *The Seasons*, p. xxxii.

5. Quoted in J. R. Watson, *Picturesque Landscape and English Romantic Poetry* (London, 1970) p. 16.

6. *Correspondence of Thomas Gray*, edited by P. Toynbee and L. Whibley, 3 vols (Oxford, 1935), III, 1090.

7. All references are to the first edition, 2 vols (London, 1786).

8. William Gilpin, *Essay on Prints* (London, 1768), p. xii.

9. W. K. Wimsatt, 'The Structure of Romantic Nature Imagery' in *English Romantic Poets*, edited by M. H. Abrams (New York, 1960), p. 31.

10. *Biographia Literaria*, II, 5 (Ch. XIV).

11. David Hartley, *Observations on Man, His Frame, His Duty and His Expectations* (London, 1749), p. 420.

12. See also Coleridge, *'Frost at Midnight'* (ll. 58–62).

13. Erasmus Darwin, *Zoonamia*, 2 vols (London 1794), I, 208.

14. Darwin, I, 208.

15. *The Letters of William Blake*, edited by Geoffrey Keynes, third edition (Oxford 1980), p. 48.

16. *Fish's Outline of Psychiatry*, edited by Max Hamilton (Bristol 1978), pp. 264, 267.

17. Darwin, I, 203.

18. All references are to the second edition (London, 1737).

19. Sigmund Freud, *The Interpretation of Dreams*, translated by James Strachey (Harmondsworth, 1980), p. 129: 'There lies in dreams a marvellous poetry, and apt allegory, an incomparable humour, a rare irony.'

20. Freud, p. 468.

21. Freud, p. 312.

22. Freud, pp. 671–72.

23. See the Three-text edition of *The Prelude*, edited by Jonathan Wordsworth, M. H. Abrams, and Stephen Gill (New York and London, 1979).

24. J. W. Smyser, 'Wordsworth's Dream of Poetry and Science', *PMLA*, 81 (1956), 269–75.

25. *The Collected Writings of Thomas de Quincey*, edited by David Masson 14 vols (London, 1896), II, 268.

26. *The Complete Poetical Works of Samuel Taylor Coleridge*, edited by E. H. Coleridge, 2 vols (Oxford, 1912), I, 295.

27. Keats to Benjamin Bailey, 22 November 1817; *The Letters of John Keats*, edited by H. E. Rollins 2 vols (Cambridge, 1958), I, 185.

28. *Biographia Literaria*, II, 6 (Ch. XIV).

29. Lamb to Wordsworth, 30 January 1801; *The Letters of Charles and Mary Anne Lamb*, edited by E. W. Marrs, Jr. (Ithaca and London, 1975–), I, 266.

30. David Simpson, *Irony and Authority in Romantic Poetry* (London, 1979), I, p. 129.

31. Wolfgang Iser, 'Indeterminacy and the Reader's Response in Prose Fiction', in *Aspects of Narrative*, edited by J. Hillis Miller (New York, 1971), p. 11.

32. Gilbert Slater *The English Peasantry and the Enclosure of Common Fields* (London, 1907), p. 85. See also W. E. Tate, *The English Village Community and the Enclosure Movements* (London, 1967), pp. 174–75.

33. R. J. White, *The Age of George III* (London, 1968), p. 226.

34. *Poetical Works*, II, 386.

35. Bertram H. Davis, *Thomas Percy* (Boston, Mass., 1981), p. 84.

36. Davis, p. 134.

37. 'Essay, supplementary to the Preface', *Poetical Works*, II, 425.

38. Keats to George and Georgiana Keats, 14 Feb. to 3 May 1819; *Letters of John Keats*, II, 101–02.

39. For a discussion of this theme see W. B. Carnochan. *Confinement and Flight* (Berkeley and Los Angeles, 1977).

40. *Byron's Letters and Journals*, edited by Leslie A. Marchand, 12 vols (London. 1973–82), III, 225.

41. *Byron's Letters*, V, 105.

42. The title of Kathleen Coburn's bicentenary study of Coleridge's notebooks (London, 1974).

43. Harold Bloom. 'The Internalization of Quest Romance', *Yale Review*, 58 (1969), 526–36.

44. *Poetical Works*, II, 393.

45. Anne K. Mellor, *English Romantic Irony* (Cambridge, Mass., and London, 1980), p. 11.

46. Ibid., p. 18.

47. Viktor Shklovsky, 'Art as Technique' (1917), reprinted in David Lodge, ed., *Modern Criticism and Theory* (London, 1988), p. 27.

48. Rene Girard, *Violence and the Sacred*, translated by Patrick Gregory (Baltimore and London, 1977), p. 207.

49. David Simpson, *Irony and Authority in Romantic Poetry* (London, 1979), p. xi.

50. Ibid., p. 11.

51. Roland Barthes, 'From Work to Text', reprinted in Josue V. Harari, *Textual Strategies* (London, 1979), p. 76.

52. Terry Eagleton, *Literary Theory* (Oxford, 1983), p. 76.

53. Mikhail Bakhtin, 'The Problem of Speech Genres', reprinted in extracts in G. S. Morson, ed., *Bakhtin, Essays and Dialogues on His Work* (Chicago, 1986), p. 92.

54. Roland Barthes, 'The Death of the Author', from *Image-Music-Text*, reprinted in Lodge, *Modern Criticism and Theory*, p. 170.

55. Bakhtin, in G. S. Morson, *op. cit.*, p. 95.

56. See Roland Barthes, *Le Plaisir du texte* (Paris, 1973).

57. Stanley Fish, *Is There a Text in This Class?* (Cambridge, Mass. and London, 1980), p. 305.

58. Ibid., p. 171.

59. Anne K. Mellor, *English Romantic Irony*, pp. 4–5.

Chapter 4
Some Poets

In the second part of this book, I shall consider the work of six great
Romantic poets. Their imaginative energy and their originality require
full acknowledgement. But it is important to understand that their
originality depends upon a specific and often inspired insight into the
conditions of the time: they share feelings and prejudices with many
other poets – and with others, of course, fellow-citizens who took part
in the same events and who were implicated in the same assumptions
and actions. In his study, *Romanticism*, David Morse argues that the
artist's literary activity

> is always inserted into particular fields of literary discourse
> that themselves define the nature of what can be and
> what is said; that he will share many thoughts, feelings,
> and preoccupations with other writers and with those
> who have never put pen to paper; that we understand his
> literary productions not as and how we like but within the
> parameters of the discourses in terms of which they are
> constructed.[1]

This argument would place the emphasis firmly on historicism,
understanding the writers of the period 'within the parameters of the
discourses' of that period; and although it is not easy to identify the
ideas of those who have never put pen to paper, there is evidence of those
discourses in the work of those poets who were not members of the
visionary company, who did not possess the individual prophetic voice,
the charismatic seizing and proclaiming of their individual insight. To a
contemporary, too, the poetic scene would have seemed very different
from the way in which it appears nearly two hundred years later. The
two major publishing events in 1812, for example, were Byron's *Childe
Harold's Pilgrimage*, Cantos I and II, and Crabbe's *Tales*; and in his Journal
for 1813, Byron schematized the contemporary poetic scene by means
of a pyramid, as follows:[2]

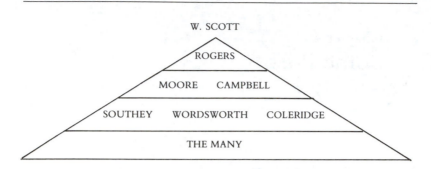

In such a crowded profession there is a struggle for imaginative space, and the lesser poets go under: the Romantic period shows particularly clearly Harold Bloom's distinction between strong and weak poets, between those who wrestle with their poetic father-figures and carve out their own space, and those who do not. In the hard world of poetic reputation, the lesser poets are diminished by the greater, as Southey was by Wordsworth or Scott by Byron. Southey is a particularly good example: he does not have his own individual note, something he does exceptionally well (as, for instance, Scott and Crabbe and Clare do); and his *A Vision of Judgement* is the most conspicuous example in the period of a poem which is destroyed by comparison (or in this case direct attack) with the work of a major poet. Another example is 'The Sailor who served in the Slave-Trade', a poem in the style of 'The Ancient Mariner' which completely lacks that poem's magic and mystery. The sailor had been compelled to flog a woman slave to death, and is subsequently pursued by the devil:

> I shut my eyes, . . . it matters not . . .
>   Still, still the same I see, . . .
> And when I lie me down at night,
>   'Tis always day with me.
>
> He follows, follows everywhere,
>   And every place is hell!
> O God . . . and I must go with him
>   In endless fire to dwell.
>
> He follows, follows everywhere,
>   He's still above . . . below
> Oh tell me where to fly from him!
>   Oh tell me where to go!
>
> But tell me, quoth the stranger then,
>   What this thy crime hath been, . . .
>   (ll. 37–50)

The device of the interlocutor and the agonized confession is clearly modelled on Coleridge's poem, and because of its subject-matter it has its moments of power:

> I see the sea close over her,
>   Yet she is still in sight;
> I see her twisting everywhere;
>   I see her day and night.
>
> (ll. 101–4)

The word 'twisting', with its vivid portrayal of the woman writhing under the lash, is a fine visual image; but the poem as a whole suffers because we know that there is another poem entitled 'The Ancient Mariner' (which, unfortunately, Southey dismissed as 'a Dutch attempt at German sublimity').[3] Southey's poem becomes a limited and explicable exercise, an outburst against a social evil which is moving because of the appalling situation rather than the poetry. Southey often deals finely with crime and punishment, as he does in 'The Grandmother's Tale', in which a smuggler murders an old woman; the murder cannot be proved against him, but

> A guilty conscience haunted him; by day
> By night, in company, in solitude,
> Restless and wretched, did he bear upon him
> The weight of blood; her cries were in his ears;
> Her stifled groans, as when he knelt upon her
> Always he heard; always he heard her stand
> Before his eyes; even in the dead of night . . .
>
> (ll. 77–83)

Similarly, Southey has a compassion for the old, the poor, and for convicts (shown in the Eclogues on the Convicts in New South Wales). The suicide and death of young girls appear in 'The Funeral' and 'The Cross Roads', while 'Mary the maid of the inn' is a variation on the theme of the pure girl and the wicked young man. Southey was an expert also in parody, and in metrical experiment, and is consequently capable of producing occasional effects of great beauty, as in the description of the wild beasts enchanted by Kailyal in *The Curse of Kehama*:

> Lo! as the voice melodious floats around,
>   The Antelope draws near,
> The Tigress leaves her toothless cubs to hear;
> The Snake comes gliding from the secret brake,
> Himself in fascination forced along

By that enchanting song;
The antic Monkies, whose wild gambols late,
When not a breeze waved the tall jungle grass,
Shook the whole wood, are hush'd, and silently
Hang on the cluster'd tree.
All things in wonder and delight are still.

(XIII. 177–87)

The Curse of Kehama is only one of the long poems which has an exotic setting: *Madoc* is set mainly among the Aztecs of Mexico, and *Thalaba* in Arabia. As Jean Raimond has observed, they are no longer widely read. He quotes Peacock's harsh judgement:

Mr Southey wades through ponderous volumes of travels
and old chronicles, from which he carefully selects all that
is false, useless and absurd, as being essentially poetical; and
when he has a commonplace book full of monstrosities,
strings them into an epic.[4]

One of their problems is the sheer length of the narrative; Byron saw them as heavy (and portrayed them as sinking to the bottom of Derwentwater). Together with this, there is a certain absence of fineness in Southey, an ordinariness of feeling. This sometimes results in downright complacency, as it does in the extraordinary banality of 'The Poet's Pilgrimage to Waterloo':

Me most of all men it behoved to raise
The strain of triumph for this foe subdued,
To give a voice to you, and in my lays
Exalt a nation's hymn of gratitude,
And blazon forth in song that day's renown, . . .
For I was graced with England's laurel crown.

(Part I, 'Flanders', ll. 31–36)

To a nineteenth-century editor Southey seemed admirable: 'the life of Robert Southey', he wrote, 'is a picture the very first sight of which elicits boundless satisfaction'.[5] At the present time we are more likely to see his life as one of profound conventionality. His poetry fails to take account of his innermost self; as Lionel Madden has written, 'there is among contemporary critics a frequent sense of frustration that Southey, while willing to write so much, should usually be so unwilling to involve his deepest mental and emotional impulses in his poetry'.[6] The consequence was that Southey became a prose writer, and a very good one.

There are no such problems with Scott. It is tempting to say that his poetry is one grand self-indulgence, in the sense that its subject-matter and treatment are assertions of that which is dear to his heart; certainly his poetry is Romantic, in that it treats of a world remote from the concerns and constraints of the day in a manner that indicates Scott's love of imaginative freedom. His poems have affinities with the world of legend and folk-tale: they are associated with an ideal world, with history seen as excitement, tragedy, and romance. As a young man Scott escaped each summer from the discipline of the Edinburgh law courts and travelled through the remote parts of the Borders collecting stories and poems, publishing them as *Minstrelsy of the Scottish Border* (1802–3); his poetry inherits the tradition of the story-teller and ballad-maker, and represents Scott's Romantic side in its purest form. In his novels the Romance is tempered by a lawyer's respect for order, progress, and stability; in the poems, the imagination is given its holiday freedom.

Scott had been fascinated by Percy's *Reliques of Ancient English Poetry* when he first came across it as a boy of twelve. The attraction of the ballads lay in their simplicity and directness, in the sharp and bare presentation of events, and also in the magic by which the folk-tale is often conducted. To this Scott added the tradition of picturesque landscape, transformed by his passion for his native land. His affection for the Scottish landscape, like that of Wordsworth for the Lake Country, may be said to have begun with the picturesque, but in both cases the maturing vision transcended it: by the time of *The Lady of the Lake* (1810), Scott had become a master of local description, of the Scottish landscape seen through eyes that made it peculiarly meaningful and full of power. These eyes belong to the figure of the poet-minstrel, who was inherited from James Beattie's *The Minstrel*.

Scott's first success, *The Lay of the Last Minstrel* (1805), deals with 'scenery and manners' as the Preface admits, but the last minstrel has unmistakable affinities with Gray's figure of the Bard. He is an outsider, neglected since the arrival of a new regime, the last of an old breed:

> Old times were changed, old manners gone;
> A stranger filled the Stuarts' throne;
> The bigots of the iron time
> Had called his harmless art a crime.
>
> (Introduction, 19–22)

The conception of the poet in an iron time (later borrowed by Matthew Arnold for his memorial verses on Wordsworth) is characteristic of Scott's Romantic impulse to prefer the folk-tale to the reality. He knew the short-comings of the Stuart line, and the benefits that had accrued to Scotland since the Act of Union in 1707; and yet here he places the Hanoverian dynasty in the position of those who would preside over the death of art. *The Lay of the Last Minstrel* is thus escapist, preferring a legendary interpretation of history to the recognizable fact; it has its own atmosphere of magic and mystery, imported at the outset from Coleridge's 'Christabel':

> The feast was over in Branksome tower,
> And the Ladye had gone to her secret bower;
> Her bower, that was guarded by word and by spell,
> Deadly to hear, and deadly to tell –
> Jesu Maria, shield us well!
> No living wight, save the Ladye alone,
> Had dared to cross the threshold stone.
>
> (I. st. 1)

The story which follows is exciting and well told, with its appropriate quantity of Romantic exaggeration. The knights, for example, sleep in their armour (for the absurdity of this, the reader is referred to Chapter 13 of Mark Twain's *A Connecticut Yankee in King Arthur's Court*); they

> carved at the meal
> With gloves of steel,
> And they drank the red wine through the helmet barred.
>
> (I. st. 4)

The wars and skirmishes which are described took place in the same Border landscape that Scott knew. The description of the River Teviot at the opening of Canto IV contrasts the period of 'steel-clad warriors' with the peace of Scott's own day, and the extensive notes are a mine of information about the history of the area which allow the reader to appreciate the country with more understanding. This focus on the locality and its meaning reaches a climax in the celebrated opening of Canto VI:

> Breathes there the man, with soul so dead,
> Who never to himself hath said,
> This is my own, my native land!

The poet goes on to pay specific tribute to 'Caledonia! stern and wild,/Meet nurse for a poetic child!' The connection between poets and places goes directly back to Gray, and his vision of the Welsh bards; it was taken up by Byron two years later in *Hours of Idleness*. The appeal is obvious: the actions of Scott's poem may be remote, but the scene is intimately known and loved. Scott is using his historical imagination to link the present with the past, to give the traveller to the Scottish Border country a sense that he is escaping from the limitations of the present: he is using his poetry to allow the sympathy and understanding to be enlarged, so that the appreciation of landscape becomes an understanding of past and present in fertile interaction and superimposition. *The Lady of the Lake* (1810) performed a similar function for the Highlands, especially the countryside around Loch Katrine. In *Marmion* (1808) the six cantos are concerned with the events leading up to the battle of Flodden Field, with the battle itself forming the climax in the final canto; but each section is enclosed within personal introductions, epistles to friends. These are among the most pleasant pieces that even Scott ever wrote, short verse letters of considerable urbanity and charm: they raise the expression of friendship to high art. Scott is being more daring than before in *Marmion*: he is prepared to break the illusion by addressing his friends and by referring to contemporary events, such as the deaths of Pitt and Fox. He is a Scottish lawyer and poet, addressing his friends of a later generation; centuries have passed since Flodden, and the days of enchantment are over:

> No fairy forms, in Yarrow's bowers,
> Trip o'er the walks, or tend the flowers
>
> (Introduction to Canto II)

Like Fielding in *Tom Jones*, Scott intervenes between each part of his work: the fiction, we are assured, *is* fiction, but its foundation on historical fact is sufficient to give it credibility. The author himself, meanwhile, acts as an intermediary between the past and the present, and in so doing he demonstrates one view of the Romantic artist in a particularly clear form. 'The artist', says David Morse, 'is essentially a *mediator*, a go-between, who connects the natural with the civilized, the imaginary with the real.'[7] Scott is so confident of his abilities in this respect that he can afford to demonstrate this process at work. The prefaces describe the immediate surroundings, the garden at Ashestiel, the November weather in the Scottish Border country, or (most vividly) the pleasures of Edinburgh in December. The poet enjoys the company of friends and the pleasures of books, and then proceeds to transport the reader out of this world into the sixteenth century. The Christmas introduction to Canto VI, addressed to Richard Heber, is a spectacular example, for in the middle of the conversation (as it were) Scott hears the drums of Flodden. The present fades before the reality of the past: social intercourse is suspended by the dictates of the historical imagination. Scott was fascinated by time, by the shaping of the present by the past, and by the present becoming past even as it is being experienced. Like

Byron and Southey he visited the battlefield of Waterloo, and saw the trampled grain, the wheelmarks in the mud made by the artillery, and the dents made by the cannonballs; in the conclusion to *The Field of Waterloo*, he muses sombrely:

> Stern tide of human Time! that know'st not rest,
> But, sweeping from the cradle to the tomb,
> Bear'st ever downward on thy dusky breast
> Successive generations to their doom. . . .
>
> (Conclusion to *The Field of Waterloo*, 1–4)

At the end of all time there is the Day of Judgement, the *Dies Irae* which Scott translated so memorably and wove into the final scene of *The Lay of the Last Minstrel*. Human life is humbled before it, and time is an ever-present reminder of transience and death. In 'The Aged Carle', a song from *The Antiquary*, Time itself speaks:

> 'Before my breath, like blazing flax,
> Man and his marvels pass away!
> And changing empires wane and wax,
> Are founded, flourish, and decay.
>
> Redeem mine hours – the space is brief –
> While in my glass the sand-grains shiver,
> And measureless thy joy or grief
> When Time and thou shall part for ever!'
>
> (ll. 9–16)

The Waverley Novels are, of course, the work of Scott the writer of historical fiction; but it is important to remember that Scott was a poet before he was a novelist, and a ballad-collector before he was a poet. The songs, snatches of rhyme, and fragments of ballads which are scattered through the novels give a strange and often sinister ring to the action. *The Bride of Lammermoor*, for instance, enacts the prophecy of the four macabre lines:

> When the last Laird of Ravenswood to Ravenswood shall ride,
> And woo a dead maiden to be his bride,
> He shall stable his steed in the Kelpie's flow.
> And his name shall be lost for evermoe!

The poetry of the Waverley Novels has been studied in detail by Clare Lamont,[8] and I do not wish to add to her account; except to say that in the context of Romantic poetry as a whole, Scott's verse is flexible, daring, and often exotic. Rebecca's Hymn, from *Ivanhoe*, is as noble as one of Byron's *Hebrew Melodies*:

> When Israel, of the Lord beloved,
> Out from the land of bondage came,
> Her fathers' God before her moved,
> An awful guide in smoke and flame.
> By day, along the astonish'd lands
> The cloudy pillar glided slow;
> By night, Arabia's crimson'd sands
> Return'd the fiery column's glow.

and in his largeness of sympathy and wide humanity Scott resembles Byron more than he does any other of the major Romantic poets.

Scott's poetry has many features that are central to the Romantic movement. Two other poets stand on its edge rather than its centre: they are Samuel Rogers and George Crabbe. Rogers was placed by Byron at the apex of his pyramid, above all the others (Scott stood alone, in a class by himself); Byron described Rogers as 'the last of the *best* school',[9] by which he meant that Rogers was the last of the Augustans, whom Byron continued to admire in preference to his contemporaries. Rogers's *The Pleasures of Memory* (1792) clearly indicates his affinities with eighteenth-century modes of thought, as its 'Analysis' demonstrates:

> The Poem begins with the description of an obscure
> village, and of the pleasing melancholy which it excites
> on being revisited after a long absence. This mixed
> sensation is an effect of the Memory. From an effect we
> naturally ascend to the cause; and the subject proposed
> is then unfolded with an investigation of the nature and
> leading principles of this faculty.
>
> It is evident that our ideas flow in continual succession, and
> introduce each other with a certain degree of regularity.[10]

The process which Rogers is describing here is fundamentally Hartleian, and has affinities with the mechanical and regular models of the mind. When Coleridge described fancy as 'no other than a mode of Memory' and as having 'no other counters to play with, but fixities and definites',[11] he was undermining Rogers's whole acceptance of the traditional pattern of mental activity. Similarly, Rogers's poetry seems predictable:

Childhood's loved group revisits every scene;
The tangled wood-walk, and the tufted green!
Indulgent MEMORY wakes, and lo, they live!
Clothed with far softer hues than Light can give.

(*The Pleasures of Memory*, I. 81–84)

His description of the workings of the mind is traditional and unimaginative:

Lulled in the countless chambers of the brain,
Our thoughts are linked by many a hidden chain.
Awake but one, and lo, what myriads rise!
Each stamps its image as the other flies.

(I. 171–4)

Rogers's poetry is unassuming and unexciting, but he has one individual characteristic, and that is a certain rather delightful sentimentality. He lived on well into the Victorian age, and it is almost as if he has one foot in the eighteenth century and one in the nineteenth, bestriding the Romantic movement not like a colossus but like one who seems not to know that it is there. Where one expects to find an eighteenth-century poet developing into a Romantic one, there is nothing: Rogers moves straight from late-Augustan predictability to Victorian sentimentality. Sometimes his verse has considerable charm:

Mine be a cot beside the hill;
A bee-hive's hum shall sooth my ear;
A willowy brook, that turns a mill,
With many a fall shall linger near.

The swallow, oft, beneath my thatch,
Shall twitter from her clay-built nest;
Oft shall the pilgrim lift the latch,
And share my meal, a welcome guest.

('Mine be a cot', ll. 1–8)

The pleasantness of this cannot really disguise its lack of substance, its habit of turning rural life into a series of pretty pictures. As an antidote the reader is advised to turn to Crabbe.

Byron described Crabbe as 'Though nature's sternest painter, yet the best'[12]; as a young poet Crabbe had won the approval of Dr Johnson for the uncompromising severity of his portrayal of ordinary life in *The Village*. Like Johnson, Crabbe disliked pastoral poetry, believing it to be a fiction where

> the Muses sung of happy Swains
> Because the Muses never knew their pains: . . .
>
> (*The Village*, I. 21–22)

Instead, Crabbe robustly asserted:

> I paint the Cot
> As Truth will paint it and as Bards will not.
>
> (I. 53–54)

In the heavy but effective antithesis of these extracts, Crabbe may be seen as using the best traditions of satire for a moral purpose; and during the Romantic period, when he was publishing alongside Wordsworth, Byron, and Keats, he continues to impress because he seems to know what he is talking about. *The Borough*, for instance, is a substantial achievement: it presents a detailed portrait of a small town, with subdivisions into trades, professions, the law, the church, and so forth, followed by case histories. Crabbe is a sociologist among poets: his work has an integrity which comes from a clear-sighted presentation of evidence, and he has a healthy scorn for the fabrications of literature when they gloss over the truth. The attack on Romantic fiction in 'Ellen Orford' is a classic of its kind, worthy to rank with Jane Austen's *Northanger Abbey*; and Crabbe's special quality, both in his descriptive pieces and his tales, is an unsentimental clarity which allows him to see not only the situations themselves, but also the motives behind them. A tale such as 'Procrastination' is an example: it describes with an almost classical restraint and austerity the process by which love is driven out by selfishness and materialism. Dinah and Rupert, encouraged by their elderly relatives, put off their marriage, and then Rupert is sent abroad; in his absence, Dinah becomes more and more addicted to a life of ease and material comfort, and when Rupert returns, older and poorer, she breaks her promise to marry him. The sterility of her life is reflected by the possessions with which she surrounds herself – carpets, books, a silver urn and a silver lamp, and, above all, a beautiful clock:

> A stag's-head crest adorn'd the pictur'd case,
> Through the pure crystal shone th'enamelled face;
> And while on brilliants moved the hands of steel,
> It click'd from pray'r to pray'r, from meal to meal.

The progress of the clock through the day records the emptiness of Dinah's life, its narrowness and comfortable piety (one senses the experience of Crabbe the clergyman at this point, and also in 'The

Parish Clerk', where a man is ruined by stealing money from the church collection).

Although Dinah rejects Rupert, she still sees him in the streets of the little town; and the tale ends with a sharp reminder of the parable of the Good Samaritan (Luke 10):

> Religion, duty urged the maid to speak
> In terms of kindness to a man so weak:
> But pride forbad, and to return would prove
> She felt the shame of his neglected love;
> Nor wrapp'd in silence could she pass, afraid
> Each eye should see her, and each heart upbraid;
> One way remain'd – the way the Levite took,
> Who without mercy could on misery look;
> (A way perceived by craft, approved by pride),
> She cross'd, and pass'd him on the other side.

Crabbe's tales are sometimes thought of as short stories which would be equally good in prose, but the neatness of this last line – and of many others – suggests that by writing in verse Crabbe has succeeded in adding a precise quality, a sharp edge, to his observation, deriving from the way in which his acute insights fit in to the rhythms and rhymes of the Heroic Couplet. His best-known poem, 'Peter Grimes', which is about a sadistic fisherman who beats his apprentices, is full of such moments:

> some, on hearing cries,
> Said calmly, 'Grimes is at his exercise.'

The word 'exercise' has a precise and very frightening double meaning here; although Crabbe is not just condemning Grimes, but the society which allows boys to be bound to such cruel masters and which does not interfere. His concerns look forward to Dickens's in *Oliver Twist*.

At last, after three boys have died under such treatment, Grimes is forbidden to take any more. He becomes a lonely figure, sitting idly in his boat surrounded by the flat sea-scape:

> There hang his head, and view the lazy tide
> In its hot slimy channel slowly glide;
> Where the small eels that left the deeper way
> For the warm shore, within the shallows play;
> Where gaping mussels, left upon the mud,
> Slope their slow passage to the fallen flood; –
> Here dull and hopeless he'd lie down and trace

How sidelong crabs had scrawl'd their crooked race;
Or sadly listen to the tuneless cry
Of fishing gull or clanging golden-eye;

The dullness of the scene reflects the fixed depression of Peter's mind, condemned forever to its loathing of life and terror of death. His dying speech describes the way in which his father (whose death he had hastened) and the three boys appear to him, and throw what seems to be red-hot water over him:

'All days alike! for ever!' did they say,
'And unremitted torments every day' –

In its portrayal of isolation and of hellish imaginings, 'Peter Grimes' is a remarkable example of the way in which Crabbe's psychological insight into the individual consciousness joins with his natural tendency towards a poetry about society, a poetry which is keenly observant and sharpened by its metrical effectiveness.

Crabbe's sociological poetry has been mistaken for social science. Wordsworth said that 'nineteen out of 20 of Crabbe's pictures are mere matters of fact',[13] thus interestingly paralleling Coleridge's criticism of his own poetry as having 'not seldom a matter-of-factness in certain poems'.[14] Wordsworth felt that in his own verse he added something to Crabbe's perception: he spoke to Isabella Fenwick in 1843 of 'the imaginative influences which I have endeavoured to throw over common life' contrasting it 'with Crabbe's matter of fact style of treating subjects of the same kind'.[15] However patronizing it may seem, and however vague, Wordsworth's view has some truth in it: the reader looks in vain in Crabbe for surprise, or for the intimations of radiance and awe, or for that kind of poetry which is formed by the interaction of the internal mind and the external world, the apprehension of

all the mighty world
Of eye and ear – both what we half create
And half perceive –
                          ('Tintern Abbey', ll. 105–7)

Although there are points at which Crabbe appears to come close to the other Romantics, as in the portrayal of Sir Eustace Grey in the madhouse, his poetry is usually governed by a conventional point of view (which makes him end 'Sir Eustace Grey' with an admonition to trust in God through Jesus Christ) and by a decorous and appropriate diction; it seems unlike that of the other poets of his time, except in its determination to identify the true state of poverty, misery, and unhappiness. Even so, his poetry is not as radical and reforming as might be expected; it is impressive because it uncovers the truth, not because it sets that truth in the visionary context of a better society as Shelley or Blake do.

Nevertheless, Crabbe is an individual voice in the period, a poet of integrity and modesty whose work is a significant part of the pattern. As we have seen, the other poets knew about him and measured themselves against him: like Scott, he contributes to the spirit of the age. This is not the case with poets such as Landor (who is neo-Classical), Campbell, or Thomas Moore, even though Moore's lyrics have a touching plangency and Campbell's poetry can be mildly stirring. Neither is ever as effective as the 'one-poem' poet, Charles Wolfe, whose poem on 'The Burial of Sir John Moore at Corunna' was recited by Byron during a conversation on 'the most perfect Ode that had been produced'.[16] Its effect, like that of pictures of the death of Nelson at Trafalgar, is due almost entirely to the potent combination of death and heroism, together with the provision of realistic detail. Wolfe had read the account of the burial in the *Edinburgh Annual Register*, from which he took the atmosphere and circumstances:

> Not a drum was heard, not a funeral note,
> As his corse to the rampart we hurried;
> Not a soldier discharged his farewell shot
> O'er the grave where our hero we buried.
>
> We buried him darkly at dead of night,
> The sods with our bayonets turning;
> By the struggling moonbeam's misty light,
> And the lantern dimly burning.
>
> (ll. 1–8)

By placing the poem in the mouth of a soldier of the burial party, Wolfe has given it an immediacy and apparent authenticity which is extremely effective; more important, however, is the combination of the obscure grave and the hero who lies in it:

> Slowly and sadly we laid him down,
> From the field of his fame fresh and gory;
> We carved not a line, and we raised not a stone –
> But we left him alone with his glory.
>
> (ll. 29–32)

The last line is almost an oxymoron: to be alone with one's glory is a contradiction in terms. Yet, in the Romantic period, with its interest in the self and its admiration for heroes, it becomes a powerful example of individual and lonely magnificence. We may add to this the feeling that the poem itself is satisfying, because it adds the memorial which is missing; it is a testimony to greatness.

'The Burial of Sir John Moore at Corunna' is an example of the Romantic capacity for admiration. It is found in Shelley's celebration of the Prometheus myth, in Blake's and Wordsworth's feeling for Milton, even in such things as Keats's and Byron's fascination with prize-fighting. Even John Clare, the Northamptonshire poet, had delusions that he was a champion boxer such as Tom Spring.[17]

John Clare is the most remarkable of the poets of the Romantic period, apart from the six great ones. Since the pioneering work of J. W. and Anne Tibble in the 1930s his work has more and more come to be seen as authentic, if not exactly central, as a response to the age. Curiously enough, it is the authenticity which is the problem: Clare writes so well about the places and the life which he knew that his poetry seems too local and circumscribed. 'Insofar as Clare was successful in expressing his own sense of place', John Barrell has written, 'he was writing himself out of the main stream of European literature.'[18] Yet Clare expresses in miniature and local form the same problems that are found on the much wider canvas of the major Romantics: problems of loneliness, of poverty, of helplessness in the face of tyranny, and problems of the self.

Above all, Clare was a peasant poet. This does not mean that he was ignorant, for he read widely among the English poets; what it does mean is that his descriptions of rural life are controlled by his own experience, and given validity by it. He knew country life in all the seasons, and not just the pleasures of it: he knew cold, and rain, and boredom, and the fatigue of a heavy day's labour. He wrote of Keats:

> . . . his descriptions of scenery are often very fine but as
> it is the case with other inhabitants of great cities he often
> described nature as she appeared to his fancies & not as he
> would have described her had he witnessed the things he
> describes – Thus it is he has often undergone the stigma
> of Cockneyism & what appears as beautys in the eyes of a
> pent-up citizen are looked upon as consciets by those who
> live in the country –[19]

While Keats described Autumn as 'sitting careless on a granary floor', Clare knew that threshers, at the end of the day's work, always took off their boots:

The weary thresher leaves his barn
And emptys from his shoes the corn
That gathers in them thro the day
                    (*The Shepherd's Calendar*, July, ll. 611–13)

Clare was unusual not only in knowing about work in the country, but in being able to express his feelings. Poetry was a joy and comfort to him during boring and heavy work, as he indicates in 'The Progress of Ryhme', but he knew that most countryfolk could not express themselves very well. The ploughman, in 'Dawnings of Genius', sees the daisy or a well-shaped stone and is delighted:

Raptures awhile his inward powers inflame,
And joys delight him which he cannot name;
Ideas picture pleasing views to mind,
For which his language can no utterance find;
Increasing beauties, fresh'ning on his sight,
Unfold new charms, and witness more delight; . . .

Thus pausing wild on all he saunters by,
He feels enraptur'd though he knows not why,
And hums and mutters o'er his joys in vain,
And dwells on something which he can't explain.
                                        (ll. 23–28, 31–34)

Even Clare's earliest poetry, which is often written in such conventional verse-form, has a freshness and originality which comes from direct observation and direct address. Like Wordsworth, he is not afraid to declare his love for the scenes of his infancy:

Hail, scenes obscure! so near and dear to me,
The church, the brook, the cottage, and the tree:
Still shall obscurity rehearse the song,
And hum your beauties as I stroll along.
                                        ('Helpstone', ll. 31–34)

The life of the village, and Clare's ability to express his feelings for it, are seen at their best in *The Shepherd's Calendar* (1827). The months are described one by one, with the weather, the work, and the natural appearances described in intimate but never boring detail. Throughout his poetry Clare's enthusiasm reaches out to all natural things, but he has a particular affinity with creatures who are defenceless or small or delicate. In 'Summer Images', for instance, he describes the frog and the snail:

I love at early morn from new mown swath
To see the startled frog his rout pursue
And mark while leaping oer the dripping path
  His bright sides scatter dew
And early lark that from its bustle flyes –
   To hail his mattin new
   And watch him to the skyes

And note on hedgerow baulks in moisture sprent
The jetty snail creep from the mossy thorn
In earnest heed and tremolous intent
  Frail brother of the morn
That from the tiney bents and misted leaves
   Withdraws his timid horn
   And fearful vision weaves . . .
      (ll. 99–112)

The description of the snail as a 'frail brother' suggests that Clare feels a special relationship with it. Similarly there is in his poetry a love of small flowers, and of birds' nests with eggs in them. The lark's nest, for instance, is for Clare a small miracle, discovered with four eggs in the early morning and then revisited later in the day:

Behind a clod how snug the nest
Is in a horse's footing fixed!
Of twitch and stubbles roughly dressed,
With roots and horsehair intermixed.
The wheat surrounds it like a bower,
And like to thatch each bowing blade
– And here's an egg this morning laid!
    ('The Lark's Nest', ll. 7–14)

Such innocent joy is characteristic of Clare's poetry. As David Constantine has pointed out, his opening words are often 'I love . . . I love to see'[20]; and even in a poem of depression like 'The Flitting', he can write of love and joy:

Een here my simple feelings nurse
A love for every simple weed
And een this little shepherds purse
Grieves me to cut it up – Indeed
I feel at times a love and joy
For every weed and every thing.
    (ll. 185–90)

In the same poem Clare writes of his old pleasures at Helpstone, seeing himself as alone, yet not alone for he was in communication with the ordinary things of nature: such solitude was a necessary element of Clare's work, caused in part by the alienation which he felt from the changes in rural life and landscape, and in part by the intensity of his own feelings. In 'Autumn' he seeks the 'solitudes where no frequented paths/But what thine own feet makes betray thy home' (i.e. Autumn's feet), following the paths across the hills and hollows

> Where step by step the patient lonely boy
>   Hath cut rude flights of stairs
>   To climb their steepy sides . . .
>   (ll. 26–28)

Clare has a special sympathy with solitary creatures and lonely people, especially country children forced to lead isolated lives stone-picking or rook-scaring. In 'October' from *The Shepherd's Calendar* he describes different birds in flight, and concludes

> These pictures linger thro the shortning day
> And cheer the lone bards mellancholy way
> And now and then a solitary boy
> Journeying and muttering oer his dreams of joy.
>   (ll. 112–15)

His own sense of solitude turned to isolation in the years that followed the unsuccessful *Shepherd's Calendar*. His removal from Helpstone to Northborough, three miles away, was a particularly disorientating experience: at Helpstone he had felt that

>   every weed and blossom too
> Was looking upward in my face
> With friendship's welcome 'how do ye do'
>   ('The Flitting', ll. 126–28)

but now everything was strange and unfamiliar. He describes the effect with an extraordinary adjective that powerfully suggests an undermining of his self-hood:

> Strange scenes mere shadows are to me
>   Vague unpersonifying things . . .
>   ('The Flitting', ll. 89–90)

In the process of removal he has become an unperson, thus anticipating the rootless and nomadic sensibility of modern society. He also anticipates the feeling of powerlessness in the face of change, because his awareness of his own village and its immediate vicinity is given a special poignancy by his experience of enclosure. The Enclosure Act for Helpstone was published in 1809, when Clare was sixteen,[21] and he saw the subsequent alterations with a despair that was partly political and partly aesthetic. In 'The Mores', for instance, he describes the way in which the eye could, at one time, range freely across the Northamptonshire countryside:

> Unbounded freedom ruled the wandering scene
> Nor fence of ownership crept in between
> To hide the prospect of the following eye
> Its only bondage was the circling sky . . .
>
> (ll. 7–10)

The freedom of the eye is symbolic of another freedom. that of the poor to walk in the countryside and graze their animals there. The equivalent of this in nature was the freedom of clouds and wild flowers; now man is confined, and nature is faded, in a new version of the fall of mankind:

> Now this sweet vision of my boyish hours
> Free as spring clouds and wild as summer flowers
> Is faded all – a hope that blossomed free
> And hath been once no more shall ever be
> Inclosure came and trampled on the grave
> Of labours rights and left the poor a slave . . .
>
> (ll. 15–20)

Clark was deeply conscious that he belonged to the very poor, and he resented the power, condescension, and complacency of the landowning classes. His bitter satire, 'The Parish', has something of Crabbe's dedication to truth. Clare writes:

> The meanest dregs of tyranny and crime
> I fearless sing: let truth attend my rhyme . . .
>
> (ll. 7–8)

but his criticism is more savagely detailed than Crabbe's, more sharply focused on figures of luxury and pride. In a note on the poem Clare said that it had been begun and finished

under the pressure of heavy distress, with embittered
feelings under a state of anxiety and oppression almost
amounting to slavery, when the prosperity of one class was
founded on the adversity and distress of the other.[22]

The names of the characters tell their own story: Miss Peevish Scornful,
the farmer's daughter given to fashion and tittle-tattle, Squire Dandy,
'Just returned from France', Farmer Bigg, young Headlong Racket,
Dandy Flint Esquire, proud Farmer Cheetum, Old Saveall, Young
Bragg; they are the principal members of a rotten and corrupt society,
which includes a whole pyramid of tyrants:

> Churchwardens, constables, and overseers
> Make up the round of commons and of peers;
> With learning just enough to sign a name,
> And skill sufficient parish rates to frame,
> And cunning deep enough the poor to cheat . . .
>
> (ll. 495–99)

In the parish the workhouse is 'a makeshift shed for misery'; the
woodman stops the poor from gathering fuel; and religion 'now is
little more than cant':

> A cloak to hide what godliness may want;
> Men love mild sermons with few threats perplexed,
> And deem it sinful to forget the text;
> They turn to business ere they leave the church,
> And linger oft to comment in the porch
> Of fresh rates wanted from the needy poor
> And list of taxes nailed upon the door . . .
>
> (ll. 264–70)

Clare's 'The Parish' is Crabbe turned Marxist: the description of the
inexorable rise of Farmer Thrifty is a savage indictment of bourgeois
capitalism. This kind of perception gives a sharp edge to Clare's poetry
and a deeper meaning to his natural descriptions: a wild flower is not
just pretty, but it is part of an unfettered existence, while a baited badger
is an example of the abuse of power. The badger tries to reach the wood
where he will be free, but he is set upon by men and boys and dogs:

> Till kicked and torn and beaten out he lies
> And leaves his hold and cackles groans and dies . . .
>
> ('The Badger', ll. 53–54)

Some people, Clare goes on, keep tame badgers; and we may read into
the description of a once noble animal reduced to slavery Clare's own
hatred of the power exercised by one individual over another. The
opposite of the badger is the skylark, which

> oer her half formed nest with happy wings
> Winnows the air till in the clouds she sings
> Then hangs a dust spot in the sunny skies . . .

The bird, however, is vulnerable too. The boys who watch it forget

> That birds which flew so high would drop agen
> To nests upon the ground where any thing
> May come at to destroy . . .
>
> ('The Sky Lark', ll. 13–15, 18–20)

The fact that the lark can fly so high, and can also be destroyed, is an
apt emblem for Clare's poignant awareness of the possibilities of life
and also the sufferings of it. The vision and the realism belong to the
same person: Clare, who suffered the privations of the poor, had his
own visionary sense of happiness, associated with childhood, freedom,
and love. In his own life, he believed, he had experienced paradise; and
he came to know what it was to be shut out from paradise, to lose love,
and freedom, and youth. The myth of Eden is re-enacted in the patterns
of his life and especially the effects of enclosure upon his village.

Throughout his life he struggled: as Mark Storey has written, 'Clare's
life becomes, in effect, an attempt to return to the shell, [the snail shell]
to rebuild the nest scattered by the plough.'[23] His failure to do this may
have been one of the reasons for his madness: the famous certification of
madness on account of 'years addicted to poetical prosings'[24] may not
have been entirely without foundation, in that the distance between his
hopes and his disappointments (not least in the sales of his later books)
was large enough to drive anyone mad. Clare's illness, however, may
have had other causes, and his anger at the way in which his world did
not conform to his desires suggests a predisposition to instability.

The poems of John Clare's madness are often vividly intense, and
sometimes piercing and direct:

> This life is made of lying and grimace
> This world is filled with whoring and deceiving
> Hypocrisy ne'er masks an honest face
> Story's are told – but seeing is believing

And I've seen much from which there's no retrieving
I've seen deception take the place of truth . . .
>   (from 'Child Harold': 'Now harvest smiles', ll. 10–15)

The consciousness of such intractable wickedness pressed upon Clare, and in his later verse he sought ways of escaping from it. The first is through the harmless delights of sexual fantasy:

I'll come to thee at even tide
When the west is streaked wi grey
I'll wish the night thy charms to hide
And daylight all away

I'll come to thee at set o'sun
Where white thorns i' the May
I'll come to thee when work is done
And love thee till the day
>   ('Song: I'll come to thee at even tide', ll. 1–8)

In 'An invite to Eternity' the relationship becomes associated with death, in an annihilation of lover and loved one:

Wilt thou go with me sweet maid
Say maiden wilt thou go with me
Through the valley depths of shade
Of night and dark obscurity
Where the path hath lost its way
Where the sun forgets the day
Where there's nor life nor light to see
Sweet maiden wilt thou go with me . . .
>   (ll. 1–8)

The landscape becomes distorted and fantastic, full of strange shapes and movements; now the 'unpersonifying' scenes of 'The Flitting' turn into a strange darkness, a landscape of 'non-identity'. It is a weird and terrible ecstasy, a death-in-life that is also a life-in-death:

Where stones will turn to flooding streams
Where plains will rise like ocean waves
Where life will fade like visioned dreams
And mountains darken into caves
Say maiden wilt thou go with me
Through this sad non-identity
Where parents live and are forgot
And sisters live and know us not

> Say maiden wilt thou go with me
> In this strange death of life to be
> To live in death and be the same
> Without this life or home or name
> At once to be and not to be
>
> (ll. 9–21)

This is, says Harold Bloom in a memorable phrase, 'something like a vertigo of vision' which is necessary to affirm both of Hamlet's contraries.[25] Clare can suggest a joyful union which is both a life in death, a being, and which yet is itself a dying, a death-in-life. In the fourth verse, the poem goes a stage further; for he and his love will be together in death, yet unable to know one another:

> The land of shadows wilt thou trace
> And look nor know each others face
> The present mixed with reasons gone
> And past and present all as one
> Say maiden can thy life be led
> To join the living with the dead
> Then trace thy footsteps on with me
> We're wed to one eternity
>
> (ll. 25–32)

The final verse provides a terrifying consummation, as the poet and his love walk forward to be united to one eternity. That eternity appears to be life, but it is death also; in no sense is it a Christian heaven. It is closer to the pagan association after death that is found in *Wuthering Heights*, where Heathcliff intends his dust to be mingled with Cathy's.

If the first escape from pressing circumstances is into the strange landscape of love, the second is into nature. Clare continues to write delicately about the appearances of natural scenes, as in 'Martinmas' or his very last poem, 'Birds' Nests'. He can also lose his identity by entering into the life of small creatures, as he does with the ladybird in 'Clock-a-Clay':

> In the cowslips peeps I lye,
> Hidden from the buzzing fly,
> While green grass beneath me lies,
> Pearled wi' dew like fishes' eyes,
> Here I lie a Clock a clay
> Waiting for the time o'day . . .
>
> (ll. 1–6)

The fragile life of the ladybird is emphasized in the fourth stanza:

My home it shakes in wind and showers
Pale green pillar topt wi' flowers
Bending at the wild winds breath
Till I touch the grass beneath
Here still I live lone clock a clay
Watching for the time of day
                    (ll. 19–24)

The Lilliputian imaginings of Clare have great charm and delicacy: often in his later poetry, however, the landscape itself is changed, transformed by an imagination that starts with a simile and then blurs the comparison into a literal description. On a hot day in early autumn the landscape is dried and glittering, and by the end of the poem the rivers are burning gold: the air has turned to liquid gold, the hills are like hot iron. As in Psalm 97 the hills melted like wax at the presence of the Lord, so now Clare sees a landscape that is vibrating in the heat so that it becomes the landscape of eternity:

AUTUMN

The thistledown's flying, though the winds are all still,
On the green grass now lying, now mounting the hill,
The spring from the fountain now boils like a pot;
Through stones past the counting it bubbles red-hot.

The ground parched and cracked is like overbaked bread,
The greensward all wracked is, bents dried up and dead
The fallow fields glitter like water indeed,
And gossamers twitter, flung from weed unto weed.

Hill-tops like hot iron glitter bright in the sun,
And the rivers we're eying burn to gold as they run;
Burning hot is the ground, liquid gold is the air;
Whoever looks round sees Eternity there.
                    (ll. 1–12)

Clare's 'Whoever looks round' here is a defiant reassertion of the Romantic imagination, comparable with Blake's insistence on seeing 'through the eye' rather than 'with the eye', and this poem is Clare's equivalent of seeing a world in a grain of sand or a heaven in a wild flower.

One result of this transforming Blakean imagination is the third major escape from circumstances, into the abiding self-hood of the solipsist. Geoffrey Grigson has emphasized the loneliness of Clare's life in the asylum at Northampton[26]; because of the absence of friends (although he was well treated) he was driven back upon himself. In his poetry he seems to be acutely conscious of his own identity, not because he thinks (*cogito ergo sum*) but because he remembers and feels:

> I feel I am, I only know I am
> And plod upon the earth as dull and void
> Earth's prison chilled my body with its dram
> Of dullness, and my soaring thoughts destroyed
>
> ('Sonnet: I am', ll. 1–4)

The phrase 'I am' recurs in this later poetry, almost as if Clare is having to insist that he exists against a conspiracy to forget him. In the poem entitled 'I am' he feels himself forgotten, estranged from those whom he loves, and tossed like a vapour into nothingness:

> I AM – yet what I am, none cares or knows;
>   My friends forsake me like a memory lost:
> I am the self-consumer of my woes –
>   They rise and vanish in oblivions host,
> Like shadows in love's frenzied stifled throes
>   And yet I am, and live – like vapours tost
> Into the nothingness of scorn and noise,
>   Into the living sea of waking dreams,
> Where there is neither sense of life or joys,
>   But the vast shipwreck of my lifes esteems;
> Even the dearest that I love the best
> Are strange – nay, rather, stranger than the rest.
>
> (ll. 1–12)

He wishes only to escape from earth, into a sleep which is like the sleep he remembers from childhood, a natural sleep in the open air:

> I long for scenes where man hath never trod
>   A place where woman never smiled or wept
> There to abide with my Creator God,
>   And sleep as I in childhood sweetly slept,
> Untroubling and untroubled where I lie
>   The grass below, above, the vaulted sky.
>
> (ll. 13–18)

This longing to be taken into the presence of God, to be part of an eternity, is not just fuelled by a desire to escape. Clare can claim it as his right as a visionary poet, one who is able to lift himself above his circumstances by the energy of his Blakean vision:

> I lost the love of heaven above
> I spurned the lust of earth below
> I felt the sweets of fancied love
> And hell itself my only foe
>
> I lost earth's joys but felt the glow
> Of heaven's flame abound in me
> Till loveliness and I did grow
> The bard of immortality
>
> ('A Vision', ll. 1–8)

This is Clare the peasant poet turned prophet: nothing is more dramatic in English Romantic poetry than the transformation of a figure who was oppressed, poor, and unable to lead a normal life, into this visionary. In the assured rhythms of the four-line stanza Clare rises in triumph above his circumstances:

> I loved but woman fell away
> I hid me from her faded fame
> I snatched the sun's eternal ray
> And wrote till earth was but a name
>
> In every language upon earth
> On every shore, o'er every sea,
> I gave my name immortal birth,
> And kept my spirit with the free
>
> August 2nd 1844
>
> ('A Vision', ll. 9–16)

The spirit can be kept if the body cannot; Clare's insistence is as thrilling and dramatic as Ezekiel's; it is an archetypal statement of the continuing vitality of the imagination, a fundamental assertion of man's unconquerable mind.

Two other poets require a brief mention: George Darley and Thomas Lovell Beddoes. Darley was born in Ireland, and had the characteristic Romantic attachment to his childhood surroundings ('I have been to *la belle France* and to *bella Italia*, yet the brightest sun which ever shone upon me broke over Ballybetagh mountains').[27] He suffered from a debilitating stammer which he described as 'a hideous mask upon my mind',[28] and which caused him to be almost incapable of holding a conversation[29]; and although he led a successful life as a literary journalist, he seems to have developed an independent and original mind. He published his most remarkable poem, *Nepenthe*, in a manner later to be made famous by Ezra Pound in *Blast*:

> with the most imperfect and broken types, upon a coarse, discoloured paper, like that in which a country shopkeeper puts up his tea, with two dusky leaves of a still dingier hue at least a size too small for the cover, . . .[30]

The failure of *Nepenthe* and his masque-drama *Sylvia* depressed Darley: the images of drowning that are found everywhere in his poetry are evidence of a fascination with a strange and imaginative life-in-death. 'The Sea-Bride' sequence, for instance, includes the seductive words of 'The Temptress of the Cave', imploring the youth to dive:

> 'Neath the wave there is no sorrow,
> Love the only pain we know,
> Jocund night brings joyful morrow
>   To the bowers below.
>   (ll. 8–12)

Under the smooth sea the figures glide in 'When Nestling Winds':

> How sweet to glide from smooth to smooth,
>   The halcyons of the under sea!
>   (ll. 3–4)

And in 'Dirge' the mermen bury the dead:

> Prayer unsaid and mass unsung,
> Dead man's dirge must still be rung;
> Dingle-dong the dead-bells sound!
> Mermen chant his dirge around!
>
> Wash him bloodless, smooth him fair,
> Stretch his limbs and sleek his hair:
> Dingle-dong the dead-bells go!
> Mermen swing them to and fro!
>   (ll. 1–8)

The enchantment of the bottom of the sea in 'A Sea Dream' is a similar piece of fantasy. To it must be added Darley's Celtic love of romance and chivalry: his 'The Flight of the Forlorn' is subtitled 'A Romantic Ballad founded on the History of Ireland', and it anticipates the admiration for failure that is later found in Matthew Arnold's *The Study of Celtic Literature*. Similarly the lyric 'It is not beauty I demand' looks forward to Yeats and 'the last romantics':

> Did Helen's breast though ne'er so soft
> Do Greece or Ilium any good?
>
> (ll. 19–20)

Darley had an eye for the exotic and a free-ranging imagination, both of which are seen in *Nepenthe*. The description of the Phoenix is an example:

> O blest unfabled Incense Tree,
> That burns in glorious Araby
> With red scent chalicing the air,
> Till earth-life grow Elysian there!
>
> Half buried to her flaming breast
> In this bright tree, she makes her nest,
> Hundred-sunned Phoenix! when she must
> Crumble at length to hoary dust!
>
> (I. 147–54)

Here the legend of the Phoenix, building itself a nest of spices in a palm tree before dying and being reborn, is given a kind of life: Darley invents his own time-scheme for this (100 years instead of the normal 500 or 1000) and his peculiar myth-making is again Yeatsian; the poem was clearly influenced by Keats's *Endymion* but it has its own atmosphere caused by its perpetual need to escape from the ordinary. Hence its dream-like imagery of flying or living beneath the sea. 'The general object or mythos of the poem', said Darley, 'is to show the folly of discontent with the natural tone of human life.'[31] It attempts to do so by painting, in Canto I, the effects of too much joy; in Canto II, the effects of too much sadness; but the imagery suggests that Darley himself is more in love with the effects than with the discipline of living a contented human life.

The problem with *Nepenthe* is that, in Harold Bloom's words, 'it is *Alastor* and *Endymion* with the informing control gone'.[32] He says, I think rightly, that 'it represents a waste of imagination',[33] and he brackets it with Beddoes's *Death's Jest-Book* in this respect. Unfortunately Beddoes's idea of the poet was that of a maker of sweet thoughts, 'like rainbow-fringed clouds':

> Their delicate pinions buoy up a tale
> Like brittle wings, which curtain in the vest

Of cobweb-limbed ephemerae, that sail
In gauzy mantle of dun twilight dressed,
Borne on the wind's soft sighings . . .

('Thoughts', from *Quatorzains*, ll. 9–13)

Beddoes greatly admired Shelley, but as these lines suggest, his verse is lacking in Shelley's reforming and pragmatic drive. In his 'Lines, written on a Blank Leaf of the "Prometheus Unbound"', Beddoes commends Shelley as

An Intellect ablaze with heavenly thoughts,
A soul with all the dews of pathos chiming,
Odorous with love . . .

Angelic sounds
Alive with panting thoughts sunned the dim world.
The bright creations of an human heart
Wrought magic in the bosoms of mankind.

(ll. 2–4, 6–9)

We can see Shelley being refashioned in Beddoes's image: it is one step from this to Matthew Arnold's beautiful and ineffectual angel. Only when he writes about time and death does Beddoes rise above such mediocrity. In 'A Clock Striking Midnight' he manages to give life to an old image:

Hark to the echo of Time's footsteps; gone
Those moments are into the unseen grave
Of ages. They have vanished nameless.

(ll. 1–3)

In 'Resurrection Song' a Stanley-Spencer-like treatment of the idea of resurrection is carried out with energy and aplomb:

Thread the nerves through the right holes,
Get out of my bones, you wormy souls.
Shut up my stomach, the ribs are full:
Muscles be steady and ready to pull.
Heart and artery merrily shake
And eyelid go up, for we're going to wake. –
His eye must be brighter – one more rub!
And pull up the nostrils! his nose was snub.

('Resurrection Song', ll. 1–8)

Death's Jest-Book is a complicated and overelaborate play, in which some of the choruses use rhythm and line endings with consummate skill. The song from Act IV, where the female voices sing under Amala's window, show extraordinary control and variation:

> We have bathed, where none have seen us,
>   In the lake and in the fountain,
>   Underneath the charmed statue
> Of the timid, bending Venus,
>   When the water-nymphs were counting
> In the waves the stars of night,
>   And those maidens started at you,
> Your limbs shone through so soft and bright.
>   But no secrets dare we tell,
>   For thy slaves unlace thee,
>   And he, who shall embrace thee,
>   Waits to try thy beauty's spell.
>   (IV. iii. 165–76)

Of a different character is the song of the death-figures in Act V, but the same control is present:

> Mummies and skeletons, out of your stones;
>   Every age, every fashion, and figure of Death:
> The death of the giant with petrified bones;
>   The death of the infant who never drew breath.
> Little and gristly, or bony and big,
>   White and clattering, grassy and yellow;
> The partners are waiting, so strike up a jig,
>   Dance and be merry, for Death's a droll fellow.
> The emperor and empress, the king and the queen,
>   The knight and the abbot, friar fat, friar thin,
> The gipsy and beggar, are met on the green;
>   Where's Death and his sweetheart? We want to begin.
> In circles, and mazes, and many a figure,
>   Through clouds, over chimneys and cornfields yellow,
> We'll dance and laugh at the red-nosed gravedigger,
>   Who dreams not that Death is so merry a fellow.
>   (V. iv. 11–26)

At the end of the play it is possible to see why Beddoes is so often called 'the last Elizabethan'; he has a fine talent for blank verse, which is seen in the speech by Wolfram's ghost. But Beddoes catches more than an

Elizabethan tone: the opening of this speech sounds like the dramatic verse of T. S. Eliot, as the ghost speaks:

> Wolfram: Did I say so? Excuse me, I am absent,
> And forget always that I'm just now living.
> But dead and living, which are which? A question
> Not easy to be solved. Are you alone,
> Men, as you're called, monopolists of life?
> Or is all being living?
>
> (v. iv. 204–9)

Beddoes's fascination with death, which led to his eventual suicide, leads him to ask, through the ghost, some searching questions about life:

> Or is all being, living? and *what is*,
> With less of toil and trouble, more alive,
> Than they, who cannot, half a day, exist
> Without repairing their flesh mechanism?
> Or do you owe your life, not to this body,
> But to the sparks of spirit that fly off,
> Each instant disengaged and hurrying
> From little particles of flesh that die?
> If so, perhaps you are the dead yourselves:
> And these ridiculous figures on the wall
> Laugh, in their safe existence, at the prejudice,
> That you are anything like living beings.
>
> (v. iv. 209–20)

The question is teasing, open-ended, yet also peculiarly loaded with the suggestion that death is somehow more central than life. It is a suggestion that is found also in Shelley, but there it engenders none of the morbid curiosity that is displayed in Beddoes, the strange fascination with death and its secrets. Shelley's Platonic tradition has been lost, and so has the reckless courage of the end of *Adonais*; now there is a flickering, diseased interest, that can allow Wolfram's ghost to speak thus to Sibylla:

> The dead are ever good and innocent,
> And love the living. They are cheerful creatures,
> And quiet as the beauty, and so be remembered
> And quiet as the sunbeams, and most like,
> In grace and patient love and spotless beauty,
> The new-born of mankind. 'Tis better too

To die, as thou art, young, in the first grace
And full of beauty, and so be remembered
As one chosen from the earth to be an angel;
Not left to droop and wither, and be borne
Down by the breath of time.
(v. iii. 112–21)

We are on the edge of the Victorian rejoicing at the deaths of young
children; in Beddoes's hands the life-giving impulse of the Romantic
movement, the desire to experience and record all varieties of joy and
pain, has become a sickly and seductive traffic with death and decay.

I now wish to examine six Romantic period poets in some detail;
bearing in mind that each is part of a complex literary scene in which the
poets discussed in this chapter, and many others whom I cannot discuss
for reasons of space, are engaged in formulating their own responses
to legends, social conditions, or personal and emotional problems, in
their own ways – yet within the 'parameters of the discourse' (to use
Morse's phrase) of the time – so that, for instance, the poets share
certain assumptions about both human life and the ways of writing
about it. What distinguishes the six poets to be discussed in the next
six chapters, however, is the strong individuality of vision, and the glad
assumption of the prophetic role, as the poet sees himself as crucial to
the health of society and as speaking for – and attempting to safeguard
– the future of the human race.

Notes

Note on the texts of John Clare's poetry used in this chapter.

In the present incomplete state of Clare editions, I have used where possible
Selected Poems and Prose of John Clare edited by E. Robinson and G. Summerfield
(1967); when poems do not appear in this selection, I have used *John Clare,
Selected Poems*, edited by J. W. and A. Tibble (1965). All quotations from *The
Shepherd's Calendar* are from the edition by E. Robinson and G. Summerfield
(1964).

1. David Morse, *Romanticism* (London, 1982), p. 3. See also Morse's
   companion study, *Perspectives in Romanticism* (London, 1981).

2. *Byron's Letters and Journals*, edited by Leslie A. Marchand, 12 vols (London,
   1973–82), III, 220.

3. *Coleridge, the Critical Heritage*, edited by J. R. de J. Jackson, (London, 1970).
   p. 53.

4. Jean Raimond, *Robert Southey* (Paris, 1968), p. 232n.

5. Robert Southey, *Joan of Arc and Minor Poems* (London, 1854), p. v.

6. *Robert Southey, the Critical Heritage*, edited by Lionel Madden (London, 1972), p. 9.

7. Morse, *Romanticism*, p. 193.

8. Clare Lamont, 'The poetry of the early Waverley Novels', *Proceedings of the British Academy*, 61 (1975), pp. 315–36.

9. *Byron's Letters*, III, 220.

10. Samuel Rogers, *Poems* (1834), p. 5.

11. *Biographia Literaria*, edited by James Engell and W. J. Bate (London, 1983), 305 (Ch. XIII).

12. *English Bards and Scotch Reviewers*, 1. 858.

13. *The Letters of William and Dorothy Wordsworth, The Middle Years*, Part I, edited by E. de Selincourt, second edition, revised by Mary Moorman (Oxford, 1969), p. 268.

14. *Biographia Literaria*, II, 126 (Ch. XXII).

15. *The Poetical Works of William Wordsworth*, edited by E. de Selincourt and H. Darbishire, 5 vols (Oxford, 1940–49), I, 360.

16. *Medwin's Conversations of Lord Byron*, edited by Ernest J. Lovell, Jr (Princeton, 1966), p. 114.

17. Mark Storey, *The Poetry of John Clare* (London, 1974), p. 152.

18. John Barrell, *The Idea of Landscape and the Sense of Place, 1730–1840* (Cambridge, 1972), p. 188.

19. *The Prose of John Clare*, edited by J. W. and Anne Tibble (London, 1951), p. 223.

20. David Constantine, 'Outside Eden: John Clare's Descriptive Poetry', in *An Infinite Complexity*, edited by J. R. Watson (Edinburgh, 1983), p. 200.

21. An extract will be found in *Selected Poems and Prose of John Clare*, edited by Eric Robinson and Geoffrey Summerfield (London, 1967), p. 169.

22. John Clare, *Selected Poems*, edited by J. W. and Anne Tibble (London, 1965), p. 140.

23. Storey, p. 12.

24. J. W. and Anne Tibble, *John Clare, a Life* (London, 1932), p. 454.

25. Harold Bloom, *The Visionary Company*, revised edition (Ithaca and London, 1971), p. 453.

26. *Poems of John Clare's Madness*, edited by Geoffrey Grigson (London, 1949), p. 40.

27. *Selections from the Poems of George Darley*, edited by R. A. Streatfeild (London, 1904). pp. ix–x.

28. *Selections*, p. xxvi.

29. *Selections*, p. xii.

30. *Selections*, p. xix.
31. Quoted in John Heath-Stubbs, *The Darkling Plain* (London, 1950), p. 29.
32. Bloom, p. 458.
33. Bloom, p. 458.

Chapter 5
Blake

'Well done Paine': Blake's pat on the back for the great ideologist of the American Revolution is a fair indication of his sympathies. He supported the London riots against the American war, and was present at the burning of Newgate in 1780; like Godwin, he regarded wars as the work of kings, and monarchy as an unjustified evil. The tyranny of George III, and the almost universal corruption of justice, were highlighted for Blake as a young man not only by the American war but by social conditions in England and by the undemocratic exclusion of the radical John Wilkes from Parliament. Later, during the French Revolution, Blake saw the fall of the Bastille as a great symbol of a nation rousing itself to throw off the chains of monarchy and oppression. He was one of a group of radicals which included Paine and the publisher Joseph Johnson: and, as David Erdman has pointed out,[1] he quoted (in his 1793 notebook) Ezekiel's prophecy to the Prince of Tyre, seeing it as a warning to the prosperous nations of Europe of impending revolution (Ezekiel 27. 2; 28. 5, 7–8). Blake's view of the American and French Revolutions as the first of many is fundamental to an understanding of the earlier Prophetic Books. It is associated with his hatred of established forms of government and justice.

This is accompanied in all Blake's work by his unique capacity for vision, a capacity which makes him at once the most original and the most exclusive of the Romantic poets, and – in one sense – the purest, the most uncompromising of them. As a child he saw God at the window, and a tree full of angels; while the death of his brother Robert, in 1787 (Blake was twenty-nine, Robert nineteen) convinced him of the reality of the world of his imagination in which he could 'converse daily and hourly in the spirit' with Robert after his death. Such visions of infancy, and such intimations of immortality, are not uncommon: what is extraordinary about Blake's visions is the unquestioning elaboration of them, and their continuation throughout his life. In 1825, for instance, he was visited by Henry Crabb Robinson, a lawyer who was friendly with a number of poets, including Wordsworth and Coleridge:

Shall I call him artist or genius – or mystic – or madman? . . .

Of the faculty of vision he spoke as one he had had from early infancy. He thinks all men partake of it, but it is lost by not being cultivated. . . .[2]

Blake can be understood as a radical, and admired as a visionary; but he can only be fully appreciated if the two sides of his nature are seen as continuously interacting in his work. Blake is a revolutionary because he is a visionary: his work appears visionary partly because it expresses, in idea and technique, a revolutionary mind, prepared to be utterly original and to take nothing in the material world for granted. The result is that Blake is (as the titles of some of his works indicate) a prophet, an 'individual bearer of charisma'[3] who is a seer of visions and communicator of them to society. 'Would to God that all the Lord's people were prophets!' he wrote in *Milton*, immediately after the best-known expression of his own prophetic mind:

> And did those feet in ancient time
> Walk upon England's mountains green?
>
> (Pl. 1, ll. 21–22)

and Blake suffered throughout his life from being a solitary prophet, one to whom very few would listen. There are signs in his later work of a certain impatience at this situation, which leads to an even greater reliance on his own visions, however complex and sibylline they may be. Even the most riddling and labyrinthine structures of the later Prophetic Books, however, contain some of the most mature and sensitive understanding of human behaviour and the most inspiring descriptions of a better world, created by imagination and love. Blake had an extraordinary ability to see the world transformed, shown in question-and-answer form in 'A Vision of the Last Judgement':

> 'What', it will be Question'd, 'When the Sun rises, do you not see a round disk of fire somewhat like a Guinea?'
> O no, no, I see an Innumerable company of the Heavenly host crying 'Holy, Holy, Holy is the Lord God Almighty.'
>
> (p. 95)

It is important to realize that Blake sees the material world accurately and clearly: the shape and colour of the rising sun are instantly recognizable. But at the same time it is transformed into the company of the heavenly host, so that there is a simultaneous portrayal of the sun in two ways. The twofold vision is contrasted, in Blake's mind, with the 'single vision' of the scientist or materialist:

> May God us keep
> From Single vision and Newton's sleep!
>> (To Thomas Butts, 22 November 1802)

Blake claimed further complex ways of seeing in the immediately preceding lines of the same letter-poem to Butts:

> Now I a fourfold vision see,
> And a fourfold vision is given to me;
> 'Tis fourfold in my supreme delight
> And threefold in soft Beulah's night
> And twofold Always.

This is a testimony to the creative power of the imagination. Blake sees a fourfold vision in the supreme unity of heaven; a threefold vision in Beulah, the earthly paradise which Blake identified with the subconscious and with dreams; and twofold always on earth, never the single vision of the materialist. In 'Auguries of Innocence' Blake described the process as seeing 'through the eye' not 'with the eye'; seeing 'with the eye' is the materialist's way, the way of Newton and Locke, but seeing 'through the eye' allows the imagination to work upon the created world and reveal the latent wonder within it:

> To see a world in a grain of sand
> And a heaven in a wild flower,
> Hold infinity in the palm of your hand
> And eternity in an hour.
>> ('Auguries of Innocence', ll. 1–4)

As an example, we may take a very attractive and simple poem from *Songs of Innocence*, 'The Lamb'. It presents a pleasing description of a lamb, together with a child's natural affection for it and a child's simple but pure understanding of God. The poem gives expression to this quite beautifully: the simple metre and rhythm, and the repetitions, reproduce something of the earnest prattle of the child; meanwhile the lamb is described in terms of its soft woolly coat, its baaing which echoes in the vales, and its feeding 'by the stream and o'er the mead'. If we consider the poem further, it becomes a brilliant exercise in Christian theology: the child asks the lamb about God the Creator in the first verse ('Dost thou know who made thee?') and answers his own question in the second verse by referring to God, in Jesus Christ, as Redeemer. The God who made the lamb is called a lamb Himself, because He was crucified ('Worthy is the Lamb that was slain'), and because He became a little child at the Incarnation. Both child and lamb are called by God's name because two of the crucial attributes of God are His Incarnation and His Passion. So when the poem ends

> Little Lamb, God bless thee,
> Little Lamb, God bless thee!

the understanding of the nature of God infuses and directs these lines with a force that gathers into itself all the accumulated attributes of God as Creator and God as Redeemer which have been outlined in the poem. As a threefold vision 'in soft Beulah's night' the poem celebrates an earthly paradise in which animals and human beings live in complete love and harmony under the protection of a benevolent God. The illustration reinforces this: the naked child is stroking one of a flock of sheep, under a canopy of entwining trees; behind is a byre with an open door (compare the closed door in 'The Chimney Sweeper' from *Songs of Experience*) and on the roof of the byre are two doves, again symbolic of harmony and love. Behind is a tree in full leaf.

The fourfold vision in the poet's supreme delight is an amalgam of this, a radiance which Blake clearly feels and manages to convey in the poem through the use of words such as 'rejoice' and 'delight'. The lamb has a clothing not just of wool but of delight, and the vales do not merely echo to the tender cries but rejoice in them. The Creator gave the lamb life, and it is the simplicity of the word 'life' in line 3 which is so important, carrying as it does the accumulated experience of youthful delight. The result is a kind of radiant joy, the joy of just being a lamb: it is a quality that can perhaps only be expressed by another poem (and a recent article has pointed to the affinity between Blake and the American poet Theodore Roethke):

> The Lamb just says, I AM!
> He frisks and whisks. *He* can.
> He jumps all over. Who
> Are *you*? You're jumping too![4]

The delight in such natural life is found in some of the poems of Blake's first printed work, *Poetical Sketches* (1783). These have been dismissed as immature, but had Blake published nothing else they would have displayed a certain individuality which can be detected through the conventional phrases. There are three elements in particular which anticipate Blake's later poetry: one is the use of personification and symbol, the second is the note of social and political concern, and the third is the discovery of an original prophetic voice.

Personification was a natural eighteenth-century habit, but in Blake's hands it is extended into an enlivening myth-making. Spring looks down through the windows of the morning, and England, the western isle, looks longingly for the coming of spring like an expectant lover. Summer also pitches his golden tent on the earth, and Autumn sings a song of fruits and flowers:

> The narrow bud opens her beauties to
> The sun, and love runs in her thrilling veins;
> Blossoms hang round the brows of morning, and
> Flourish down the bright cheek of modest eve,
> Till clustering Summer breaks forth into singing,
> And feathered clouds strew flowers round her head.
>
> ('To Autumn', ll. 7–12)

Not only do these lyrics have such moments of individual beauty: they anticipate Blake's later Prophetic Books in possessing their own system of symbols, moving during the four poems from morning to darkness and round the four points of the compass. *Poetical Sketches* also contains a 'Song' which anticipates Blake's later concern with a wrong kind of love, jealous and possessive. In 'How sweet I roam'd', the singer is captured by the prince of love and shut in his golden cage:

> He loves to sit and hear me sing,
> Then, laughing, sports and plays with me;
> Then stretches out my golden wing,
> And mocks my loss of liberty.
>
> (ll. 13–16)

This poem is reminiscent of a sinister fairy-tale, and Blake often employs fairy-tale elements, recognising instinctively their power to enter both the darker and the more hopeful places of the human mind. The Prophetic Books are Blake's own fairy stories, and his creation of original legends is a feature of his work throughout; in *Poetical Sketches*, as elsewhere, this is linked with a concern for social issues which is found transmuted into ballad form in 'Gwin, King of Norway' where Gwin, the cruel tyrant, is overcome by Gordred, the sleeping giant who is awakened by the cries of the starving people. Its hatred of war comes through convincingly: this hatred is also found in the unfinished drama of King Edward the Third, which is set on the eve of the battle of Crécy and is obviously influenced by Act IV of Shakespeare's *Henry V* in its portrayal of medieval warfare and the questioning of its values.

Poetical Sketches was printed for Blake by two of his friends, John Flaxman the sculptor and the Rev. A. S. Matthews; Blake must have been unsure about its quality, for he retained all the copies in his hands and the book was never published. Blake may have had doubts about its

reception in an age which he thought of as unpoetical; this is the force
of the best-known poem from the collection. 'To the Muses', which is
a cry to the 'fair Nine' who have forsaken poetry:

> How have you left the ancient love
> That bards of old enjoyed in you!
> The languid strings do scarcely move,
> The sound is forced, the notes are few.
>
> (ll. 13–16)

Blake here glances at Gray's *The Bard* and 'The Progress of Poesy',
and at the whole prophetic tradition. His complaint about the state
of contemporary poetry is the outburst of a young rebel, and this is
echoed in 'An Island in the Moon' (*c.* 1784–87) in which a farrago of
nonsense is suddenly interrupted by a new lyric voice, when Obtuse
Angle sings a version of 'Holy Thursday':

> Upon a Holy Thursday, their innocent faces clean,
> The children walking two and two in grey and blue and green;
>
> (Chapter 11, ll. 8–9)

The effect is like cool clear water: the babble of voices ceases at this point,
and 'they all sat silent for a quarter of an hour. And Mrs Nannicantipot
said, "It puts me in mind of my mother's song: . . .".' There follows
the 'Nurse's Song' from *Songs of Innocence*, and then Quid the Cynic
(Blake himself) sings 'The Little Boy Lost'. In each of these poems we
hear a new note, a sudden pure simplicity in the middle of the trivial
chatter of 'An Island in the Moon'. It is as if Blake was testing out the
Songs of Innocence against a background of a society to which poetry has
become nonsense, and even the benevolent characters of the amiable
circle of Blake's friends are struck dumb by the advent of a new kind
of poetry.

To invent an absolutely new voice, an original way of expressing
oneself in poetry, is an extraordinary achievement; and this is what Blake
did in *Songs of Innocence* (1789). It is sometimes said that these poems
resemble Isaac Watts's *Divine and Moral Songs for the Use of Children*
(1715), but if they do it is a resemblance which has its own irony:
Blake is using Watts, or the nursery-rhyme form, to break through
to a new expression of experience, in which the playful is profound,
and the profound playful, in which the speech of children and the tone
of childlike utterance carry with them ideas that are archetypal in their
simplicity.[5] Above all, what the *Songs of Innocence* do is to break the
mould of eighteenth-century poetry. If the nine Muses have fled, they
must be sought with fresh means: poets much unthink their traditional

ways, must become as little children: they may even need to rethink the whole business of book-making, and ask themselves whether it is not likely to produce something mechanical, a book which when held in the hand is exactly like all the other books with that title. And so Blake produced his own, illuminated and engraved, each one hand-coloured so that no two copies are identical. His books are individual productions of a poet-craftsman, each one having its unique characteristics.

The new pure voice is heard immediately in the 'Introduction' to *Songs of Innocence*:

> Piping down the valleys wild,
> Piping songs of pleasant glee,
> On a cloud I saw a child,
> And he laughing said to me:
>
> 'Pipe a song about a lamb.'
> So I piped with merry cheer;
> 'Piper, pipe that song again.'
> So I piped, he wept to hear.
>
> (ll. 1–8)

The immediate impression is one of a childlike simplicity, in which the piper becomes a figure who writes to dictation. The child 'calls the tune', literally, and weeps with joy when he hears it piped: he then demands that it should be sung, and finally that it should be written down. His peremptory demands are exactly like those of small children, and the songs are those which 'Every child may joy to hear'; yet in that simple process from the dictating child through the adult back to the hearing child there is a complex and profound truth. The child speaks to other children with a directness and simplicity, a straightforward and simple honesty, which is revealing and illuminating. The adult exists in a benevolent relationship to this because he is the communicator and preserver; but the essential perception and reception are those of the little child, and the adult who reads these poems is only an eavesdropper. What he hears is the wisdom of children, the voices of those who have not been corrupted by the complexities and pretensions of adult life: it is their innocence which is found in 'The Shepherd', the second poem of the collection, in which the child who speaks and the child who listens can both take pleasure in the peace and safety of the lambs while they are being watched over. The adult understanding can, if it wishes, add to this: its awareness of the good shepherd as the figure of Jesus Christ and of mankind as the sheep complicates the poem and makes it one of many in *Songs of Innocence* that are concerned with the relationship between the protector and the protected. Examples of this include shepherd and lamb, parent and child, God and man; a recurring figure in the illuminations (beginning with the title page) is the child at the parent's knee, or watched over by a loving figure (as in 'Spring', 'A Cradle Song', and 'Infant Joy'). In 'The Little Black Boy' there is a moving transition from the black boy talking to his mother on the first page of the illumination, and the black and white boys together at God's knee on the second page. Again the black boy's innocence is deeply touching, as he imagines himself and the little English boy together:

> I'll shade him from the heat, till he can bear
> To lean in joy upon our father's knee;
> And then I'll stand and stroke his silver hair,
> And be like him, and he will then love me.
>
> (ll. 25–28)

The trustful and loving spirit of this poem is likely to be read with some wistfulness by the adult: if only white and black could live together with this kind of open goodwill, the hatred and bitterness of racial prejudice would disappear. The innocence here cuts like a scalpel through the qualifications and hesitations of the usual attempts at reconciliation, and through the jealousy and fear which prevent the simple love of the children for one another from taking effect.

In this way Blake's 'Innocence' becomes the most powerful commentary imaginable upon a stale and war-torn adult world. The eyes of the children look out upon a society which is corrupt, vicious, and unjust, and their very trust is itself a denunciation. This is particularly true of those poems in which the children are exploited or neglected by the adults: the innocence which the children display on these occasions is an ingenuous confidence which exposes the true relationship in a particularly effective way. Two poems of *Songs of Innocence*, for instance, concentrate on grave social evils of Blake's own time: 'The Chimney Sweeper' concerns the employment of small boys to climb and sweep chimneys, and 'Holy Thursday' the number of orphan or uncared-for children in charitable institutions.

Like some of Blake's other songs, 'The Chimney Sweeper' begins with an authentic child's voice. The first lines sound dispassionate, almost as if the child is too bewildered to feel the trauma of losing his parents; and, like many other little children, he cannot sound the letter 's' at the beginning of his words:

> When my mother died I was very young,
> And my father sold me while yet my tongue

> Could scarcely cry "'weep! 'weep! 'weep! 'weep!'
> So your chimneys I sweep, & in soot I sleep.
>
> (ll. 1–4)

The chimney-boys' cry of 'Sweep! Sweep!' is here given a pathetic ring as the child attempts to pronounce it, and the double meaning is unmistakable to the adult reader. The poem continues to work in this way, providing a sharp contrast between what the child says, taken at its face value, and what the reader perceives:

> There's little Tom Dacre, who cried when his head,
> That curl'd like a lamb's back, was shav'd; so I said,
> 'Hush, Tom, never mind it, for when your head's bare,
> You know that the soot cannot spoil your white hair.'
>
> (ll. 5–8)

Now the child who spoke the first verse is engaged with another, even younger child; his protective comfort is reassuring, until we realize with a shock that the soot cannot spoil Tom's hair because it has already been ruined. Tom has been shorn, like a recruit in the army or like a lamb (and the fact that he does not speak suggests that he may have been dumb before his shearers, like the sacrificial lamb who is identified with Jesus Christ). At this point Tom's dream is recounted: the children are released from their coffins of black (probably their bodies, covered in soot; Blake is here, as elsewhere, drawing on Platonic and neo-Platonic tradition) and find themselves in a children's paradise:

> Then down a green plain leaping, laughing they run,
> And wash in a river and shine in the Sun.
>
> (ll. 15–16)

The dream, like the remainder of the poem, is told in a childlike sing-song:

> And the Angel told Tom, if he'd be a good boy,
> He'd have God for his father & never want joy.
>
> (ll. 19–20)

The simplistic nature of this is a fitting parody of a certain kind of Sunday-school teaching: its application to Tom can be read as true and comforting, but it also points to the enormous distance that exists between 'being a good boy' and Tom's actual situation. Its simplicity prepares the way for the last verse, in which the distance between what is said and what is understood becomes sharply poignant:

And so Tom awoke: and we rose in the dark,
And got with our bags and our brushes to work.
Tho' the morning was cold, Tom was happy & warm;
So if all do their duty, they need not fear harm.

The dream has turned into reality, into the dark morning and the chimney-sweeper's equipment; yet the boy who speaks these lines does so without comment, as if accepting the whole thing as normal. He also thinks Tom is happy and warm: if he is happy it is because he knows no other life except in dreams (which is a pathetic state of happiness to be in) and if he is warm it is probably because the chimneys that he has to climb are still hot. The last line sounds comforting, but is almost unbearably painful: the speaker has become so contented with his condition that he accepts it without question and without complaint. If the boys do as the sweep-master tells them, no doubt they will be unharmed: but the state of slavery which this suggests is terrifying.

'The Chimney Sweeper' is about innocence, but it is an innocence which is exploited and which is unaware of the exploitation. 'Holy Thursday' is another poem in which the scene appears pleasing and attractive, and which is about innocence; but once again the distance between what is perceived at first sight and the reflective adult reading of the poem is immense. The children of the charity institutions who are going to St Paul's for their annual service (probably on Ascension Day, which gives an added point to the final verse) look beautiful, in their fresh faces and different-coloured uniforms. The picture is presented with a completely ingenuous, unprejudiced eye, with an 'innocent' eye, as if the spectator were concerned only with the attractions of the scene. It is the reader who has to supply the questions: who are all these children? why do so many of them come to be in institutions? It is at this point that the details of the poem become significant in a new way: is it right that children should wear uniforms and walk in crocodiles (Coleridge, too, hated children in crocodiles, calling them 'walking advertisements')? What is their relationship to the greyheaded beadles? The poem does not answer these questions, or even raise them: but its innocence prompts the reader to raise them. And then comes the third verse:

Now like a mighty wind they raise to heaven the voice of song,
Or like harmonious thunderings the seats of heaven among.
Beneath them sit the aged men, wise guardians of the poor;
Then cherish pity, lest you drive an angel from your door.

The crucial word of this verse is 'Beneath'. As in 'Auguries of Innocence', where the crucial distinction is between seeing 'through' and not 'with' the eye, Blake rests his case on the apparently unimportant word (so, too, in *The Book of Thel*, he uses, as an image of caring, the unimportant clod of clay, which looks after the worm). In their radiance and their singing on Holy Thursday, the children ascend into heaven: they become like angels, and their voices become like the harmonious thunderings of the heavenly host The aged men, meanwhile, remain earth-bound; there can be no other explanation for 'Beneath', because the seating in St Paul's is not banked in tiers. The grey-headed beadles may be 'wise', perhaps in a worldly sense, but it is as if the earth-bound are trying to control the angelic; and this is given more point by the last line, with its reference to driving an angel from the door. It refers to the story of Lot (Genesis 19) and the use of it in the Epistle to the Hebrews ('Forget not to shew love unto strangers: for thereby some have entertained angels unawares.') (13. 2). The children-angels are in institutions because they are uncared-for, turned-away, orphans. The fact that they seem beautiful and radiant is an accident, though one which Blake uses to advantage: they look like angels, for one thing, with their fresh faces and innocent hands; on another level they make a fine sight for a spectator, but this hides a world of neglect and indifference. The 'innocence' of this poem, therefore, is the innocence of the completely vulnerable, the lambs, the 'little boys and girls' who have never known the love of parents and the care of home.

In these two poems the innocence of *Songs of Innocence* has a sharp and poignant under-side to it. But this does not invalidate the quality of innocence itself: in poems such as 'The Lamb', 'The Echoing Green', 'Laughing Song', 'A Cradle Song', 'Spring', and 'Infant Joy' Blake successfully portrays a world in which happiness is genuine and 'innocent', in the sense that it is not based upon anything harmful, such as the exploitation of one human being by another, or the inequality between individuals. This innocence is founded upon a vision of everything in its right relationship: mankind with nature, God with mankind and the creation, the protector with the protected. This is a kind of heaven on earth, as the illumination of 'The Divine Image' suggests: the radiant flame travels across and upwards from the bottom right-hand corner, in which God is raising up a human figure, while at the top left-hand corner there are figures walking, dancing, and praying. It is as if earthly things are happening in heaven, and heavenly things on earth; and the poem testifies to this in its recital of the four virtues:

> For Mercy, Pity, Peace, and Love
> Is God, our father dear,
> And Mercy, Pity, Peace, and Love
> Is Man, his child and care.

For Mercy has a human heart,
Pity, a human face,
And Love, the human form divine,
And Peace, the human dress.

                                    (ll. 5–12)

These four virtues are beautifully enclosed and expressed in the four
lines of each verse: the balance and harmony of each line, and of each
line within each verse, are evident. Blake is here celebrating the divine
qualities that can be found in human beings, the paramount virtue being
that of love, the 'human form divine'. This is an inspired borrowing
from *Paradise Lost* Book III, where Milton describes the 'human face
divine' which he can no longer see: it is now the human form divine,
God incarnate in the love of human beings for one another. In the final
verse Blake takes the collect for Good Friday from the *Book of Common
Prayer* (which quaintly asks for mercy 'upon all Jews, Turks, Infidels,
and Hereticks') and uses it in an all-embracing God-centred vision of
human love:

And all must love the human form
In heathen, turk or jew.
Where Mercy, Love & Pity dwell
There God is dwelling too.

The idea of 'Innocence', therefore, contains many things: the new-born
innocence of children and lambs, the vulnerable and exploited innocence
that shows children neglected and enslaved, and this mature vision of
a world of love in which God is found in the merciful and peaceful
works of men and women on earth. *Songs of Experience*, engraved
probably from 1791 to 1793, completes and deepens the pattern; for
as Blake recognized, and made explicit in *The Marriage of Heaven and
Hell*, 'without contraries is no progression' – that is, 'Innocence' cannot
be fully apprehended in human terms without an understanding of
'Experience', the familiar reality of life in a fallen world. Without
Experience, Innocence can become prettiness: with an awareness of
Experience, it becomes an ideal which may be attained in certain
moments, notably in childhood or in the love between human beings,
but which is for the most part an ideal to be struggled for in a corrupt
and wicked world. Blake had been reading Milton, whom he regarded
as the greatest English poet, and the structure of contraries in *L'Allegro*
and *Il Penseroso* is applied to *Songs of Innocence and of Experience*; but
the paramount influence on *Songs of Experience* is *Paradise Lost*. Milton's
great attempt to 'justify the ways of God to men' is heroic because he is
so powerfully aware of the fallen nature of the world: the Fall is a cosmic

event, but it is also manifest in personal and contemporary terms, in Milton's own blindness, in the collapse of the Commonwealth, and in the Restoration of the monarchy. For Blake too the Fall was evident around him, in the cries of the children, the complacency of the church, the despair of the soldier, the failures of love. So the 'Introduction' to *Songs of Experience* has a very different tone from the piping of the piper in *Songs of Innocence,* and an unmistakable reference to the Fall of Adam and Eve and the judgement of God in the garden of Eden:

> Hear the voice of the Bard!
> Who Present, Past, & Future sees,
> Whose ears have heard
> The Holy Word
> That walk'd among the ancient trees,
>
> Calling the lapsed Soul
> And weeping in the evening dew,
> That might controll
> The starry pole,
> And fallen, fallen light renew!
> (ll. 1–10)

The Bard is Milton's prophet-figure, Gray's Bard given a cosmic instead of a national role, Ezekiel, Isaiah, the visionary or seer calling to the earth to arise (as in Isaiah 60: 'Arise, shine . . .'):

> O Earth, O Earth return!
> Arise from out the dewy grass;
> Night is worn,
> And the morn
> Rises from the slumbrous mass.
> (ll. 11–15)

But the Earth's reply, in the poem which follows, 'Earth's Answer', is that

> 'Prison'd on wat'ry shore
> Starry Jealousy does keep my den
> Cold and hoar
> Weeping o'er
> I hear the father of the ancient men.'
> (ll. 6–10)

The father of the ancient men here is a restrictive father-God figure; this is the voice which Earth, 'her locks cover'd with grey despair', hears. Meanwhile the virgins of youth and morning are 'chain'd in night', their love 'with bondage bound'. It is, says Earth, profoundly unnatural:

> 'Does spring hide its joy
> When buds and blossoms grow?
> Does the sower
> Sow by night?
> Or the plowman in darkness plow?'
>
> (ll. 16–20)

The unnatural proceedings of the fallen world are a recurring theme in *Songs of Experience*: in 'The Garden of Love' the chapel is built over the garden of love where the child used to play, and in 'A Little Boy Lost' the priest tortures and burns the child for saying that he loves his father as he loves all created things. Similarly in 'Holy Thursday', the neglect of children is seen as unbelievably unnatural:

> Is that trembling cry a song?
> Can it be a song of joy?
> And so many children poor?
> It is a land of poverty!
>
> (ll. 5–8)

The sun can never be shining, and it must always be winter in that country; there is no other possible explanation for the neglect of so many children. In this poem, which is the counterpart to its namesake in *Songs of Innocence*, the reality behind the charming picture of the children at St Paul's is harshly exposed (the illumination shows a mother being forced to reject a child, and others crying and clinging to a weeping mother); the singing of the children on Ascension Day turns into the trembling cry of an orphan, almost as if one is superimposed upon the other, so that the reader ceases to hear the singing and all that remains is the crying. Blake's use of such metamorphoses is common in *Songs of Experience*, where his images often take on an almost surrealist quality, as they do, for instance, in 'London':

In every cry of every Man,
In every infant's cry of fear,
In every voice, in every ban,
The mind-forg'd manacles I hear:

(ll. 5–8)

'London' works by a gradual change from an ordinary compassionate perception to the most strange and terrifying vision. In the first verse the poet looks at the faces of those who pass him in the street and sees there 'Marks of weakness, marks of woe'; in the second verse he hears the cries and curses, like the sound of chains in the mind; and in the third verse, strange occurrences take place:

> the Chimney-sweeper's cry
> Every blackening Church appalls,
> And the hapless Soldier's sigh
> Runs in blood down Palace walls;
>
> (ll. 9–12)

The universe seems for a moment to be governed by a moral law, which makes the church pale, or faint, and translates sighs into blood on a palace wall; and in the final verse these laws become terrifying, as words and tears have their own devastating effect:

> But most through midnight streets I hear
> How the youthful harlot's curse
> Blasts the new-born infant's tear
> And blights with plagues the marriage-hearse.
>
> (ll. 13–16)

The last image is the most compressed and violent of all, turning a marriage into a funeral: as the eye watches the happy couple drive away from the church, the carriage suddenly becomes a funeral car. It is like a shifting image in a Bergman film: Blake is saying that a loveless marriage can be a living death, and that it can also be a physical death, brought on by the plagues of venereal disease which the young prostitute has already contracted. Venereal disease is a destroyer here, but it is also a symbol of the diseased relationship of the cursing harlot, whose curse can blast the new-born baby's tears. The first cry of the unwanted baby takes us back to the cries of verse two: the child's first cry as it enters the world should be natural and good, but it is a sign of life which the mother curses because it may prevent her from earning a living; later the child will cry for other reasons, as the mind-forged manacles take their grip.

In this poem, with its strong patterns of repetition, Blake mixes literal and metaphorical meaning in a disturbing and powerful way. Faces bear marks (as they do); marriage is destroyed; both are signs of the corruption and decay of a city whose streets are 'charter'd' (bought up) and whose river is even chartered too. The chartered river is one of the images of natural life turned rotten and corrupt. Another is the central image in the poem 'The Sick Rose', whose beauty is destroyed by the workings of a dark secret love instead of an open and free love:

> O Rose, thou art sick.
> The invisible worm,
> That flies in the night
> In the howling storm,
>
> Has found out thy bed
> Of crimson joy;
> And his dark secret love
> Does thy life destroy.

It is impossible to describe with any precision what is being referred to here: to reduce the poem to a set of symbols and a paraphrase would destroy its magic and mystery. It is probably a contrary poem to 'The Blossom' in *Songs of Innocence*, a poem which happily and healthily accepts merriment and sorrow. 'The Sick Rose', with its short and rhythmically flaccid lines, feels far less open, energetic, and healthy: in the illumination its dull crimson contrasts with the brilliant scarlet of 'The Blossom'. What is clear, however, is that 'The Sick Rose' deals with a sickness that can eat at the heart of the beautiful, and that the rose is dying because it is consumed by a secret passion, a dark love which flies in the night. A similar difficulty of interpretation is found in the most celebrated of the *Songs of Experience*, 'The Tyger'. Like 'The Sick Rose', it has its counterpart in *Songs of Innocence* ('The Lamb'); and like 'The Sick Rose' it eludes paraphrase and symbolic interpretation:

> Tyger, Tyger, burning bright
> In the forests of the night,
> What immortal hand or eye
> Could frame thy fearful symmetry?
>
> (ll. 1–4)

The poem consists almost entirely of questions, which point towards the unseen power behind the tiger, God the Creator seizing the fire that is the spirit of the tiger from out of the unformed creation where it existed:

> In what distant deeps or skies
> Burnt the fire of thine eyes?
> On what wings dare he aspire?
> What the hand dare seize the fire?
>
> (ll. 5–8)

Having seized the fire, the Creator then handles it and shapes it, twisting
the sinews, making the heart beat, and hammering out the shape of the
tiger like some celestial blacksmith:

> And what shoulder, & what art,
> Could twist the sinews of thy heart?
> And when thy heart began to beat,
> What dread hand? & what dread feet?
>
> What the hammer? what the chain?
> In what furnace was thy brain?
> What the anvil? what dread grasp
> Dare its deadly terrors clasp?
>   (ll. 9–16)

The effect of so many unanswered questions is to make them rhetorical,
so that the question marks become something like exclamation marks
(What dread hand! & what dread feet!). There follows a change of
mood, a moment of extraordinary daring, as the beating of the verse
changes to a more extended syntactical pattern:

> When the stars threw down their spears
> And water'd heaven with their tears,
> Did he smile his work to see?
> Did he who made the Lamb make thee?
>   (ll. 17–20)

The first two lines of this verse are a complete surprise. At first sight
they appear so remote from the tiger which has been described as
vibrating with an energy that only the Creator can handle; now the
rhythm and pattern of the words along the line, so different from
the stabbing questions of the previous verses, are part of the sudden
transference from the tiger itself into another experience – the tradition
of the weeping angels after the battle in heaven, crying for the loss of
a third of their number. The verse then turns to a question, but not
before the image of the weeping angels as stars has left an indelible
impression on the mind. It is as though their victory has shown the
limitations of force: they do not rejoice, but weep. In *Paradise Lost*,
as Blake knew, the battle in heaven was followed by the Creation of
the world: the reference here is to the moment at which the end of the
battle led into the creation of all things, and the moment at which the
tiger first appeared. Then, as the account in Genesis (1. 10) informs us,
'God saw that it was good.' Blake turns this into a penetrating question
which has all kinds of implications:

Did he smile his work to see?
Did he who made the Lamb make thee?

Was God the Creator pleased with the tiger? Or was it something so terrifying and energetic that even He stood aghast? And what kind of a Creator was he, who could make something as docile and unaggressive as the lamb and as powerful and dangerous as the tiger? Truly, the question implies, he is a Creator whose range is vast and whose power is unimaginable: He can contain within His nature such opposites, can exercise his creative power in such contrary and limitless ways.

And, finally, what of the tiger? For the poem, having raised all sorts of questions about God, ends with the tiger, returning to the arresting first verse but altering 'Could' to 'Dare', thus underlining the accumulated awe for the Creator which has been acquired during the poem. This return is significant and memorable, for it enables the reader to return to the images of the first verse with a new understanding. The images themselves are startling enough: the eyes, burning in the dark forest, suggest that the tiger is looking out of the darkness straight at the reader (not, as in the peculiar illumination, looking sideways out of the picture), and so does the 'fearful symmetry'. The threatening implications of this image suggest that Blake may be challenging the eighteenth-century complacency which saw God as presiding amiably over a beneficent and harmonious creation; but at the same time there is no evidence that Blake saw the tiger as evil.[6]

Blake habitually endorsed energy as one of the great enlivening and moral qualities[7]: if it is associated with anger, then anger too can be a moral virtue (not, as in the teachings of the church, one of the Seven Deadly Sins). In *The Marriage of Heaven and Hell* we are told that 'The tygers of wrath are wiser than the horses of instruction', and in a poem such as 'A Poison Tree' Blake argues in favour of an open anger rather than a concealed resentment:

I was angry with my friend;
I told my wrath, my wrath did end.
I was angry with my foe;
I told it not, my wrath did grow.

(ll. 1–4)

All these support the idea that the tiger is to be associated with forces that are at the furthest remove from the gentleness of the lamb, and that those forces are not to be seen as evil. They are part of the contraries of the world, without which there is no progression: and without them the fallen world may well be deprived of the anger and violence which is needed to change society. Above all, the tiger's force is open, burning and recognizable; it is totally opposed to deceit, concealed resentment, and mystery. These last qualities Blake saw as encouraged by conventional religion, which specialized in thwarting and controlling the natural instincts. So, in 'My Pretty Rose Tree', the rose turns away in jealousy, and in 'Ah! Sunflower' the youth has 'pined away with desire' and the pale Virgin is 'shrouded in snow'; all are affected by ideas of conventional morality and religion, the 'Thou Shalt Not' of the chapel in 'The Garden of Love'. Such a morality can infuse itself through all life and affect all ideas; indeed, one of the most painful oppositions of *Songs of Experience* comes when the lovely 'The Divine Image' of *Innocence* is twisted into the sceptical and cynical 'The Human Abstract':

> Pity would be no more
> If we did not make somebody Poor;
> And Mercy no more could be
> If all were as happy as we;
>
> And mutual fear brings peace,
> Till the selfish loves increase.
> Then Cruelty knits a snare
> And spreads his baits with care.
>
> (ll. 1–8)

Where can such a jaundiced view have come from? Clearly it is Mercy, Pity, Peace, and Love seen from a different, exclusively human, angle, one in which they are not divine qualities so much as consequences of a fallen and evil world. Mercy, it seems to say, is only the result of uneven happiness; pity, of poverty; peace, of mutual fear; and love is self-love. Blake explores the origins of such an appalling reductiveness in the stanzas which follow, which show religion not concerning itself with the practical and divine qualities of mercy, pity, peace, and love, but with traditional religious abstractions such as humility and mystery. Humility takes root in the ground watered with Cruelty's tears:

> Soon spreads the dismal shade
> Of Mystery over his head;
> And the Catterpiller and Fly
> Feed on the Mystery.
>
> (ll. 13–16)

The 'catterpiller' appears elsewhere in Blake's poetry as the destroyer of the rose; here the feeding on the tree of mystery has the perverse effect (since it is the opposite of a normal and healthily growing plant) of making it grow. It thrives on the work of its parasites, and bears the fruit of Deceit; it grows and is sought for by the earth-bound gods 'of the earth and sea'

> But their search was all in vain:
> There grows one in the Human Brain.
>
> (ll. 23–24).

The last three words make an extraordinary and forceful conclusion: the whole process that has been so vividly described in vegetable terms is revealed as being the product of the human brain. We have no one to blame but ourselves: it is our habits of mind that allow society to be corrupt and rotten, and that see religion as the worship of a mystery rather than the creation of the kingdom of God upon earth. *Songs of Experience* leaves us in no doubt that it is such false ways of thought that lead to evil and destruction.

This becomes clear if we consider some of the other poems that Blake was writing at this time, *Tiriel* (written 1789 but not engraved), *The Book of Thel* (1789), and *The French Revolution* (1790–91). *Tiriel* is the portrait of an aged tyrant, blind and bald, 'king of rotten wood & of the bones of death'.[8] The poem was never published or engraved, and it is certainly less attractive than *The Book of Thel*, which describes Thel, a young girl, and her encounters with the created world. She is distressed by its transience, but is answered by the lowly things of creation, the lily of the valley and the cloud. The lily's humility (different from the pious humility of the religious in 'The Human Abstract') is touching in its simplicity:

> I am a wat'ry weed,
> And I am very small and love to dwell in lowly vales;
> So weak the gilded butterfly scarce perches on my head;
> Yet I am visited from heaven, and he that smiles on all
> Walks in the valley and each morn over me spreads his hand . . .
>
> (Pl. 2, ll. 16–20)

This acceptance is also found in the cloud, which is a striking example of the transience which Thel complains of; yet the cloud also rejoices in its usefulness, and sees its own disappearance as natural and good. In the Platonic tradition which Blake inherited and admired, the cloud rejoices in the disappearance of its material form, for

> when I pass away,
> It is to tenfold life, to love, to peace, and raptures holy.
>
> (Pl. 3, ll. 10–11)

Thel reflects that, unlike the cloud, she is unable to feed the flowers,

> And all shall say 'Without a use this shining woman liv'd –
> Or did she only live to be at death the food of worms?'
>
> (Pl. 3, ll. 22–23)

In its selflessness and simplicity the cloud reflects that to be the food of worms is itself a great use and blessing; it then calls upon the worm itself to speak. Thel pities the worm for being, as she thinks, so helpless and unloved; but she then learns that the clod of clay looks after the worm. The clod of clay speaks:

> 'O beauty of the vales of Har, we live not for ourselves.
> Thou seest me the meanest thing, and so I am indeed:
> My bosom of itself is cold, and of itself is dark,
> But he that loves the lowly pours his oil upon my head,
> And kisses me, and binds his nuptial bands around my breast,
> And says: "Thou mother of my children, I have loved thee,
> And I have given thee a crown that none can take away."
> But how this is, sweet maid, I know not, and I cannot know;
> I ponder, and I cannot ponder; yet I live and love.'
>
> (Pl. 4, ll. 10–12; Pl. 5, ll. 1–6)

The clod of clay invites Thel to enter the world of earth, the world of the grave. From this she hears the voice of sorrow which is lamenting over the earth, posing a series of rhetorical questions: it is as though in death she discovers a reality which had been hidden from her on earth, and that new perception suggests fresh dangers and difficulties. Thel has disposed of her previous problems, those of transience and of lowly things in the scheme of creation: now she is faced with something which Blake found far more problematical, the deceptions and fears of life, together with the constraints upon the freedom of love:

> Why are Eyelids stor'd with arrows ready drawn,
> Where a thousand fighting men in ambush lie?
> Or an Eye of gifts & graces, show'ring fruits and coined gold?
> Why a Tongue impress'd with honey from every wind?
> Why an Ear a whirlpool fierce to draw creations in?
> Why a Nostril wide inhaling terror, trembling and affright?
> Why a tender curb upon the youthful burning boy?
> Why a little curtain of flesh on the bed of our desire?
>
> (Pl. 6, ll. 13–20)

The questions are too much for Thel, who flees back to the vales of

Har from which she came. Clearly she is an innocent, but in the wrong sense, in that she cannot face the complexities of life: she enjoys hearing the lily of the valley, the cloud, and the worm, but not the voice of sorrow with its message of frustration and fear. Her retreat is a refusal to become involved: it is an implied contrast to the service in the world performed by the created things in the poem. The clod of clay, for instance, is Blake's symbol for unselfishness, here acting as the worm's protector and in *Songs of Experience* (in 'The Clod and the Pebble') being soft and yielding as opposed to the hard pebble.

If *The Book of Thel* is the philosophical complement of *Songs of Innocence and of Experience*, *The French Revolution* is a reminder of the political upheavals of the time, and also a foretaste of one of Blake's later methods in the Prophetic Books: he takes an historical event, or a place, and invests it with his own mythological significance, giving it a name, or the form of an animal, and devising an appropriate atmosphere.

The key work of these years, however, is *The Marriage of Heaven and Hell* (1790–93). It begins with a promise of revolution, like a thunderstorm in the air, as Rintrah, the wrathful figure, appears angry and frustrated by the domination of the villain and the sneaking serpent; but in subsequent sections it develops Blake's ideas on morality and religion in ways that confirm and explain *Songs of Innocence and of Experience*. If Innocence and Experience are, as the title page of the joint work says, 'two contrary states of the human soul', in *The Marriage of Heaven and Hell* they are seen as part of the necessary pattern of life:

> Without contraries is no progression. Attraction and repulsion, reason and energy, love and hate, are necessary to human existence.
>
> From these contraries spring what the religious call *good* and *evil*.
> Good is the passive that obeys reason: Evil is the active springing from energy.
>
> (Pl. 3, ll. 7–12)

With the definition of 'good' as passive (that is 'what the religious call good') Blake identifies a religious morality that he campaigns against continually: it is the 'Thou shalt not'; what Blake sees as the repressive, anti-life doctrine of self-control and reason. So 'the religious' call energy evil: and in Plate 4 Blake suggests that they think of it as particularly associated with the body. The Plate is entitled 'The Voice of the Devil', but this devil is what the religious call the devil, and therefore good. 'Energy', the devil tells us, 'is eternal delight', and 'Those who restrain desire do so because theirs is weak enough to be restrained.' In support of this argument Blake enrols Milton, suggesting (in common with other readers, notably Shelley) that Satan was the true source of energy in *Paradise Lost* and that 'The reason Milton wrote in fetters when he wrote of angels and God, and at liberty when of devils and Hell, is because he was a true poet, and of the Devil's party without knowing it.' Thus the 'Proverbs of Hell' which form the third section are in effect articles of Blake's belief, gnomic and sometimes shocking:

> The road of excess leads to the palace of wisdom.
>
> (Pl. 7, 1. 7)
>
> Prudence is a rich ugly old maid courted by incapacity.
>
> (Pl. 7, 1.8)
>
> Sooner murder an infant in its cradle than nurse unacted desires.
>
> (Pl. 9, 1. 27)

The exaggeration of these is characteristic of Blake in this section; it is part of the exuberance of *The Marriage of Heaven and Hell*, a zest and flavour which is demonstrated in the parodies of Swedenborg. At least one of these parodies is hilarious (Pl. 17–20): its title (and that of other sections) is 'A Memorable Fancy', which is an ironic imitation of Swedenborg's 'A Memorable Relation'. Emmanuel Swedenborg (1688–1772) was a Swedish scientist who claimed to have seen many visions, and whose New Church in England was founded in 1788. Blake was interested in his work, and found his visionary gospel attractive; but in *The Marriage* he uses even Swedenborg as a type of religious writer who needs to be exposed. As S. Foster Damon has pointed out,[9] Blake's ridiculing of Swedenborg needs to be set beside his description of him as 'strongest of men' (*Milton*, Pl. 22, 1.50) and his adoption of at least one of Swedenborg's beliefs, that Jesus is the only God. But in Plate 2 of *The Marriage*, his writings are described as 'the linen clothes folded up' beside the tomb of the risen Christ. This suggests that they are empty, and that the true divinity is elsewhere: Blake may have been particularly disturbed by Swedenborg's *Heaven and Hell* (from which the title of Blake's work comes) which suggested a predestination that he found 'more abominable than Calvin's'.[10]

Swedenborg had claimed a Second Coming in 1757 (the year of Blake's birth). Now, in 1790, Blake grimly and humorously notes, thirty-three years, the length of the life of Jesus, have elapsed and 'the eternal Hell revives'. In this case we are probably to understand the eternal 'Hell' as figuring the energies of the French Revolution, a very different phenomenon from that envisaged by Swedenborg, but welcome to Blake, who saw it as evidence of a true religious event, the energetic emergence of a new world. It is an energy which the religious (many of whom were opposed to the French Revolution) would have thought of as 'hellish' but which Blake thought of as leading to a new heaven on earth, a heaven of liberty and equality. Hence the *marriage* of heaven and hell, the vision which sees the energy of hell producing a true heaven; and hence the presence in the poem of the prophetic element, in which Blake questions Isaiah and Ezekiel. The two prophets dine with him, making (one is meant to suppose) a trinity of prophets, and Isaiah explodes the normal ideas about God:

> 'I saw no God, nor heard any, in a finite organical
> perception; but my sense discover'd the infinite in every
> thing, and as I was then perswaded & remain confirm'd,
> that the voice of honest indignation is the voice of God, I
> cared not for consequences, but wrote.'
>
> (Pl. 12, ll. 5–11)

Similarly Ezekiel desires by various strange means to raise men into a perception of the infinite. Blake then enters the poem himself, as the third prophetic voice:

> the notion that man has a body distinct from his soul is
> to be expunged. This I shall do, by printing in the infernal
> method, by corrosives, which in Hell are salutary and
> medicinal, melting apparent surfaces away, and displaying
> the infinite which was hid.
>
> (Pl. 14, ll. 10–14)

This direct description of Blake's method as an engraver (the opposite of the usual method) ingeniously points to it as a symbol of uncovering truth; and the Prophetic Books attempt to fulfil the promise which is made here of cleansing the doors of perception, so that the material world shall seem infinite. According to Blake, man has 'closed himself up': the five senses prevent him from seeing the infinite in every thing. So he asks dramatically:

> How do you know but ev'ry Bird that cuts the airy way,
> Is an immense world of delight, clos'd by your senses five?
>
> (Pl. 6, ll. 26–27)

Religion is one of the closing-up agents, as the later Plates make clear: another comic episode, in Plates 22–24, describes the 'conversion' of a (conventional) angel into a devil, who then becomes Blake's particular friend:

We often read the Bible together in its infernal or diabolic sense, which the world shall have if they behave well.

I have also: The Bible of Hell, which the world shall have whether they will or no.

One Law for the Lion & Ox is Oppression.

This last line of text comes below the figure on all fours of Nebuchadnezzar, whose rigid application of the laws of the Medes and Persians led to the persecution of Daniel and the throwing of Shadrach, Meshach, and Abednego into the burning fiery furnace (Daniel, Ch. 3). Nebuchadnezzar as imprisoner and tyrant is an apt figure to introduce 'A Song of Liberty' which concludes *The Marriage* with a contemporary portrayal of the French Revolution at the point when the young republic drove off the invasion of 1792. But the portrayal of successful revolutionary energy is not left there, as Blake returns in the final chorus to the priests and the tyranny of religion:

> Let the Priests of the Raven of dawn no longer, in deadly black, with hoarse note curse the sons of joy. Nor his accepted brethren, whom, tyrant, he calls free, lay the bound or build the roof. Nor pale religious lectchery call that Virginity that wishes but acts not!

> For every thing that lives is Holy.

The Marriage of Heaven and Hell opens the way to the Prophetic Books. In its free-ranging, combative way it denounces false thinking and unimaginative religion, and holds up for our admiration the visions of prophecy. In its Swedenborgian imitations it is humorous and local in effect, but the overall meaning is clearly wider, dismissing all orthodox religions in favour of the individual vision. Clearly, this is dangerous ground, and it is at this point that the Romantic poet's celebration of prophecy begins to be suspect. If we believe, with Isaiah, that 'a firm perswasion' that a thing is so makes it so, then we have an antinomian problem on our hands (no doubt Hitler had firm persuasions). The problem is one that continues to beset the Prophetic Books which follow: their visions are individual, communicated through line and word but essentially representing Blake's own systems which for him represent the central truth but which are unchallengeable. Prophets do not abide our question; they dictate.

The first to be called 'a Prophecy' was *America* (1793), based loosely upon the American Revolution and (in its illuminations) brilliant with the bright colours of youth and hope. It describes the coming of Orc, the spirit of revolution in the material world, who is united with the daughter of Urthona ('earth-owner') symbolizing the natural life of North America, chained by the British occupation. The 'Guardian Prince of Albion' burns with 'sullen fires' (the adjective perhaps taken from Paine's description of George III as a 'sullen Pharaoh') and confronts the American leaders: the coming of Orc is seen as a kind of resurrection, a release of the 'fiery joy' that Urizen ('your reason') perverted 'to ten commands' (Pl. 8, l. 61). Urizen is here the law-maker, the limiter, the imposer of a control which leads to tyranny. In *America* he intervenes in the conflict between Albion's Angel (the spirit of colonializing England) and Orc; the Angel uses pestilence, and Orc uses fire, until Urizen (seeing that Albion's Angel is having the worst of it) freezes the action

> Till angels and weak men twelve years should govern o'er
> the strong,
> And then their end should come, when France received the
> demon's light.
> (Pl. 16, ll. 14–15)

The obvious reference is to the revolution in France, which broke out twelve years after the American war ended; and Blake ends *America* with a description of European countries shuddering with terror at the approaching dawn of a new age which would overthrow their 'law-built heaven'. In *Europe* (1794), the idea continues: the frontispiece shows Blake's most celebrated illumination, the God-figure of Urizen measuring the heavens (sometimes known as 'The Ancient of Days'), and the title page which follows shows the great serpent figure of Orc, rising up with unbounded energy (its tail symbolically disappears off the page because the page is not big enough to hold it) and embodying, in David Erdman's words, 'energy, desire, phallic power, the fiery tongue'.[11] Then the mythological turns into the historical: the Preludium contains a cartoon-like drawing of Burke, the anti-Jacobin, waiting in a cave to assassinate the pilgrim who passes by (dressed in the colours of George Washington which were adopted by the Whigs, led by Fox, who supported the French Revolution).

Europe is dominated by the figure of Enitharmon, later (in *The First Book of Urizen*) representing pity, but here a female figure who has lost her true nature and turned tyrannical. She sends her sons, Rintrah and Palamabron, to 'tell the human race that Womans love is Sin'. In the poem she dreams for 1800 years, laughing in her sleep to see

> (O woman's triumph)
> Every house a den, every man bound; the shadows are fill'd

With spectres, and the windows wove over with curses of iron:
Over the doors Thou shalt not; & over the chimneys Fear is
written;
(Pl. 12, ll. 25–28)

She awakens, unaware that the time of the end of that world has come, and inviting Orc to smile upon her children; but her children are now the corrupted and materialistic, and Orc rises up 'in the vineyards of red France' so violently that she is dismayed. Enitharmon has accepted a perversion of the normal imaginative and sympathetic processes: she presides over an insidious materialism which overwhelms earth-born humanity with the five senses and which turns the infinite into a serpent-figure, no longer a rearing serpent but a brazen, regular form, coiled in seven coils to represent the seven days of material creation:

> Then was the serpent temple form'd, image of infinite
> Shut up in finite revolutions, and man became an Angel;
> Heaven a mighty circle turning, God a tyrant crown'd.
> (Pl. 10, ll. 21–23)

Europe is concerned with the way in which the destruction of the imagination, the natural, the free, becomes accepted. Thus Albion's Angel is (as in *America*) tyrannical, and Rintrah and Palamabron subjected to the power of Enitharmon. Similarly in *The Song of Los* (1795), subtitled 'Africa: Asia' (to connect it to *Europe* and *America*), the original power of the imagination gives way to laws and religion, and to a deadening materialism which makes Urizen weep: nature shrinks 'before their shrunken eyes' until

> a Philosophy of Five Senses was complete.
> Urizen wept & gave it into the hands of Newton and Locke.
> (Pl. 4, ll. 47–48)

Like Enitharmon, Urizen is not essentially evil: his weeping here is the lament of a great figure who beholds his own downfall. In the 'Asia' section he weeps for a different reason, for the renewal of the dry bones of the world by Orc. Urizen is a complex figure in Blake's mythology, whose story is told in *The First Book of Urizen* (1794) and in *Vala, or The Four Zoas* (1797–1803). It has parallels with the story of Satan, in that Urizen was the 'first born Son of Light' (*FZ*, ll. 108) who desired dominion and became jealous of man, and so limited man's imaginative life and power (some critics, notably Kathleen Raine, derive the word from the Greek οὑρίζειν to limit). He is associated with materialism and becomes the God of this world, the jealous God

of the Old Testament. In so doing he splits off from Los, the spirit
of imagination and poetry, and a further consequence of this Fall is
the splitting off from Los of the female form Enitharmon (*The First
Book of Urizen*, Ch. 5). In *The First Book of Urizen*, the son of Los and
Enitharmon is Orc. Los is jealous of Orc, and chains him to a rock;
and with the coming of unimaginative man the Fall is complete:

> Six days they shrunk up from existence
> And on the seventh day they rested;
> And they bless'd the seventh day, in sick hope:
> And forgot their eternal life.
>   (*The First Book of Urizen*, Pl. 25, ll. 39–42)

The image of shrinking and the destructive force of jealousy recur
throughout, and the Fall is accompanied by a recognizable pattern of
religious behaviour associated with prudence, selfishness, and materialism. It marks a grand and terrible division, a splitting apart which is
charted in *The Four Zoas*, subtitled 'The Torments of Love & Jealousy
in The Death and Judgement of Albion the Ancient Man', and given a
deeply moving particularity in Enion's lament (at the end of the Second
Night). Albion is both man and country, England and Englishmen
corrupted from their true condition and with their true nature split
into abstractions. So *The Four Zoas* begins with a gloss on two passages
from St John's Gospel, both of which emphasize the unity of God and
man in Jesus Christ:

> Four mighty ones are in every man;
>   a perfect unity
> Cannot exist, but from the universal
>   brotherhood of Eden,
> The universal man, to whom be
>   glory ever more. Amen.
> What are the natures of those living creatures the
>   Heavenly Father only
> Knoweth; no individual knoweth nor can know in all Eternity.
>   (I. 1–8; marginal glosses refer to John 17. 21–23 and John 1.14)

The four mighty ones of the first line are Urthona/Los (imaginative),
Luvah/Orc (passionate), Urizen (rational and limiting), and Tharmas
(compassionate). Each has a compass point and an element, and the
division is seen in global and material terms as well as in national and
personal ones. At every level the Fall brings division and jealousy; it is
only ended in 'Night the Ninth, being the Last Judgement', when Blake
describes (as in the Book of Revelation) the coming of the heavenly

city. This section of the poem is a song of the new creation, on the
mythological level (with the cleaning of Urizen's plough), in a symbolic
form (with the rising sun and the beautiful morning, the animals all at
play), and thirdly on a literal level that expresses Blake's contemporary
view of political and religious events:

> 'Let the slave grinding at the mill run out into the field;
> Let him look up into the heavens & laugh in the bright air;
> Let the enchained soul, shut up in darkness & in sighing,
> Whose face has never seen a smile in thirty weary years,
> Rise & look out – his chains are loose, his dungeon doors
> are open.
> And let his wife & children return from the oppressor's scourge.
>
> 'They look behind at every step & believe it is a dream:
> Are these the slaves that groaned along the streets of Mystery?
> Where are your bonds & taskmasters? Are these the prisoners?
> Where are your chains, where are your tears? Why do you
> look around?
> If you are thirsty, there is the river: go bathe your
> parched limbs.
> The good of all the land is before you, for Mystery is no more!'
> (IX. 667–78)

The image of grinding at the mill comes from *Samson Agonistes*, a poem
which furnished Blake with material for his two major prophecies about
the coming to England of the new Jerusalem, *Milton* and *Jerusalem*.
Milton begins with the poem which compresses its theme into a form
which is forceful and immediately compelling – 'And did those feet in
ancient time/Walk upon England's mountains green?' At this point the
prophecy is immediately accessible, even if the full significance of the
'dark Satanic mills' is usually missed. It is easy to scoff at the use of
this poem, but for a moment, while singing it, all the Lord's people
become prophets (as Blake suggested that they should in the line which
follows):

> Bring me my bow of burning gold;
> Bring me my arrows of desire;
> Bring me my spear – O clouds unfold!
> Bring me my chariot of fire!
> (Pl. ii. 29–32)

Although Blake is attacking the evils of his own day, the vision is
so strong that anyone can partake for a moment of the prophetic
role, even though the details may be blurred. The poem is contrasting

an England before the Fall, when Christ was present, with the same country filled with 'dark Satanic mills'. These are possibly the factories of the Industrial Revolution, but more probably the mills of mental slavery (the image comes from Milton's *Samson Agonistes*); it is against these that the 'arrows of desire', the spear of the warring angel, and the chariot of the prophet are assembled.

Blake's declaration that he 'will not cease from mental fight' is a good indication of the combativeness of *Milton*. The trust in the individual vision is here complete. *Milton* itself celebrates this in the references to the two personal experiences of Blake, the shaft of light striking his foot as he was fastening his shoe at Lambeth and a moment of ecstasy at Felpham, when a lark sang and he smelt the wild thyme. Both occur in the poem[12]: the shadow of Milton enters Blake's foot (Pl. 15, l. 49 and Pl. 21, l. 4) and the lark and wild thyme are discovered in Book II, in Plates 35–36, and at the end:

> Immediately the lark mounted with a loud trill from Felpham's
> vale,
> And the wild thyme from Wimbledon's green and empurpled hills:
> (Pl. 42, ll. 29–30)

Milton's problem, according to Blake, was an over-confidence in reason. In a fallen world, his trust in reason led naturally to a legalized religion: this is associated not only with the tyranny of kings and priests, but also with the tyranny of time and space. Thus the spirit of Milton can transcend the limitations which he knew in bodily form, and it can appear in different places simultaneously. This makes the reading of the poem difficult, but it is part of Blake's refusal to admit the primacy of 'the sea of time and space' (the use of water in this image may be compared with its use in the engraving of 'Newton'). So Milton's spirit can return to earth as a reforming spirit (as Wordsworth, in his September 1802 sonnet, wished) and it can inspire Blake himself; it can also remain in heaven as an immortal soul, and simultaneously with these two states it can be a sick soul, 'a wanderer lost in dreary night' (Pl. 15, l. 16).[13]

Milton descends to earth, in an obvious parallel to Christ's descent to redeem mankind promised in *Paradise Lost*. He comes to convince mankind, through Blake (whom he inspires) of the great possibilities of true religion, the full imaginative life of the created world (as opposed to the orthodox teaching of his epic poem):

> Seest thou the little winged fly, smaller than a grain of sand?
> It has a heart like thee, a brain open to Heaven & Hell,
> Withinside wondrous and expansive. Its gates are not closed;

I hope thine are not. Hence it clothes itself in rich array;
Hence thou art clothed with human beauty, O thou mortal man.
Seek not thy heavenly father then beyond the skies; . . .

(Pl. 20, ll. 27–32)

The poem speaks of the possibility of a heaven upon earth, of a religion which is utterly different from the usual church doctrine, in which 'everything that lives is holy' and the prophet can see eternity through space and time. Blake describes a moment in which he cannot comprehend the descent of Milton:

for man cannot know
What passes in his members till periods of Space & Time
Reveal the secrets of Eternity: for more extensive
Than any other earthly things, are Man's earthly lineaments.

And all this vegetable world appeared on my left Foot
As a bright sandal form'd immortal of precious stones & gold:
I stooped down & bound it on to walk forward thro' Eternity.

(Pl. 21, ll. 8–14)

He goes forward in faith, until the moment in Plate 36 when Ololon descends into the garden of Blake's cottage at Felpham. The illustration in Plate 40 showing the cottage and its water-pump in the garden with Ololon gliding to earth between two branches of a tree, is a touching example of the non-earthly emanation entering the sphere of ordinary domestic life. Ololon is part of the complex mythological structure of Milton: she is the ideal, the woman Milton loved on earth but never found (instead he found the Sixfold Emanation, his three wives and three daughters). When she meets Milton their love is so great that to Blake

Wondrous were their acts – by me unknown
Except remotely;

(Pl. 40, ll. 2–3)

This is because in a mortal form (as opposed to the eternal form) the vision is inevitably incomplete and the good corrupted. Even a great and inspired figure such as Milton is likely to be condensed on earth into the Covering Cherub (Pl. 37), beautiful but deadly. This sense of Milton's work as magnificent but corrupting is paralleled in the Bard's song of Book I, which relates the quarrel between Satan (Blake's friend Hayley) and Palamabron (Blake himself). Hayley's friendship, kind and useful though it was, appears in the end to be destructive; what is required is a total sacrifice of the self, the self which inevitably partakes of the natural world, as Milton's shadow (as opposed to the true Milton, the spirit of Milton) does:

> Milton's shadow, who is the Covering Cherub
> The Spectre of Albion, in which the spectre of Luvah inhabits,
> In the Newtonian voids between the substances of creation.
> (Pl. 37, ll. 44–46)

Luvah is the spectre of the evil possessing Britain, and is perhaps associated with William Pitt; the individual purification which is the subject of *Milton* (the spirit of the dead poet returning to earth to inspire mankind but also to unite with Ololon and be purged of error) is also a national cleansing, signalled at the beginning by 'And did those feet . . .' and returned to at the end when

> Los listens to the cry of the poor man, his cloud
> Over London in volume terrific, low bended in anger.
> (Pl. 42, ll. 34–35)

The image of a great thunderstorm, about to break, is part of the promise at the end of *Milton*. Milton himself is so great in his self-annihilation that he terrifies that part of Ololon which is the Sixfold Emanation so that the three wives and three daughters flee repentant into his bosom. At the end love and wisdom are combined in a new relationship: the 'Starry Eight' (Milton's Humanity and his seven guardian angels) become Jesus and

> Round his limbs
> The clouds of Ololon folded as a garment dipped in blood.
> (Pl. 42, ll. 11–12)

The prophecy at this point is of war and judgement, of a terrifying moment of the second coming of Jesus to England, walking forth

> From Felpham's vale, clothed in clouds of blood, to enter into
> Albion's bosom, the bosom of death, . . .
> (Pl. 42, ll. 20–21)

The complete statement of this coming in love and judgement is found in *Jerusalem, The Emanation of The Giant Albion* (1804–20). Blake's idea of the emanation (as found also in *Milton*) is of a part of a person, belonging to him but separated from him; and *Jerusalem* deals with the separation of Jerusalem, the holy city, from Albion, or England. Albion is preoccupied with its own materialism, and with conquest

and warfare: Los, the spirit of the imagination, rages in frustration
(Pl. 6 shows him idle at his anvil, looking up at the horrible spectre
which darkens the scene). The spectre is a kind of vampire figure,
terrible when in power, though it can be used (as material things
can) for good, as it is by Los in Plate 8; it is also a 'spectre', an
empty ghost-figure, and is a kind of under-side to Los himself, his
own 'Pride and self-righteousness' (Pl. 8, l. 30). Los begins to build
his city of art and manufacture, Golgonooza, which is to cover the
whole of Britain; its elaborate structure is described in *Jerusalem*, Plates
12–14. Albion's failure to unite with Jerusalem is all the more tragic
when compared with its past: just as the holy lamb of God walked in
England in *Milton*, in Chapter 2 of *Jerusalem* Blake sees a London that
was once transfigured:

> The fields from Islington to Marybone,
> To Primrose Hill and Saint John's Wood,
>   Were builded over with pillars of gold,
> And there Jerusalem's pillars stood.

Chapter 2 of *Jerusalem* describes the weakening of Albion, although
there is (as there is in *Milton*) a gate which cannot be found

> By Satan's watch-fiends; though they search numbering every
>   grain
> Of sand on earth every night, they never find this gate.
> It is the gate of Los.
>   (Pl. 35, ll. 1–3)

Albion comes to the gate, speaking (to Los's despair) in traditional
religious terms of himself as a sinner needing the ransom of the sacrifice
of Jesus. This is part of Albion's surrender to the disease of his own
affections, the corruptions of the natural world. Only when Albion
says 'Hope is banished from me' (Pl. 47, l. 17) does a true religion
appear, when

>   the merciful Saviour in his arms
> Received him, in the arms of tender mercy, & reposed
> The pale limbs of his eternal individuality
> Upon the Rock of Ages.
>   (Pl. 48, ll. 1–4)

But in Chapter 3 Albion falls under the power of the spectre, and
becomes entirely corrupt. An example is Plate 70, in which a huge
stone trilithon, dwarfing the humans underneath, accompanies the text

describing the coming of Bacon, Newton, and Locke, the philosophical trilithon that Blake detested. Not until the second part of Chapter 4 does Albion awake, beginning at Plate 94. Thereafter there is a resurrection of the dead, and the final vision of the inspired prophet:

> The four living creatures, chariots of Humanity Divine
> incomprehensible,
> In beautiful paradises expand. These are the four rivers of paradise
> And the four faces of humanity fronting the four cardinal points
> Of heaven, going forward, forward – irresistible from eternity
> to eternity.
> And they conversed together in visionary forms dramatic, which
> bright
> Redounded from their tongues in thunderous majesty, in visions,
> In new expanses, creating exemplars of memory & of intellect –
> Creating space, creating time according to the wonders divine
> Of human imagination, . . .
> (Pl. 98, ll. 24–32)

In this new creation there is a new time and new space, the work of the imagination which is human and also divine, the 'divine image' of *Songs of Innocence* that has become active and creative.

The achievement of Blake's Prophetic Books is not in their constructions of a mythology that is complex (and occasionally obscure), nor in what the poet himself described as 'the energetic exercise of my talent' (*Jerusalem*, Pl. 3, l. 21); although both of these are impressive enough, the truly remarkable feature of the Prophetic Books is their ability to relate these things to a moral and spiritual world that can be recognized and understood. Blake opens out an imaginative world, in which he sees the cities of Britain as part of a gigantic pattern of good and evil, of possessiveness and self-deception, of materialism, and corruption, and possibility. The reader uses Blake's mythological universe for the sake of the truths which it contains, the insights into patterns of false religion and unimaginative materialism; and beyond those obvious evils there are other moral perceptions, into manipulation, narcissism, passive aggression, and selfishness masquerading as kindness. Blake's moral incisiveness is terrifying: a reading of his Prophetic Books is a progress through a labyrinth that is a continual education in self-knowledge. At the beginning of Chapter 4 of *Jerusalem*, there is a verse addressed 'to the Christians', which uses this labyrinth image:

> I will give you the end of a golden string,
> Only wind it into a ball:

It will lead you in at Heaven's gate,
Built in Jerusalem's wall.

(Pl. 77, ll. 1–4)

And in the passage which follows, Blake claims that 'I know of no other Christianity and no other Gospel than the liberty both of body and mind to exercise the divine arts of imagination' (Pl. 77, ll. 12–13). The primacy of the imagination is paramount: it is human and divine. His works, astonishing in their originality, are his evidence: and they are not needed just for their moral insights, accurate though they are. They are needed for their own sakes, for their extraordinary testimony to the energy and vision of the human spirit. Blake offers his work itself as a witness of the divine spirit in human living, as a counterblast to the materialism of Newton and Locke, and as an example of life as opposed to death.

Notes

1. David Erdman, *Blake, Prophet against Empire* (Princeton, 1954), pp. 185–88.

2. *Henry Crabb Robinson on Books and their Writers*, edited by Edith J. Morley, 3 vols (London, 1938), I, 325–31.

3. Max Weber, *The Sociology of Religion*, translated by E. Fischoff (London, 1965), p. 46.

4. Jenijoy La Belle, 'William Blake, Theodore Reothke and Mother Goose: The Unholy Trinity', *Blake Studies*, 9 (1980), pp. 74–86.

5. See John Holloway, *Blake, The Lyric Poetry* (London, 1968), p. 28.

6. David Erdman has said that the poem 'remains one of Blake's contrived enigmas – a contrivance forced upon him by the truth, one feels'. See *The Illuminated Blake* (London, 1975), p. 84.

7. See Peter Butter's note to the poem in *William Blake, Selected Poems* (London, 1982), p. 207.

8. *The Complete Writings of William Blake*, edited by Geoffrey Keynes (London, 1966), p. 101.

9. S. Foster Damon, *A Blake Dictionary* (London, 1973), pp. 392–94.

10. Peter Butter's reading: *William Blake, Selected Poems*, p.214.

11. Erdman, *The Illuminated Blake* p. 157.

12. See *Milton* Plate 15, ll. 47–50; Plate 21, ll. 4–14; Plate 42, ll. 24–30.

13. For the form of the poem, see David Fuller, '*Milton* and the Development of Blake's Thought', in *An Infinite Complexity*, edited by J. R. Watson (Edinburgh, 1983), pp. 46–94.

Chapter 6
Wordsworth

Wordsworth is always known as the poet of nature. There is something rather strange about this, because he thought of himself as writing principally about humanity:

> the Mind of Man –
> My haunt, and the main region of my song.
> (Preface to *The Excursion*, ll. 40–41).

When he is considered alongside the other Romantic poets, what is so extraordinary about Wordsworth is not his evocation of nature but his insight into the nature of man, both individually and in society. His poetry is filled with characters, as sharply defined as those in Greek tragedy (and sometimes as tragically): Michael at the sheepfold, the Solitary among the mountains, the discharged soldier, Martha Ray crying

> 'Oh misery! oh misery!
> Oh woe is me! oh misery!'
> ('The Thorn', ll. 65–66)

And in addition to these individual figures, Wordsworth has an extraordinary ability to foresee the present problems of human beings in society. He is interested, for instance, in the problems of living in cities; in the relationship between money and the individual personality; in the relationship between the individual and the state, and the state's responsibility towards its members; and in the way in which certain pressures tend to reduce the individual to a machine, or at least to something less than his or her full individuality. In his own life he experienced (during his stay in London) the sudden transition from a moral and agricultural society to a 'mass society'[1]; and Wordsworth's experience of London gave him an insight into these problems, and a lifelong attachment to the values which the mass society denied: individuality, local loyalty, the spirit of community. His ability to see these matters clearly and to devise a poetry which expresses his beliefs about human beings in society is one of the reasons why he is a central poet of the modern tradition. His preoccupations are those which lie at the heart of the human reaction to a technological, urbanized, and industrialized society.

The demagoguery which is associated with mass society was also experienced by Wordsworth during the French Revolution. Alone among the principal Romantic poets, he was actually there, living in the provinces during the September massacres and subsequently (through his relationship with Annette Vallon and their child) having a deep emotional involvement and interest in the country's progress. In 1790 he witnessed the first anniversary of the Fall of the Bastille, when the country was full of life and hope; he lived in France from the autumn of 1791 to December 1792; he subsequently heard of (and perhaps witnessed) the overthrow of the Girondins (some of whom he is supposed to have known) and the reign of terror under Robespierre. Of all the Romantic poets, therefore, Wordsworth is the one whose radical and reforming sympathies were most vigorously tested by first-hand experience and consequent reflection.

The course of the French Revolution and the life in London confirmed Wordsworth's earliest intuitions of health and happiness, the life he had found as a child at school in Hawkshead. His relief at returning there during the first long vacation from Cambridge is another example of the fundamental opposition which was developing in his experience between the simple benevolence of an organic lakeland community and the life of an acquisitive and confused university society beyond; and the later return to Grasmere in December 1799 was a very important homecoming after many years of wandering. It is celebrated in 'Home at Grasmere', a poem which does not ignore human misery but which really does see the value of Grasmere as 'home', not only in the sense of habitation but also in the deeper sense that the poet feels at peace with himself and at home with his surroundings in ways which he could never feel elsewhere.

The opposition between the individual happiness with the good community on the one hand, and the restless egoism with the failure of community on the other, is fundamental to Wordsworth's poetry. It is easy, unfortunately, to see this as reclusive: Wordsworth can seem to be retreating back into himself, to be returning to the Lake District in order to write contentedly about nature and to denounce the evils beyond. This would be a mistake, and a serious one. Wordsworth is charging himself with the duty of making such sense of his own experience that he will have something important to say to mankind: his energies are to be devoted to a radical programme of reform both of the individual and of the nation. In the process, he has to draw upon his own experience, and trust that experience: it may seem like egotism, but it involves also integrity and courage, a willingness to undertake the role of the prophet. And what the prophet sees is evil as well as good: Wordsworth is a great tragic poet as well as a great visionary.

The return to Grasmere was thus a decisive step. It indicated the poet's unqualified acceptance of his high office, and it may be compared to a religious commitment to a divine call. From henceforth Wordsworth was to live out consciously the life of a dedicated spirit, prophet, teacher: and because his teaching and prophecy were based on his own experience, and that experience was so accidentally and peculiarly central to the discontents of modern industrial society, Wordsworth is a figure of fundamental importance. It is significant that the lines which were used for the Preface to *The Excursion* when it was published in 1814 formed originally the concluding section of 'Home at Grasmere', for they celebrate magisterially the mind

> intent to weigh
> The good and evil of our mortal state.
>
> (ll. 8–9)

His intention is to sing

> Of truth, of Grandeur, Beauty, Love and Hope,
> And melancholy Fear subdued by Faith;
> Of blessed consolations in distress;
> Of moral strength, and intellectual Power;
> Of joy in widest commonalty spread;
> Of the individual Mind that keeps her own
> Inviolate retirement, subject there
> To Conscience only, and the law supreme
> Of that Intelligence which governs all
>
> (ll. 14–22)

– and the programme is staggering in its comprehensiveness. What kind of poet can sing of these things, not to mention the others, the 'solitary anguish' (l. 77) of humanity and the 'living Presence' (l. 44) of paradisal beauty? Wordsworth's answer is the poet on whom the great power of prophetic insight may fall:

> Descend, prophetic Spirit! that inspir'st
> The human Soul of universal earth,
> Dreaming on things to come; and dost possess
> A metropolitan temple in the hearts
> Of mighty Poets: upon me bestow

A gift of genuine insight; that my song
With star-like virtue in its place may shine,
Shedding benignant influence, . . .

                                    (ll. 83–90)

Wordsworth's courage and aspiration here come from the example of his great master Milton, poet and patriot; he was singularly struck, he told Landor, with 'the style of harmony, and the gravity, and republican austerity' of Milton's sonnets.[2] Milton, like Wordsworth, had seen the rise and fall of a great revolution: he had responded with the great justification of the ways of God to men, *Paradise Lost*, and with the tragic defiance of *Samson Agonistes*. Wordsworth, who began the first attempt at *The Prelude* with an echo of Samson, also saw himself as a chosen figure from whom something great was expected.

When Wordsworth writes about nature, therefore, he is doing so in the context of his own beliefs and experience, and of his consciousness of the prophetic role. His writings about nature must not be understood superficially: when he describes nature, as he does in 'Tintern Abbey', as

                    the nurse,
The guide, the guardian of my heart, and soul
Of all my moral being. . . .

                                    (ll. 109–11)

he is using precise language for a process which he wishes, as prophet, to declare to the world: that in contrast to the mechanical, diseased waste of life that is encouraged by modern urban society, there are ways of living that allow the fuller development of the mind and heart:

Knowing that Nature never did betray
The heart that loved her; 'tis her privilege,
Through all the years of this our life, to lead
From joy to joy: for she can so inform
The mind that is within us, so impress
With quietness and beauty, and so feed
With lofty thoughts, that neither evil tongues,
Rash judgments, nor the sneers of selfish men,
Nor greetings where no kindness is, nor all
The dreary intercourse of daily life,
Shall e'er prevail against us, or disturb
Our cheerful faith, that all which we behold
Is full of blessings.

                    ('Tintern Abbey', ll. 122–34)

Wordsworth is here similar to Blake and Byron as a critic of society, though with his own individual poetic expression; like them he sees the need for a radical change of heart, a complete rejection of contemporary assumptions and habits of thought. Where Blake found in every London face 'marks of weakness, marks of woe', Wordsworth found 'greetings where no kindness is' and 'the dreary intercourse of daily life'. It is the sheer waste and sadness of life that angers him:

> The world is too much with us; late and soon,
> Getting and spending, we lay waste our powers:
> Little we see in Nature that is ours;
> We have given our hearts away, a sordid boon!
>
> (Miscellaneous Sonnets, xxxiii)

In this manner the doctrine of nature in Wordsworth's poetry is an unremitting campaign against the destruction of the individual by material and social pressures. To this end, he described the poet as 'the rock of defence for human nature; an upholder and preserver, carrying everywhere with him relationship and love'. He saw himself and Coleridge as prophets of nature, not so much to propagate a gospel as to demonstrate the power and beauty of the mind of man when influenced by nature:

> Prophets of Nature, we to them will speak
> A lasting inspiration, sanctified
> By reason and by truth; what we have loved,
> Others will love; and we may teach them how;
> Instruct them how the mind of man becomes
> A thousand times more beautiful than the earth
> On which he dwells, . . .
>
> (The Prelude, 1805, XIII. 442–48)

This mind, exalted above the material world, is 'Of substance and of fabric more divine' (l. 452); and the use of the word 'divine' as the final word of The Prelude suggests that Wordsworth is a poet who, like the other Romantics, is celebrating the God-like imagination of the creative mind. It is this mind which he sees as capable of looking out on the world and perceiving a relationship of an 'infinite complexity' between the internal mind and the external world. It produces poetry, and through poetry, pleasure – a pleasure which is

> an acknowledgment of the beauty of the universe, an
> acknowledgment the more sincere, because not formal,
> but indirect; it is a task light and easy to him who looks

at the world in the spirit of love: further, it is a homage
paid to the native and naked dignity of man, to the grand
elementary principle of pleasure, by which he knows, and
feels, and lives, and moves.[3]

Wordsworth's phraseology here is indicative of his poetic concerns.
His poetry can be seen to be expressing the native and naked dignity
of man, and also the world seen 'in the spirit of love'; some of the
Lyrical Ballads are patently concerned with a native and naked dignity
('Simon Lee', 'Goody Blake and Harry Gill', 'The Idiot Boy'), and
others, such as 'Tintern Abbey', are involved with the world seen in
a spirit of love. The finest of Wordsworth's nature poetry explores
the relationship between these two great themes, in the attempt to
demonstrate the power of nature in the rescuing of the individual mind
from degradation, materialism, selfishness, and despair.

Wordsworth's early poetry demonstrates his two great preoccupations, the predicaments of human life and the beauty of the natural
world; but in *An Evening Walk* and *Descriptive Sketches* (published
together in 1793, shortly after the poet's return from France) the two
things are held in the same poem without any attempt at integration.
An Evening Walk, written at school and during the Cambridge vacations,
describes the Lake District in the tradition of picturesque landscape,
interrupted by the terrible portrayal of the soldier's widow and her
two starving children. Her husband has been killed in the American
War of Independence, and she is left destitute. Yet after the description
of the deaths of her children, Wordsworth turns back to the twilight
landscape without a flicker of hesitation:

> Sweet are the sounds that mingle from afar,
> Heard by calm lakes, as peeps the folding star, . . .
>
> (1793 text, 301–2)

Similarly in *Descriptive Sketches*, which is an exercise in the sublime
rather than the picturesque, the difficulties of the Swiss mountaineers
and the desperation of the begging children is juxtaposed to the alpine
scenery rather than integrated with it in the poem. Wordsworth refers
to a legend of a golden age among the Alps, and sees the Swiss as
nobly free and independent; but dreadful happenings, such as the death
of the chamois-chaser and the ever-present threat of avalanches, reveal
the tragic possibilities of life in the midst of sublime scenery. As well
as being sublime, the Alps become a symbol of struggle:

> – Alas! in every clime a flying ray
> Is all we have to chear our wintry way,

> Condemn'd, in mists and tempests ever rife,
> To pant slow up the endless Alp of life.
>
> (1793 text, 590–93)

The 1793 text, from which these quotations are taken, is illuminating in another direction, as evidence of Wordsworth's eighteenth-century stylistic inheritance. The heroic couplets are rich with borrowings from seventeenth- and eighteenth-century poetry, and contain a fair proportion of personifications, inversions, Latinate constructions, and other features of contemporary poetic diction; although to the perceptive reader (such as the young S. T. Coleridge) the style was far from commonplace:

> In the form, style, and manner of the whole poem, and in
> the structure of the particular lines and periods, there is an
> harshness and acerbity connected and combined with words
> and images all a-glow, which might recall those products
> of the vegetable world, where gorgeous blossoms rise
> out of the hard and thorny rind and shell, within which
> the rich fruit was elaborating. The language was not only
> peculiar and strong, but at times knotty and contorted,
> as by its own impatient strength; while the novelty and
> struggling crowd of images acting in conjunction with
> the difficulties of the style, demanded always a greater
> closeness of attention, than poetry, (at all events, than
> descriptive poetry) has a right to claim.[4]

During the years that followed, Wordsworth found ways of expressing himself more variously. From the heroic couplet he turned to the other tried and conventional forms, the Spenserian stanza (in the 'Salisbury Plain' poems), blank verse (in 'The Ruined Cottage', 'The Pedlar', and the first fragments of *The Prelude*) and the ballad (in *Lyrical Ballads*). In each case the process which Coleridge observed with respect to *Descriptive Sketches* is repeated: a traditional form is taken but it is used with remarkable energy, originality, and power.

The 'Salisbury Plain' poems[5] are an example. They have their inspiration in Wordsworth's remarkable experience of 1793, when he found himself alone on Salisbury Plain, compelled to fend for himself and sleep rough like a vagrant. Fifty years later he remembered the occasion vividly: 'my rambles over Salisbury Plain', he told Isabella Fenwick in 1843, 'left on my mind imaginative impressions the force of which I have felt to this day'.[6] He walked alone across the Plain, then north-west to the Wye valley, and finally to North Wales, where his friend Robert Jones lived. The journey was rich with significant moments, which were later used in Wordsworth's poetry: he met the little girl of 'We are Seven', and the tinker who became Peter Bell; he had strange hallucinations of ancient Britons, Druids, and human sacrifice (described in the 1805 *Prelude*, Book XII); and he visited Tintern Abbey for the first time. It was a well-known beauty-spot for the traveller in search of picturesque landscape, but Wordsworth saw it in a very different frame of mind from the sophisticated appreciation of the connoisseur:

> more like a man
> Flying from something that he dreads, than one
> Who sought the thing he loved. For nature then
> (The coarser pleasures of my boyish days,
> And their glad animal movements all gone by)
> To me was all in all. – I cannot paint
> What then I was. The sounding cataract
> Haunted me like a passion: the tall rock,
> The mountain, and the deep and gloomy wood,
> Their colours and their forms, were then to me
> An appetite; a feeling and a love,
> That had no need of a remoter charm,
> By thought supplied, nor any interest
> Unborrowed from the eye.
>
> (ll. 70–83)

The intensity of passion described here is an indication of Wordsworth's extraordinary state of mind at this time. He had returned from France in the previous December, leaving behind Annette who was about to give birth to their child. In January 1793 the King was guillotined; in February war was declared between England and France. Because of his political support for the revolution, and his emotional attachment to France, Wordsworth was deeply shocked by England's declaration of war; and it was in this frame of mind that Wordsworth began to compose 'Salisbury Plain' (1793), the first version of the poem that was later to be drawn upon for 'The Female Vagrant' in 1798 and published as 'Guilt and Sorrow' in 1842. His experience of life as a solitary wanderer not only gave him the intense feeling towards nature that is described in *Lyrical Ballads*, but it also may have increased his identification with the poor and houseless. The prehistoric remains on Salisbury Plain (he tells us in the Preface to 'Guilt and Sorrow') drew him to compare the warlike and barbarous savagery of those times with the conditions of his own day. In both times it is the weak who suffer:

> The monuments and traces of antiquity, scattered in
> abundance over that region, led me unavoidably to
> compare what we know or guess of those remote times
> with certain aspects of modern society, and with calamities,
> principally those consequent upon war, to which, more
> than other classes of men, the poor are subject.[7]

In this first version, the desperate poet throws himself headlong at the
established political and social system:

> Heroes of Truth pursue your march, uptear
> Th' Oppressor's dungeon from its deepest base;
> High o'er the towers of Pride undaunted rear
> Resistless in your might the herculean mace
> Of Reason; let foul Error's monster race
> Dragged from their dens start at the light with pain
> And die; pursue your toils, till not a trace
> Be left on earth of Superstition's reign,
> Save that eternal pile which frowns on Sarum's plain
>
> (ll. 541–49)

Similarly the unpublished 'Letter to the Bishop of Llandaff' (1793) is
written with a bitterness that is perceptible and even frightening. In
it, as we have seen, Wordsworth confessed himself 'the advocate of
Republicanism' and approved the use of force by the revolutionary
power. The subsequent events of the French Revolution led him to
alter course somewhat: not losing the ultimate aim of a fairer society,
but condemning the use of violence by desperate and determined men.
The motives of the revolution had been so noble, and the outcome so
disastrous, that an explanation was needed: in *The Borderers*, therefore,
Wordsworth portrays a good man (Marmaduke) who is led to commit
an awful crime against humanity (leaving an old blind man to die
without shelter) under the influence of the unprincipled Oswald.
We learn that Oswald had many years earlier been manipulated into
committing a similar crime, and that since then he had become one of
the 'Restless Minds'

> Such Minds as find amid their fellow men
> No heart that loves them, none that they can love, . . .
>
> (III. 1452–53)

and he urges Marmaduke to free himself from the tyranny of custom.
He praises Marmaduke's action in terms that suggest he (Oswald) is a
psychopath:

Today you have thrown off a tyranny
That lives but in the torpid acquiescence
Of our emasculated souls, the tyranny
Of the world's masters, with the musty rules
By which they uphold their craft from age to age:
You have obeyed the only law that sense
Submits to recognise; the immediate law,
From the clear light of circumstances, flashed
Upon an independent Intellect.

(III. 1488–96)

Here revolution has become associated (as it was habitually by the Parisians themselves) with reason, but it is a reason without human feeling or restraint. In the Preface to *The Borderers*, Wordsworth describes Oswald as 'a young man of great intellectual powers, yet without any solid principles of genuine benevolence'; his action shows 'the dangerous use which may be made of reason when a man has committed a great crime'.[8] This suggests that Wordsworth was reacting against the Godwinism of the 'Salisbury Plain' poems. This reaction is confirmed by the first examples of Wordsworth's mature style and preoccupations, 'The Ruined Cottage' and 'The Pedlar' (written 1797–98). 'The Ruined Cottage' was later incorporated into the first book of *The Excursion*, where it is softened by a Christian conclusion and by the philosophy of the Wanderer; in its earlier version it is taut, intense, and agonizingly painful. Like the 'Salisbury Plain' poems it deals with the suffering caused by war, together with those of bad harvests; Robert, the husband and breadwinner, falls ill, the family's small savings are consumed, and the result is disaster. The poem underlines how precarious a family's economy is; and when Robert disappears, the ones who suffer are his wife and his children. Wordsworth has Blake's ability to see the effect of poverty on innocent children: their unemployed father becomes irritable, and (in one of the fragments from which the poem originated) the loaded baker's van refuses to stop, as if, says Margaret,

You were not born to live, or there had been
No bread in all the land.[9]

Margaret's fortitude in the face of her desertion, of the death of one of her children, and of the loss of her other child who is sent away as a parish orphan, is remarkable. She lives on in the disintegrating cottage with 'torturing hope', refusing to move in case Robert returns, until her death. The ruined cottage is a symbol of the destruction of the family's life; beyond it, somewhere where Robert has gone, is an inhuman society which leaves people destitute through no fault of their own.

In the same blank-verse form Wordsworth adds to this tragedy the fragment describing the Pedlar, written between January and March 1798. The Pedlar has described the tragedy of Margaret in 'The Ruined Cottage', and now the reader learns something of the secret of his equanimity in the face of such suffering. This is one of the central mysteries of Wordsworth's poetry, and he comes nearer to explaining it in 'The Pedlar' than anywhere else. The problem is one of appropriate consolation: how can the Pedlar end his description of Margaret with the lines describing the beauty of the ruin covered with weeds, so beautiful

> That what we feel of sorrow and despair
> From ruin and from change, and all the grief
> The passing shews of being leave behind,
> Appeared an idle dream that could not live
> Where meditation was. I turned away,
> And walked along my road in happiness.
>
> (ll. 513–25)

The transition from the wretchedness of Margaret (however compassionately viewed) to such a contentment is very difficult to explain. In can be seen as a great overview of human life, in which it all appears transitory; or it can be seen as inspired by the power of human love to endure so much; or it can be seen as a bold admission of the pleasure which is to be had from tragedy, the cathartic effects of pity and fear described by Aristotle. In Wordsworth's description of the Pedlar, however, all these are subordinated to the character of the Pedlar himself, as an example of the resilience of the human mind. His mind is kept 'in a just equipoise of love' (l. 268) by reflection and by the influences of his early childhood, and the result is that

> He could afford to suffer
> With those whom he saw suffer. Hence it was
> That in our best experience he was rich,
> And in the wisdom of our daily life.
> For hence, minutely, in his various rounds
> He had observed the progress and decay
> Of many minds, of minds and bodies too;
> The history of many families,
> And how they prospered, how they were o'erthrown
> By passion or mischance, or such misrule
> Among the unthinking masters of the earth
> As makes the nations groan.
>
> (ll. 283–94)

As at other times, we may conjecture the interaction between this
and Wordsworth's own experience: his despair at the progress of the
French Revolution and at his failure to make sense of the political
and social developments of his time, together with his ability to
survive (supported by Dorothy and by Coleridge). The survival of
his imaginative powers becomes for Wordsworth a great source of
wonder, pleasure, and celebration. It is part of the exuberance of the
1798 *Lyrical Ballads*, and part of the joy in the fruitful partnership with
Coleridge during this period. I have argued elsewhere[10] that the Pedlar
is an example of a prophet, an individual with charisma (as described by
Max Weber); and Wordsworth and Coleridge themselves are prophetic
in their ability to transform experience, however painful, into instructive
and inspiring poetry. Similarly the Pedlar's inspiration is in the natural
life of his childhood, and his transforming power is nature:

> To every natural form, rock, fruit, and flower,
> Even the loose stones that cover the highway,
> He gave a moral life; he saw them feel,
> Or linked them to some feeling. In all shapes
> He found a secret and mysterious soul,
> A fragrance and a Spirit of strange meaning.
>
> (ll. 332–37)

The 'strange meaning' here is the kind of discovery which comes from
the shorter poems of *Lyrical Ballads*, and the 1800 Preface, concerned as
it is with matters of language and expression, is also concerned with
the charismatic figure of the prophet-poet. Instead of the blank-verse
characterization of the Pedlar, we have the prose description of the
poet as

> a man speaking to men: a man, it is true, endowed with
> more lively sensibility, more enthusiasm and tenderness,
> who has a greater knowledge of human nature, and a more
> comprehensive soul, than are supposed to be common
> among mankind; a man pleased with his own passions
> and volitions, and who rejoices more than other men in
> the spirit of life that is in him; delighting to contemplate
> similar volitions and passions as manifested in the
> goings-on of the Universe, and habitually impelled to
> create them where he does not find them.[11]

The concept of relationship which is behind the marvellous simplicity
of the first phrase is suggested in 'The Pedlar' by the Pedlar's relationship
with Margaret, and also by his relationship with the poet to whom he is

telling the story of the ruined cottage. In the same way in *Lyrical Ballads*, the poet looks two ways: towards the subject-matter, and towards the audience. An obvious example is 'Simon Lee'. In this poem the narrator describes Simon in his old age, and his own meeting with him; he also turns directly to the 'gentle reader', and points out unusual features of the story – that it is no tale, but

> Should you think
> Perhaps a tale you'll make it.
>
> (ll. 72–73)

Lyrical Ballads is sometimes seen as a landmark in English Romantic poetry, a clear break with the eighteenth century in terms of diction and subject-matter. Since Robert Mayo's article on 'The Contemporaneity of the *Lyrical Ballads*' in 1954,[12] it has been clear that the subject-matter was not particularly new: but it is important to recognize that *Lyrical Ballads* is still a profoundly original work. Coleridge described its genesis in *Biographia Literaria*:

> During the first year that Mr. Wordsworth and I were neighbours, our conversations turned frequently on the two cardinal points of poetry, the power of exciting the sympathy of the reader by a faithful adherence to the truth of nature, and the power of giving the interest of novelty by the modifying colours of imagination. The sudden charm, which accidents of light and shade, which moon-light or sun-set diffused over a known and familiar landscape, appeared to represent the practicability of combining both. These are the poetry of nature.[13]

Truth and imagination; the transformation of reality; these are to be the aims of the volume. Coleridge was to direct his attention 'to persons and characters supernatural, or at least romantic'; Wordsworth

> was to propose to himself as his object to give the charm of novelty to things of every day, and to excite a feeling analogous to the supernatural, by awakening the mind's attention from the lethargy of custom, and directing it to the loveliness and the wonders of the world before us; an inexhaustible treasure, but for which in consequence of the film of familiarity and selfish solicitude we have eyes, yet see not, ears that hear not, and hearts that neither feel nor understand.[14]

This is a very accurate description of the kind of 'consciousness-raising' that goes on in the 1798 *Lyrical Ballads*. The poems are not like those of Wordsworth's contemporaries except in the superficialities of style and subject-matter, because what is new is the awakening of the mind's attention from the lethargy of custom. The reader is made to contemplate the subjects as if for the first time, often by the arresting first line:

> Oh! what's the matter? what's the matter? . . .

> There is a thorn; it looks so old, . . .

> 'Tis eight o'clock, – a clear March night, . . .

The first lines introduce portrayals of considerable force and simplicity. Wordsworth is using the ballad form to present a state of human life which is common, unpadded by art (poetic diction, or any of the other conventional beauties of poetry), and revealing. So when he writes of Simon Lee he is writing of old age, and deliberately avoiding a story-line. There is an 'incident', as the poem's subtitle informs us, but that is all:

> My gentle Reader, I perceive
> How patiently you've waited,
> And I'm afraid that you expect
> Some tale will be related.
>
> O reader! had you in your mind
> Such stores as silent thought can bring,
> O gentle reader! you would find
> A tale in every thing.
> What more I have to say is short,
> I hope you'll kindly take it;
> It is no tale; but should you think
> Perhaps a tale you'll make it.
>   (ll. 69–80)

The intervention, with the direct appeal to the reader, seems clumsy, but it is in fact of great significance. The poet is drawing attention to the lack of a story: this is because he does not want to provide a story in the traditional sense, for that would allow the reader to escape. Instead, the reader is to be confronted with the simple fact of old age: that a man who was once athletic and energetic is now old and feeble. The tale itself is there, if we only allow ourselves to think about it: it tells us of human need, of reduced circumstances, of an old man who was once tall and is now bent double, of a gratitude that is paradoxically more upsetting than ingratitude:

> – I've heard of hearts unkind, kind deeds
> With coldness still returning;
> Alas! the gratitude of men
> Has oftener left me mourning.
>
> (ll. 93–96)

The neatness of the paradox comes as a shock after the earlier simplicity of the poem. Wordsworth has portrayed an old man in all the unconcealed nakedness of his poverty and need; now he reflects on his own reactions to Simon Lee's outburst of gratitude. The result is a poem which is memorable not only for its stark portrayal of human suffering but also for its establishing of a relationship between narrator and subject. It also becomes interestingly intimate with the reader, not only in the 'My gentle Reader' passage quoted above, but also in the reflective ending, which is communicated as if to a sympathetic listener; and Wordsworth relies on that listener being able to pick up the reference to ingratitude (from *As You Like It* and *King Lear*). His ballad is speaking in a dialogue with earlier expressions of ingratitude, its intertextuality sharpening the force of what is said.

A number of the poems in *Lyrical Ballads* present memorable figures, so that their plight is unignorable. Martha Ray in 'The Thorn' has been seduced, betrayed, and has lost her child; Goody Blake is an old poor woman gathering sticks from under a hedge; the old shepherd has one lamb from his flock, having been forced to sell the others to feed his children. They are all memorable and pitiable: their situations reflect the fundamental problems of human nature. In publishing poems about them, Wordsworth was appealing over the heads of connoisseurs and poetasters to the fundamental sympathies of the human heart. He is unequivocally 'a man speaking to men', as he makes clear in the celebrated letter to John Wilson of June 1802. Wilson, then an undergraduate at Glasgow, had written to Wordsworth praising *Lyrical Ballads* with the exception of 'The Idiot Boy', which he thought would not please. Wordsworth's reply was 'please whom? or what?'

> I answer, human nature, as it has been and ever will
> be. But where are we to find the best measure of this? I
> answer, from within; by stripping our own hearts naked,
> and by looking out of ourselves towards men who lead
> the simplest lives most according to nature: men who have
> never known false refinements, wayward and artificial
> desires, false criticisms, effeminate habits of thinking

and feeling, or who, having known these things, have outgrown them. [15]

'The Idiot Boy', which was the cause of this fine statement of faith, is a very interesting example of Wordsworth's ability to transform an apparently unpromising subject into a great poem. It is also significant in its moral insight, which directs the reader to see madness as potentially more valuable than sanity. We who think of ourselves as sane, and as living by the direction of reason, have no conception of the possible power of madness, or of its imaginative qualities:

> I have often applied to Idiots, in my own mind, that
> sublime expression of Scripture, that 'their life is hidden
> with God'. They are worshipped, probably from a feeling
> of this sort, in several parts of the East. Among the Alps
> where they are numerous, they are considered, I believe,
> as a blessing to the family to which they belong. I have,
> indeed, often looked upon the conduct of fathers and
> mothers of the lower classes of society towards Idiots as
> the great triumph of the human heart. It is there that we
> see the strength, disinterestedness, and grandeur of love,
> nor have I ever been able to contemplate an object that
> calls out so many excellent and virtuous sentiments without
> finding it hallowed thereby, and having something in me
> which bears down before it, like a deluge, every feeble
> sensation of disgust and aversion. [16]

The inference here is twofold: that the idiot boy may have insights beyond our normal capability, and that the care of idiot children is a deeply moving example of human love at its most noble. Both are found in the poem: the whole situation is worked back from the dropped grain of suggestion, the story told to Wordsworth of the idiot child's description of the moon and the owls:

> 'The cocks did crow to-whoo, to-whoo,
> And the sun did shine so cold.'
>
> (ll. 450–51)

In one respect this is nonsense, but in another it represents an imagination that perceives the moon and the owls in a new way. It discovers a new relationship between things: the owls are the cockerels of the night, the moon is the cold sun in the night sky. This is Johnny's story, as the last two lines tell us: he returns home happily with his three companions, his mother, Susan Gale, and the pony. Human and animal are united in relationship and love:

The owls have hardly sung their last,
While our four travellers homeward wend;
The owls have hooted all night long,
And with the owls began my song,
And with the owls must end.

(ll. 432–36)

The simple happiness of the four travellers, out in the night with the owls, is contrasted with the normal restraints of reason, especially those shown by the doctor when he is knocked up in the middle of the night. He is questioned by Betty about her idiot boy: she has lost him, and does the doctor know where he is? Not unreasonably, the doctor goes back to bed; it is, after all, hardly a medical emergency. Yet Wordsworth explores the serious side of the comic situation, and indicates just how much human love the doctor is missing. The joyful reunion of Johnny and his mother, and the spontaneous recovery of Susan Gale, are evidence of a power of love, selflessness, and healing that the doctor knows nothing about.

The part played by the narrator in this and the other lyrical ballads is extremely important. It is through the narrator's eyes that the whole action of 'The Idiot Boy' is seen, and those eyes are amused and benevolent. His description of Betty Foy in such a bustle is one of pretended alarm, and throughout the poem his interventions provide a comic element. He addresses the reader in tones that anticipate Byron:

Oh reader! now that I might tell
What Johnny and his horse are doing!
What they've been doing all this time,
Oh could I put it into rhyme,
A most delightful tale pursuing!

(ll. 312–16)

On a subsequent occasion, the narrator has some kind of argument with the Muses which goes on off-stage and between the stanzas; it is like hearing one half of a telephone conversation (ll. 337–46). This subcomedy of the ingenuous narrator helps to establish a relationship between him and the protagonists: he seems to be harmless, inquisitive, and simple-minded, and the poem is a testimony of his love and admiration for Betty, Susan, and Johnny (and the pony). He can afford to laugh at them from time to time because of his love for them (just as, in *The Prelude* Book IV, Wordsworth can afford to poke fun at Ann Tyson: he can permit himself to be amused by the behaviour of someone whom he loves and admires very deeply).

A similar relationship exists between the narrator of 'Simon Lee' and the old man of the poem, although in this case it is a relationship which sees the narrator as acting within the poem; it is a kind action which is a minor parallel to that of the Good Samaritan, and it has serious and compassionate overtones. The difference between the two poems is that Johnny is loved and cared for, in a way which Wordsworth finds wholly admirable and even inspirational, while Simon Lee is old, feeble, and destitute. There are numerous figures in Wordsworth's poetry like him, and the way in which the poet (carrying everywhere with him relationship and love) speaks to them is crucial. In the 1798 version of 'Animal Tranquillity and Decay' (then called 'Old Man Travelling'), for instance, the old man's suffering and loneliness are portrayed through the interlocution with a severe restraint:

> – I asked him whither he was bound, and what
> The object of his journey; he replied
> 'Sir! I am going many miles to take
> A last leave of my son, a mariner,
> Who from a sea-fight has been brought to Falmouth,
> And there is dying in an hospital.'
>   (ll. 15–20)

Here the simplicity is quite sufficient. The very fact that the narrator thinks it worth recording is an indication of his sympathy. He can vary his approach from the actively concerned (as in 'Simon Lee') to the amused and loving (in 'The Idiot Boy') to the didactic (in 'Goody Blake and Harry Gill'):

> Now think, ye farmers all, I pray,
> Of Goody Blake and Harry Gill.
>   (ll. 127–28)

The poem has been a moral tale of a well-to-do farmer and a poor old woman. Her curse on Harry Gill suggests the supernatural (since it is a prayer addressed to God), but there is no suggestion that she is a witch. She is a representative of oppressed, cold, and desperate humanity while Harry is a representative of the acquisitive and possessive property-ownership denounced by Rousseau. The ballad, said Crabb Robinson, showed qualities that were 'truly Shakespearian', in its repetition of simple phrases and dwelling on simple incidents.[17] Merely by recording the story, the narrator is indicating his moral position, especially when he alters the original narrative in Goody Blake's favour.[18]

'The Thorn', on the other hand, shows what can happen when this relationship ceases to exist. Once again it is a story about desperate humanity, but one in which the narrator has to be imagined (as Wordsworth indicated in the 1800 note) as

> a Captain of a small trading vessel, for example, who being past the middle age of life, had retired upon an annuity or small independent income to some village or county town which he was not a native, or in which he had not been accustomed to live. Such men having little to do become credulous and talkative from indolence.[19]

The captain sees Martha Ray on the hilltop, and hears her dreadful cry, but he cannot help her or enter into any kind of relationship with her. He becomes one with the judgemental villagers who discuss her. The clumsy attempts to find out exactly what happened are thwarted by the mysterious quaking of the ground, but not before the community of villagers has been revealed as unsympathetic and even punitive:

> 'And some had sworn an oath that she
> Should be to public justice brought;
> And for the little infant's bones
> With spades they would have sought.'
>
> (ll. 221–24)

The narrator's apparent complacency about the whole proceedings is underlined by the horrific juxtaposition of 'spades' and 'little infant's bones'. It emphasizes the lack of any relationship in the poem between Martha Ray and the remainder of the human species, and it demonstrates her isolation more effectively than anything else could have done.

It is in the context of this subtle relationship between narrator, subject, and reader, that the language of *Lyrical Ballads* has to be considered. Wordsworth stubbornly defended it, even when friends like Henry Crabb Robinson told him that they dared not read certain lines aloud. 'They ought to be liked', said the poet,[20] and in this statement we can find not only the authoritative voice of the prophet-teacher, but also the voice of the poet, insisting on the authenticity of his expression. With their peculiar infelicities (when judged by certain traditional critical standards) they appear strange and sometimes odd: generations of students (and lecturers who ought to have known better) have cackled over Simon Lee's weak ankles or the dimensions of the little pond beside which Martha Ray sits. But when read as they should be read, as expressions of human compassion and concern, they become profoundly impressive, even in such moments. The language is a direct appeal to awareness of others, an appeal which intentionally undercuts the ities of art. There is no elegance in 'The Thorn', because elegance is not required; there is no tale in 'Simon Lee', because a tale would allow the reader to enjoy something other than the dreadful contemplation of old age. These *Lyrical Ballads*, in short, are radically new because they challenge the reader in ways that are unknown to the hundreds of contemporary examples. They are uncompromisingly appealing: they shout for attention. In their patterns of speech and techniques of narration they demonstrate the vital quality of *relationship*, the human interaction and the vital sense of communication between individuals

The poet is present throughout *Lyrical Ballads*, commenting, portraying, as he does in 'The Idiot Boy' or 'Simon Lee'; only in a dramatic monologue such as 'The Thorn' or 'The Mad Mother' does he remain outside the poem, and those instances serve to indicate a lack of community and a failure of communication. On two occasions, 'We are Seven' and 'Anecdote for Fathers', the poet humorously casts himself in the role of unfeeling and dried-up adult narrator confronted with the intuitive vision and imaginative instinct of children; these poems form one end of a spectrum in *Lyrical Ballads*, which at one end shows the poet as unimaginative, and at the other shows him triumphing in his special powers. Between, there are various stages, all illustrating the importance of relationship, the *I-Thou* of Martin Buber's distinction between the *I-Thou* and the *I-It* ('that wisdom which perceives a closed compartment in things, reserved for the initiate and manipulated only with the key'[21]). The world of relationship, the *I-Thou* of community between human beings, and between human beings and the external world, is the subject of those poems from *Lyrical Ballads* which most openly celebrate Wordsworth's beliefs. These are the 'credal lyrics' and 'Tintern Abbey'; in the lines 'It is the first mild day of March', for instance, the poet describes a moment of intense joy in the natural world, a moment which is part of a time that is utterly different from the mechanical time of January to December:

> No joyless forms shall regulate
> Our living Calendar:
> We from to-day, my friend, will date
> The opening of the year.
>
> Love, now a universal birth,
> From heart to heart is stealing,
> From earth to man, from man to earth,
> – It is the hour of feeling.
>
> (ll. 17–24)

It is this ability to respond to a moment of love, an hour of feeling, that is central to the patterned interchange of 'Expostulation and Reply' and

'The Tables Turned'. In these poems Matthew first questions William about his apparent idleness one morning, and receives a reply:

> 'The eye it cannot chuse but see,
> We cannot bid the ear be still;
> Our bodies feel, where'er they be,
> Against, or with our will.
>
> 'Nor less I deem that there are powers,
> Which of themselves our minds impress,
> That we can feed this mind of ours,
> In a wise passiveness.'
>
> (ll. 17–24)

In the evening William 'turns the tables' on Matthew; after his day spent in allowing his mind and senses to develop in relationship with nature, he now has a superabundant energy which mocks Matthew's 'toil and trouble'. Now he can say, with pardonable exaggeration:

> One impulse from a vernal wood
> May teach you more of man,
> Of moral evil and of good
> Than all the sages can.
>
> (ll. 21–24)

The claim appears absurd ('outrageous', A. C. Bradley called it[22]) unless we see that it is part of the crucial discovery of relationship, without which all study is vain. The essential first step is the cultivation of the human heart:

> Enough of Science and of Art;
> Close up those barren leaves;
> Come forth, and bring with you a heart
> That watches and receives.
>
> (ll. 29–32)

The greatest celebration in *Lyrical Ballads* of the watching and receiving heart is the final poem, 'Lines written a few miles above Tintern Abbey'. I have already suggested, in quoting the full title, that this is a poem which arouses expectations of the picturesque only to concern itself with something more important: Wordsworth is concerned to explore the effects of memory, time, and the landscape itself upon the human heart. The poem does not lose sight of the scene entirely, and returns to it with a delightful allusion at the end; but it also records, with great sensitivity and passion, the developing power of a mind and heart that are affected by nature. In this process the style and language are important: 'Tintern Abbey' is written in blank verse, but it is used differently from the blank verse in *The Prelude* (except in certain impassioned and rapturous sections of *The Prelude*) and 'Michael'. Its special characteristic, as Geoffrey Hartman has noted,[23] is the doubling of words to give a rich and cumulative effect of abundance, which corresponds to the sense of overflowing beneficence in the poet's mind. His greatest passages move towards the sublime with a gradual development through the sentence: an early phrase is picked up and echoed, given a stronger expression, and then completed, as it is when Wordsworth discusses the effect of nature on his moral actions, and continues:

> Nor less, I trust,
> To them I may have owed another gift,
> Of aspect more sublime; that blessed mood,
> In which the burthen of the mystery,
> In which the heavy and the weary weight
> Of all this unintelligible world,
> Is lightened: - that serene and blessed mood,
> In which the affections gently lead us on, –
> Until, the breath of this corporeal frame
> And even the motion of our human blood
> Almost suspended, we are laid asleep
> In body, and become a living soul:
> While with an eye made quiet by the power
> Of harmony, and the deep power of joy,
> We see into the life of things.
>
> (ll. 35–49)

The movement of the verse here is in three parts, each depending on the introductory two and a half lines. The first signifies the blessed mood, and grows in strength through the double 'In which'; this is then taken up and amplified by 'that serene and blessed mood' and the complex suspension which follows it; and then there is a graceful diminuendo in the simple description of the inward eye 'made quiet by the power/Of harmony, and the deep power of joy', which is succeeded by the simple daring totality of 'We see into the life of things'. This follows on from the climax of the passage, when we 'become a living soul'; it is the natural, quietly stated consequence. The same three-part structure is found in the central climax of the poem, where 'And I have felt' (which itself echoes 'For I have learned', five lines previously) has three separate sections depending upon it. One begins 'A presence', the second 'a sense sublime', and the third 'A motion and a spirit':

> And I have felt
> A presence that disturbs me with the joy
> Of elevated thoughts; a sense sublime
> Of something far more deeply interfused,
> Whose dwelling is the light of setting suns,
> And the round ocean and the living air,
> And the blue sky, and in the mind of man:
> A motion and a spirit, that impels
> All thinking things, all objects of all thought,
> And rolls through all things.
>
> (ll. 93–102)

Here again there is a crescendo and diminuendo, with the force reserved for the 'something' whose dwelling is everywhere, within and without. From the glimpse of this power, the poet brings us gently back to himself:

> Therefore am I still
> A lover of the meadows and the woods,
> And mountains; and of all that we behold
> From this green earth;
>
> (ll. 102–5)

The way in which 'Tintern Abbey' moves from such moments of vision to the commonplaces of human affection for the landscape is sure-footed and essential to the poem's effect. It enables Wordsworth to turn an eighteenth-century poem in the loco-descriptive mode into a nineteenth-century example of self-discovery and celebration. For the poem is an utterance of joy and celebration: its language is enriched with words such as 'blessings', 'blessed', 'genial', 'sweet', 'delightful', 'joy'. The poet is reflecting on his good fortune in being present before the same beautiful landscape which he remembered from the previous visit; now he has his sister with him, and is aware of the blessing to her. His own joy is in having survived: not merely in physical survival, but in the preservation of his spirit of love, his enthusiasm for nature, and his imaginative power. In 1793 he had been

> more like a man
> Flying from something that he dreads than one
> Who sought the thing he loved.
>
> (ll. 70–72)

Now he finds a new maturity, accompanied by the sense of

> The still, sad music of humanity
> Nor harsh nor grating, though of ample power
> To chasten and subdue.
>
> (ll. 91–93)

His enthusiasm for nature is no longer the frantic escape of 1793, when he was bewildered and shocked by the war, the progress of the revolution, and the separation from Annette; now, in 1798, he is recording his gratitude for his survival as a poet, and his sense of the value of nature in relation to human life. Its place at the end of *Lyrical Ballads* is entirely appropriate, even though it is not a ballad, for it describes with fervour and sensitivity the convictions which have underpinned so many of the preceding poems. It celebrates the poet's own sense of the relationship between one human being and another, his conviction that nature influences the conduct of one person towards another, and his joy at being able to apprehend the sublime sense of a living presence in the active universe. It is in many ways a pivotal poem, for it looks back to 1793 and also to the eighteenth-century tradition while it looks forward to the confidence of *The Prelude*, to the way in which that poem can incorporate the disturbances (both within and without) of Wordsworth's early years and see them as part of a pattern of ultimate good.

The Prelude was begun during the winter of 1798–99. Following the publication of *Lyrical Ballads*, Coleridge, Wordsworth, and Dorothy Wordsworth went to Germany; Coleridge went to Göttingen, and the Wordsworths to Goslar, where they were kept indoors for long periods by the coldest winter of the century. After the intense excitement of the previous year's companionship with Coleridge, the isolation (in Stephen Parrish's words) 'drove Wordsworth back to the sources of memory and led him to trace in wondering and thankful tones the beginnings of the growth of a poet's mind'.[24] In this two-part version, the poet assembles various episodes (spots of time) which demonstrate the interaction between himself and nature and the providential power of certain moments. By the end of Part I many of the most vivid of these incidents have been set down, with a freshness and an immediacy which comes from the pleasures of memory. As in 'Tintern Abbey', the poet is clearly enjoying his work, and Part I ends with an acknowledgement that he is

> loth to quit
> Those recollected hours that have the charm
> Of visionary things, and lovely forms
> And sweet sensations that throw back our life

> And make our infancy a visible scene
> On which the sun is shining – . . .
>
> (ll. 459–64)

This part of the original attempt contains many of the moments which
are later distributed into the various parts of the larger work and which
form the most memorable testimonies to the childhood experience. Part
II is more complicated, because it acknowledges two things: first, that
the past is past, and irrecoverable; second, that the process of influence
and development is mysterious and indefinable. The first of these is
evidenced by the change in Hawkshead, discovered by Wordsworth
during a walking tour with Coleridge in 1799, when he found the old
grey stone at the centre of the village had been replaced by 'A smart
assembly-room that perked and flared' (II. 37). The second is connected
with this, for the disappearance of the old grey stone while the memory
remains in the mind indicates the curious and inexplicable relationship
between past and present, inner and outer. In 'Tintern Abbey' the
landscape was the same, though the poet was more mature; now the
memory remains, but the evidence of the place itself has gone. But these
things cannot be charted with any exactitude:

> Who knows the individual hour in which
> His habits were first sown, even as a seed;
> Who that shall point as with a wand and say,
> This portion of the river of my mind
> Came from yon fountain?
>
> (II. 245–49)

The river is a favourite image of Wordsworth's; it is the same, yet
different, continually changing yet always present. To describe it at any
moment as *the* river is impossible, for at the moment of describing it a
transition has occurred, and it is no longer the same river; yet it can be
traced from mouth to source (as Wordsworth and Coleridge had been
fond of doing in north Somerset, to the alarm of the authorities). In Part
II of the two-part *Prelude* Wordsworth goes back to the source, seeking
to identify the first processes of infant consciousness. The babe gathers
'passions from his Mother's eye' (l. 273), and when he is 'subjected
to the discipline of love' (l. 281) he reaches out in love to the whole
visible world:

> No outcast he, bewildered and depressed:
> Along his infant veins are interfused
> The gravitation and the filial bond
> Of nature that connect him to the world.

> Emphatically such a being lives
> An inmate of this *active* universe; . . .
>
> (ll. 291–96)

The language of this passage is suggestive of powerful but imprecise forces. The interfusing of a gravitation and a bond, the inhabiting of an active universe, are phrases by which Wordsworth seeks to give expression to the most mysterious of all processes, the early development of the human mind. In this, and in all his descriptions of the mind's relationship with the circumambient universe, Wordsworth is breaking new ground. He is describing something beyond the reach of sense, but he is not being a mystic, and the language of Christian thought or neo-platonic myth will not suffice. Wordsworth is engaged in something different from these traditional activities, celebrating the activity of something which is beyond sight and beyond all knowledge, but which is also contained within the visible and active universe. 'What is new in Wordsworth', writes Peter Malekin, 'is his treatment of the mind of man.'[25] In Part II of the two-part *Prelude*, therefore, there is a bold statement of the joy of the universe, invisible to the eye yet living to the heart:

> I was only then
> Contented when with bliss ineffable
> I felt the sentiment of being spread
> O'er all that moves, and all that seemeth still,
> O'er all that, lost beyond the reach of thought
> And human knowledge, to the human eye
> Invisible, yet liveth to the heart,
> O'er all that leaps, and runs, and shouts and sings
> Or beats the gladsome air, o'er all that glides
> Beneath the wave, yea, in the wave itself
> And mighty depth of waters: wonder not
> If such my transports were, for in all things
> I saw one life and felt that it was joy.
>
> (*The Prelude*, 1798–99, II. 448–60)

This rapturous passage is central for an understanding of Wordsworth's mature thinking. He turns from it in due course to celebrate the gratitude he feels towards his native hills, but not before these lines have established the true source of power as within but also beyond the normal associative strength of local landscape. The integration of that which is intimate and local with that which is universal and sublime is also the larger achievement of *The Prelude* itself: it is the record of a life, but it is also a testimony to a power in the universe and a vision of that power in the human mind.

Wordsworth worked on the amplified versions of *The Prelude* mainly during 1804 and 1805. At first it was a five-book version, containing Wordsworth's childhood up to and including his time at Cambridge; then it was extended to thirteen books, recording his experiences in London and France, his comments on the French Revolution, his commitment to the philosophy of Godwin, his subsequent despair; and finally, his recovery of confidence under the benign influence of Dorothy and Coleridge. The thirteen-book *Prelude* (fourteen in the first printed text of 1850, dividing Book x into two parts) thus contains a much more extensive and elaborate pattern, a structure which makes the poem much more than a record of early influences. It now becomes a poem of first experience giving way to wider influences; of loss and gain; and of the most notable and immediate political events. It is sometimes forgotten, I suspect, that *The Prelude* was written in the shadow of the French Revolution, and while Napoleon was in his prime: to this extent it is a poem which articulates with careful honesty the hopes and fears of a young man looking back on his own life in the France of 1791–92, and his developing ideas in the rapidly-changing years that followed.

The Prelude is thus a private poem, about the growth of an individual poet's mind; it is also (although it was not published in Wordsworth's lifetime) a public and representative poem, one which expresses the hopes and fears of all those who grow up and have to leave home for the outside world. In Wordsworth's case the 'home' was his Lake District childhood, and the outside world was London and the French Revolution, which made the process especially meaningful in terms of his own generation; the journey of his life was a journey into the biggest city and the most earthshaking event in modern history. In his efforts to come to terms with British opposition to France, Wordsworth found himself in a dilemma, unable to pray for a British victory yet distraught at his isolation from his fellow churchgoers.

> It was a grief –
> Grief call it not, 'twas my thing but that –
> A conflict of sensations without name,
> Of which he only who may love the sight
> Of a village steeple as I do can judge,
> When in the congregation, bending all
> To their great Father, prayers were offered up
> Or praises for our country's victories,
> And, 'mid the simple worshippers perchance
> I only, like an uninvited guest
> Whom no one owned, sate silent – shall I add,
> Fed on the day of vengeance yet to come!
>
> (*The Prelude*, 1805, x. 264–74)

In moments such as these Wordsworth conveys an authentic and touching sense of his own difficulty: the reactions to the political events involve no easy radicalism but a painful choice. *The Prelude* convinces because it does not shirk such moments: Wordsworth records the uncomfortable moments of his later life (in Cambridge or in London) and the disappointing ones (the crossing of the Alps) as well as the serene and confident ones. Similarly, his attitude to London is complex: he sees its excitement and variety, as well as its confusion.

The only place where such completeness is absent is in the account of his childhood. It is known that this period of Wordsworth's life was not as happy as it appears in the poem: the death of his parents, the splitting up of the family, his uncomfortable relations with the grandparents, aunts, and uncles at Penrith – all these are quietly omitted from the first two books of *The Prelude*. According to these opening books, the child was surrounded by love and by beneficent influences of nature: he was given plenty of freedom, and learned by experience to live wisely and well, because he was brought up by nature

> Fostered alike by beauty and by fear.
>
> (I. 306)

He was allowed to feel the beauty of the created world, and the joy of games and friendships; he was also made to feel fear, but a healthy and a useful fear, one that convinced him that he was being watched by benevolent and corrective natural powers. In both ways he felt himself privileged, from the early days when he was to be found bathing in the stream at Cockermouth to the more mature experiences at Hawkshead. The image he uses of himself at this stage is characteristically natural: he is a flower, sown in the right conditions and safely moved:

> Fair seed-time had my soul, and I grew up
> Fostered alike by beauty and by fear,
> Much favored in my birthplace, and no less
> In that beloved vale to which erelong
> I was transplanted.
>
> (I. 305–9)

In the growth of this child there are naturally mistakes and failures, but they are part of a learning process which (as in Rousseau's *Émile*) is far better than a purely docile and disciplined existence in which childhood becomes a kind of premature adulthood. Wordsworth rejoices in the fact that as a child he enjoyed himself, energetically and wholeheartedly, and that he and his companions were

A race of real children, not too wise,
Too learned or too good, but wanton, fresh,
And bandied up and down by love and hate;
Fierce, moody, patient, venturous, modest, shy,
Mad at their sports like withered leaves in winds;
Though doing wrong and suffering, and full oft
Bending beneath our life's mysterious weight
Of pain and fear, yet still in happiness
Not yielding to the happiest upon earth.

(v. 434–44)

In the last line we glimpse the true argument of the extended *Prelude*:
it deals with the kind of happiness which only some fortunate children
know, and with the vision, hope, mistakes and enthusiasm which are
part of it; it then deals with this in relation to what follows, to the
necessary movement out of childhood, the inevitable journey away
from the enchanted land. In the retrospective Book VIII, Wordsworth
looks back at this period (and place):

Beauteous the domain
Where to the sense of beauty first my heart
Was opened – . . .
(VIII. 119–21)

In an extended piece of Miltonic pastiche, he says that his childhood
place was

tract more exquisitely fair
Than is that paradise of ten thousand trees
Or Gehol's famous gardens
(VIII. 121–24)

and so on for some twenty tortured and elaborate lines; then suddenly
he takes up a mode of sublime simplicity:

But lovelier far than this the paradise
Where I was reared, . . .
(VIII. 144–45)

and it becomes clear that the pattern of *The Prelude* is that of an individual
Paradise Lost. Wordsworth has conceived of the major process of his life
as a myth: the child is in paradise, and steps out of it into the turbulent
world of the 1790s.

The circumstances in which he finds himself are also those of the fallen world, the world in which we as human beings have to live: it is a world of struggle, of ideals that are thwarted, of confusion of mind, of societies that are life-denying, and of political institutions that are corrupt. The young man's experience of this world is at once an unhappy one and also a necessary one: in his own life he encounters a 'fall', but it is a fall from which he can, if preserved by the right spirit and temper, emerge stronger than before.

Wordsworth is therefore extending the first two parts of *The Prelude* into an epic which in its own way parallels and enacts *Paradise Lost*. Just as Milton described the 'fortunate fall', so Wordsworth describes the process of growing up as one of loss and gain. In his own life he demonstrates what is shown at the end of *Paradise Lost*, Adam and Eve going out into the world to make their own lives with their own choices:

> The world was all before them, where to choose
> Their place of rest, and providence their guide . . .
>
> (XII. 646–47)

Wordsworth echoes this in his own 'glad preamble' to *The Prelude*, when he writes 'The earth is all before me' (I. 15)

> – with a heart
> Joyous, nor scared at its own liberty,
> I look about, and should the guide I chuse
> Be nothing better than a wandering cloud
> I cannot miss my way.
>
> (ll. 15–19)

Where *Paradise Lost* ends, *The Prelude* begins. The important difference is that Adam and Eve are guided by providence, and Wordsworth by a wandering cloud. The orthodox Christian message has become something else, a simple rejoicing in freedom of action. Choice itself becomes a delight when the poet is surrounded by nature.

So the poet opens his epic. In making the poem into an epic he was challenging comparison with Milton, even as Milton had challenged comparison with Homer and Virgil. Milton had asserted his right to make an epic out of the Christian themes of patience and heroic martyrdom rather than out of heroes and battles; now Wordsworth asserts his right to make an epic out of the life of a child and young man in the 1770s, 1780s, and 1790s. It was, he said, 'unprecedented in Literary history that a man should talk so much about himself',[26] but it was also, he knew, heroic. He makes this claim for the process of child development:

O heavens, how awful is the might of souls,
And what they do within themselves while yet
The yoke of earth is new to them, the world
Nothing but a wild field where they were sown.
This is in truth heroic argument,
And genuine prowess – which I wished to touch
With hand however weak – but in the main
It lies far hidden from the reach of words.

(III. 178–85)

If *Paradise Lost* lies behind *The Prelude*, so does *Samson Agonistes*. Once again Milton was attempting a *tour de force*, a rendering of an old classical form. Wordsworth, as John Woolford has argued,[27] echoes Samson's first speech in which he wonders why special powers have been given to him if he is now lying captive in a Philistine gaol. Wordsworth feels like Samson, given great gifts which he has failed to use: he was being pressed throughout this period by Coleridge, who wanted him to write *The Recluse*, 'the first great philosophical poem'. Wordsworth side-steps this, and turns aside to write what was to him far more important, an epic poem in which his childhood and youth are seen in terms of the myth of the lost paradise. The subject is nothing less than becoming human, as Adam and Eve become human after the Fall.

It is this which gives point to the episodes which are so brilliantly described in Book I, such as the skating and boat-stealing. They are part of the pattern of memories, the 'spots of time' which are so important to the poet because they are evidence of a sustaining and guiding power, that of nature. This has preserved the poet through all his subsequent vicissitudes, until his final stability and emergence as a prophet. The 'spots of time' contain what Wordsworth in the 1798–99 *Prelude* first called 'a fructifying virtue' (l. 290), and later changed to 'a vivifying virtue'. The change is significant because it means that the spots of time are no longer associated with creative moments, but with the process of keeping the spirit alive from which such moments can come, against the pressures from without:

There are in our existence spots of time,
Which with distinct pre-eminence retain
A vivifying virtue, whence, depressed
By false opinion and contentious thought,
Or aught of heavier or more deadly weight,
In trivial occupations, and the round
Of ordinary intercourse, our minds
Are nourished and invisibly repaired;

A virtue, by which pleasure is enhanced,
That penetrates, enables us to mount,
When high, more high, and lifts us up when fallen.

(XI. 257–67)

The poet is now aware, as he was not as a child, of the forces working against him: he reassures himself by his memory of certain moments, such as the one described in Book XI, when he is lost and then regains the path, seeing a girl with a pitcher on her head. He revisits the spot later, and asserts

So feeling comes in aid
Of feeling, and diversity of strength
Attends us, if but once we have been strong.

(XI. 325–27)

This is one reason why he dislikes the changes at Hawkshead, because they may interrupt, if not destroy, the way in which 'feeling comes in aid/Of feeling' (as it did, for instance, near Tintern Abbey). But the state is a complex one: he remembers being lost, as a child, and now looks back as an adult, and finds it all a profound mystery:

Oh mystery of man, from what a depth
Proceed thy honours! I am lost, but see
In simple childhood something of the base
On which thy greatness stands – but this I feel,
That from thyself it is that thou must give,
Else never canst receive.   (XI. 328–33)

The whole of this passage is probing the deepest areas of experience, as Wordsworth engages in this enquiry into his past:

the hiding places of my power
Seem open, I approach, and then they close;

(XI. 335–36)

but he presses on to a further 'spot of time', remembering his brothers and himself waiting for the horses to take them home at the Christmas holidays. Again, looking back at the event and its unhappy ending (his father's death), he recognizes that the mist, the single sheep, the one blasted tree, and the old stone wall

All these were spectacles and sounds to which

> I often would repair, and thence would drink,
> As at a fountain; . . .
> > (XI. 382–48)

to these and the many other mysteriously working moments of childhood must be added the most memorable experiences of adult life. Two, in particular, affirm the poet's cognizance of a power beyond himself which is yet within him. In Book VI, in the passage about crossing the Alps (ll. 494–548), he is lost but recovers. He describes how imagination 'came/Athwart me':

> > I was lost as in a cloud,
> Halted without a struggle to break through;
> And now recovering, to my soul I say –
> 'I recognize thy glory': in such strength
> Of usurpation, in such visitings
> Of awful promise, when the light of sense
> Goes out in flashes that have shown to us
> The invisible world, doth greatness make abode,
> There harbours, whether we be young or old.
> Our destiny, our nature, and our home
> Is with infinitude, and only there;
> With hope it is, hope that can never die,
> Effort, and expectation, and desire,
> And something evermore about to be.
> > (VI. 529–42)

The other experience is described in the climbing-of-Snowdon passage. This took place in 1791, and therefore precedes some of the episodes in earlier books. It is held back to the last book to provide a fitting climax to the whole endeavour. Not only is it a spectacular and memorable event in itself, but the process of climbing out of the mist into the moonlight is an illuminating and symbolic one. The landscape of clouds and mountain-tops under the moon is truly transformed, as Coleridge said it would be; and just visible within the mist is a chasm

> A deep and gloomy breathing-place, through which
> Mounted the roar of waters, torrents, streams
> Innumerable, roaring with one voice.
> > (XIII. 57–59)

The chasm is an emblem of the profound grandeur and awful sublimity of the mind:

it appeared to me
The perfect image of a mighty mind,
Of one that feeds upon infinity,
That is exalted by an underpresence,
The sense of God, or whatsoe'er is dim
Or vast in its own being . . .

(XIII. 68–73)

In all of these cases the moments come spontaneously, irrationally, unexpectedly. The mind responds with its own power to the spots of time, which often arrive with great suddenness: the child who has stolen the boat on Ullswater is astonished to see what he thinks is the mountain coming after him; the child who is hooting to the owls (V. 389–413) suddenly hears something else when the owls cease:

Then sometimes, in that silence, while he hung
Listening, a gentle shock of mild surprize
Has carried far into his heart the voice
Of mountain torrents; or the visible scene
Would enter unawares into his mind,
With all its solemn imagery, its rocks,
Its woods, and that uncertain heaven, received
Into the bosom of the steady lake.

(V. 406–13)

In each of these cases the mind can receive, as Coleridge knew, because it can give: and *The Prelude* is an extraordinary record of this process. The child, the fortunate child, has put away childish things but has retained the vital power that will make him a visionary and a prophet.

I have dealt with *The Prelude* extensively because it is a crucial poem of self-discovery and self-analysis, shaped into a coherent and meaningful pattern. It is now necessary to return to the poet of the 1798–99 *Prelude*, and of the 'Lucy' poems, most of which were written in Germany. They deal with the growth of the poet's love for a pure young girl, and the loss of the beloved. Lucy is a child of nature, and lives in a simple perfection. Her beauty is that of other lovely things:

'The floating clouds their state shall lend
To her; for her the willow bend;
Nor shall she fail to see
Ev'n in the motions of the storm
Grace that shall mould the maiden's form
By silent sympathy.

> 'The stars of midnight shall be dear
> To her; and she shall lean her ear
> In many a secret place
> Where rivulets dance their wayward round,
> And beauty born of murmuring sound
> Shall pass into her face.'
>
> ('Three years she grew in sun and shower', ll. 19–30)

and yet Lucy dies: I have argued elsewhere[28] that her death is a return to
the nature to which she truly belongs, but it is painful nevertheless, and
mysterious. In these short poems, the language is simple, yet intense
and moving:

> A slumber did my spirit seal;
> I had no human fears:
> She seemed a thing that could not feel
> The touch of earthly years.
>
> (ll. 1–4)

Almost any line of this verse is elusive and difficult to interpret,
expressed in ambiguous language; in the next verse, by contrast, the
language seems simple, but the idea is difficult to grasp:

> No motion has she now, no force;
> She neither hears nor sees;
> Rolled round in earth's diurnal course,
> With rocks, and stones, and trees.
>
> (ll. 5–8)

From a personal and human point of view, the poet may be feeling the
pain of loss; from the understanding of the world as an active universe,
full of power, in which transience is part of the changeful energy of
the world, we may see Lucy's transition from life to death as part of
a natural assumption into magnificence. She is now one with the rocks
and stones and trees, ever moving in a majestic diurnal course.

Her stillness in the earth contrasts with her activity when alive; and
in the poems of the years which follow, Wordsworth often draws
out this contrast between movement and stillness. Trees and streams
move; rocks and mountains seem permanent and still. In the landscape
of two of his most memorable poems stand figures who are motionless,
Michael and the leech-gatherer.

'Michael' (written in 1800) is written in blank verse, though of a
very different kind from that of 'Tintern Abbey' and *The Prelude*
(where different kinds of blank verse, narrative, reflective, philosophical,

rapturous, exist together). It begins with the landscape, the boisterous brook of Greenhead ghyll, but at the centre of the landscape and the poem is the unfinished sheepfold, a symbol, like the ruined cottage, of a failure of hope. The figure of Michael himself is still, sitting beside the sheepfold and unable to bring himself to go on working. The memorable line

> And never lifted up a single stone
> (l. 466)

is characteristic of a certain kind of Wordsworthian effect, a sudden stillness which is extraordinarily moving because it carries with it the corresponding sense of the failure of all the activity of the poem. It has all come down to the figure by the sheepfold, in whose form are concentrated all the events which led up to this moment – the financial arrangements which broke down the hopes of success for Luke, the bustle of preparation, the hectic life in the city and his flight. In opposition to these is the simple way of life of the family, and Michael's attachment to his patrimonial fields. He has a straightforward and simple code of conduct, and the family life is unaffected by change or fashion. Michael is 'of a stern unbending mind' (l. 161), but part of that severity is an attachment to Luke that is lasting. So when the news of Luke's downfall reaches him, he is not overcome but continues with his work:

> There is a comfort in the strength of love;
> 'Twill make a thing endurable, which else
> Would overset the brain, or break the heart:
> (ll. 448–50)

it is only after we learn of Michael's stoical continuing with his work that we are told that he goes to the unfinished sheepfold and lifts no stone. The effect is even more powerful than it might have been because of this: if a man of Michael's strength is bowed down, then the affliction must indeed be great.

The solitary and still figure of Michael is not the final picture of the poem. After his death the cottage is destroyed, and only the oak tree and the unfinished sheepfold remain. The fact that the plough goes over the spot where Michael and his wife lived and hoped and died is a reminder of human transience; it puts the tragedy into the past, still remembered but having that air of history about it, a told tale of human stubbornness and frailty and love. In 'Resolution and Independence' there is another solitary figure, but he is very much part of the present; his encounter with the poet is seen against a background of immediate worries and

fears on the poet's side. It is known that the leech-gatherer is based on a
beggar who came to the door of Dove Cottage and who is described in
Dorothy Wordsworth's journal[29]; in Wordsworth's hands he becomes
a strange, solitary, motionless figure out on the moor. He is described
in physical and bodily terms, but he also has an air of the other world
about him:

> Now, whether it were by peculiar grace,
> A leading from above, a something given,
> Yet it befell that, in this lonely place,
> When I with these untoward thoughts had striven,
> Beside a pool bare to the eye of heaven
> I saw a Man before me unawares:
> The oldest man he seemed that ever wore grey hairs.
>
> (ll. 50–56)

The language of the first lines suggests an over-seeing providence
which ordains that the poet shall meet the leech-gatherer. But he is
unmistakably human, and not an angelic visitor: he may be strange,
but he is a man, the oldest man there has ever been, one might say.
The poet stumbles across him on a fine morning, after heavy rain; it is a
most beautiful day, but the poet cannot enjoy it because of his 'untoward
thoughts' – his worries about the future and his sadness about great poets
(Chatterton, Burns) who died young. Now he meets this strange and
solitary figure:

> As a huge stone is sometimes seen to lie
> Couched on the bald top of an eminence;
> Wonder to all who do the same espy,
> By what means it could thither come, and whence;
> So that it seems a thing endued with sense:
> Like a sea-beast crawled forth, that on a shelf
> Of rock or sand reposeth, there to sun itself;
>
> Such seemed this Man, . . .
>
> (ll. 57–64)

The strange comparisons of the old man to a stone which is in turn
compared to a sea-beast make us realize his oddness: yet he is present
in the poem, entering into conversation with the narrator; he is stoical
and cheerful, firm in his mind and dignified in his conversation in spite
of his hard life and dwindling profession of leech-gathering.

He is resolute and independent, and his resolution communicates
itself to the poet who makes a 'resolution' at the end:

'God', said I, 'be my help and stay secure;
I'll think of the Leech-gatherer on the lonely moor!'

The poet is being taught the lessons of experience. He is still growing
towards maturity, in the way that *The Prelude* explores; the finest
example of this is the 'Immortality Ode'.

The 'Immortality Ode' (written 1802–4) is, as Lionel Trilling observed, 'a poem about growing': 'some say it is a poem about growing
old, but I believe it is about growing up'.[30] It begins with the radiance
of the childhood vision, described with such delicate rhythm in the first
five lines:

There was a time when meadow, grove, and stream,
The earth, and every common sight,
To me did seem
Apparelled in celestial light,
The glory and the freshness of a dream.

The secret of this is in the pauses, the line-endings, and the following
of the single definitive nouns with the sudden transformation in line
form. After the catalogue of ordinary things, summed up in the phrase
'every common sight', comes the elaborate word 'Apparelled' followed
by 'celestial': the line is held back through the necessary connecting 'To
me did seem', but its sudden use of a word as consciously unusual as
'Apparelled' is enough to transform all that has gone before. Similarly,
the nature of the apparel –

in celestial light
The glory and the freshness of a dream

– is able to continue the transforming work: in the world of vision,
these are the ways in which common things appear. Childhood, and
dreams, show us things in their radiance. But the last part of the stanza
abandons the delicate rhythm of the first five lines:

It is not now as it hath been of yore; –
Turn wheresoe'er I may,
By night or day,
The things which I have seen I now can see no more.
(ll. 6–9)

The monosyllabic alexandrine at the end of the verse signifies the
ordinariness of the present vision; and yet not so ordinary:

> The Rainbow comes and goes,
> And lovely is the Rose,
> The Moon doth with delight
> Look round her when the heavens are bare,
> Waters on a starry night
> Are beautiful and fair;
> The sunshine is a glorious birth;
> But yet I know, where'er I go,
> That there hath past away a glory from the earth.
>
> (ll. 10–18)

If the common things of nature are as beautiful as this, then the 'glory' which has passed away must have been even more remarkable. Once again the rhythms carry the simplicity of the verse and the boldness of the idea ('The Rainbow comes and goes' must be one of the simplest conceptions ever to find expression in English poetry).

The first four verses provide a complex interaction between what remains and what is remembered. At one point the energy of natural life takes over and almost obliterates the memory of past glory, until the other voice of remembrance of things past returns:

> I hear, I hear, with joy I hear!
> – But there's a Tree, of many, one,
> A single Field which I have looked upon,
> Both of them speak of something that is gone:
>
> (ll. 50–53)

The Ode is filled with different voices, as the poet's mood changes. From the exultation of 'I feel – I feel it all', to

> Whither is fled the visionary gleam?
> Where is it now, the glory and the dream?
>
> (ll. 56–57)

the poem oscillates between joy and despair: indeed one of its salient characteristics is the way in which this powerful swinging sensation is resolved into something more philosophical. In the first four stanzas, written in 1802, there is not only a recapturing of the moments of vision but a series of powerful sensations and responses:

> The cataracts blow their trumpets from the steep;
> No more shall grief of mine the season wrong;
> I hear the Echoes from the mountains throng,

> The Winds come to me from the fields of sleep,
> And all the earth is gay;
>
> (ll. 25–29)

After the fourth stanza the poem employs another voice, philosophical and analytical: Wordsworth is now writing a parallel to the first four stanzas, which deals with the process of losing vision but discusses it in neo-Platonic terms.

This third voice is a necessary complement to the first two: through it the reader is introduced to the thinking behind the sensation, and the sensation becomes no longer personal but universal. It is no longer the record of one poet's vision, but of the necessary process of human life, seen as a movement away from the first impressions of being still close to a radiance that is God. The subsequent loss is then described as if Wordsworth were considering the child from outside; the earth makes the child feel at home, and the child responds by imitating the actions of his elders; in one of the most unusual and rhetorical of his long sentences,[31] Wordsworth asks *why?*, both in terms of genuine enquiry and also in a tone of anguish. The end of stanza VIII gathers into itself both the personal note and the philosophical, and prepares the way for the poem's resolution. Once again the opening word is 'joy':

> O joy! that in our embers
> Is something that doth live,
>
> (ll. 130–31)

The word 'joy' has appeared four times before; the Shepherd-boy is 'Thou Child of Joy', and the poet hears the sounds of spring:

> I hear, I hear, with joy I hear!
>
> (l. 50)

The growing boy still sees the light of his infant vision 'in his joy', but the child who is acting is doing so with 'joy and pride'. In the last example it is *his* joy, a joy which is unfortunately leading him (as Wordsworth thinks) in the wrong direction. On the other occasions joy is associated with the life of nature, and with the radiant vision. Now Wordsworth returns to it in a different context: it is a joy that something remains in the memory, some recollection of the complex and fugitive sensations of childhood. These are not just the moments of delight and liberty, but those of high and holy vision, in which the normal powers of sense and knowledge are put away:

> Blank misgivings of a Creature
> Moving about in worlds not realised,

High instincts before which our mortal Nature
Did tremble like a guilty Thing surprised . . .

(ll. 145–48)

The other consolation of maturity beside this remembering is the sense
of shared humanity which comes from an infancy which has known
vision:

In the primal sympathy
Which having been must ever be;
In the soothing thoughts that spring
Out of human suffering;
In the faith that looks through death,
In years that bring the philosophic mind.

(ll. 182–87).

This allows the poet, like the pedlar, to find soothing thoughts even
out of human suffering, to find faith and to find the philosophic mind.
As with *The Prelude*, the process is one of loss and gain: the childhood
vision, so movingly and vividly portrayed in the first part of the poem,
is succeeded by an adult state which has two consolations: that the
memory of the early intimations is still present in the mind, and that an
awareness of suffering and death can be added to the childhood vision
in order to complete it.

The irregular stanzas of the Pindaric ode are very important in
establishing the authentic combination of feeling and thought which
is found in the 'Immortality Ode'. They provide a sense of experience
which is quite different from the unfolding revelations of the blank
verse *Prelude* and from the graceful Authorized Version modulations
of 'Resolution and Independence'. The 'Immortality Ode' approaches
a new freedom and suggests a spontaneity and confidence which is
confirmed by the poems of these years. Wordsworth was 'at home'
at Grasmere, secure in the love of his family and friends, rejoicing in
his natural powers and their effect upon human beings. The event
which brought this to an end was the death of his brother John, who
was drowned at sea in February 1805. His premature death touched
William and Dorothy deeply: he was the most beloved of their brothers,
a man who shared many of their loves and concerns. His death turned
Wordsworth from a prophet into a human being: that is not to say that
he had not had his share of human feeling before, or that prophets are
not human beings as well as prophets, but that instead of the charismatic
power of the prophet (evidenced by the pedlar) there is a powerful
sense of individual vulnerability. The prophetic claims disappear and
a touching humanity takes their place:

A power is gone, which nothing can restore;
A deep distress hath humanised my Soul.

(ll. 35–36)

The poem from which these lines come, 'Elegiac Stanzas, suggested by
a Picture of Peele Castle in a Storm, painted by Sir George Beaumont',
is an interesting and significant pointer to the later years. It is in part a
tribute to Beaumont, a generous friend but an indifferent painter, whose
friendship at this time was so helpful to the bereaved Wordsworth
(it is a possible speculation that the friendship of conventional and
conservative Beaumont replacing that of brilliant Coleridge may have
helped to accelerate Wordsworth's own later decline into ordinariness).
The painting shows a castle, beaten by the waves, with a ship going
down in sight of shore (as John Wordsworth's ship, the *Earl of
Abergavenny*, had done); not only did the shipwreck have an obvious
point for Wordsworth, but the castle itself had been seen by him during a
period of calm weather in 1794. All the elements of the painting therefore
combined to mark Wordsworth's own state of mind, and especially the
storm instead of the calm. The weather is obviously symbolic; the castle,
beaten upon by the waves, is a figure representing fortitude. This is a
world which has now changed for the poet:

Not for a moment could I now behold
A smiling sea, and be what I have been:
The feeling of my loss will ne'er be old;
This, which I know, I speak with mind serene.

(ll. 37–40)

As Wordsworth has maintained all along, there is a happiness which
persists through human suffering: now he asserts this in his own personal
experience, explicitly condemning the reclusive mode of existence:

Farewell, farewell the heart that lives alone,
Housed in a dream, at distance from the Kind!
Such happiness, wherever it be known,
Is to be pitied; for 'tis surely blind.

But welcome fortitude, and patient cheer,
And frequent sights of what is to be borne!
Such sights, or worse, as are before me here. –
Not without hope we suffer and we mourn.

(ll. 53–60)

The poet is bidding farewell to a heart 'at distance from the Kind',
although he himself never had such a heart. The 'human heart' is an

important phrase for Wordsworth, as John Beer has indicated.[32] It is 'the human heart by which we live', the shared organ of feeling, the evidence of our proper humanity,

> That we have all of us one human heart.
>
> ('The Old Cumberland Beggar', l. 153)

Wordsworth's grand simplicity is found in a line such as this which asserts the basic and universal characteristic of human feeling, which can be used for good or ill. In *The Excursion* (1814), the major poem published in Wordsworth's own lifetime, he demonstrated this in the persons of the Solitary, the Wanderer, and the Pastor. The Wanderer (the Pedlar of 1797) is a figure of charismatic and prophetic power, whose role as prophet-wanderer gives him an insight into the afflictions of mankind without overcoming his fundamental benevolence. The Solitary, on the other hand, is misanthropic and grief-stricken, overcome by the failure of the French Revolution and his personal bereavement. The Pastor, most important of all, is the figure engaged in living a life at the centre of a community. If the Wanderer finishes his long discourse in Book IV with the idea that nature is the inspiration of human love, the Pastor demonstrates that love in action. The Pastor is urged by the Wanderer to describe the lives of those who have died, in order that his hearers (and especially the Solitary) may be led

> To prize the breath we share with human kind;
> And look upon the dust of man with awe.
>
> (v. 656–57)

The Pastor's examples lead to a conception of national life as founded on the idea of responsible living within the community. The examples which he gives are of lives that are far from ideally happy; the inhabitants that he has known are as subject as any to the fluctuations of fortune. And yet within this awareness of human instability and obscure suffering, there is also a knowledge that life can be well spent. And so *The Excursion*, which began with a ruined family, ends with the Pastor's family and home.

That ending is fundamental to Wordsworth's thinking and feeling. In the Pastor's home, and in the vision of a national life of happiness and benevolence (as opposed to the national life of France, for example), he catches a glimpse of what he seeks and hopes to find, an earthly paradise, a restoration of the fallen world with the grace to perceive that restoration. Given the right frame of mind, the world can be perceived as it should be: not as a bed of roses, where pain and suffering are ignored, but as a world in which they are part of the very business of being human. Wordsworth was writing, as Edwin Muir was to write, of a world outside Eden:

> What had Eden ever to say
> Of hope and faith and pity and love . . . ?
>
> ('One Foot in Eden', ll. 24–25)

and he was writing, as Milton had written, of a fallen world that was nevertheless the only and right one for human beings to live in:

> then wilt thou not be loath
> To leave this Paradise, but shalt possess
> A paradise within thee, happier far.
>
> (*Paradise Lost*, XII. 585–87)

Milton described the human condition in orthodox Christian terms; Wordsworth saw it more immediately in terms of his own experience. He had human moments of deprivation, sadness, bereavement, and despair: but he had also human moments in which he had seen the earth as transfigured by the power of nature and a concomitant human love. He writes about them in the Miltonic and sublime Preface to *The Excursion*:

> Paradise, and groves
> Elysian, Fortunate Fields – like those of old
> Sought in the Atlantic Main – why should they be
> A history only of departed things,
> Or a mere fiction of what never was?
> For the discerning intellect of Man,
> When wedded to this goodly universe
> In love and holy passion, shall find these
> A simple produce of the common day.
>
> (ll. 47–55)

The last beautiful line, with its reverberant simplicity, is the kind of effect which Wordsworth achieves at his best. It is only achieved by the utmost boldness, by the inspirational power of a conviction which at other times makes him seem humourless, or authoritarian, or dull. But Wordsworth is great enough to accommodate this: and in his exploration of the self, and his understanding of the problems of modern society in relation to the individual, he is the most far-seeing and large-minded of Romantic poets. He is the poet of grandeur and tenderness,[33] the one who most lives up to his own definition of the poet, that definition of the poet in relation to his fellow human beings which is most needed in our own day: he is 'the rock of defence for human nature; an upholder and preserver, carrying everywhere with him relationship and love'.

Notes

1. See Edward Shils, 'The Theory of Mass Society', in *The Concept of Community*, edited by David W. Minar and Scott Greer (Chicago, 1969), p. 299.

2. Wordsworth to Landor 20 April 1822; *The Letters of William and Dorothy Wordsworth, The Later Years, Part I, 1821–1828*, edited by Alan G. Hill, second edition (Oxford, 1978), p. 126.

3. *The Poetical Works of William Wordsworth*, edited by E. de Selincourt and H. Darbishire, 5 vols (Oxford, 1940–49), II, 395. All references are to this edition except when texts have been published in *The Cornell Wordsworth*.

4. *Biographia Literaria*, edited by James Engell and W. J. Bate (London, 1983), I, 77 (Ch. IV).

5. See the edition by Stephen Gill (1975) in *The Cornell Wordsworth*.

6. *Poetical Works*, I, 330.

7. *Poetical Works*, I, 95.

8. The *Prose Works of William Wordsworth*, edited by W. J. B. Owen and J. W. Smyser, 3 vols (Oxford, 1974), I, 76, 79.

9. Fragment printed in Jonathan Wordsworth, *The Music of Humanity* (London, 1969), pp. 5–6. All line references to 'The Ruined Cottage' and 'The Pedlar' are taken from the texts printed in this volume. Both poems are available (1979) in *The Cornell Wordsworth*, edited by James A. Butler.

10. J. R. Watson, *Wordsworth's Vital Soul* (London, 1982), pp. 83–90.

11. *Poetical Works*, II, 393.

12. Robert Mayo, 'The Contemporaneity of the *Lyrical Ballads*', *PMLA*, 69 (1954), pp. 486–522.

13. *Biographia Literaria*, II, 5 (Ch. XIV).

14. *Biographia Literaria*, II, 6–7 (Ch. XIV).

15. Wordsworth to John Wilson, 7 June 1802; *The Letters of William and Dorothy Wordsworth, The Early Years, 1787–1805*, revised by Chester L. Shaver, second edition (Oxford, 1967), p. 355.

16. *Letters, Early Years*, p. 357.

17. Henry Crabb Robinson to Thomas Robinson, 6 June 1802; printed in *William Wordsworth, a Critical Anthology*, edited by Graham McMaster (Harmondsworth, 1972), p. 72.

18. The story was taken from Erasmus Darwin's *Zoonamia* (1794), in which

the old woman breaks the hedges and appears 'like a witch in a play'. See *Poetical Works*, IV, 439–40.

19. *Poetical Works*, II, 512.

20. Quoted by Helen Darbishire, *The Poet Wordsworth* (Oxford, 1950), p. 49.

21. Martin Buber, *I and Thou*, translated by R. Gregor Smith (Edinburgh, 1937), p. 5.

22. A. C. Bradley, *Oxford Lectures on Poetry* (London, 1909), note to p. 102.

23. Geoffrey Hartman, *The Unmediated Vision* (New Haven, 1954), pp. 21–25.

24. *The Prelude, 1798–1799*, edited by Stephen Parrish, *The Cornell Wordsworth* (Ithaca and Hassocks, Sussex, 1977), p. 3.

25. Peter Malekin, 'Wordsworth and the Mind of Man', in *An Infinite Complexity*, edited by J. R. Watson (Edinburgh, 1983), pp. 1–25.

26. Wordsworth to Sir George Beaumont, 1 May 1805: *Letters, Early Years*, p. 586.

27. John Woolford, 'Wordsworth Agonistes', *Essays in Criticism*, 31 (1981), pp. 27–40.

28. J. R. Watson, 'Lucy and the Earth-Mother', *Essays in Criticism*, 27 (1977), pp. 187–202. Reprinted in Watson, *Wordsworth's Vital Soul*, Ch. 9.

29. *Journals of Dorothy Wordsworth*, edited by E. de Selincourt (London, 1941), I, 63.

30 Lionel Trilling, 'The Immortality Ode', in *The Liberal Imagination* (London, 1951), p. 131.

31. See Robert Rehder, *Wordsworth and the Beginnings of Modern Poetry* (London, 1981), Ch. 3 ('Wordsworth's Long Sentences').

32. See John Beer, *Wordsworth and the Human Heart* (London, 1978), pp. 4–17 especially, but also throughout.

33. The title of a sensitive study on Wordsworth, by David B. Pirie: *William Wordsworth, the Poetry of Grandeur and of Tenderness* (London, 1982).

Chapter 7
Coleridge

As to me, my face, unless when animated by immediate
eloquence, expresses great Sloth, a great, indeed almost
ideotic, good nature. 'Tis a mere carcase of a face: fat,
flabby, and expressive chiefly of inexpression. Yet I
am told, that my eyes, eyebrows, and forehead are
physiognomically good –; but of this the Deponent
knoweth not. As to my shape, 'tis a good shape enough,
if measured – but my gait is awkward, & the walk, & the
Whole man indicates *indolence capable of energies*.[1]

This description, eloquent as a Rembrandt self-portrait, tells us a good
deal about Coleridge, not only in his physical appearance but also in his
attitude to himself: the self-deprecating, half-humorous characterization
of his face as 'a mere carcase of a face' and the admission that it is 'fat,
flabby, & expressive chiefly of inexpression', these are evidence of an
endearing refusal to take himself too seriously. Coleridge is the most
unthreatening of Romantic poets: the one whose riches of mind and
sensibility are displayed most unceremoniously, the one who least claims
the prophetic fire; and yet his poems are curiously and quintessentially
Romantic, for two reasons. The first is that he captures, better than
any of the others except Shelley, the strange magic of the world of
the supernatural; the second is that his poems have a remarkable and
touching intimacy, a revelation of personal feeling and circumstance
which makes Coleridge known to his readers in a way that is quite
different from the way that the others are known. Coleridge's own
difficulties and hesitations, his aspirations and failures, his limitations,
his family problems, his hopes and fears – all can be discovered in
his poetry, in the letters and notebooks, and in what we can deduce
from other evidence: the result is a figure whose life and work arouse
admiration and pity – admiration for the extraordinary mind that he
obviously possessed and for the amount that he did achieve, pity for
his distress, for his unfinished work, and for the mess that he often got
himself into.

Some of these muddles are a source of laughter, as when he enlisted in the 15th King's Light Dragoons in December 1793 under the name of Silas Tomkyn Comberbache. He proved an impossible soldier, and had to be extracted by his friends (with the connivance of his Commanding Officer, who agreed to describe him as insane); on his return to Cambridge in April 1794, he plunged with enthusiasm into the Pantisocracy scheme, in which 'a small but liberalized party' intended to emigrate to the banks of the Susquehanna 'on the principles of an abolition of individual property'.[2] He hoped to learn the theory and practice of agriculture and carpentry in preparation for this; when the scheme collapsed, Coleridge found himself firmly committed to marry Sara Fricker (whose two sisters had been married to Pantisocrats). In due course, the marriage proved unhappy, but one can only wonder if any single individual could have made Coleridge happy and contented. Certainly his relationships with Southey and Wordsworth were marked by a passionate love which could easily be hurt. He was so enthusiastic, so chaotic, and so open in his affections, that he was especially vulnerable; and in addition his mind was a continual ferment of ideas. He wrote to Josiah Wade in February 1796:

> I verily believe no poor fellow's idea-pot ever bubbled up
> so vehemently with fears, doubts and difficulties, as mine
> does at present. Heaven grant it may not boil over, and put
> out the fire! I am almost heartless! my past life seems to
> me like a dream, a feverish dream! all one gloomy huddle
> of strange actions, and dim-discovered motives! Friendships
> lost by indolence, and happiness murdered by mismanaged
> sensibility! The present hour I seem in a quickset hedge of
> embarrassments! For shame! I ought not to mistrust God!
> but indeed, to hope is far more difficult than to fear.[3]

In the following month, March 1796, comes the first reference to the regular use of opium as a relief from stress.[4] Its subsequent domination over Coleridge's mind, and the effect on his poetry, are difficult to assess[5]; but what seems to have happened, in Alethea Hayter's words, is that 'opium, which had given or promoted the dreams, had taken away the power to profit from them poetically'. What is clear is that for much of his life Coleridge was especially subject to moods of energetic activity, and to other moods of helplessness and despair. Coleridge's poetry is like his life: it is enthusiastic, open to experience, uneven, sometimes chaotic, and even annoying; but it is always touchingly human and vulnerable.

The early poems are those of the Christ's Hospital schoolboy; in them Coleridge experimented with all kinds of verse-forms and linguistic registers. His most spectacular attempt is 'A Mathematical Problem', a poem which attempts jocularly to do something which Coleridge later engaged upon seriously, 'to assist Reason by the stimulus of Imagination':

> Because the point A. is the centre
>   Of the circular B.C.D.
> And because the point B. is the centre
>   Of the circular A.C.E.
> A.C. to A.B. and B.C. to B.A.
> Harmoniously equal for ever must stay;
>   Then C.A. and B.C.
>   Both extend the kind hand
>   To the basis, A.B.
> Unambitiously join'd in Equality's Band.
>
> (ll. 32–41)

In contrast to this light-heartedness there is an underlying political and humanitarian seriousness in poems such as the ingenuous 'To a Young Ass' (a poem which provoked Byron's ridicule):

> Poor Ass! her Master should have learnt to shew
> Pity – best taught by fellowship of woe!
> For much I fear, that He lives, ev'n as she,
> Half famish'd in a land of luxury!
>
> (ll. 19–22)

The contrast between the ideal and the actual, between the beauty of creation and the injustices of contemporary life, is found in 'Religious Musings' (Christmas Eve, 1794), in which 'Ev'n now the storm begins' (l. 328) of the French Revolution; it is seen as the coming of the Millennium, with the destruction of evil religious and political establishments:

> The THOUSAND YEARS lead up their mystic dance,
> Old OCEAN claps his hands! The DESERT shouts!
> And soft gales wafted from the haunts of Spring
> Melt the primaeval North! The mighty Dead
> Rise to new life, who'er from earliest time
> With conscious zeal had urged Love's wondrous plan
> Coadjutors of God.
>
> (ll. 373–79)

The verse sounds like inflated James Thomson, while dependence on the Revelation of St John the Divine is similar to Blake's habit of reading current events in mythological and biblical terms. The blending of various elements is typical of the poetry which Coleridge was writing at this period. In the volume of 1796, in which 'Religious Musings' appeared, it is possible to detect the influence of Gray and Collins (in the 'Monody on the Death of Chatterton'), of Pope (in 'To a Young Lady, with a Poem on the French Revolution'), and Spenser ('Lines in the Manner of Spenser'). But the most significant influence is that of Cowper, whose poetry, and especially *The Task*, indicated to Coleridge a way of poetically expressing his most informal and discursive thoughts: Coleridge described Cowper as 'the best modern poet', and his poetry as 'divine Chit chat'.[6] The result is 'The Eolian Harp' (August 1795), the most delightful of Coleridge's early poems and the one which looks forward most clearly to his later work, both the later 'conversation poems' and the supernatural ones.

It is a poem whose crescendos and diminuendos are most delicately controlled; it seems almost to breathe more deeply in places, so natural is its movement. It conveys quite beautifully the workings of a benign intelligence, as the poet describes the landscape and adds his own commentary on its emblematic significance:

> My pensive SARA! thy soft cheek reclin'd
> Thus on mine arm, most soothing sweet it is
> To sit beside our cot, our cot o'er grown
> With white-flower'd Jasmin, and the broad-leav'd Myrtle,
> (Meet emblems they of Innocence and Love!)
> And watch the clouds, that late were rich with light,
> Slow sad'ning round, and mark the star of eve
> Serenely brilliant (such should Wisdom be)
> Shine opposite!
> (ll. 1–9)

Just when the poet appears to be becoming didactic, his awareness of the outside world becomes simply appreciative, a joy in the scents of the evening and the quietness of the place:

> How exquisite the scents
> Snatch'd from yon bean-field! and the world *so* hush'd!
> The stilly murmur of the distant Sea
> Tells us of Silence.
> (ll. 9–12)

The silence is broken only by the Aeolian harp in the window-casement, giving out sound as the wind blows upon it, as if caressed by nature itself:

> Like some coy Maid half-yielding to her Lover,
> It pours such sweet upbraidings, as must needs
> Tempt to repeat the wrong!
>
> (ll. 15–17)

The image of the coy maid takes the mind back to Sara herself at the beginning of the poem: Coleridge is establishing a parallel between the music of the natural world, the union of the free wind with the man-made harp, and the love of man for woman. As the wind rises, so the syntax becomes more elaborate and the sentence longer:

> And now, its strings
> Boldlier swept, the long sequacious notes
> Over delicious surges sink and rise,
> Such a soft floating witchery of sound
> As twilight Elfins make, when they at eve
> Voyage on gentle gales from Faery Land,
> Where *Melodies* round honey-dropping flowers,
> Footless, and wild, like birds of Paradise,
> Nor pause, nor perch, hovering on untam'd wing.
>
> (ll. 17–25)

The sustained movement of this passage carries the mind through the delight in witchery of sound into the elfins of fairyland and the image of the bird of paradise: it is as though the simple action of sitting outside the cottage on a fine summer evening has turned into a labyrinthine journey of the mind, which still keeps in touch with the original sensation, so that the journeying mind and the feeling senses are united. Coleridge may have had in mind a passage from Cowper's *The Task* which does something similar:

> Mighty winds
> That sweep the skirt of some far-spreading wood
> Of ancient growth, make music not unlike
> The dash of ocean on his winding shore,
> And lull the spirit while they fill the mind, . . .
>
> (*The Task*, I. 183–87)

As Mary Jacobus has pointed out, the last line could almost have been written by Wordsworth, 'with its transference of sensation to inner life, its merging of natural and internal landscapes'.[7] In 'The Eolian Harp' Coleridge puts his own individual stamp on the transference by carrying the reader into worlds of fairyland and paradise: Cowper's straight comparison of sound between the wind in the wood and the breaking of waves on the shore becomes a witchery, in a paradise where the flowers are dropping honey and the birds of paradise fly for evermore. This in turn sends the attention back to the scents of the bean-field, to the jasmine and myrtle, and these are associated with innocence and love. The result is a complexity of response, which allows the mind to be filled and the spirit lulled (as Cowper's was), and the senses to play a part in this process. The result seems more active than Cowper's 'lulling', however: it is a response of joy to the time, the place, and to the love in his own life which is reflected in the world of nature. It is a response, too, to the rhythms of his own thought which occur simultaneously with the sense-impressions of the evening; so that all things come together to make what Coleridge called, in a later version of the poem, 'the one Life' (in lines not printed until 1817, which means that they could not be a climax in the 1796 editition):

> O! the one Life within us and abroad
> Which meets all motion and becomes its soul,
> A light in sound, a sound-like power in light,
> Rhythm in all thought, and joyance every where –
>
> (ll. 26–29)

The rhythms of the verse here indicate the love for all created things and the joy of life which is both 'within us and abroad'. There is a kind of diffusive unity of the spirit, a filling of the world with love, which gives everything that moves a soul and spirit. In this process light and sound become one, united in 'the one Life', the great animating spirit which makes 'a light in sound, a sound-like power in light'. The phraseology is strange, and so unscientific as to be challenging[8]: and yet it is possible to see through its strangeness the quality of experience which Coleridge is seeking to represent, the unity of all physical things. So light has a kind of sound-like power, and sound affects the mind as light does: they join in a creative harmony, as the wind and the harp do, and as Coleridge and Sara do. All things, human and natural, celebrate a life of interconnection, and the result is a sense of universal benevolence and love:

> Methinks, it should have been impossible
> Not to love all things in a world so fill'd;
> Where the breeze warbles, and the mute still air
> Is Music slumbering on her instrument.
>
> (ll. 30–33)

Coleridge brings the poem back to himself and Sara in the next line: he is creating a pattern which Wordsworth was to follow so magisterially in 'Tintern Abbey', in which the reflections of the mind arise from the circumstances, and the poem moves out from the circumstantial situation and then returns to it. So Coleridge has been speculating on the life of nature and on the benevolent universe of love from his own situation with Sara in a summer evening beside their cottage, with the Aeolian harp making music in the window. Now he returns to her, only to describe himself at another moment, on a hillside at noon watching the sunlight on the sea. At this point, the thoughts traverse his brain idly: his brain is 'passive' and the ideas impress themselves upon it rather as the wind makes music on the harp, the 'subject Lute'. Yet it is this passive brain which suddenly breaks into an active and creative thought, one which presents the reader with the greatest synthesis of all: the poem has been dealing throughout with relationships between different things in the world, and between the mind and the external world; now Coleridge proposes a speculation which is undeniably grand, of the animating power breathing life into the universe:

> And what if all of animated nature
> Be but organic Harps diversly fram'd,
> That tremble into thought, as o'er them sweeps
> Plastic and vast, one intellectual Breeze,
> At once the Soul of each, and God of all?
>
> (ll. 44–48)

The secret of this passage is the use of the two verbs 'tremble' and 'sweeps': in both cases they are surrounded by concepts which allow them a peculiar meaning and power. Nature becomes a harp trembling into thought, as an ordinary harp trembles into sound (here the earlier 'light in sound' has an important effect, allowing the reader to accept the integration here of 'sound' and 'thought' in the metaphor), swept by a breeze which is itself two things, within and without:

> At once the Soul of each, and God of all.

At this point the gradual process of building up relationships and resemblances, the beautiful process of fusing the internal and external, reaches its climax. The animating and breathing spirit is the power of God, functioning outside nature as 'one intellectual Breeze' (the mind which gives life) and within nature as its very soul. In the same way the secondary imagination, as Coleridge defined it in *Biographia Literaria*, is 'essentially *vital*, even as all objects (*as* objects) are essentially fixed and dead'. What Coleridge is suggesting here, therefore, is a pattern of creative interaction which is found in the relationship of God to the created world; this is reflected and paralleled in the love of the poet for the world, and from this we can deduce that the poetic imagination (a repetition in the finite mind of the eternal act of creation in the infinite I AM) is related to this love, as it seems to be here. Coleridge is synthesizing the work of God, the work of the poet, and the love of man and woman, all found together in a universe filled with love.

It is at this point that the poem turns back to Sara, and to her reproof. It is a striking moment: the picture which Coleridge has built up so carefully and sensitively is disturbed, as Sara's 'more serious eye' darts 'a mild reproof'. At first sight this looks as if Sara is a complete brake on the poet's imagination, a destroyer of the poem; the orthodox Christianity which the poet offers at the end of the poem seems a very inadequate substitute for the vision of the world filled with love. And yet there are two things to be said in qualification of this. The first is that Coleridge's description of Sara's mind as 'more serious' indicates that he rather deprecatingly saw the early part of the poem as playful: if he were really to think about the world it would not be seen as a world of love but as a world of sin and pain, in which the only discussable role for God is that of Saviour and Redeemer. Seen in this light the peace which he feels at the beginning of the poem, and celebrates in the last line, becomes more sensibly and stably based. It is the gift of God, a tranquil moment in an untranquil world. The poem, therefore, is a poem of relaxation, *Coleridge ludens*, in which he tranquilly muses on tranquillity (the phrase itself is playful). The second complicating factor is that Coleridge, faced with a choice, has to decide to agree with Sara. The last section, with its 'well hast thou said', is an acknowledgment of the demands of human company, of the other that is Sara, of her way of thinking, and of the peace that comes through mutual agreement and understanding.

The end of the poem, therefore, may seem a retreat, a failure of the imagination; it does, in fact, make the poem more mature by placing the playful element in the context of a more difficult and demanding world and it makes the poem less selfish by acknowledging the beliefs of another person. The fact that the end comes as a surprise, and seems to jar on the multiple simultaneous awareness of the early part of the poem, is a testimony to the strength of Coleridge's playful imagination: its movement is that of a going-out from the 'My pensive Sara!' of the first line and a return to 'THEE, heart-honored Maid!' at the end, and in this movement, as so often happens in Romantic poetry, the free-running imagination is able to capture the attention (as it does, for instance, in Keats's 'Ode to a Nightingale') and enchant the mind. What is significant about Coleridge's imaginative progress here, and what sets him apart from other poets throughout, is his ability to create worlds of his own that have an unmistakable originality and yet also have a kind of affinity with the ordinary world in which we live. Again and again, Coleridge's greatest poems are elusive, neither of this world nor not of it; they are the world seen with new eyes, as it is in 'The Eolian Harp', so that it appears different and strange, yet often extraordinarily beautiful. The best way to describe this is in Coleridge's own image of landscape seen by moonlight, in *Biographia Literaria*, as truth transformed by imagination into 'the poetry of nature'.[9] Nature itself acts as changer and enchanter, supplying qualities of light unknown before. So the poet, by the power of his imagination, changes the familiar into something rich and strange.

All Coleridge's finest poems do this: even 'The Rime of the Ancient Mariner' is filled with images that we recognize but which are transformed by the context and narrative; 'Kubla Khan' is a dream-poem, but one in which the dream has images of great clarity which we can recognize as having beauty and terror; 'Christabel' seems to have a story-line which makes sense, but we are never quite sure. These poems are like 'The Eolian Harp' in one respect, however different they may seem: they contain that unmistakable evidence of a transforming imagination, of Coleridge's especial gift for drawing magic out of the ordinary, of a mind playing upon the external world.

'Reflections on having left a Place of Retirement', written in 1795 when the 1796 collection was in the press, makes clearer the distinction which is found in 'The Eolian Harp' between the freedom of the speculative mind and the world of pain and suffering which is hinted at in the 'more serious' mind of Sara and in the references to God as Saviour. Now Coleridge remembers the rural tranquillity of the cottage at Clevedon, the song of the 'viewless' skylark (in which Coleridge gropes rather ineffectually at the idea later achieved so triumphantly by Shelley) and the view from the hill above. The description of the view is much more successful than the description of the skylark; Coleridge puts his individual and transforming stamp on the conventional prospect-poem of the eighteenth-century:

> *Here* the bleak mount,
> The bare bleak mountain speckled thin with sheep;
> Grey clouds, that shadowing spot the sunny fields;
> And river, now with bushy rocks o'erbrow'd,
> Now winding bright and full, with naked banks;
> And seats, and lawns, the Abbey and the wood,
> And cots, and hamlets, and faint city-spire;
> The Channel *there*, the Islands and white sails,
> Dim coasts, and cloud-like hills, and shoreless Ocean –
> It seem'd like Omnipresence! God, methought,
> Had built him there a Temple: the whole World

Seem'd *imag'd* in its vast circumference:
No *wish* profan'd my overwhelméd heart.
Blest hour! It was a luxury, – to be!

(ll. 29–42)

The sense of being overwhelmed, as though the whole world was imaged there and was the temple of God, is as momentarily convincing as the visions of nature and the animating breath in 'The Eolian Harp'. In this case it awakens feelings of guilt, that the poet should be so filled with love and joy while his fellow men suffer:

> Was it right,
> While my unnumber'd brethren toil'd and bled,
> That I should dream away the entrusted hours
> On rose-leaf beds, pampering the coward heart
> With feelings all too delicate for use?

(ll. 44–48)

So the poet decides to renounce comfort and beauty, to go out and fight for the betterment of mankind, although he promises to revisit the cottage in spirit

> when after honourable toil
> Rests the tir'd mind, and waking loves to dream,
> My spirit shall revisit thee, dear Cot!

(ll. 63–65)

As with 'The Eolian Harp' the contrast is between the playing imagination, the dream, and the work of life, the reality of the world. 'Reflections' ends with a quotation from the Lord's Prayer; if only all could enjoy such dreaming, playful, free happiness, in a free and equitable world:

> Ah! – had none greater! And that all had such!
> It might be so – but the time is not yet.
> Speed it, O Father! Let thy kingdom come!

(ll. 69–71)

In 1796 Coleridge left Clevedon, the 'place of retirement', for Nether Stowey, in the Quantock Hills of Somerset. His acquaintance with Wordsworth began probably in 1795 and ripened in June 1797 when he visited William and Dorothy at Racedown (in Dorset). There is a delightful picture of Coleridge arriving there, jumping a gate and cutting across a field in his impatience to arrive; by July he had persuaded them to move near him at Alfoxden. The result was a year of stimulating companionship, of high poetic hopes, and (for Coleridge especially) a new accuracy in the observation of nature. This last was probably due to the influence of Dorothy Wordsworth, whose acute perception of natural appearances transferred itself to Coleridge in many places, most notably in the 'one red leaf' image in 'Christabel', which is directly borrowed from her journal. Coleridge's delight in natural appearances is found in 'This Lime-Tree Bower my Prison' which dates from the summer of 1797, when Charles Lamb visited Coleridge. Lamb and the Wordsworths went walking; Coleridge could not accompany them, because 'dear Sara accidentally emptied a skillet of boiling milk on my foot',[10] but during their evening walk Coleridge wrote 'This Lime-Tree Bower my Prison' in a way which shows his imagination as still buoyant and playful.

The poem describes in detail the walk which the Wordsworths and Lamb took, along the hilltop, into the dell, out on to the eminence with a view of the hills and the sea; Coleridge longs for a fine sunset, that Lamb may be as deeply impressed as he has been, that its colours may seem like those of heaven:

> Ah! slowly sink
> Behind the western ridge, thou glorious Sun!
> Shine in the slant beams of the sinking orb,
> Ye purple heath-flowers! richlier burn, ye clouds!
> Live in the yellow light, ye distant groves!
> And kindle, thou blue Ocean! So my friend
> Struck with deep joy may stand, as I have stood,
> Silent with swimming sense; yea, gazing round
> On the wide landscape, gaze till all doth seem
> Less gross than bodily; and of such hues
> As veil the Almighty Spirit, when yet he makes
> Spirits perceive his presence.
>
> (ll. 32–43)

Contemplating this in his mind, the poet feels a delight 'As I myself were there!' His mind has broken out of the prison of the lime-tree bower; even there, he reflects, nature is very beautiful, so that the heart can be kept awake to love and beauty. Both present and absent, nature is a source of abundant joy to 'the wise and pure'. Coleridge evidently thinks of himself and his friends in this category; the poem is a celebration of a joy which comes from within as well as without, from a poet who can enjoy a lime-tree-bower prison, and a clerk from the India office

>   to whom
>   No sound is dissonant which tells of Life.
>
>   (ll. 75–76)

The 'one Life' of which Coleridge was to write in the later version of
'The Eolian Harp' is 'within us and abroad'; it suggests a relationship, a
heart at peace with itself which responds to the beauty and benevolence
of nature. This is the true significance of 'This Lime-Tree Bower my
Prison': its intimacy and openness are evidence of a mind that can
declare itself as tranquil, joyful, buoyant, playful, in a way which is
vital for the relationship between the poet and the external world. When
Coleridge writes that the poet 'described in ideal perfection, brings the
whole soul of man into activity', he is thinking of a soul in good repair,
filled with benevolence and love which goes out to the external world
and comes from it. Without the power of the soul, the external world
is dead:

>   we receive but what we give,
>   And in *our* Life alone does Nature live.
>
>   ('Letter to Sara Hutchinson', ll. 296–97)

'This Lime-Tree Bower my Prison' celebrates a constructive and positive
relationship with nature, a happy set of friendships, and a shared pleasure
in the external world. Similarly, in 'Frost at Midnight', which dates
from the following winter (February 1798), the mind is tranquil and
beautifully related to its memories and to nature. In this poem there
are two clearly distinguished fields of force: first, the scene within the
cottage, in which the poet sitting by the fire next to his sleeping baby
has a series of recollections of his earlier life; second, the mysterious
life of nature outside, the 'secret ministry' of the frost and the cry of
the young owl. The poem's fascination depends upon the powerful
contrast between the silent workings of nature and the busy processes
of the poet's mind; it is so still and calm outside

>   that it disturbs
>   And vexes meditation with its strange
>   And extreme silentness.
>
>   (ll. 8–10)

Within, the poet's mind sets off on its own journey, impelled by the
sight of the film of ash fluttering on the grate: it goes back to seeing
the same kind of film at school, where it was thought to herald the
arrival of some friend. In turn this leads him to reflect on his own
son, the sleeping baby in the cradle, and his future education; this will

be a very different kind of experience, one in which the child will be surrounded by nature and be free to wander where he will.

The processes of the mental activity in this poem are Hartleian: that is, they suggest a journey of the mind which is linked by an identifiable chain of ideas and memories. It is entirely different from the greater, stranger, more awe-inspiring, and more beautiful world outside, the world of summer and winter; while the poet has been thinking his thoughts, the strange and silent workings of nature have been going on outside:

> whether the eave-drops fall
> Heard only in the trances of the blast,
> Or if the secret ministry of frost
> Shall hang them up in silent icicles,
> Quietly shining to the quiet Moon.
> (ll. 70–74)

The strange and mysterious beauty of these final lines takes the reader back to the opening of the poem: the power of the frost encloses the mental activity of the poem, surrounds it; nature outside the cottage is secretly and magically active, transforming the world of water and eave-drops into icicles shining in the moonlight. The poet meanwhile has been active also, his memories and hopes blending with the stillness to produce an atmosphere in which the various elements of the poem exist together in harmony: the indoors and the outdoors; warmth and cold; the inner world of past and future, and the outer world of the present moment; the owl in the night, the poet and his babe by the fire; all these combine to suggest a peace of mind and spirit, a harmony which is not unlike that in 'The Eolian Harp'.

But as in that poem, and in 'Reflections on having left a Place of Retirement', Coleridge was aware of another side to the story, so in 'The Ancient Mariner' he writes of a man no longer at peace with himself, and no longer an integrated member of a community. The stillness and domesticity of 'Frost at Midnight' and 'The Eolian Harp' have given way to the nomadic restlessness of the guilty and penitent mariner.[11]

To the extent that he is a sinner, guilty and penitent, the ancient mariner is representative of a fundamental human attribute of which Coleridge was only too well aware. He knew periods in which

> all the realities about me lose their natural *healing* powers,
> at least, diminish the same, and become not worthy of a
> Thought. Who that thus lives with a continually divided
> Being can remain healthy![12]

At other times he had to struggle 'day after day with life-loathing Sickness, as my first Good-Morning to you!'[13] To escape from the self and from its attendant and inescapable evils was, for Coleridge, a hopeless task and an ideal to be attained only momentarily: and one of the major components of 'The Rime of the Ancient Mariner' is its sense that the mariner cannot avoid himself. It is his own consciousness and his own experience that he carries around with him. The realities about him lose their healing powers when he shoots the albatross, and the healing powers are only recovered when he blesses the water-snakes: even then he has to undergo the penance for his crime, and his experience cuts him off from the stable domestic life of family and community.

Such an approach to the poem leaves many questions unanswered, and to call the shooting of the albatross a crime is itself an over-simplification. As William Empson has pointed out, many animals and birds are killed for food; he points rather to the mariner's guilt as the fundamental concern of the poem, a guilt which he was constrained to feel just as Coleridge in his own life was made to feel guilty by the Wordsworths and Southey (among others). It is difficult to refute this, though difficult to feel that it is entirely right: what is clear is that the poem is not a warning against shooting albatrosses any more than Wordsworth's boat-stealing episode in *The Prelude* is a caution against stealing boats. Nor is it a poem which can be adequately summed up by the moral at the end:

> He prayeth well, who loveth well
> Both man and bird and beast.

> He prayeth best, who loveth best
> All things both great and small;
> For the dear God who loveth us,
> He made and loveth all.
> (ll. 612–17)

Coleridge is supposed to have repudiated this as a moral summary when he told Mrs Barbauld that 'The Rime of the Ancient Mariner' had too much moral 'in a work of such pure imagination'.[14] Certainly the punishment which the mariner receives, and even more the punishment which his fellow mariners receive, seems inconsistent with the idea of a God 'who made and loveth all'. But to say that the poem is one of 'pure imagination', and to imply by this that it has no specific meaning, is to go too far in the other direction, and turn it into an exercise of the poet's free-wheeling mind, without reference to the human condition of which Coleridge was so powerfully aware.[15]

The customary interpretation of 'The Rime of the Ancient Mariner' is that in shooting the albatross the mariner commits a crime against the 'one life'. Since that one life is 'within us and abroad' (as described in 'The Eolian Harp'), the mariner's crime is against the created world and also against himself. But the crime (if it is a crime) is part of a larger process of human experience which the mariner goes through and which is contrasted with the world and the experience of the wedding-guest. The wedding-guest plays an important part in the poem, acting as an ordinary and ingenuous figure who is held by the glittering eye of the mariner; beside his limited experience, we are to set the strange journey of the mariner, a journey which is not just geographical but which moves into strange worlds of the mind. The key to the poem is the fact that it is a ballad, and also a poem concerned with a long journey by sea. Through the use of these forms, Coleridge has been enabled to convey what George Whalley calls 'the most intense personal suffering, perplexity, loneliness, longing, horror, fear'.[16]

Travel has often been used as a metaphor for experience. Nowhere is the contrast between the man who stays at home and the man who goes out into a wider world more clearly expressed than in 'The Rime of the Ancient Mariner'. The mariner puts out to sea, leaving behind him the well-known landmarks:

> 'The ship was cheered, the harbour cleared,
> Merrily did we drop
> Below the kirk, below the hill,
> Below the light house top.
> (ll. 21–24)

The absence of land is emphasized by the presence of the elemental power of sun and sea:

> The Sun came up upon the left
> Out of the sea came he!
> And he shone bright, and on the right
> Went down into the sea.
> (ll. 25–28)

The ship, therefore, is sailing south, into storms and then ice; the momentary vision of the bride pacing into the hall behind 'the merry minstrelsy' gives way to the mariner's relentless narrative:

> And now the STORM-BLAST came, and he
> Was tyrannous and strong:
> He struck with his o'ertaking wings,
> And chased us south along.

With sloping masts and dipping prow,
As who pursued with yell and blow
Still treads the shadow of his foe,
And forward bends his head,
The ship drove fast, loud roared the blast,
And southward aye we fled.

And now there came both mist and snow,
And it grew wondrous cold:
And ice, mast-high, came floating by,
As green as emerald.

(ll. 41–54)

The seascape is fearful and strange; the pack-ice which surrounds the ship 'cracked and growled, and roared and howled'. It is into this alien universe that the albatross comes, a sign of life in the midst of the frozen waste, and the ice splits to allow the ship through. When the mariner shoots the bird he does so with no apparent motive or premeditation; the memory of it causes his face to show signs of torment, as the wedding-guest observes in the brilliant last verse of Part I:

'God save thee, ancient Mariner!
From the fiends, that plague thee thus! –
Why lookst thou so?' – With my cross-bow
I shot the ALBATROSS.

(ll. 79–82)

Coleridge's development of the ballad form is shown in the brief but telling exchange between the two characters here: question and answer each contain the most powerful resonances, as they do (for example) in a ballad such as 'Lord Randal'. There the question and answer contain the foundation of the whole experience; so here the question and answer provide a similar focal point, sharpening our sense of the mariner's state of mind and of the central action of the poem.

So far the poem has been concerned with the experience of a voyager, as opposed to the land-based wedding-guest. Now the voyage becomes even stranger, a journey into another ocean of the mind, into a silent sea where there is no wind and no water, where the very deep rots, and slimy things crawl upon the surface, where the mariners have strange dreams and where the ancient mariner himself, having been cursed and then praised, is now used as a scapegoat:

Instead of the cross, the Albatross
About my neck was hung.

(ll. 141–42)

The moment is strange, ritualistic, tribal: we have moved from the sophisticated world of the wedding-guest, worried about being late for the wedding, to the bedrock of human nature, caught in an alien universe where

> The water, like a witch's oils,
> Burnt green, and blue and white.
>
> (ll. 129–30)

We then move still further, as the spectre-ship comes into sight, the skeleton ship with Death and Life-in-Death casting dice. What happens at this point in the poem has caused problems because of its element of chance: the mariner's punishment should not be seen, it is argued, as depending on the fall of dice. Yet in a curious way the sheer arbitrariness of the fate of the mariner and his fellows is all part of the unpredictable world in which the sea-voyagers find themselves. The landmarks (kirk, hill, lighthouse) have long since disappeared, and the journey has taken them further and further into the heart, not of darkness, but of the inscrutable and ultimately incomprehensible. The death of the mariners is certainly undeserved; it is related to Coleridge's idea that the poem had 'no more moral than the *Arabian Nights'* tale of the merchant's sitting down to eat dates by the side of a well and throwing the shells aside, and lo! a genie starts up, and says he *must* kill the aforesaid merchant, *because* one of the date shells had, it seems, put out the eye of the genie's son' (*Table Talk*, 31 May 1830). So the mariners, 200 of them, drop down dead at the rising of the moon:

> The stars were dim, and thick the night,
> The steersman's face by his lamp gleamed white;
> From the sails the dew did drip –
> Till clomb above the eastern bar
> The hornéd Moon, with one bright star
> Within the nether tip.
>
> (ll. 206–11)

The awful moment of death is suspended, while the ship in the night is described with the marvellously economical series of images that Coleridge uses; then, with an extraordinary use of 'language really used by men', the deaths occur:

> Four times fifty living men,
> (And I heard nor sigh nor groan)
> With heavy thump, a lifeless lump,
> They dropped down one by one.

The souls did from their bodies fly, –
They fled to bliss or woe!
And every soul, it passed me by,
Like the whizz of my cross-bow!

(ll. 276–23)

The souls fly like arrows into eternity, leaving the mariner for seven days in his own appalling waste land, with the dead around him, the rotting sea, his prayers stifled. Only when he unthinkingly blesses the water-snakes is the spell broken and the albatross falls from his neck.

Thus far the poem has been a journey into the unknown. Now in Part v we discover that the world contains spirits, of whose presence we are usually unconscious, safely fixed as we are in our material world. Coleridge took the hint from Thomas Burnet, whose *Archaeologiae Philosophicae* is quoted at the head of the poem: 'Facile credo, plures esse Naturas invisibiles quam visibiles in rerum universitate' ('I readily believe there to be more invisible natures than visible ones in the universe of things'). In this case the mariners rise up as ghosts, inspirited by 'a blessed troop of angelic spirits, sent down by invocation of the guardian saint': these govern, among other things, the Polar Spirit, who seeks vengeance for the killing of the albatross, and the guardian spirit, who promises that a further penance will be required. What that penance is becomes clear when the mariner finds himself, to his immense joy, back in his own country: he meets the hermit, the pilot, and the pilot's boy, but can communicate properly with none of them, except possibly the hermit, whose strength is enough to challenge the mariner to tell his story. But that story is not really a piece of true communication: it has too much of the air of compulsion about it. The wedding-guest has been detained against his will, and so will others be:

I pass, like night, from land to land;
I have strange power of speech;
That moment that his face I see,
I know the man that must hear me:
To him my tale I teach.

(ll. 58–90)

The final burst of noise from the wedding serves only to illuminate the great gulf of experience between the mariner and the wedding-guest:

O Wedding-Guest! this soul hath been
Alone on a wide wide sea:

So lonely 'twas, that God himself
Scarce seemèd there to be.

(ll. 597–600)

It emphasizes the absolute remoteness of the mariner's mind, the mind that has been so deeply touched by a series of terrible and inexplicable experiences. After his journey, his awareness is sharpened, especially of the joys and delights of community and family life: but he has been so altered by experience that he cannot integrate properly into the community again. He remains a marginal figure, possessed by a power over which he has no control, haunted and solitary.

Certain critics, notably George Whalley, have seen in 'The Rime of the Ancient Mariner' a poem which allegorizes Coleridge's own feelings of guilt and loneliness. This has been given a psychoanalytical justification by David Beres, in 'A Dream, a Vision, and a Poem'[17]: he sees the killing of the albatross as related to Coleridge's unsatisfactory and ambivalent relationship with his mother (who is killed as the albatross and who returns as the Nightmare Life-in-Death). Others, such as Marius Bewley, have condemned the poem as sacrificing a moral theme to the dramatic excitement of the action: Coleridge's motive, he argues, 'was not substantially different from Mrs. Radcliffe's or Monk Lewis's'.[18] Certainly 'The Ancient Mariner' has affinities with the Gothic; but its ultimate significance as a poem lies not in this, nor in any theme or 'message', but in the portrayal of desperation, guilt, and loneliness. To this, as D. W. Harding has suggested, the poem directs our attention in its form. He writes of Part IV:

> This, the central experience, comes almost at the middle of
> the poem. It is the nadir of depression to which the earlier
> stanzas sink; the rest of the poem describes what is in part
> recovery and in part aftermath.[19]

Harding seems to me to be right here: the poem's form is its own journey of the mind, a going out from safety into a sea-world of unmarked and unbelievable horror, in which causeless and terrible events take place and the central figure is so marked by them that he can never be quite the same again, can never be a contented, ordinary member of society.

'The Ancient Mariner' dates from a walk which Coleridge took with William and Dorothy Wordsworth in November 1797 (indeed, it seems to have been Wordsworth, who had been reading of such things in Shelvocke's *Voyages*, who suggested the shooting of the albatross as a pivotal moment in the action). 'Kubla Khan' probably dates from the same period. Like 'The Rime of the Ancient Mariner', it depends for its effect upon a quite extraordinary power and clarity of image, and an elusive sense that the poem is concerned with areas of vital human experience. Instead of guilt and loneliness, 'Kubla Khan' is concerned with vision, with the prophetic trance-like role and the kinds of experience which it can bring, with the role of the poet-bard in a fallen world.

The circumstances of its composition and publication have already been referred to. They seem to affect the very meaning and 'feel' of the poem, so that even without knowing that Coleridge had fallen asleep while reading *Purchas his Pilgrimage* the reader might have gained the impression of an involuntary effusion, of a dream-poem which fused together elements of Coleridge's mind in a way that was quite unexpected. In 'Frost at Midnight', we can observe the stages of the travelling imagination; in 'Kubla Khan' the transitions and fusions are more mysterious and magical. The sheer beauty of the lines, the contrasting rhythms, and the relationships of parts of the poem to each other, all contribute to its total effect: it would be a mistake to talk of its 'meaning', because the poem is its irreducible self, a work of strange power and beauty. Yet it is not meaningless: it exists somewhere in the world where dreams relate to our waking life, yet are more beautiful, more exciting, and more mysterious. Kathleen Raine has pointed this out most eloquently in her article, 'Traditional Symbolism in *Kubla Khan*',[20] which relates the poem to the world of dream and symbol.

The first sentence is a good example:

> In Xanadu did Kubla Khan
> A stately pleasure-dome decree:
> Where Alph, the sacred river, ran
> Through caverns measureless to man
> Down to a sunless sea.
>
> (ll. 1–5)

According to Coleridge, he was reading the following sentence from Purchas when he fell asleep: 'In Xanadu did Cublai Can build a stately Palace.' Somehow his imagination seized upon the first five words and saw in them the dactylic possibilities of the first two lines, with the crucial word (for the poem's rhythm) 'decree':

> In Xānădŭ did Kubla Khan
> A stately Plēasŭre-dŏme decree:

As J. B. Beer points out, the memory of Milton's line in *Paradise Lost*, 'Of Cambalu, seat of Cathaian Can' involuntarily drew Coleridge's attention to the symbolic meaning of Milton's poem,[21] to ideas of the lost paradise, and to attempts to make an earthly pleasure-garden that would recapture some of the qualities of the original paradise (Coleridge would have known that the word comes from the Greek παραδεισοƒ and Old Persian *pairidaeza*, an enclosed garden or park).

Kubla's domain is a delicately drawn scene, with its gardens, trees blossoming with incense, and forests enclosing sunny spots of greenery: it is its own enclosed garden, girdled round with walls and towers, and contrasted with the landscape which follows:

> But oh! that deep romantic chasm which slanted
> Down the green hill athwart a cedarn cover!
> A savage place! as holy and enchanted
> As e'er beneath a waning moon was haunted
> By woman wailing for her demon-lover!
>
> (ll. 12–16)

The language is now entirely different. In place of the words of enclosing, 'girdled round' and 'Enfolding', the magical and primitive suggestions begin to take over. Now the place is 'savage', 'holy', 'enchanted'; instead of the cultivation of Kubla's garden, there is a new kind of wild experience, a deep chasm. It is too simple to describe this as the sublime as opposed to the beautiful, but there is an element of this contrast in it. Coleridge's imagery is opening up areas of the dream-world of the mind that are stranger and more wonderful than the enclosed garden: and the passage which follows, in which the fountain rises from the chasm, adds an excitement which is conveyed in sexual images, as if the earth were moving to some climax. The movement and excitement contrast strongly with the life within the walls and towers: now all is energetic, forced, bursting, dancing, flying through the air:

> And from this chasm, with ceaseless turmoil seething,
> As if this earth in fast thick pants were breathing,
> A mighty fountain momently was forced:
> Amid whose swift half-intermitted burst
> Huge fragments vaulted like rebounding hail,
> Or chaffy grain beneath the thresher's flail:
> And 'mid these dancing rocks at once and ever
> It flung up momently the sacred river.
>
> (ll. 17–24)

Now the precision of Kubla's pleasure-dome and its garden has disappeared. The movement of the earth, the flying fragments, and the dancing rocks, are all part of a great passionate upheaval, a profoundly shaking experience, in which the river is flung up, only to sink later 'to a lifeless ocean'.

The interpretation of the fountain is doubtful, and it should not be pressed into any specific meaning: one of the elements of greatness in 'Kubla Khan' is that the centre of it remains a mystery. But it is possible to see it as one kind of energy, a violent and daemonic energy,[22] something which is itself yet also something beyond itself. As Coleridge pointed out, in his distinction between allegory, which he saw as 'picture-language', and symbol, the latter

> is characterized by a *translucence* of the Special in the
> Individual, or of the General in the Especial, or of the
> Universal in the General; above all by the translucence of
> the Eternal through and in the Temporal. *It always*
> *partakes of the Reality which it renders intelligible*; and while
> it enunciates the whole, abides itself as a living part in that
> unity of which it is the representative.[23]

'Kubla Khan' is full of such symbols, whose meaning is elusive, and whose presence in the poem abides beyond any thematic meaning. Nevertheless, we may say that in contrast to Kubla's pleasure-dome there is another kind of energy, a powerful and momentary energy: the possibility that this is akin to poetic inspiration should not be ruled out, especially if we accept Humphry House's interpretation of the poem as 'a poem about the act of poetic creation'.[24] The poet's excitement is itself a moment of holiness and enchantment, a place and a time of joy in which he is scarcely in control of what happens. The inspiration takes over, as it does in the case of Wordsworth's breeze at the beginning of *The Prelude* that becomes 'A tempest, a redundant energy,/Vexing its own creation' (1805 text, 1. 46–47). Coleridge, like Wordsworth, is recognizing a power which has an element of danger as well as excitement in it:

> And 'mid this tumult Kubla heard from far
> Ancestral voices prophesying war!
>
> (ll. 29–30)

The 'ancestral voices' are a further puzzle in this enigmatic poem: they add to the fascination of it by suggesting a relationship between the tumult of the savage chasm and the tranquillity of the pleasure-garden. Possibly the two modes of being are complementary though opposed, a way of recovering the lost paradise through peaceful art, and another way of doing so through passion, inspiration, and nature. Then follows the surrealistic passage, in which the two appear to be unified:

> The shadow of the dome of pleasure
> Floated midway on the waves;

> Where was heard the mingled measure
> From the fountain and the caves.
> It was a miracle of rare device,
> A sunny pleasure-dome with caves of ice!
>
> (ll. 31–36)

Here after the surprising 'war!' we have a sudden tranquillity, a waterborne image of the dome of pleasure casting a shadow on the waves, and of the mingled measure: it can be seen as 'the conjunction of pleasure and sacredness', as House saw it,[25] a moment in which opposites are reconciled, the images of peace and the sounds of war.

So far the poem has been releasing its energy in different directions, in the tight garden of the pleasure-dome, the earthquake of the savage chasm, and the mingled measure. At this point Coleridge appears to go off in yet another direction, although what is actually happening is that the poem is about to be knitted together in a manner that is breathtaking. Coleridge suddenly remembers the vision of a damsel with a dulcimer, 'Singing of Mount Abora'; this is the mountain which is compared to Eden by Milton in *Paradise Lost*:

> where *Abassin* Kings thir issue Guard,
> Mount *Amara*, though this by som suppos'd
> True Paradise
>
> (IV. 280–82)

Coleridge's echo of this moment in *Paradise Lost* not only links the poem back to the Eastern inspiration of the Khan and his pleasure-dome; it is also a reminder of the great poem about paradise, and of Milton's prophetic inspiration. The last part of 'Kubla Khan' is clearly a celebration of a lyrical moment, which is of such force and beauty that it would be too holy and powerful to look upon. In turn this glances back to the description of the breaking earth, and the flinging up of the sacred river among the dancing rocks. The final section, in other words, suggests a vision which is so glorious that most people would think it dangerous: it is part of the unified pattern of the poem, that the reader is moved from a contemplation of serenity to a violent agitation of mind, an activity which is consuming and terrifying. As with the worst moment in 'The Rime of the Ancient Mariner' when we read the agony in the mariner's face from the reactions of the wedding-guest, so here we read the passion in the poet's countenance from the reactions of those around him:

> And all who heard should see them there,
> And all should cry, Beware! Beware!

His flashing eyes, his floating hair!
Weave a circle round him thrice,
And close your eyes with holy dread,
For he on honey-dew hath fed,
And drunk the milk of Paradise.

(ll. 48–54)

The poet seems here to be like some primitive figure who has to be
kept apart from society: in his holiness and sacred inspiration he seems
dangerous, inspired by a paradisal vision that most of us would find
intolerably beautiful and fearful. The final section therefore captures the
sense which is symbolically represented in the earlier part of the poem:
that there is a vision which is able to transcend the ordinary vision of
beauty and become holy, enchanted, violent, and even terrifying. And
in its last two lines this is marvellously concluded, when the poet relates
it to the recovered paradise. The poet-prophet experiences the vision
which is itself a moment of paradise, as Ezekiel saw 'visions of God':
that vision is suggested in the imagery which fills the poem, exotic,
attractive, terrifying.

'Kubla Khan', therefore, is a poem which both describes and enacts
the process of vision, the way in which poetry can possess some
person and the way in which, in that possession, he or she becomes
transformed. The poet, we remember, brings the whole soul of man
into activity, and

> diffuses a tone, and spirit of unity, that blends, and (as it
> were) *fuses*, each into each, by that synthetic and magical
> power, to which we have exclusively appropriated the
> name of imagination.[26]

'Kubla Khan', by this definition, is the most imaginative of poems: its
fusion, its synthetic and magical power, means that it is truly a 'mingled
measure', a mysterious miracle of rare device whose meaning is elusive
but whose visionary import is unmistakable. The poet of 'Kubla Khan',
like the ancient mariner, has been vouchsafed a vision of beauty and
terror, and returns from it different from other men. The result, as
Swinburne said, is a poem in which 'all the least details and delicacies
of work are worth notice when the result of them is so transcendent'.
He continues:

> Every line of the poem might be subjected to the like
> scrutiny, but the student would be none the nearer to
> the master's secret. The spirit, the odour in it, the cloven
> tongue of fire that rests upon its forehead, is a thing neither
> explicable nor communicable.[27]

Swinburne went on to describe 'Christabel' (1797–1801) as the loveliest of Coleridge's poems. Certainly it has some images of the most piercing accuracy, and observations of nature which are extremely effective. Coleridge himself, however, said that he would rather have written Wordsworth's 'Ruth' and 'Three years she grew in sun and shower' than 'a million such poems'.[28] It was, he told Southey, unsuitable for an anthology which Southey was editing because 'it would still not harmonize with the *real-life* Poems that follow'.[29] His deprecating remarks about the poem contrast with the very real pleasure he must have obtained from the Wordsworths' applause for it, and with his trouble in transcribing a copy for Lady Beaumont 'to do the thing in a handsome way to her Ladyship'.[30] These disparate feelings about the poem reflect an ambivalence which can still be felt: there is so much brilliant imagery, the superb catching of an atmosphere of foreboding, and yet there are also elements which seem stagey and Gothic, and a plot which is fragmentary and incomplete.

Of all these qualities the one which stands out is the creation of atmosphere. The setting, the staging, the properties of the poem are among the finest things that Coleridge ever did, for they have just the right quality of suggestiveness. When he writes

> The night is chill, the cloud is gray:
> 'Tis a month before the month of May,
> And the Spring comes slowly up this way.
>
> (ll. 20–22)

the sense of a certain kind of weather, of the rawness of winter's end, links with the northern-ness of 'up this way'; its coldness and remoteness links up with the owls and the moon, the toothless mastiff bitch in its kennel beneath the rock, Sir Leoline the Baron, and the thin grey cloud. All these impressions suggest a far-off land, in place and in time: it is in this landscape that the figure of Christabel is found, strangely vulnerable 'a furlong from the castle gate' and stealing out to pray 'for the weal of her lover that's far away'. The sounds of the night surround her as she steals along, and the mastiff bitch howls, some say, because 'she sees my lady's shroud', the shroud in which Christabel's mother lies. It is important to establish the loneliness and vulnerability of Christabel at this point. With a mother dead, a father weak in health, and a lover far away, she is defenceless in the night forest when she hears a groan; so the cry 'Jesu, Maria, shield her well!' is very appropriate.

There is something sinister about the figure of Geraldine, 'beautiful exceedingly' and distressed; as she is lifted over the threshold by Christabel she seems to gain strength, as something evil might do when admitted by the good. This is confirmed when the mastiff bitch moans and the light flickers as Geraldine passes by, and made explicit when Geraldine drives off the guardian spirit who is Christabel's mother. From this point onward, Geraldine seems to be completely in control of Christabel, in a way which is at first disquieting and then terrifying: at her command Christabel undresses and gets into bed, and then watches as the lady herself strips:

> Behold! her bosom and half her side –
> A sight to dream of, not to tell!
> O shield her! shield sweet Christabel!
>
> (ll. 252–54)

Whatever the horror here, like the look on the ancient mariner's face, it is the more effective for being undescribed and unspecific. So when Geraldine takes Christabel in her arms, and touches her, there is an immediate and frightening piece of thought-control. All Christabel will be able to recount is, Geraldine tells her,

> That in the dim forest
>   Thou heard'st a low moaning,
> And found'st a bright lady, surpassingly fair;
> And didst bring her home with thee in love and in charity,
> To shield her and shelter her from the damp air.
>
> (ll. 274–78)

The breaking-off at this point is very dramatic. From the moment of being rescued, Geraldine has steadily gained an ascendancy over Christabel, has exploited her natural goodness, and now seems to have taken the place of Christabel's mother, like some kind of evil surrogate. In this strange ballad-like atmosphere, good seems to be giving way to evil; Coleridge said at one point that Crashaw's verses on St Theresa beginning:

> Since 'tis not to be had at home
> She'l travel to a martyrdome

'were ever present to my mind whilst writing the second part of Christabel; if, indeed by some subtle process of the mind they did not suggest the first thought of the whole poem'.[31] Christabel is, of course, at home: but in other respects she endures a kind of martyrdom in which, in Part II, Geraldine charms her father and isolates Christabel. The Bard Bracy's dream of the snake killing the dove, which we apply to Geraldine and Christabel, is wrongly interpreted by Sir Leoline as applying to the capturers and Geraldine: and at this point Christabel sees clearly the snake-eye. Her reaction is a powerful piece of dramatic irony, entirely comprehensible to the reader but outrageous to Sir Leoline and to all the traditional laws of hospitality that he knows. He is ashamed of her apparent lack of generosity, seeing it only as dishonourable; and turning from Christabel, he leads out Geraldine.

The poem ends at this point, apart from the enigmatic lines on the little child which forms the coda to Part II. They refer to Coleridge himself, and his delight in his little child, Hartley. They refer, too, to a strange paradox of loving attention:

> pleasures flow in so thick and fast
> Upon his heart, that he at last
> Must needs express his love's excess
> With words of unmeant bitterness.
>
> (ll. 662–65)

This may have affinities with Sir Leoline's anger with Christabel, but I am inclined to think that they go deeper, to a difficulty which Coleridge was painfully wrestling with at this time, the coexistence in his mind of love and anger, and the reciprocal action between them, so that the more one loved a person the more likely one was to be involuntarily angry with him for not living up to the ideal. This was a difficult period for Coleridge: the struggle to finish 'Christabel', and its rejection by Wordsworth for the second edition of *Lyrical Ballads*, were accompanied by emotional and financial problems.[32] It is possible, therefore, that the reference to the 'unmeant bitterness' of the father in the 'Conclusion' is a parallel to the sense of possession of Christabel by Geraldine: as Christabel is powerless in the face of such strength, especially after it has been carried across the threshold, so the poet, and all human beings, are possessed by something in them that can turn even parental love into rage and pain. Another notebook entry suggests the same preoccupation: a Greek quotation from Josephus is concerned with 'the spirits of wicked men which enter the living'. The victims can be cured only by the application of the root of rue, and Kathleen Coburn suggests that Coleridge may have seen this as a possible way to an ending of 'Christabel'. Certainly it points, as the 'Conclusion' does, to a kind of 'possession', and Professor Coburn provides several references to the subject of daemoniacs, good men possessed by the spirits of wicked men.[33]

The outcome of the first two parts of the poem seems a clear enough triumph of evil over good. But how evil is Geraldine? At one point she seems to have benevolent instincts, telling Christabel:

'All they who live in the upper sky,
Do love you, holy Christabel!
And you love them, and for their sake
And for the good which me befel
Even I in my degree will try,
Fair maiden, to requite you well.
But now unrobe yourself; for I
Must pray, ere yet in bed I lie.'

(ll. 227–34)

Either Geraldine is untruthful here, or she is seeing her visitation to Christabel as having some ultimately benevolent effect. It has been argued[34] that Geraldine comes to rescue Christabel from a disabling innocence, and that Christabel will be stronger from the encounter, especially when she is reunited with the lover for whom she is praying. Various accounts exist of how Coleridge intended to continue the poem, none of them particularly satisfactory[35]; but there does seem to have been an awareness of the paradox that good without evil is (as Blake saw) not fully good. Geraldine can therefore be seen as performing a necessary office, and her whole nature as ambivalent. Beneath the 'Conclusion' of the poem (and the conduct of the whole story) may lie Coleridge's problems: his conflict between his duty as a husband and father and his love for Sara Hutchinson, whom he had met in 1799, and who became a devoted member of the Wordsworth household when William married her sister Mary in 1802. The struggle, suppressed for so long beneath Coleridge's notebook descriptions of Lake District scenery and his voluminous philosophical and scientific reading, bursts out in the verse 'Letter to Sara Hutchinson' of 4 April 1802. There he describes how distress, misfortunes, and ill tidings turn him from his true nature:

each Visitation
Suspends what Nature gave me at my Birth,
My shaping Spirit of Imagination!

(ll. 240–42)

And while Coleridge can imagine a hope for Christabel, in the unfinished schemes of the poem, the 'Letter to Sara Hutchinson' sees hope for Sara but not for the poet. As George Dekker has written, 'She epitomizes everything that is missing from his own domestic life'[36] and the poem vividly emphasizes Coleridge's doctrine that the imagination is 'essentially *vital*':

O Sara! we receive but what we give,
And in *our* Life alone does Nature live.

> Our's is her Wedding Garment, our's her Shroud –
> And would we aught behold of higher Worth
> Than that inanimate cold World allow'd
> To the poor loveless ever-anxious Crowd,
> Ah! from the Soul itself must issue forth
> A Light, a Glory, and a luminous Cloud
>   Enveloping the Earth!
>   (ll. 296–304)

Because of his own distress, Coleridge finds that he cannot respond
to the beauty of the natural scene. He can see, but not feel: the eye,
which Wordsworth described in *The Prelude* as 'the most despotic of
our senses' (1805, XI. 173) is active, but the feelings are dead:

> All this long Eve, so balmy & serene,
> Have I been gazing on the western Sky
> And it's peculiar Tint of Yellow Green –
> And still I gaze – & with how blank an eye!
> And those thin Clouds above, in flakes & bars,
> That give away their Motion to the Stars;
> Those Stars, that glide behind them, or between
> Now sparking, now bedimm'd, but always seen;
> Yon crescent Moon, as fix'd as if it grew
> In it's own cloudless, starless Lake of Blue –
> A boat becalm'd! dear William's Sky Canoe!
> – I see them all, so excellently fair!
> I see, not feel, how beautiful they are.
>   (ll. 31–43)

The sky canoe is a reference to the Prologue to Wordsworth's *Peter
Bell*, in which Wordsworth jocularly imagines a journey through the
stars and clouds in a boat shaped like a crescent moon. Coleridge's
mind, on seeing the moon and stars, naturally remembered the peculiar
imaginative confidence of the opening of *Peter Bell*, if only because it
contrasted with his own sense of failure. Indeed one of the complex
emotional strands which go to make up the poem may be a comparison
with Wordsworth: when Coleridge considered the valleys, woods, and
lakes, he used a line from the 'Immortality Ode':

> But oft I seem to feel, & evermore I fear,
> They are not to me now the Things, which once they were.
>   (ll. 294–95)

The relationship between the two poems is difficult to determine exactly, but I accept Mark Reed's dating of the first four stanzas of the 'Immortality Ode' on 27 March 1802[37]; Coleridge's letter, therefore, with its despairing self-portrait, is not a response, as is sometimes thought, to the whole of the 'Immortality Ode' but to that part which ends

> Whither is fled the visionary gleam?
> Where is it now, the glory and the dream?
> (ll. 56–57)

Wordsworth, it is true, was making great poetry out of his sense of loss; but Coleridge's 'Letter', and its subsequent transformation into 'Dejection: an Ode', should be seen as complementary to Wordsworth's poem rather than in opposition to it.[38] Coleridge is going much further than Wordsworth, characteristically being more intense and self-regarding. The interaction between the self and the external world now only serves to illuminate the face of failure: Coleridge in the 'Letter' is painting yet another self-portrait, of a man whose energy has gone, whose ability to respond has disappeared. The sacred river, the fountain image of 'Kubla Khan' is now lifeless:

> I may not hope from outward Forms to win
> The Passion and the Life, whose Fountains are within!
> (ll. 50–51)

The reasons for this are given at various points in the poem, in a way which is so explicit as to be embarrassing:

> My own peculiar Lot, my house-hold Life
> It is, & will remain, Indifference or Strife –
>
>   my coarse domestic Life has known
> No Habits of heart-nursing Sympathy,
> No Griefs, but such as dull and deaden me,
> No mutual mild Enjoyments of it's own,
> No Hopes of its own Vintage. None, O! none –
> (ll. 164–65, 258–62)

In this way the 'Letter' is the most self-revealing of Romantic poems. Coleridge sees himself as an Aeolian harp, but one which 'better far were mute', since it is blown upon by the winds of the approaching storm and it gives out harsh music.

And yet the poem is not all self-pity and potential embarrassment. It is saved by a certain heroism, in which Coleridge, overwhelmed though he is by his marriage problems, can still write a love poem to

Sara Hutchinson, and can conclude with a vision of the radiant earth
in harmony with her life and joy:

> To thee would all Things live from Pole to Pole,
> Their Life the Eddying of thy living Soul. –
> O dear! O Innocent! O full of Love!
> A very Friend! A Sister of my Choice –
> O dear, as Light & Impulse from above,
> Thus may'st thou ever, evermore rejoice!
>
> (ll. 335–40)

The adaptation of the 340 lines of the 'Letter' into the 139 lines of
'Dejection: An Ode' is a process which yields a very different kind
of poem. In some respects the shortening leads to a more economical
and austere poem, with less of the incidental detail and conversational
reminiscence: in others it produces a poem which is less arresting,
because Coleridge's problems are buried in the discreet reticence of
'now afflictions bow me down to earth'. It is best not to try to compare
them, but to regard one as a verse letter and the other as an example of
what M. H. Abrams calls 'the greater Romantic lyric'.[39] In this reading
'Dejection' becomes a public possession in a way that the verse letter can
never be: it functions in a different manner, and is developed, as George
Dekker has shown, from the eighteenth-century ode and conversation
poem. It still possesses the pulsing note of personal experience, but in
this version the grief is an unspecified though powerful presence which
has destroyed the poet's power to appreciate nature. The 'Aeolian lute'
of the first verse becomes a general image for the nature-poet, affected
by everything around him and responsive to the wild weather that is
increasing throughout the poem. As in 'Christabel', the atmosphere of
the scene is extremely effective, beginning with the sinister picture of
the new moon 'with the old moon in her arm'. This was a prelude to
disaster in the old ballad of Sir Patrick Spens, and it suggests disaster
now, though the poet argues that anything would be better than the
fixed expression of his current mood. The structural pattern of the
poem is alternate: Grief-Joy-Grief-Joy. After the initial description of
his own uncreative despair, the poet turns naturally to the alternative,
unrealizable by him but known to the 'Lady':

> Ah! from the soul itself must issue forth
> A light, a glory, a fair luminous cloud
>   Enveloping the Earth –
>   (ll. 53–55)

The imagery of light emphasizes the oppositions through which this poem works, contrasting grief and joy, 'the poet' and 'the lady', darkness and light, death and life, sterility and creativity. At the centre of it all, the key to the whole process, is the image of the 'great consummation' which Wordsworth was to use at the end of 'Home at Grasmere' (and as the Preface to *The Excursion*), of the creative interaction between the kind of man and the natural world:

> Joy, Lady! is the spirit and the power,
> Which wedding Nature to us gives in dower
>   A new Earth and new Heaven,
>   Undreamt of by the sensual and the proud –
>
> (ll. 67–71)

While Wordsworth sees this as the recovery of the lost paradise, Coleridge sees it in the imagery of the young idealist, the supporter of the French Revolution, the creator of the new heaven and new earth, the enthusiastic supporter of Pantisocracy. The poet is turning the knife in his own wound: for although he knows that nature works with 'us' and 'We in ourselves rejoice', the next section (VI) makes it clear that he is himself no longer able to engage in such hope. It is the darkest section of the poem, given more poignancy by the remembrance of an earlier life of idealism and hope. It is Coleridge's version of *Samson Agonistes*, though with an opening phrase from Wordsworth:

> There was a time when, though my path was rough,
>   This joy within me dallied with distress,
> And all misfortunes were but as the stuff
>   Whence Fancy made me dreams of happiness:
> For hope grew round me, like the twining vine,
> And fruits, and foliage, not my own, seemed mine.
> But now afflictions bow me down to earth. . . .
>
> (ll. 76–82)

The recovery from this section of the poem, the banishing of the snake-thoughts that coil around my mind' (a recurrence of the image of the snake and bird from 'Christabel') provides the only distraction from the beautifully poised oppositions of the rest of the poem. It could be said that the lute, which gives out a scream of torture, is an emblem of the poet's own mind; and certainly the listening to the wind returns the attention to the weather of the first section. But the comparison of the wind to a mad lutenist making a Devils' yule in April is unnecessary, and so is the remainder of this section, with its descriptions of two tales, one of a battle and the other of a lost child. George Dekker has argued that this (which he calls 'the "sublime" cadenza') meant more to Coleridge and his contemporaries than it does to a twentieth-century reader,[40] but his defence is surely too generous. In the poem's delicate balance between hope and despair, this section is an awkward interruption, a cliché-ridden idea of a 'mighty Poet, e'en to frenzy bold'. Only after this frenzy does the poem again touch the intimate, delicate note:

> 'Tis midnight, but small thoughts have I of sleep:
> Full seldom may my friend such vigils keep!
>
> (ll. 126–27)

and the final blessing moves out brilliantly from the personal to the universal and back to the personal again:

> May all the stars hang bright above her dwelling,
>   Silent as though they watched the sleeping Earth!
>   With light heart may she rise,
>   Gay fancy, cheerful eyes,
>   Joy lift her spirit, joy attune her voice;
> To her may all things live, from pole to pole,
> Their life the eddying of her living soul!
>   O simple spirit, guided from above,
> Dear Lady! friend devoutest of my choice,
> Thus mayst thou ever, evermore rejoice.
>
> (ll. 130–39)

'Dejection: an Ode' is a watershed in Coleridge's poetry. Before it lies the hope of 'Frost at Midnight' and the magic of 'Kubla Khan'; after it the shame of 'The Pains of Sleep', the awful cry of 'The Blossoming of the Solitary Date-Tree':

> Why was I made for Love and Love denied to me?
>
> (l. 80)

and the sense of sterility in the poem written to Wordsworth after the latter had recited the poem on the growth of his own mind later entitled *The Prelude*. Once again, as with 'Dejection', Coleridge's self-pity goes hand in hand with an endearing recognition of others; so Wordsworth's poem is 'an Orphic song' (Coleridge himself having abandoned the role of Orpheus) and his poem is more than historic, 'that prophetic Lay'. In these lines, Coleridge gets to the heart of Wordsworth's poem with a sharp immediacy: it is a poem of the inner life of the poet, but also

> of the Social Sense
> Distending wide, and man beloved as man
>
> (ll. 27–28)

and especially with regard to the great event of the French Revolution, of its hopes and

> Of that dear Hope afflicted and struck down
> (l. 38)

leading to the final theme of duty. Coleridge perceived at once that the poem had its own architecture, building up into a 'linkéd lay of Truth' from 'her own natural notes'. It is at this point that Coleridge is unable to resist the comparison with himself: that he could not do so tells us a great deal about him as a poet. Again and again his work is enthusiastic, engaged with the world, full of hope and interest, theorizing, admiring, loving; but accompanying this is his introspection, his self-pity, his expressions of unhappiness. The reader comes across these with (I suggest) a mixture of compassion and exasperation: Coleridge's very openness is part of his vulnerability and is endearing, but it is also intrusive. Here he turns the experience of hearing Wordsworth's poem into a painful one: he is making a hell in heaven's despite, as Blake would have said, by being unable to escape from the imprisonment of his own self. The joy of hearing Wordsworth's poem addressed to himself was like being given new life, but

> Life's joy rekindling roused a throng of pains –
> (l. 64)

The rebirth is cruel and painful, for in the end it becomes only a reminder of the death-in-life which Coleridge is leading. Among the 'throng of pains' are

> Hope that scarce would know itself from Fear;
> Sense of past Youth, and Manhood come in vain,
> And Genius given, and Knowledge won in vain;
> And all which I had culled in wood-walks wild,
> And all which patient toil had reared, and all,
> Commune with thee had opened out – but flowers
> Strewed on my corse, and borne upon my bier,
> In the same coffin, for the self-same grave!
> (ll. 68–75)

The moment of the reading, 7 January 1807, was a significant one. Coleridge had just returned from an absence of more than two years, which he had hoped would send him 'back to dear old England, a sample of the first Resurrection'.[41] He seemed to have had some hope that his marital and personal problems would somehow have sorted themselves out, and that his health would have improved in a drier and warmer climate. But the stay in Malta and the return through Italy were powerless to cure the deep-seated problems, and during the years that followed he continued to be hopelessly in love with Sara Hutchinson; the Latin poem 'Ad Vilmum Axiologum' (to William Wordsworth) implies that Wordsworth tried to warn him off, and this may have been one element in the misunderstanding which led to the break between the two poets in 1810.

Much of Coleridge's finest prose work, his best lecturing, and the performances of his plays date from the following years. His poetry, however, is occasional and fragmentary, the perception of a moment; it is sometimes whimsical, but more often despairing. In 'Youth and Age' he reflects

> When I was young? – Ah, woful When!
> Ah! for the change 'twixt Now and Then!
>> (ll. 6–7)

and his images for his own condition are often memorable, single reminders of the buoyant magic of earlier years. So 'Work without Hope' (composed 21 February 1825) ends:

> Work without Hope draws nectar in a sieve,
> And Hope without an object cannot live.
>> (ll. 13–14)

Similarly in the 'Song' of around that date Coleridge likens love to a sword

> By rust consumed or snapt in twain:
> And only hilt and stump remain.
>> (ll. 7–8)

The condition of being loveless, and without hope, shows Coleridge in a pitiable state: he becomes a type of the penitent and helpless man of evangelical religious teaching, dependent on God, as poems such as 'My Baptismal Birth-Day' suggest. And, in addition to the consolations of religion, he attempts to find other associated comforts. In 'The Improvisatore' hope has gone, but

> The certainty that struck Hope dead,
> Hath left Contentment in her stead:
>> And that is next to Best!
>> (ll. 65–67)

and in the 1829 poem, 'Love, Hope, and Patience in Education', the final lines suggest that Patience remains when Love and Hope are gone. The frightening image of these lines is that of Patience as a statue, mute, smiling, and strong; this is so different from the living, breathing energy of Coleridge's earlier nature poetry that it is a consolation only in name:

> Yet haply there will come a weary day,
>   When overtask'd at length
> Both Love and Hope beneath the load give way.
> Then with a statue's smile, a statue's strength,
> Stands the mute sister, Patience, nothing loth,
> And both supporting does the work of both.
>
>   (ll. 21–26)

Coleridge's image is doubtless derived from Viola's speech in *Twelfth Night*, in which the hopeless lover

>   sat like Patience on a monument
>   Smiling at grief.
>   (II. 4. 122–23)

and Coleridge's own capacity to smile at his own condition is nowhere better seen than in his 'Epitaph'. In lines such as

>   Beneath this sod
>   A poet lies, or that which once seem'd he;
>   (ll. 2–3)

we sense the slight comicality of some epitaphs,[42] which is taken up by Coleridge in order to give it a deeper and more serious meaning. He really did seem to have promise, now dissipated; so the joke dies away on the reader's lips. So too the comic rhyme of the next line

>   O, lift one thought in prayer for S.T.C.;
>   (l. 4)

is a piece of amused and amusing self-reference that overlays the very real need for prayer. Then come the neat antitheses of line 6:

> That he who many a year with toil of breath
> Found death in life, may here find life in death!
>   (ll. 5–6)

The art seems almost to take over, to shape out the seriousness; and yet the reader suddenly becomes aware that Coleridge is reviewing his life, and seeing all of the last part of it – certainly the years since 1810 and the parting from Sara Hutchinson – as really a death-in-life, a condition like that of the ancient mariner, condemned to live on.

The epitaph begins with a call to the passer-by to stop 'and read with gentle breast'. It is a cry which is appropriate to much of Coleridge's poetry, because his openness makes him so vulnerable. He is a poet of an extraordinary charm because of this: of all the Romantic poets he is the one who most often allows himself to be caught in situations where he could well seem ridiculous – being reprimanded by his wife for having original thoughts about nature, sitting in a lime-tree bower with a scalded foot. Except in 'Kubla Khan' (and there the 'Could I revive within me' is ambiguous), he declines to be prophetic. And perhaps because of this refusal to adopt the role of the great individual seer, Coleridge succeeds in responding to and re-creating the elusive magic of certain kinds of experience; the haunting qualities of 'The Rime of the Ancient Mariner' (praised by the painter Constable as 'the very best modern poem'[43]), of 'Christabel' and of 'Kubla Khan' make them the most mysterious yet also the most memorable of all Romantic poems.

Notes

1. Coleridge to John Thelwall, 19 November 1796; *Collected Letters of Samuel Taylor Coleridge*, edited by E. L. Griggs, 6 vols (Oxford, 1956–71), I, 259.

2. *Collected Letters*, I, 96.

3. *Collected Letters* I, 184–85.

4. *Collected Letters* I, 188.

5. But see Alethea Hayter, *Opium and the Romantic Imagination* (London, 1968), Ch. 9.

6. Quoted by Mary Jacobus, in *Tradition and Experiment in Wordsworth's Lyrical Ballads (1798)* (Oxford, 1976), pp. 44–45.

7. Jacobus p. 48.

8. M. H. Abrams has related this, however, to Coleridge's attempts to unite scientific phenomena in one great natural science. See 'Coleridge's "A Light in Sound": Science, Metascience, and Poetic Imagination', *Proceedings of the American Philosophical Society*, 116 (1972), 458–76.

9. *Biographia Literaria*, edited by James Engell and W. J. Bate (London, 1983), II, 5 (Ch. XIV).

10. *Collected Letters*, I, 334.

11. See the chapter on 'Domesticity and Retirement in Coleridge's Poetry', in Kelvin Everest, *Coleridge's Secret Ministry* (Hassocks, Sussex, 1979).

12. Quoted in *Inquiring Spirit*, edited by Kathleen Coburn (London, 1951), p. 37.

13. *Inquiring Spirit*, p. 40.

14. *Table Talk*, 31 May 1830.

15. See the contrary views, among others, of Robert Penn Warren, 'A Poem of Pure Imagination', in *Selected Essays* (London, 1964); and Edward E. Bostetter, 'The Nightmare World of the Ancient Mariner', *Studies in Romanticism*, 1 (1962), pp. 351–98.

16. George Whalley, 'The Mariner and the Albatross', *University of Toronto Quarterly*, 16 (1946–47), pp. 381–98.

17. David Beres, 'A Dream, A Vision, and a Poem: a psychoanalytic study of the origins of *The Rime of the Ancient Mariner*', *International Journal of Psychoanalysis*, 32 (1951), pp. 97–116.

18. Marius Bewley, 'The Poetry of Coleridge', *Scrutiny*, 8 (1940), pp. 406–20.

19. D. W. Harding, 'The Theme of "The Ancient Mariner"', *Scrutiny*, 9 (1941), pp. 334–42.

20. Kathleen Raine, 'Traditional Symbolism in *Kubla Khan*', *Sewanee Review*, 72 (1964), pp. 626–42.

21. See J. B. Beer's Everyman edition (revised) of Coleridge's *Poems* (London, 1974), p. 165.

22. See J. B. Beer, *Coleridge the Visionary* (London, 1959), p. 237.

23. 'The Statesman's Manual', in *Lay Sermons*, edited by R. J. White (London, 1972), p. 30 (*Collected Works of Samuel Taylor Coleridge*, Vol. 6); quoted in this context by Elisabeth Schneider, in *Coleridge, Opium and 'Kubla Khan'* (Chicago, 1953), p. 257.

24. Humphry House, *Coleridge* (London, 1953), p. 118.

25. House, p. 119.

26. *Biographia Literaria*, II, 16 (Ch. XIV).

27. A. C. Swinburne, 'Coleridge', *Essays and Studies* (London, 1875); reprinted in *The Ancient Mariner and other Poems*, edited by Alun R. Jones and William Tydeman (London, 1973), pp. 85–95.

28. Coleridge to Humphry Davy, 9 October 1800; *Collected Letters*, I, 631–32.

29. Coleridge to Southey, 10 November 1799; *Collected Letters*, I, 545.

30. Coleridge to John Rickman 17 March 1804; *Collected Letters*, II, 1095.

31. *Letters, Conversations and Recollections of S. T. Coleridge*, edited by Thomas Allsop (London, 1864), pp. 104–05.

32. See Notebook entry 834 and note 901 and note *The Notebooks of Samuel Taylor Coleridge*, edited by Kathleen Coburn (London, 1962–).

33. Note to entry 851.

34. See two articles by Macdonald Emslie and Paul Edwards: 'The Limitations of Langdale: a reading of "Christabel"', *Essays in Criticism*, 20 (1970), 57–70, and '"Thoughts so all unlike each other": the paradoxical in "Christabel"', *English Studies*, 52, (1971), pp. 236–46.

35. See J. B. Beer, *Coleridge the Visionary* (London, 1959), pp. 176–77, 187–88.

36. George Dekker, *Coleridge and the Literature of Sensibility* (London, 1978), p. 23.

37. Mark Reed, *Wordsworth, The Chronology of the Middle Years*, 1800–1815 (Cambridge, Mass., 1975), p. 156.

38. Wordsworth may have composed stanzas v–viii on 17 June 1802, before Coleridge published 'Dejection' on 4 October, but this does not affect the argument, since the consolatory conclusion was still to come. Stephen Prickett, in *Coleridge and Wordsworth, The Poetry of Growth* (Cambridge, 1970), discusses the relationship between the two poems. See also Lucy Newlyn, *Coleridge, Wordsworth, and the Language of Allusion* (Oxford, 1986).

39. M. H. Abrams, 'Structure and Style in the Greater Romantic Lyric', in *From Sensibility to Romanticism*, edited by F. W. Hilles and H. Bloom (New York, 1965), pp. 527–60.

40. George Dekker, *Coleridge and the Literature of Sensibility* (London, 1978), pp. 239–40.

41. Alethea Hayter, *A Voyage in Vain* (London, 1973), p. 18.

42. Coleridge and Wordsworth were both deeply interested in epitaphs and inscriptions on tombstones. See the Introduction to Wordsworth's three *Essays on Epitaphs* (the first of which was published in Coleridge's *The Friend* in 1810) in *The Prose Works of William Wordsworth*, edited by W. J. B. Owen and J. W. Smyser (Oxford, 1974), II, 45.

43. *John Constable's Correspondence, VI, The Fishers*, edited by R. B. Beckett (Ipswich, 1968), p. 186.

Between the Acts: 1812

It is customary to speak of the first- and second-generation Romantic poets, although the two overlap. It is, of course, impossible to point to any single moment and say

> 'Tis well an old age is out
> And time to begin a new . . .

Just as it is impossible to imagine the Romantic movement through the eyes of those who took part in it, except with the hindsight of literary history and the convenience of cultural labels. However, there is one significant change between the conditions in which the first-generation Romantic poets wrote and those in which their successors, Byron, Keats and Shelley, wrote *Don Juan*, *Hyperion*, or *Prometheus Unbound*. This was the failure of the French Revolution. As Hazlitt, for one, was never tired of emphasizing, the French Revolution had come and gone by 1800: its catastrophic course, and the consequences of that course, made the world seem a very different place in 1810 from the Europe of 1789.

The French Revolution looms so large in the poetry of Wordsworth, Blake, and Coleridge, and in the consciousness of Shelley (who tried to excuse it in the Preface to *The Revolt of Islam*) that it is not always easy to remember that it was one spectacular event among many changes. There were underlying shifts of social and industrial structure which were largely unaffected by the events in France, although the war which followed had serious consequences for the British economy. The forces for social change were present in the growth and development of industry, and in the enclosure system, which has already been briefly referred to in Chapter 3.

In the present interlude between two generations of poets, I wish to focus primarily on the year 1812: it was a year of some importance, later made famous by Tchaikovsky in his Overture '1812' saluting the defeat of Napoleon and the emergence of a Russian pride and confidence; it was also, as we shall see, a year of some importance in the world of English literature. But 1812 must also be seen as one year in a continuum, and in that continuum there occurred the Industrial Revolution, roughly from about 1760 to about 1830. Its beginnings have been briefly mentioned in Chapter 3, when it was noted that Abraham Darby's iron bridge was dated 1779, and Richard Arkwright was setting up spinning mills at Cromford in 1771. The great Carron Ironworks in the Clyde Valley, which Burns facetiously likened to the fires of Hell, began work in 1760. These developments, and others like them, succeeded because there was capital to finance the building of factories and the employment of workers, and the result was an economic system which was much more complex than the earlier one. Instead of working to grow food for himself and his family, the labourer worked to get money to buy food, and thus became subject to economic misfortunes caused by unemployment or bad harvests, as well as enjoying periods of relative prosperity.

A primary cause of this was the enclosure system. J. L. and Barbara Hammond began their classic study, *The Village Labourer* (1911), with the sentence: 'At the time of the great Whig revolution, England was in the main a country of commons and of common fields; at the time of the Reform Bill, England was in the main a country of individualist agriculture and of large or medium-sized farms.'[1] The Hammonds saw this as part of a process, in which the enclosure system led to impoverishment of the rural poor, which in turn led to the riots of the 1830s, violent outbursts from people who had nothing to lose. Similarly, the Hammonds' companion study, *The Town Labourer* (1917), suggested that the development of machinery could have been used for the good of society, but was instead exploited for the benefit of a few enterprising capitalists. This view of the Industrial Revolution was developed by E. P. Thompson in *The Making of the English Working Class* (1963), which argued that between 1790 and 1840 'there was a slight improvement in average material standards' but that at the same time 'there was intensified exploitation, greater insecurity, and increasing human misery'.[2]

Thompson's argument is an attempt to make sense of the evidence, which is abundant and sometimes conflicting. As he points out,

> It is at times as if statisticians have been arguing: 'the indices reveal an increased *per capita* consumption of tea, sugar, meat and soap, *therefore* the working class was happier', while social historians have replied: 'the literary sources show that people were unhappy, *therefore* their standard-of-living must have deteriorated'.[3]

Thompson is certainly right about literary sources, as we shall see. His and the Hammonds' view of the miseries attendant upon the Industrial

Revolution has not gone unchallenged, however, for other economic historians such as T. S. Ashton and G. E. Mingay have stressed the increased production of food consequent upon enclosures and the new opportunities provided by improved travel, movement of goods, and chances of work.[4]

Certain things seem to be clear. The long war with France, which lasted with only two short breaks from 1793 to 1815 sent up prices, and made exports and imports more difficult. When there were bad harvests, the farmers held on to their money, or had none to spend, and this led to a stagnation of trade, which in turn led to a falling of wages and to the laying-off of workmen. There were bad harvests from 1799 to 1801, in 1804 and 1805, and again in the years from 1809 to 1813. The anger and frustration of workers led to anti-government conspiracies, frame-breaking riots and other violent outbreaks, and these fuelled fears that a Revolution, similar to that in France, was about to start in Britain. And in all these matters, whether in the country or the city, it was the poor who suffered. The Speenhamland system of 1795, so named after the village near Newbury in Berkshire where it was conceived, attempted to help the poor by giving relief when the price of bread was high: the result was that agricultural employers kept the wages low, and created a pauper class, existing on the minimum that was needed to support a family. It was this pauperism and misery that led writers such as Malthus to criticize poor relief, on the grounds that it increased the numbers of those who were unable to provide for themselves. Malthus's controversial *Essay on the Principles of Population* (1798) forecast an increase in population without a corresponding increase in food to support it, and argued that checks on the growth of population, such as famine, disease, and war, had to remain. To Malthus it seemed folly to provide relief for the poor, because it encouraged improvidence.

Malthus was writing in opposition to the benevolent optimism of writers such as Godwin and the French philosopher Condorcet, both of whom hoped for a fairer and more equitable society. All three writers were struggling to influence political economy in an era of uncertainty and instability; but it was the poets who used individual case-histories as their material. Any accident or illness, or war, or an economic recession, could prove disastrous to those who were surviving on such a fragile family economy, and in *The Excursion* Wordsworth describes the destruction of a family through just such a combination of circumstances: two bad harvests in succession, war, illness, followed by depression and inability to work. Similarly, Clare (as we have seen) attacked enclosures with a ferocity of imagery and a directness which came from bitter experience; and Byron, speaking in the House of Lords in 1812 during his brief period of interest in politics, allied himself with the Radicals in supporting the frame-breakers of Nottingham (near his own seat of Newstead). Fresh from his travels in the near East, he shocked the House of Lords by questioning the morality of a supposedly Christian society: 'I have been in some of the most oppressed provinces of Turkey; but never under the most despotic of infidel governments did I behold such squalid wretchedness as I have seen since my return in the very heart of a Christian country.'[5]

The Industrial Revolution had other consequences beside poverty. In some parts of the country families were able to support themselves by sending each member to work in the mines or factories, the women and children carrying coal that had been cut by the men, or working in shifts in factories that continued day and night. In the earliest factories, the power to run the looms had depended on water, so that they were built beside fast-flowing rivers, but the coming of steam power meant that the factories could be built anywhere. In them, human beings became the servants of the machines, rather than the other way round. As Phyllis Deane has pointed out:

> The factories used full-time labour which stayed at the
> machines as long as the machines were turning, which
> was as long as there was a demand for their products.
> While they depended on water-power there were seasonal
> interruptions in their operations, but when steam-power
> was introduced, and still more when gas was employed
> to light the factories day and night, only trade depression
> stopped them.[6]

Wordsworth's character in *The Excursion*, the Wanderer, describes such a scene, as the night-shift takes over:

> Then, in full many a region, once like this
> The assured domain of calm simplicity
> And pensive quiet, an unnatural light
> Prepared for never-resting Labour's eyes
> Breaks from a many-windowed fabric huge;
> And at the appointed hour a bell is heard,
> Of harsher import than the curfew-knell
> That spake the Norman Conqueror's stern behest –
> A local summons to unceasing toil!
> Disgorged are now the ministers of day;
> And, as they issue from the illumined pile,
> A fresh band meets them, . . .
>   men, maidens, youths,
> Mothers and little children, boys and girls,

Enter, and each the wonted task resumes
Within this temple, where is offered up
To Gain, the master-idol of the realm,
Perpetual sacrifice.

(*The Excursion*, VIII. 165–76, 179–85)

The Wanderer's argument is that this destroys 'the old domestic morals
of the land', and the whole passage is intended to draw attention not
so much to poverty as to the loss of the quality of life. It is a direct
response to the passage, written before the Industrial Revolution,
in James Thomson's *The Seasons*, which celebrates 'Industry, rough
power' which

labour still attends, and sweat, and pain;
Yet the kind source of every gentle art
And all the soft civility of life . . .

('Autumn', 44–6)

Wordsworth's view is clearly the kind of thing which E. P. Thompson
has in mind when he speaks of 'literary evidence' of exploitation and
misery. There is a note of anger in the Wanderer's description of gain,
and this section of *The Excursion* is an example – as indeed the whole
poem is – of a Romantic poet's struggling with the political, economic,
and sociological difficulties of the age.

1812 was a turning-point year; yet it also displays many of the
problems which I have been discussing in this interlude. It was one
in which the shift of political events and ideologies can be observed
with particular clarity, but where the underlying discontents can also
be found. The harvest of 1811 was a poor one, and throughout 1812 there
was a scarcity of bread in England (and in France and Spain). In January
there were reports of frame-breaking in the Midlands, principally around
Nottingham, where workers who were afraid of losing their jobs broke
into factories and smashed the new machines. When this was debated
in the House of Lords on 27 February the young Lord Byron made his
maiden speech, in which he stated his conviction that the rioters were
driven to commit such offences by desperation and want. There were
further outbreaks of machine-breaking in Yorkshire in March, and bread
riots later in the year. Other disturbances occurred in Ireland, where the
Catholics were protesting against the Protestant establishment.

The King, George III, was mentally ill, and incapable of governing.
His powers were invested in his son, the Prince Regent. Until May, the
government was carried on much as before. There was a commission to
enquire into the state of trade, which had become very bad, and a debate
on discipline in the army: a motion for reform of flogging was lost in

the House of Commons by seventy-nine votes to six. But on 11 May Spencer Perceval, the Prime Minister, was assassinated in the lobby of the Houses of Parliament. His killer, Bellingham, believed that he had many grievances and had been fobbed off by one minister after another: driven to desperation, he took a pistol into the lobby and shot Perceval. His action was something that many people would have liked to do to the head of the government, and Bellingham was cheered on his way to the scaffold. Stones were thrown at Perceval's coffin, and the *Edinburgh Review* described him as 'unquestionably the most mischievous of all the bad ministers who, for these thirty years past, have been placed at the head of affairs, in this country'.

Misery and discontent continued during Lord Liverpool's attempts to form a government in the months that followed. George III had further paroxysms in July, effectively ruling out any hope that he might be able to resume his full authority. Public subscriptions were got up for the relief of the labouring poor, but there were Luddite riots in Yorkshire again in May, and bread riots in Nottingham in August. A good harvest helped to relieve the problem at the end of the year, but the general conditions of weak government and individual hardship for the poor remained.

In Europe it was a year of extraordinary events. It began with French troops marching through Austria towards Prussia and Poland; Wellington's army was in the Iberian peninsula, and in January Wellington took Ciudad Rodrigo. The American government, ally of the French since the War of Independence, was preparing for war against Britain by preventing British ships from using American harbours. In April Napoleon entered Poland; Wellington took Badajoz. In July he won the great battle of Salamanca, taking 7000 prisoners; it was a victory on a scale not seen since the days of Marlborough, and a turning-point in the campaign. Napoleon marched into Russia, and in August Kutusov took command of the Russian army. The French entered Moscow in September, but found it destroyed and had to retreat through the Russian winter. Napoleon arrived back in Paris in December, leaving his army in ruins behind him.

The year 1812 could also be described as a decisive one in literature. In March, Byron published *Childe Harold's Pilgrimage*, Cantos I and II, which made him famous overnight and announced the arrival of a new poetry, old in form but exciting and contemporary in its descriptions, its Romantic hero, and its topical comments. It had a certain quality of immediacy which commended it to its first readers: it was easily accessible, piquant and lively, intriguing and alive. In comparison, Wordsworth and Coleridge appeared to be merely what they were coming to be called, 'Lake Poets', provincial and local experimenters. The vogue of Byron was confirmed when another reassuringly traditional but very fine work, Crabbe's *Tales*, appeared later in the year. Crabbe was old-fashioned, Byron excitingly new: he was to go on to lead the second-generation Romantic poets into new authenticities of feeling and a new revolutionary ardour. The anger which was found in Shelley, and to some extent in Keats, was given an earlier expression in Byron's daring attack on Lord Elgin for taking away the Parthenon friezes; in this section of Canto II Byron showed how contemporary discontent could be successfully incorporated into poetry.

Meanwhile Leigh Hunt, whose periodical *The Examiner* had been campaigning for the reform of Parliament and against the savagery of flogging in the army and navy, became incensed by a sycophantic article on the Prince Regent. Noting that this 'Adonis in loveliness', as he had been described, was in fact 'a corpulent man of fifty', Hunt went on to demolish him with some other unjustified epithets:

> In short, this *delightful, blissful, wise, honourable, virtuous,*
> *true* and *immortal* prince is a violator of his word, a libertine
> over head and ears in disgrace, a despiser of domestic ties,
> the companion of gamblers and demireps, a man who has
> just closed half a century without one single claim on the
> gratitude of his country, or the respect of posterity.[7]

It is not difficult to see this anger as arising out of the social and political discontents of the day: the contrast between the flattery addressed to the prince and the reality of his life was too great to be borne with equanimity. Byron's attack on cant as the 'grand *"primum mobile"* of England'[8] developed from the same perception of a deep untruth in the acceptance of establishment views.

Byron's satires fought against hypocrisy and humbug; Shelley preached revolution; Keats's friendship with Hunt was accompanied by a natural republicanism, seen in his bitter little poem on the anniversary of the Restoration of Charles II. The bells were always rung on that day, 29 May, and Keats responded to them with fury:

> Infatuate Britons, will you still proclaim
> His memory, your direst, foulest shame?
>   Nor patriots revere?
> Ah! while I hear each traitorous lying bell,
> 'Tis gallant Sidney's, Russell's, Vane's sad knell,
>   That pains my wounded ear.

Such directly expressed sympathies are an integral part of the response of the second-generation Romantic poets to the rottenness of Regency society. They continue some of the themes found in Blake, finding kings bad, church religion unacceptable, and priests an abomination; but they write more literally and less gnomically than Blake, and perhaps with more desperation. Blake had the possibility of a new dawn before him; the later poets, Shelley especially, hope for revolution but are not sure if it will happen. They seize upon isolated uprisings with enthusiasm, but have to come to terms with the fact that a major revolution is not going to happen in England.

During his period of power, Napoleon represented the one possibility of change. His defeat, and the restoration of the Bourbons,[9] signalled the end of an era of experiment and excitement. All over Europe the old kings complacently resumed their places, and the Congress of Vienna quietly restored the status quo; this was one reason why the chief architect of the Congress, Castlereagh, was so hated by the radical poets. In the emergence of these poets, and in the turn of political events, the year 1812 was a crucial beginning: it began an era in which the poet's attitude to his times is measured in his methods, and especially those of denunciation and satire. Satire had existed in an earlier generation, in the graphic work of Gillray and Rowlandson; now it was taken over by the poets and used (more directly than Blake had ever used it) because the age required it. Disillusion, and the gap between what was said and what was actually happening, were ideal conditions for the development of a new, direct, effective satirical mode; this helps to make the 'feel' of second-generation Romantic poetry different from that of those who were writing during the heady and hopeful years of the French Revolution.

Notes

1. J. L. Hammond and Barbara Hammond, *The Village Labourer* (London, 1911; re-issued, London, 1978), p. 1.

2. E. P. Thompson, *The Making of the English Working Class* (London, 1963), p. 212.

3. Ibid., p. 211.

4. See G. E. Mingay's introduction to the 1978 edition of the Hammonds' *The Village Labourer*; and T. S. Ashton, *The Industrial Revolution, 1760–1830* (London, 1947).

5. Quoted in Leslie A. Marchand, *Byron, a Portrait* (London, 1971), p. 114.

6. Phyllis Deane, *The First Industrial Revolution* (Cambridge, 1965), p. 138.

7. *The Autobiography of Leigh Hunt*, edited by J. E. Morpurgo (London, 1949), p. 231.

8. See 'Letter to – Esqre, on the Rev. W. L. Bowles's Strictures on the Life and Writings of Pope' (1821); *The Works of Lord Byron, Letters and Journals*, edited by R. E. Prothero, 6 vols (London, 1898–1901), v, 542.

9. See *Childe Harold's Pilgrimage*, Canto III, st. 36–45; and *Don Juan*, Canto IX, st. 5–9.

Chapter 8
Byron

Byron's body lies in the church at Hucknall, an undistinguished small town a few miles north of Nottingham; a polychromatic statue of him adorns the first-floor front of a nearby shop, over the Co-op sign. It is an unromantic place to find the relics of the most glamorous of Romantic poets; yet there was always a strange and even bizarre quality to Byron's career, and his final resting-place, so quintessentially English in its Midlands ordinariness, is only one more curious twist to a hectic story. A few miles away is Newstead Abbey, where the undergraduate Byron revelled with his friends; further away are Aberdeen, where his pilgrimage began, London, where he was fêted and then snubbed, Switzerland, Italy, and finally Greece, where he died a death that was unnecessary and unheroic yet which was nobly borne and vital to the cause of Greek independence. The two Hucknall Byrons are only two of many Lord Byrons, and the extreme variety of his poetry is a testimony to this. He wrote, he said at one point, 'to withdraw *myself* from *myself*'[1]; but which self? and is this always true? The answer is that there were many selves, and as many motives for writing, and if Byron said one thing at one time he was equally likely to say something else at another. He was the most various of poets, for he tried everything, in poetry and in life: at four-and-twenty, he wrote, he had taken 'degrees in most dissipations',[2] and at Carnival time in Venice, in 1818, he decided to 'work the mine of my youth to the last veins of the ore, and then – good night. I have lived, and am content.'[3]

Poetry was only one of his multifarious activities. He went in for politics, played cricket for Harrow in spite of his club foot, was a superb swimmer and a good pistol-shot, had lessons in fencing and boxing, loved travel, and enjoyed the company of men and women. As a consequence, he tended to disparage the art of writing, especially when it was practised to the exclusion of life itself. ' "Actions – actions," I say, and not writing, – least of all, rhyme. Look at the querulous and monotonous lives of the "genus" .'[4] It was not that writing itself was worthless, but it should not be taken too seriously, so that it took up the whole of life. He found 'the preference of *writers to agents* – the mighty stir made about scribbling and scribes, by themselves and others – a sign of effeminacy, degeneracy and weakness'.[5] Life, in short, was for living, and not principally for writing poetry.

Although he genuinely despised poets like Wordsworth for (as he thought) being too earnest, it would be an error to take Byron's disparaging remarks about poetry too seriously. They are the natural reactions of a good poet irritated by the solemnity of his fellows; and to see poetry as unimportant to Byron is to single out a remark or two and take them as the whole story. Moreover, Byron was often being casual, or provocative, or funny. His friend Hobhouse always remembered Byron's laugh,[6] and the reader of Byron's poetry would do well to remember it too: Byron was a sociable person, and the most unpleasant of all social tricks is to take up seriously a remark that was made in jest. In the same way, the most insensitive literary criticism of Byron is that which does not respond with the correct degree of amusement or seriousness to the tone and feel of the poetry.

The difficulty for the critic is to know where (or whether) to draw the line: whether to surrender entirely to the energy and force of Byron, or whether to express serious reservations about some of his opinions and the way of expressing them. The two best critical studies of Byron are poles apart in this respect: Andrew Rutherford's *Byron, A Critical Study* is often severe upon what is seen as superficiality, shoddy workmanship, and flashy paradox, while Bernard Blackstone's *Byron: A Survey* is much more accepting. I mention these books not as a dutiful gesture towards criticism (and a most un-Byronic thing *that* would be) but as an example of the problems which his poetry creates for the reader.

Byron's poetry varies a great deal, but it is not enough to say that it is the poetry of masks and that he has a different persona for every poem. That persona is a part of his shifting self, of his endless exploration of life, of his continual search for something that would occupy his energy. The figures of Byron's poetry are not fictions, with the artist behind, detached, like God, paring his fingernails; Francis Jeffrey, the most level-headed of critics and editor of the *Edinburgh Review*, saw this when he was knocked sideways by the force of *Childe Harold's Pilgrimage*, Canto III:

> We cannot maintain our accustomed tone of levity, or
> even speak like calm literary judges, in the midst of these
> agonizing traces of a wounded and distempered spirit. Even
> our admiration is at last swallowed up in a most painful
> feeling of pity and of wonder. It is impossible to mistake
> these for fictitious sorrows, conjured up for the purpose
> of poetical effect. There is a dreadful tone of sincerity, and
> an energy that cannot be counterfeited in the expression

of wretchedness and alienation from human kind, which
occurs in every page of this publication; and as the author
has at last spoken out in his own person, and unbosomed
his griefs a great deal too freely to his readers, the offence
now would be to entertain a doubt of their reality.[7]

Jeffrey is extraordinarily perceptive here. He sees that Byron's poetry is
not explicable in terms of masks, and that the critical habits of a lifetime
have to be abandoned in order to appreciate it properly. The 'dreadful
tone of sincerity' is one example of the directness which so often appears,
the *propria persona* that Byron often speaks in and the other *personae* that
he speaks through, because they are also a part of him. In addition,
Jeffrey's perception of the 'wretchedness and alienation' in Canto III of
Childe Harold's Pilgrimage is important. It makes Wordsworth's dismissal
of the Canto as plagiarized from himself seem superficial and mean. For
Byron, in his post-separation exile, no doubt felt some of the admiration
for nature which Wordsworth thought borrowed: it would have been an
authentic response to the external world of the Alps, particularly from
someone with such an all-enveloping sensibility as Byron's.

In the twentieth century, we are accustomed to wretchedness and
alienation, seeing them as very proper reactions to the human condition.
But we should not overemphasize this side of Byron either: he is not
just an *Angst*-laden figure. In the first place, he is a man with a huge
enjoyment of life. Not only are his satirical poems very funny, but his
letters are some of the funniest, tenderest, and most human in English
literature (the only rival as a letter-writer is Lamb). Secondly, he is a
crusader and a hero, a fighter in the cause of truth and justice. His
perception of cant is unrivalled, except by Dr Johnson, and his attacks
on complacency and inhumanity are sharp. He saw, more clearly than
any other Romantic poet except Blake, the underlying rottenness of
English society – its lack of sympathy, littleness of spirit, and poverty
of imagination. Together with his championing of Greek independence,
this made him a European figure: along with Scott, Byron was the
most admired of English writers abroad, and he was an inspiration
to authors and patriots throughout the nineteenth century. The statue
over the Co-op in Hucknall is evidence of his appeal, and it is genuinely
touching, as well as slightly comic, in its tribute to the best known poet
of his generation.

As a Romantic poet, and viewed alongside the others, Byron seems
an odd one out, as mercurial as his own personality. He was a great
admirer of certain eighteenth-century writers, regarding Pope as 'the
best of poets',[8] and having a high opinion of Fielding, whose sharp
ridicule of hypocrisy and affectation was much to Byron's taste. He
was a traditionalist in language and style, preferring the common

forms of couplet and Spenserian stanza, and having no interest in the stylistic innovations proposed by Coleridge and Wordsworth. He did not subscribe, in theory or in practice, to the doctrine of the importance of the imagination or to the idea of the poet as prophet. If he speaks with such a voice, it is likely to be a cheerful parody of the prophetic note:

> O for a *forty-parson power* to chant
> Thy praise, Hypocrisy!
>> (*Don Juan*, X. st. 34)

Nevertheless, Byron's poetry is fundamentally Romantic, partly because in his very difference from the others he is asserting his individuality, and partly because of his subject-matter. His characters, including himself, are significantly out-of-the-ordinary: Childe Harold, the restless, lonely wanderer; the heroes and heroines of the tales, courageous, glamorous, and mysterious; figures of guilt and unspecified sorrow, such as Manfred. They are unusual, deeply sensitive, brooding on the past, and above all they are outside the normal simplicities of thinking and feeling, beyond the anaesthetizing confines of society. With the exception of Blake, Byron is the Romantic poet whose work is most inclined to question the values of safety and prudence. He invites the reader continually to be adventurous, and to sympathize with those who are imprudent, exciting, sensitive, and courageous; including himself.

Byron's first volume, *Hours of Idleness* (1807) is generally regarded as apprentice work, and there is little in it which helps towards an understanding of the mature Byron. There is, as Rutherford points out, a characteristic oscillation between the poles of sentiment and satire,[9] but the sentiment is often hackneyed:

> I would I were a careless child,
> Still dwelling in my Highland cave:
>> (ll. 1–2)

and the satire is laboured, as it is in 'To a Lady, who . . . appointed a night in December to meet him in the garden':

> Why should you weep like Lydia Languish,
> And fret with self-created anguish?
> Or doom the lover you have chosen
> On winter nights to sigh half frozen;
>> (ll. 11–14)

but there is a certain robust good sense about this which anticipates the later satires, and there is one short poem, addressed to his schoolboy sweetheart (Mary Chaworth, of Annesley Hall) which is a forerunner of the wistful beauty and deep feeling expressed in the *Hebrew Melodies*:

> Hills of Annesley, bleak and barren,
> Where my thoughtless childhood stray'd,
> How the northern tempests, warring,
> Howl above thy tufted shade!
>
> Now no more, the hours beguiling,
> Former favourite haunts I see;
> Now no more my Mary smiling
> Makes ye seem a heaven to me.
>
> (ll. 1–8)

The landscape and the weather are very effectively employed here; the poem, written shortly after Mary's marriage in 1805, is a reminder, among the kilt-swinging sentiment[10] and the attempts at satire, of Byron's effectiveness at the simple statement of feeling.

The pseudo-Highland nonsense was continued in the preface, a mawkish document which emphasized that these were the poems of a young man and that they were written to pass 'the monotony of a vacant hour' or 'to divert the dull moments of indisposition'. This was plainly an attempt to construct an escape route should the poems fail; it was seen through at once by Henry Brougham, who discussed the volume in the *Edinburgh Review* for June 1807. The article itself is all the things that Byron would like to have been at this time, urbane, dismissive, poised, witty: and its effect on Byron was (according to his friend Hobhouse) devastating. The consequence was that the satire on which Byron had been working, entitled 'British Bards', became *English Bards and Scotch Reviewers* (1809). There was something of a vogue in such satires at the time, after the manner of Pope.

The poem was offered, said Byron in the Preface to the second edition, as a 'caustic', against 'the present prevalent and distressing *rabies* for rhyming' and against the debased standards of modern criticism, in which each poet had 'his separate tabernacle of proselytes'

> by whom his abilities are over-rated, his faults overlooked, and his metrical canons received without scruple and without consideration.

The religious image of the tabernacle is typical of Byron's satiric method: he loves to dress people in inappropriate clothes, as a cartoonist might do, and here the followers of certain poets are portrayed as mindless and uncritical worshippers at some shrine. If the poets are ridiculous,

the reviewers are poisonous: later in the Preface they are described
as 'the Hydra', and although Byron admits that he is no Hercules,
he declares his intention of nevertheless trying to bruise one of the
serpent's heads. The placing of himself as an author here, with an eye
for the ridiculous and an arm to fight against a terrible adversary, is very
cunning. It accounts for much of the success of *English Bards and Scotch
Reviewers*; it accounts, too, for one of the qualities which has been most
condemned by critics, a certain heavy-handedness about the satire.[11]
There is some truth in this, and Byron is certainly no Pope; but with
his feet planted so firmly on the ground, he can afford to use a cutlass
rather than a rapier. Every reader can have sympathy with a poet who
has been savagely reviewed, however poor his verse; and every reader
can laugh at the picture of other poets surrounded by adoring acolytes.
Byron's swingeing technique, therefore, has some appropriateness; and
he strengthens his hand by a tribute to Dryden and Pope:

> When sense and wit with poesy allied,
> No fabled graces, flourished side by side;
> From the same fount their inspiration drew,
> And, rear'd by taste, bloom'd fairer as they grew.
> Then, in this happy isle, a Pope's pure strain
> Sought the rapt soul to charm, nor sought in vain;
> A polish'd nation's praise aspired to claim,
> And raised the people's, as the poet's fame.
> Like him great Dryden pour'd the tide of song,
> In stream less smooth, indeed, yet doubly strong.
>
> (ll. 105–14)

In contrast to such great figures, Byron sees the new schools of poetry
as transient and ephemeral. His description of this anticipates his later
technique of satirical quotation (applying quotations, like clothes, with
mischievous inappropriateness), and his humorous use of the unlikely
analogy:

> Thus saith the Preacher: 'Nought beneath the sun
> Is new;' yet still from change to change we run:
> What varied wonders tempt us as they pass!
> The cow-pox, tractors, galvanism, and gas,
> In turns appear, to make the vulgar stare,
> Till the swoln bubble bursts – and all is air!
> Nor less new schools of Poetry arise, . . .
>
> (ll. 129–35)

This promising beginning is effectively continued in the attack on

Southey. Byron catalogues the major works – *Joan of Arc, Thalaba, Madoc* – and goes down on his knees in mock intercessory prayer:

> Oh! Southey! Southey! cease thy varied song!
> A bard may chant too often and too long:
> As thou art strong in verse, in mercy, spare!
> A fourth, alas! were more than we could bear.
>
> (ll. 225–29)

Another piece of skilful reduction is found in the couplet on Wordsworth

> Who, both by precept and example, shows
> That prose is verse, and verse is merely prose;
>
> (ll. 241–42)

although later, in the attacks on Coleridge, Wordsworth, and Scott, the limitations of Byron's methods become clear. He engages in a schoolboy pointing and baiting: Wordsworth is like his own idiot boy, Coleridge is the laureate of donkeys, Scott is writing only for the money. Much of this is coarse, though it makes for lively reading and the poem is in part rescued by its own iconoclasm and by what Bernard Blackstone has indulgently called 'a stream of fun-making, of farce, a revelling in the incongruous'.[12] Its best mood is that of a grotesque benevolence, as Byron gazes amusedly upon the Lilliputians of the literary scene, Strangford, Grahame, Bowles, and contrasts them with Crabbe, 'though nature's sternest painter, yet the best'. This muscular and austere line is a fine tribute, and underlines the balance of this section between the competent and the bogus. When he comes to the attack on the reviewers, however, Byron's animosity gets the better of him, and we lose what Rutherford calls 'the peculiar pleasure we expect from a satirical attack', the fine raillery and incisive polished wit.[13]

A free and irresponsible energy is the great virtue of *English Bards and Scotch Reviewers*. In his next satire, *Hints from Horace* (an adaptation of Horace's *Ars Poetica*) Byron was shackled by the need to follow his original. The freedom disappears, and so does some of the liveliness and energy; it is only recaptured in the freshness and variety of *Childe Harold's Pilgrimage*, Cantos I and II. Part of the freedom of that poem is due to Byron's release from the heroic couplet, the classic medium for satire. In the epigraph to *Hints from Horace*, he quotes from Fielding's *Amelia* – 'Rhymes are difficult things – they are stubborn things, sir' – and there are signs in that poem and in *The Curse of Minerva* that the form was causing him problems. He said in 1812 that he could 'weave a nine line stanza faster than a couplet, for which measure I have not the cunning',[14] and some of the success of *Childe Harold's*

Pilgrimage, Cantos I and II (1812), must be owing to Byron's ease with the Spenserian stanza form.

Childe Harold's Pilgrimage, Cantos I and II, was a turning-point in Byron's poetical career. In his own words, he awoke one morning in March 1812, and found himself famous. The poem was a highly selective account of a tour made between July 1809 and July 1811, accompanied for part of the time by his friend John Cam Hobhouse. Their course was determined by the need to circumvent the theatres of war: it included Portugal, Spain, Malta, Greece, Albania, and Turkey. From the very beginning the impressions of different countries delight the inward eye, and one of the major reasons for the immediate success of the poem was almost certainly that its freshness and novelty appealed to a public which had been prevented from travelling abroad by the Napoleonic wars.

This was only one reason for the poem's success. Its chemistry was compounded of many things: lively description, commentary on contemporary events and issues, the language and style, and even the character of the hero:

> a youth
> Who ne in virtue's ways did take delight;
>
> (Canto I, st. 2)

Childe Harold is alone (there is no reference to Hobhouse), solitary, unloved, joyless, tired of pleasure and jaded with sin ('For he through Sin's long labyrinth had run'). His boredom and guilt enclose the various experiences of Canto I, though fortunately he plays a small part in it and the travels are sensibly and naturally described. Andrew Rutherford sees this as part of the contradiction in Byron's own character: the Childe is a projection of his melancholy and disillusioned side, while 'the narrator mirrors his more normal and attractive personality'.[15] To the reader of 1812, however, the figure of Childe Harold was attractively enigmatic. Scott, who disliked it, admitted that it gave 'an odd poignancy to his descriptions and reflections',[16] and Jeffrey (who also had doubts) acutely wondered

> whether there is not something *piquant* in the very novelty
> and singularity of that cast of misanthropy and universal
> scorn, which we have already noticed as among the
> repulsive features of the composition. It excites a kind of
> curiosity, at least, to see how objects, which have been
> usually presented under so different an aspect, appear through

so dark a medium; and undoubtedly gives great effect to the
flashes of emotion and suppressed sensibility that occasionally
burst through the gloom.[17]

There are signs that Harold, however much he may resemble one side
of Byron, is something of a fabrication that the poet tires of. He is
prominent at the beginning of Canto I, but is gradually forgotten as
the narrator's interest in the changing scene takes over. At one point in
Canto II, Byron ingenuously asks 'But where is Harold?' (II. st. 16), and
his importance thereafter is minimal. In the space he leaves, the narrator
presides with an agreeable competence; the descriptions have a freshness
that comes from a quick eye and a delighted enthusiasm. Byron has a
tourist's pleasure in a fine landscape, or the first view of a city:

> What beauties doth Lisboa first unfold!
> Her image floating on that noble tide . . .
>
> (I. st. 16)

although here, as elsewhere (as in the description of 'Cintra's glorious
Eden', I. st. 18) the eye's delight is tempered by the subsequent
reflections of the mind. As he looks at Lisbon, the narrator reflects
on the Portuguese

> Who lick yet loathe the hand that waves the sword
> To save them from the wrath of Gaul's unsparing lord.
>
> (I. st. 16)

This is followed by a half-facetious stanza in archaic language, lamenting
the general dirtiness of the city. This is another tourist reaction, but it is
also typical of the way in which the poet gathers his own impressions and
adds them to the passing landscape, carrying on a commentary which is
piquant and topical. The stanza is used for indignation, as in the attack on
Lord Elgin at the opening of Canto II, or for more measured reflection –
as in the section on solitude which follows. Here the complex sentence
demands attention for almost the whole stanza:

> To sit on rocks, to muse o'er flood and fell,
> To slowly trace the forest's shady scene,
> Where things that own not man's dominion dwell,
> And mortal foot hath ne'er or rarely been;
> To climb the trackless mountain all unseen,
> With the wild flock that never needs a fold;
> Alone o'er steeps and foaming falls to lean;

This is not solitude; 'tis but to hold
Converse with Nature's charms, and view her stores unroll'd.

But midst the crowd, the hum, the shock of men,
To hear, to see, to feel, and to possess,
And roam along, the world's tired denizen,
With none who bless us, none whom we can bless;
Minions of splendour shrinking from distress!
None that, with kindred consciousness endued,
If we were not, would seem to smile the less,
Of all that flatter'd, follow'd, sought and sued;
This is to be alone; this, this is solitude!

(II. st. 25–26)

The contrast between this kind of sensitivity and the callous plunderings of Lord Elgin is clear. The Spenserian stanzas carry this contrast, and indeed the endless changes of mood and temper, with unobtrusive efficiency. Moreover, they were a conservative choice: there was a long tradition of poetry written in this metre, and one reason for the success of Byron's poem may have been that he was producing a work which was recognizably poetry in the traditional and conservative mould. He was having no truck with the *avant-garde*, with the kinds of poetic theory put forward by Coleridge and Wordsworth; here, the Spenserian stanzas affirm, is a work of endless variety, good sense, and deep feeling, in language that can be instantly recognized as the proper language of poetry.

The character of Lord Elgin, and that of the feeling narrator, are part of a perpetual opposition in these Cantos of *Childe Harold's Pilgrimage* between, on the one hand, nature and the noble individual and, on the other, man as despoiler and destroyer. Modern civilization has brought its own horrors: Canto II sets up in opposition to them two things, the wildness of Albania (where the people are savage but hospitable and comradely) and the profound sense of the glorious past that yet remains in Greece. When the poet describes the traveller as

wandering slow by Delphi's sacred side,
Or gazing o'er the plains where Greek and Persian died

(II. st. 92)

he leaves the history of Marathon and Thermopylae to speak for itself, and allows the past to echo in the mind with all its familiarity and its remoteness. Greece becomes a place that is loved, known to all students of classical literature and ancient history, and found (in the wanderer's experience) to be still moving and beautiful, in spite of 'the rifled urn,

the violated mound' (II. st. 90) To the strong imagination the power
of certain scenes is still active:

> As on the morn to distant Glory dear,
> When Marathon became a magic word;
> Which utter'd, to the hearer's eye appear
> The camp, the host, the fight, the conqueror's career, . . .
>
> (II. st. 89)

Cantos I and II work by such powerful contrasts, between then and now,
between here and there, between Sundays in England and Sundays in
Spain, between the remote and strange country of Albania and the
familiar classical sites of Delphi, or Thermopylae, or Marathon. But
behind all the variety and all the oppositions, there is heard the
unmistakable note of human transience: the broken arch and the
ruined wall are everywhere examples of change and symbols of
mortality. This might appear to be commonplace lamenting, but it
acquires a depth and authenticity when it is related to the poet's own
loss. While at Cambridge he had become attached to a young chorister
of Trinity College Chapel, John Edleston, whose death occurred while
Byron was abroad. He determined to conclude Canto II with a tribute to
Edleston, and the last stanzas form a fitting end, not just to the awareness
of mortality which is found throughout, but to the presentation of the
poet himself as a man of intense and proper feeling:

> Oh! ever loving, lovely, and beloved!
> How selfish Sorrow ponders on the past,
> And clings to thoughts now better far removed!
> But Time shall tear thy shadow from me last.
>
> (II. st. 96)

Throughout *Childe Harold's Pilgrimage* Cantos I and II the note steadily
deepens. From the opening observations of a newly-arrived visitor to
Lisbon onwards, Byron seems gradually to have become aware of
the possibilities of the form which he had chosen to render powerful
emotional states, admiration, enthusiasm, then anger, and finally grief.
The figure of Harold is left behind in the more pressing articulation of
the poet's own feelings.

Among the roles which the poet is playing at the end is that of a
man of sensitivity and experience, compelled to conceal his true nature
in a round of superficialities:

> Then must I plunge again into the crowd,
> And follow all that Peace disdains to seek?

> Where Revel calls, and laughter, vainly loud,
> False to the heart, distorts the hollow cheek,
> To leave the flagging spirit doubly weak;
>
> (II. st. 97)

Byron was speaking more truly than he knew, for the immediate and sensational success of *Childe Harold's Pilgrimage* Cantos I and II in March 1812 meant that he was swept into the glittering world of London society. During the four years which followed, filled as they were with *amours* and engagements, he wrote (between 1813 and 1816) *The Giaour, The Bride of Abydos, The Corsair, Lara, Parisina*, and *The Siege of Corinth*. In one respect they are the successors to *Childe Harold's Pilgrimage*, for they present a mode of action and a way of life which are totally outside the range of ordinary English experience and which form an implied contrast to it. The heroes and heroines are passionate, resourceful, active; they represent a side of Byron which was dissatisfied with the triviality of London society and which longed for the outlaws and warriors of Albania. He escaped from the superficiality of Regency society by writing about pirates, buccaneers, and lovers.

The tales were written with great rapidity, and they move with the same kind of speed. The octosyllabic couplet which Byron uses in most of them (*Lara* and *The Corsair* are in heroic couplets) allows the description of scenery and character to proceed with a rapidity and precision which is neat and sharp, as it is in *The Giaour*:

> And many a summer flower is there
> And many a shade that love might share,
> And many a grotto, meant for rest,
> That holds the pirate for a guest;
> Whose bark in sheltering cove below
> Lurks for the passing peaceful prow,
> Till the gay mariner's guitar
> Is heard, and seen the evening star;
> Then stealing with the muffled oar,
> Far shaded by the rocky shore,
> Rush the night-prowlers on the prey,
> And turn to groans his roundelay.
>
> (ll. 34–45)

The action and setting are economically and vividly set out; the verse is no more than competent, but it serves its purpose sufficiently and sensibly. In the sentence which follows, Byron sets out what is to become an underlying theme in these tales:

Strange – that where Nature loved to trace,
As if for Gods, a dwelling-place,
And every charm and grace hath mix'd
Within the paradise she fix'd,
There man, enamour'd of distress,
Should mar it into wilderness . . .

(ll. 46–51)

There is no Wordsworthian connection between the mind and the external world; for Byron there is only the contrast between the beauty of the Mediterranean coast, where the 'blue crystal of the seas' blends with the loveliness of the Greek landscape, and the actions that take place upon it. In the most beautiful setting, the Giaour kills Hassan, who has drowned Leila, his slave. Byron came across a similar case during his visit to Greece, saving a girl who had been sewn into a sack and was about to be thrown into the Aegean. In the contrast between the landscape and human cruelty, *The Giaour* is therefore based upon Byron's own experience.

The story of the poem is so horrible that it is told in a series of hints, images, and flashbacks. The foreground is left clear for the figure of the Giaour himself, the tormented lover of Leila who avenges her (but cannot replace her, or obliterate the memory of her death) by killing Hassan. His appearance on his black steed is terrifying, and his mind is partly revealed in his final confession:

'The cold in clime are cold in blood,
Their love can scarce deserve the name;
But mine was like the lava's flood
That boils in Aetna's breast of flame.'

(ll. 1099–1102)

It is hinted, indeed, that there are more depths of emotion than can possibly be expressed. Even Hassan, who appears brutal and unfeeling, possesses some feeling of remorse: his mind is like 'the Scorpion ringed by fire', its only relief being to dart its sting into its own brain. We only guess at the Giaour's feelings; we hear something of them, but for the most part they are shrouded in impenetrable darkness and protected by the secrecy of the confessional. So the Giaour passes into history and legend, leaving only a pieced-together tale behind him:

He pass'd – nor of his name and race
Hath left a token or a trace,
Save what the father must not say
Who shrived him on his dying day:

> This broken tale was all we knew
> Of her he loved, or him he slew.
>
> (ll. 1329–34)

The same powerful contrast between the landscape and human behaviour is found in the other tales. In the opening section of *The
Bride of Abydos*, for instance, the poet describes a land where 'all, save
the spirit of man, is divine'. The stories are of passionate love, of
cruelty and possessiveness, of individual bravery and defiance. They
end, on the whole, in death or misery; only in the more controlled
and relaxed *Mazeppa*, and the much later *The Island* (written in 1823,
and Byron's last complete poem) does the action turn out favourably.
Like the other tales, *The Island* contains cruelty, passion, and bravery,
and Byron's admiration for courage and beauty is given its final form
in the resourceful figure of Neuha. When she dives and leads Torquil
through the water into the hidden cave to escape his pursuers, she
provides an utterly escapist but obviously satisfying solution (which
need not necessarily be seen in Freudian terms).

Love and beauty are evidence of a human nature that has escaped
the usual corruption. In a fallen world, a figure like Neuha, or Haidee
in *Don Juan*, is a reminder of the pre-lapsarian time in the Garden of
Eden. It may be for this reason, because they stand apart from all
the cruelty, pretence, and hypocrisy of life, that Byron was excited
by beautiful women and able to thrill the reader by describing them.
Hebrew Melodies (1815), for instance, opens with a dazzling lyric:

> She walks in beauty, like the night
> Of cloudless climes and starry skies;
> And all that's best of dark and bright
> Meet in her aspect and her eyes:
> Thus mellowed to that tender light
> Which heaven to gaudy day denies.

The poem was written after seeing the beautiful Mrs Wilmot at a ball.
Its secret lies in its perfect unhurried pace, which contains and places the
bold imagery. The sweeping grandeur of 'like the night', and then the
held-back (across the line) qualification which follows it ('Of cloudless
climes and starry skies') are given an inevitability, a splendour which
seems to be precise and yet reverberating in the space at the end of the
line. Throughout, the abstract is related to the material (beauty – night;
dark and bright – her aspect and her eyes) which gives the poem its
unusual sense of locating these grand and mysterious qualities in one
individual. So 'She walks in beauty', walking not just beautifully but *in*

beauty, clothed with a radiance which is instantly recognizable as that of a beautiful woman, carrying it with her wherever she goes; but it is not a gaudy beauty, for it is the mysterious and magical beauty of the night, of clear skies and stars.

The movement of each line, and the accumulated grace of each stanza, suggest that Byron had learned a great deal from his study of Pope and Dryden; and the poem's daring simplicity is a feature of Byron's work that should not be forgotten in the search for a more complex poet. The *Hebrew Melodies* demonstrate this throughout: their effect comes from the same piercing directness that is found in the Old Testament, by which they were inspired. The language of the Authorized Version (now so unhappily neglected) and the ancient Jewish stories combined to inspire Byron with story and prophecy: the captivity of the Jews, the songs of Zion in a strange land, the stories of Saul and David and Belshazzar, the imagery of the psalms and the narrative of the Book of Job, all stimulated Byron's imagination because they contained themes which he was profoundly sensitive to, including exile, imprisonment, tyranny, love, and war.

A self-imposed exile became part of Byron's own experience in 1816, after the breakdown of his marriage. His departure was a new beginning, in more ways than one: when he left England he left behind a reputation as the greatest poet of the age and the ornament (somewhat dented) of Regency society; he also left behind a whole collection of restrictions and obligations. The consequences were similarly divided: from 1816 onwards, Byron delighted to portray himself as a ruin, a failure, and an incompetent (who could nevertheless write poetry better than anyone else, of course); he also acquired a sense of liberation, a freedom of speech, and a freer lifestyle, especially in Italy. He could feel able to criticize the England that he had left as full of humbugs and hypocrites, with the exception of a few close friends; 'it neither suits me – nor I it', he wrote to Douglas Kinnaird in November 1816; 'my greatest error was remaining there – that is to say – my greatest error but *one*.'[18] And although he talked about returning, he never did.

The immediate aftermath of the separation is notable for two poems, both of which reflect the stress of the summer of 1816. *Childe Harold's Pilgrimage* Canto III (1816) is a record of the journey from England to Switzerland, passing through the battlefield of Waterloo, down the Rhine, across the country made famous by Rousseau in *La Nouvelle Héloïse*, and thence to the Alps. A considerable agitation of mind is suggested by the opening stanzas, as though Byron is still recovering from the shock of the separation and his decision to leave England. He paints Childe Harold as a figure who has become rich in painful experience:

He, who grown aged in this world of woe,
In deeds, not years, piercing the depths of life,
So that no wonder waits him; nor below
Can love or sorrow, fame, ambition, strife,
Cut to his heart again with the keen knife
Of silent, sharp endurance: . . .
                                    (III. st. 5)

His isolation may be a projection of Byron's own feeling of resentment at being unjustly blamed for the breakdown of the marriage. Certainly in the assertion that 'he knew himself the most unfit/Of men to herd with Man' (st. 12) the use of the verb 'herd' suggests a proud isolation. Andrew Rutherford has criticized Byron here, saying that he 'offers us flashy paradox and large rhetorical gestures expressing a shoddy kind of self approval',[19] but this is severe. Harold's portrait is an appropriate continuation from the misanthropic individual of Canto I, here developing that portrait into one in which his experience has deepened his sensitivity and his uneasiness. He has to search for substitute friends, companions, and homes:

Where rose the mountains, there to him were friends;
Where roll'd the ocean, thereon was his home;
Where a blue sky, and glowing clime, extends,
He had the passion and the power to roam;
The desert, forest, cavern, breaker's foam,
Were unto him companionship;
                                    (III. st. 13)

In this deliberate turning away from man to nature, Harold is evidently seeking consolation for defeat; and it is oddly coincidental that one of the first places visited by Byron after leaving England was the battlefield of Waterloo, where Napoleon met his final defeat. The result is a description of the battle which fully recognizes its dramatic possibilities and its crucial role in perpetuating the status quo in Europe. Byron admired Napoleon and detested 'the cause & the victors – & the victory – including Blücher and the Bourbons',[20] even though he tells the story from the English side, recognizing the possibilities (as narrative and drama) of the Duchess of Richmond's ball. He saw Napoleon as a great man, daring, extreme, passionate, energetic, who had been destroyed by the 'whole host of hatred' (st. 39) and replaced by the nonentity Bourbon kings. In writing about him here, Byron can speculate about a greatness which carries its own isolation with it, and is certainly not associated with patience, humility, or prudence;

> He who ascends to mountain-tops, shall find
> The loftiest peaks most wrapt in clouds and snow;
> He who surpasses or subdues mankind,
> Must look down on the hate of those below.
>
> (III. st. 45)

While it is necessary to be cautious about identifying Byron himself with these figures, the construction of this part of *Childe Harold's Pilgrimage* Canto III, leads inevitably towards two things, isolation of the great, and suffering of the sensitive. The geography of the Canto confirms this: as Byron gets further away from England and the scene of his marriage failure, he becomes increasingly confident. From the plains of Belgium and the elegiac commentary on Napoleon, the poem moves towards the Swiss mountains as Byron puts the past behind him:

> I look upon the peopled desert past,
> As on a place of agony and strife,
> Where, for some sin, to sorrow I was cast,
> To act and suffer, but remount at last
> With a fresh pinion; . . .
>
> (III. st. 73)

Here time and place are one, a 'past . . . where'; in that past the poet, like Napoleon, lived uneasily, and now he begins to feel his true self in the present:

> Are not the mountains, waves, and skies, a part
> Of me and of my soul, as I of them?
> Is not the love of these deep in my heart
> With a pure passion? should I not contemn
> All objects, if compared with these? and stem
> A tide of suffering, rather than forego
> Such feelings for the hard and worldly phlegm
> Of those whose eyes are only turn'd below,
> Gazing upon the ground, with thoughts which dare not glow?
>
> (III. st. 75)

The clotted verse of the second half of this stanza is characteristic of Byron's work in this Canto. In his struggle towards a self-identity after the crisis, he is aware of the dangers of an aggressive and unsympathetic isolation. One result is that although the verse which relates to the mountain landscape is invariably clear and inspiriting, that which relates to the human beings on the plain is uneasy and unconvincing. The best solution is to work through the experience of others, and it is significant that the tribute to Napoleon is followed by one to Rousseau, another great spirit who lived uneasily among his contemporaries.

In the persons of Napoleon and Rousseau, therefore, Byron is constructing his own Pantheon of neglected heroes, with an empty plinth for himself; and *Childe Harold's Pilgrimage*, Canto III, which seems at first sight to contain some of the boldest and clearest examples of Romantic nature-worship, is in fact a poem of the struggling self. At the centre of the landscape is the hero; Byron is constructing his own mythology, with himself as the last great noble antagonist:

> I have not loved the World, nor the World me –
> But let us part fair foes;
>
> (III. st. 114)

The antithesis is powerful, if not strictly true; but the second line transforms it by making it a relationship of mutual respect. It is Byron's way out of the muddle he has got himself into in Canto III: he has appeared confused, inconsistent, posturing, but at the end he is discovered to have survived, and to have done so in a way befitting a gentleman. It is a neat ending to what Byron himself described as 'a fine indistinct piece of poetical desolation' in a letter to Thomas Moore:

> I am glad you like it. It is a fine indistinct piece of poetical
> desolation, and my favourite. I was half mad during the
> time of its composition, between metaphysics, mountains,
> lakes, love unextinguishable, thoughts unutterable,
> and the nightmare of my own delinquencies. I should,
> many a good day, have blown my brains out, but for
> the recollection that it would have given pleasure to my
> mother-in-law.[21]

Heroic, imprisoned, and isolated figures continue to feature in the poetry of 1816–17. *The Prisoner of Chillon* (1816) describes Bonnivard's helplessness and grief as those whom he loves are taken from him, and his inability to enjoy freedom when it finally comes. The poem's crisp economy suggests that Byron had found in Bonnivard another *alter ego*, more manageable and sympathetic than either Napoleon or Rousseau. The poem is in strange contrast to *Manfred* (1817), which is much more mysterious and suggestive, although it also owes much to the landscape of Switzerland. It was inspired partly by the Alps, and partly by Goethe's *Faust*: Goethe himself said that Byron had extracted from *Faust* 'the strangest nourishment for his hypochondriac humour':

He has made use of the impelling principles in his own
way, for his own purposes, so that no one of them remains
the same; and it is particularly on this account that I cannot
enough admire his genius.[22]

Byron takes over the solitude of Faust, his absolute differences from
ordinary men. Manfred's character is self-absorbed and passionate;
he desires forgetfulness of that which is within him. In the second
scene, on the Jungfrau, he is saved from suicide by the well-meaning
Chamois Hunter, whose decent ordinariness is designed to contrast with
Manfred's torment. But Manfred is seen as heroic, in that he can bear
this pain:

> I can bear –
> However wretchedly, 'tis still to bear –
> In life what others could not brook to dream
> But perish in their slumber.
>   (II. i. 76–79)

In the scene which follows, where Manfred calls up the witch of the
Alps, we learn more of this isolation:

> From my youth upwards
> My spirit walk'd not with the souls of men,
> Nor look'd upon the earth with human eyes;
> The thirst of their ambition was not mine,
> The aim of their existence was not mine;
>   (II. ii. 50–54)

Instead, his joy is in the mountain-top, in the rarefied existence of a
great spirit. His remorse is caused by some obscure and destructive
relationship with the one whom he loves ('I loved her, and destroy'd
her'). When the spirits come for him at the end of Act III, however,
Manfred is able to defy them, by asserting the inviolable self-hood that
is his (the abbot, who stands by desperately trying to intervene, is an
example of ineffective conventional religion).

Manfred's position at the end is attractive in its own stagey way,
but his character is entirely lacking in the radiance and benevolence of
Shelley's Prometheus. This is principally because Manfred is entirely
uninterested in the fate of others: he is successor to Childe Harold and
to Bonnivard in his inability to see beyond his particular problems.
Bonnivard is the most successful of the three because his condition is
the result of a cruel imprisonment: the other two appear self-indulgent
in comparison, though interestingly so.

Manfred was finished in Venice, after Byron's move there in November 1816. His arrival there seems to have quietened the disturbed spirit that is at the centre of the 1816 poems. Venice suited Byron, and he it; his lyric 'So we'll go no more a roving' is his equivalent of 'Home at Grasmere':

> So we'll go no more a roving
>   So late into the night,
> Though the heart be still as loving,
>   And the moon be still as bright.
>
> For the sword outwears its sheath
>   And the soul wears out the breast,
> And the heart must pause to breathe,
>   And love itself have rest.
>
> Though the heart was made for loving,
>   And the day returns too soon,
> Yet we'll go no more a roving
>   By the light of the moon.

The contrast with Wordsworth could hardly be stronger: 'Home at Grasmere' is an intricate, tentative, exploratory poem. Byron's lyric trembles on the edge of banality, and yet somehow succeeds in remaining moving and even serious. It was sent in a letter to Thomas Moore from Venice (28 February 1817) recording with some amusement Byron's exhaustion after the Carnival. Yet the poem extends much further than its original statement of a temporary tiredness. The sentimentality is balanced by a striking seriousness: the poem becomes almost melancholic, although its final mood seems to be contentment. This contentment is never self-indulgent or flabby, an effect for which the spare economy of the stanzas is partly responsible. Within the evenly-paced lines the imagery is suggestive, atmospheric, but firmly controlled. The night, the moon, the sword, the heart, all suggest life, feeling, romance, sexuality: they imply a whole world of experience. Together with the 'no more' of the first line, they imply a life that has been fully and excitingly spent, lived to the full: like Falstaff and Justice Shallow, Byron has heard the chimes at midnight.

The poem is a fragment of a letter, and should not be taken as a solemn declaration of retirement from loving and living. But its unmistakable tone of acceptance is indicative of a new peace of mind, which is confirmed by Canto IV of *Childe Harold's Pilgrimage* (written in 1817, published April 1818). It continues the description of travel, and is written in Spenserian stanzas, but in other respects it is as different from Canto III as Canto III is from I and II. The moody Childe has disappeared (as Byron acknowledged in the dedicatory letter to Hobhouse and in st. 164) and the poem celebrates Italy as seen through the eyes of the poet himself:

> fair Italy!
> Thou art the garden of the world, the home
> Of all Art yields, and Nature can decree;
> Even in thy desert, what is like to thee?
> Thy very weeds are beautiful, thy waste
> More rich than other climes' fertility;
> Thy wreck a glory, and thy ruin graced
> With an immaculate charm which cannot be defaced.
>
> (IV. st. 26)

Into this landscape of ruins comes the poet himself, 'A ruin amidst ruins',

> there to track
> Fall'n states and buried greatness, o'er a land
> Which *was* the mightiest in its old command,
> And *is* the loveliest, . . .
>
> (IV. st. 25)

This is much more successful than the association with the Alps. Byron's identification of himself with the ruined but beautiful landscape is a far more satisfactory way of coming to terms with his new condition. He may be ruined from the point of view of English society, but he turns this to his own advantage without the *de haut en bas* suggestion of the alpine hero. And perhaps because he sees the country as a mirror-image of his own state, he is able to write about it with a grace that he did not achieve in any of the earlier cantos. The Spenserian stanza, with its flexibility and stateliness, seems perfectly suited to the mixture of melancholy and pride which is found in Canto IV, as it is for instance in the description of Petrarch's tomb:

> They keep his dust in Arqua, where he died;
> The mountain-village where his latter days
> Went down the vale of years; and 'tis their pride –
> An honest pride – and let it be their praise,
> To offer to the passing stranger's gaze
> His mansion and his sepulchre; both plain
> And venerably simple, such as raise
> A feeling more accordant with his strain
> Than if a pyramid form'd his monumental fane.
>
> (IV. st. 31)

Classical and medieval memories mingle, heavy with associations, while
the beauty of the present landscape has its own spell to cast, as it does
in the waterfall of Velino, so 'horribly beautiful' (st. 69–72). Past and
present meet everywhere in the beholder's mind, most notably at Rome,
which makes an effective centre for the Canto, both geographically and
emotionally. Standing beside Metella's tomb, the poet reflects that

> standing thus by thee
> It seems as if I had thine inmate known,
> Thou Tomb!
> > (IV. st. 104)

His historical imagination produces a continual interplay between the
past and the present in this way, and his sense of place interacts with
his self-consciousness, so that there is a complex mixture in the Canto
of reflection, remembrance, hope, and melancholy, all inspired by the
Italian landscape itself. The Canto moves to a conclusion with a tribute
to the sea, the elemental force which is greater than man and which
beholds with indifference the rise and fall of great empires. The ending
is a natural and appropriate conclusion: from its opening in Venice, the
city of the sea which is now in decline, Byron has travelled through
Italy observing the passing of the world and hopes of mankind, and
he now returns to the sea and the earth as outlasting them all. Man
pollutes the earth, but beyond the works of his hands are the desert
and the ocean:

> Thy shores are empires, changed in all save thee –
> Assyria, Greece, Rome, Carthage, what are they?
> Thy waters wash'd them power while they were free,
> And many a tyrant since; their shores obey
> The stranger, slave, or savage: their decay
> Has dried up realms to deserts: – not so thou; –
> Unchangeable, save to thy wild waves' play,
> Time writes no wrinkle on thine azure brow:
> Such as creation's dawn beheld, thou rollest now.
> > (IV. st. 182)

Canto IV of *Childe Harold's Pilgrimage* was rapidly translated into Italian,
and it became very popular in Italy, for obvious reasons. It is superior to
the earlier cantos, because it has none of the striving for effect of the first
two or the disturbed heroism of the third. Instead it has compassionate
and sensitive tone, regarding the landscape and reflecting upon it in ways
which underline its beauty and yet see it as evidence of human grandeur
and decay. In its pervasive sense of human mortality, it anticipates the

sombre bass-notes of *Don Juan*; its achievement has probably been
under-rated because of the brilliance of *Beppo*, also written in 1817
and published in 1818. And with the composition of *Beppo* and the
discovery of *ottava rima*, Byron's poetry changes completely.

Byron discovered the comic possibilities of *ottava rima* through the
reading of John Hookham Frere's *Whistlecraft* (a comic Arthurian poem)
in September 1817. Its use of the metre of Italian burlesque poetry
demonstrated its suitability for English comic poetry, especially in
the use of rhyme: in the ABABABCC pattern, the AB rhymes are
repeated once too often for comfort, and the CC at the end provides
a 'pouncing' effect to conclude the stanza. Byron seized upon it with
an instinctive flair: he had heard the story of *Beppo* in August, read
Frere in September, and had finished the poem by 23 October. Even
by Byron's standards, this was rapid progress, and it suggests that he
was immediately at home in the new medium:

> 'Tis known, at least it should be, that throughout
> All countries of the Catholic persuasion,
> Some weeks before Shrove Tuesday comes about,
> The people take their fill of recreation,
> And buy repentance, ere they grow devout,
> However high their rank, or low their station,
> With fiddling, feasting, dancing, drinking, masking,
> And other things which may be had for asking.
>
> (st. 1)

Here there is none of the padding which is sometimes found in the
Spenserian stanzas of *Childe Harold's Pilgrimage*, when a precise first line
is often followed by a repetitive and less effective way of saying the
same thing. This stanza has a purpose which is sustained from the first
line to the last: it immediately establishes a tone, the relaxed and familiar
tone of worldly wisdom and good humour ending in an eye-twinkling
suggestiveness. The playfulness is clear from the jaunty rhymes, which
Byron plays with in *Beppo* like a child with a new toy:

> He was a Turk, the colour of mahogany;
> And Laura saw him, and at first was glad,
> Because the Turks so much admire philogyny,
> Although the usage of their wives is sad;
> 'Tis said they use no better than a dog any
> Poor woman, whom they purchase like a pad;
> They have a number, though they ne'er exhibit 'em,
> Four wives by law, and concubines 'ad libitum'.
>
> (st. 70)

The couplet rhymes at the end of the stanza can be used with particular skill to provide an element of absurdity, especially when the rhymes are feminine:

> When kneeling on the shore upon her sad knee
> He left this Adriatic Ariadne.
> > (st. 28)

> In short he was a perfect cavaliero,
> And to his very valet seemed a hero.
> > (st. 33)

The playful handling of proverb and quotation, and the ludic rhyming of individual verses, is part of a delightfully free handling of the poem's structure. It contains ninety-nine stanzas, of which less than half are directed to the telling of the story, and the poet presents a pleasing fiction of himself as an incompetent bungler:

> To turn, – and to return; – the devil take it!
> This story slips for ever through my fingers, . . .
> > (st. 63)

He presents himself not as a ruin but as 'a broken Dandy'; his rhymes come from Walker's rhyming dictionary:

> And when I can't find that, I put a worse on,
> Not caring as I ought for critics' cavils;
> I've half a mind to tumble down to prose,
> But verse is more in fashion – so here goes.
> > (st. 52)

The joke is, of course, that the poem is so full of life and energy that it could never have been written by an old failure; or, if it has been, then by all means let us have broken dandies for company rather than boring successes. Byron is not only inviting the reader to share with him the knowledge that what he says is not true, thus creating an intimacy between them; he is glancing at poets with many more pretensions who are read with much less enjoyment. He has found a way of discoursing intimately with the reader, in a way which flatters and disarms, so immediately enlisting the reader on his side. Together, poet and reader take a Cowper quotation, use it in mock solemnity, and recognize their complicity:

> 'England! with all thy faults I love thee still,'
> I said at Calais, and have not forgot it; . . .
>
> I like the taxes, when they're not too many;
> I like a seacoal fire, when not too dear;
> I like a beef-steak, too, as well as any;
> Have no objection to a pot of beer;
> I like the weather, when it is not rainy,
> That is, I like two months of every year, . . .
>
> > (st. 47–48)

Byron has discovered a way of recording his opinions without giving offence. He can make asides about critics, the weather, London's smoke, chilly women, all with the same insouciant tone which comes from an assumption of being agreed with:

> One hates an author that's *all author*, fellows
> In foolscap uniforms turn'd up with ink,
> So very anxious, clever, fine, and jealous,
> One don't know what to say to them or think,
> Unless to puff them with a pair of bellows; . . .
>
> > (st. 75)

and one of the main virtues of *Beppo* is its ability to undermine the kind of solemn seriousness about their own work that Byron associated with Wordsworth and Coleridge. 'These Scotch and Lake troubadours', he wrote, 'are spoilt by living in little circles and petty societies. London and the world is the only place to take the conceit out of a man.'[23] *Beppo* is a poem of the world: a poem in which narrow horizons give way to wider ones, and an extension of experience allows the development of a new sense of proportion. So the extended comparison between Italy and England is playful but also gently serious, a mild warning against the mindless complacency of a narrow patriotism.

The poem's delight depends on the delicate control of mood and tone, and the resourceful use of the verse form. The relationship between Laura, the Count, and Beppo is never treated solemnly: it is a delightful comedy, which reaches its climax in Laura's quizzing of Beppo after his return:

> Now Laura, much recover'd, or less loth
> To speak, cries 'Beppo! what's your pagan name?
> Bless me! your beard is of amazing growth!
> And how came you to keep away so long?
> Are you not sensible 'twas very wrong?

'And are you *really*, *truly*, now a Turk?
With any other women did you wive?
Is't true they use their fingers for a fork?
Well, that's the prettiest shawl – as I'm alive!
You'll give it me? They say you eat no pork.
And how so many years did you contrive
To – Bless me! did I ever? No, I never
Saw a man grown so yellow! How's your liver?

(st. 91–92)

Here the serious and trivial jostle each other with a comic juxtaposition, and Laura's questions tumble out without waiting for answer, like a cataract. The result is an extraordinary climax, not only to the comic treatment of the threesome, but also to the dexterity of the verse. In his discovery of *ottava rima*, Byron has hit upon a form which he can use successfully for almost anything; indeed, one of the pleasures of *Beppo* and the other satirical poems in this metre is that of seeing the verse twisted and manipulated into extraordinary and even grotesque forms. In the hands of a master craftsman, absurdity becomes high art: poetry becomes a kind of conjuring, putting on and then throwing off disguises. Throughout, the poet keeps up the pretence of ease and assurance:

I perch upon an humbler promontory,
Amidst life's infinite variety:
With no great care for what is nicknamed glory,
But speculating as I cast mine eye
On what may suit or may not suit my story,
And never straining hard to versify,
I rattle on exactly as I'd talk
With anybody in a ride or walk.

(*Don Juan*, XV. st. 19)

Yet within such a relaxed pose Byron can create effects of quite dazzling virtuosity, such as Laura's conversation at the end of *Beppo* or the doctor's prescription in Canto X of *Don Juan*:

But here is one prescription out of many:
'Sodae sulphat. 3vj. 3fs. Mannae optim.
Aq. fervent. f3ifs. 3ij. tinct. Sennae
Haustus' (and here the surgeon came and cupp'd him),
'R. Pulv. Com. gr. iij. Ipecacuanhae'
(With more beside if Juan had not stopp'd 'em).

'Bolus Potassae Sulphuret. sumendus,
Et haustus ter in die capiendus.'

(st. 41)

All the normal criteria by which poetry is considered break down in
the face of such outrageous clowning with the verse form. Any ideas
that we may have about structure are also twisted out of recognition:
Beppo, as we have seen, is a story with more digression than narrative,
and *Don Juan* is marvellously inconsequential.

Don Juan is ultimately anarchic, the poem which is closest to what
Anne K. Mellor calls 'the abundant chaos of life', which embodies most
clearly Friedrich Schlegel's theory of Romantic Irony.[24] In this sense, it
is the most Romantic of all Romantic poems because it is the wildest
and freest, because it sits most loosely to the idea of poetry while still
being poetry. It has a central figure who is hardly a hero because he is
acted upon rather than acting; he is discovered casually, when, in the
first verse of Canto I, the poet declares that he is looking round for
one – 'I want a hero' – and takes up Juan, almost, it would seem,
because he is the first one that comes to mind. The structure too, is
more like that of a picaresque novel than of a poem: 'we must I think
begin', says Jerome J. McGann solemnly, 'by renouncing our ordinary
thoughts about poetic structure'.[25] Of course we must; and a whole lot
more too. This is a poem which is against poetry, as it is sometimes
thought of: it contains some rousing abuse of contemporary authors, of
authorship generally, and (by implication) of the imagination. It affects
to despise the customary association of poetry with moral truth:

But now I'm going to be immoral; now
I mean to show things really as they are,
Not as they ought to be: for I avow,
That till we see what's what in fact, we're far
From much improvement with that virtuous plough
Which skims the surface, leaving scarce a scar
Upon the black loam long manured by Vice,
Only to keep its corn at the old price.

(XII. st. 40)

Byron is here, of course, attacking a conception of morality that would
equate it with keeping things nice and clean; his stanza goes on to
propose a far more effective morality, one which is aware of the truth
and starts from there. This is typical of the method of *Don Juan*: it
claims to have a scepticism on the surface, but then reveals its own
superior feeling. The intricate relationship between its carefree surface
and its deeper sensitivity is one of the major virtues of *Don Juan*.

Depending on which is seen to be to the fore, Byron can write that
it is intended 'to be a little quietly facetious upon every thing'[26]; or
that its only intention is 'to giggle and make giggle[27]; or that it is 'the
most moral of poems; but if people won't discover the moral, that is
their fault, not mine'.[28] These may seem to contradict each other, but
of course they are all true. The poem is facetious, and giggle-making,
and moral, all at once.

Byron may have attacked contemporary poets in *Don Juan*, and
ridiculed some precious Romantic ideas in the process. Yet he is himself
being more daringly Romantic than any of the others by choosing
to rely so much on his own independent judgement. When he says
'I mean to show things really as they are', the reader is entitled to
enquire whether or not this means 'as I (Byron) think they are'. In
other words, Byron is being defiantly heroic: these, he is saying, are
my opinions, undisguised. Instead of the Romantic imagination we
have a Romantic indignation, against Southey, against Wordsworth and
Coleridge, against Wellington, against cant and hypocrisy, against folly
and boredom, and against sloppy thinking. Even if we cannot always
agree with Byron, we can admire his willingness to defy the world
and its conventions. He has tremendous faith in his own judgement:
he sees the Lake poets as an absurd little coterie, and is convinced that
he is right.

In this process the reader is confidant, spectator, opponent, even
victim: victim for his conventional opinions, for he is an *hypocrite
lecteur*, part of the corrupt society in which he lives; victim, too, of the
poet's own unchallenged supremacy. In Canto XII, after some eleven
thousand lines, we read this:

> But now I will begin my poem. 'Tis
> Perhaps a little strange, if not quite new,
> That from the first of Cantos up to this
> I've not begun what we have to go through.
> These first twelve books are merely flourishes,
> Preludios, trying just a string or two
> Upon my lyre, or making the pegs sure;
> And when so, you shall have the overture.

> (XII. st. 54)

The whole stanza is the grin of a wrestler who has his opponent on the
floor, and at the same time it is a fine piece of straight-faced leg-pulling
which is developed with ingenious twists and turns from the first piece
of impudence. What makes it funny also is not just the side-swipe at
other poems ('some take as long as this to get going') but the possibility
that in this case, 'I've not begun what we have to go through' could

well be true. In the next stanza Byron promises us 100 cantos, and it is
perfectly possible to imagine the poem stretching out to such a length.
Its abundant fertility is such that there is no reason why it should not
go on for ever. Byron himself described it as an epic:

> My poem's epic, and is meant to be
> Divided in twelve books; each book containing,
> With love, and war, a heavy gale at sea,
> A list of ships, and captains, and kings reigning,
> New characters; the episodes are three:
> A panoramic view of hell's in training,
> After the style of Virgil and of Homer,
> So that my name of Epic's no misnomer.
>
> > (I. st. 200)

The point is, of course, that the poem is nothing like an epic. The
opening 'I want a hero' is a signal of that, and the action of Canto I
is totally unserious. The verse, therefore, actually draws attention to
Byron's disregard of poetic convention: he flaunts his difference from
others, celebrates the unpredictability and the endless possibilities of the
form which he has discovered.

Much of the pleasure of *Don Juan* comes from its surface, from
Byron's ability to describe the beautiful or the comic. The description
of the burial place of Haidee in Canto IV, for instance (st. 72–73) is
steadily moving in its grace and beauty. At other times, Byron provides
hilarity, as in the numeration of the Russian generals:

> There was Strongenoff, and Strokonoff,
> Meknop, Serge Low, Arsniew of modern Greece,
> And Tschitsshakoff, and Roguenoff, and Chokenoff,
> And others of twelve consonants apiece;
> And more might be found out, if I could poke enough
> Into gazettes; but Fame (capricious strumpet),
> It seems, has got an ear as well as trumpet.
>
> > (VII. st. 15)

If this is comedy of the ear, Byron can also transfer ideas into comic
visual images. In Canto I, for instance, he points out that the practice
of editing the classics so that passages thought improper were taken
out and printed in an appendix merely encouraged schoolboys to turn
straight to the end. There they found 'the grosser parts'

> standing staring all together,
> Like garden gods – and not so decent either.
>
> > (I. st. 45)

The visual simile is characteristic of the effect which Byron can create by caricature. Here he is a cartoonist: the obvious equivalent of *Don Juan* in the visual art of the period is the work of Rowlandson and Gillray.

Byron often draws such cartoons: his characters have exaggerated features and are found in ludicrous poses, as Juan is when hidden in the bed in Canto I or walking behind his carriage on Shooter's Hill indulging in absurd rhetoric about England as 'Freedom's chosen station':

> 'Here laws are all inviolate; none lay
> Traps for the traveller; every highway's clear;
> Here' – he was interrupted by a knife,
> With – 'Damn your eyes! your money or your life!' –
>
> (XI. st. 10)

Such vignettes are common in *Don Juan*. Yet this one is typical in the way in which it immediately gives rise to a more serious and melancholy reflection. The ridiculous situations, the brilliant surface, the verbal juggling, these are only the upper notes of a chord which has its own gravity in the bass. When Juan is set upon by the footpads, he draws his pistol and shoots one of them, who makes a brief dying speech and who is superbly described in thieves' language:

> Who in a row like Tom could lead the van,
> Booze in the ken, or at the spellken hustle?
> Who queer a flat? Who (spite of Bow-street's ban)
> On the high toby-spice so flash the muzzle?
>
> But Tom's no more – and so no more of Tom.
> Heroes must die; . . .
>
> (XI. st. 19–20)

Even in a trivial example such as this, the note of human mortality is sounded; and the phrase 'no more' or 'never more' gives a sombre ground-swell to the poem. It is found in the lament over the dead Haidee:

> Thus lived – thus died she; never more on her
> Shall sorrow light, or shame. She was not made
> Through years or moons the inner weight to bear,
> Which colder hearts endure till they are laid
> By age in earth: her days and pleasures were
> Brief but delightful – such as had not said

> Long with her destiny; but she sleeps well
> By the sea-shore, whereon she loved to dwell. . . .
>
> Ye could not know where lies a thing so fair,
> No stone is there to show, no tongue to say,
> What was; no dirge, except the hollow sea's,
> Mourns o'er the beauty of the Cyclades.
>
> (IV. st. 71–72)

The consciousness of human mortality is everywhere in *Don Juan*: human life is frail, a brief existence against the background of the passing of ages. What is to be valued in this life is love, and also heroism; but both are ultimately subject to time. In death the beautiful and the daring become one with the wicked, the hypocritical, and the ridiculous. At Canterbury, for instance, Juan sees the cathedral:

> Black Edward's helm, and Becket's bloody stone,
> Were pointed out as usual by the bedral,
> In the same quaint, uninterested tone: –
> There's glory again for you, gentle reader! All
> Ends in a rusty casque and dubious bone,
> Half-solved into these sodas or magnesias,
> Which form that bitter draught, the human species.
>
> (X. st. 73)

This Johnsonian view of human life puts a great many trivial things into proportion. Prejudice and bigotry are seen as absurd, and so are cant and hypocrisy; it is mankind's duty to be loving, and brave, and truthful. In this process Byron sees his satire as a cleansing of accumulated mental cobwebs, and he makes a daring comparison to this effect:

> a male Mrs. Fry
> With a soft besom will I sweep your halls,
> And brush a web or two from off the walls.
>
> (X. st. 74)

With a characteristic digression, Byron goes on to remark that Elizabeth Fry might find more appropriate subjects for her reforming zeal outside the prisons. She should try some of the great houses in London, to see what she could do with 'harden'd and imperial sin'. The idea is half-comic, half-serious: Byron certainly intends us to note that the aristocracy are hardened sinners, perhaps more hardened than the wretches in Newgate, but he also keeps up a kind of cheerful banter. He is posing as the shrewd, experienced man, confronting the idealist and turning off the conversation with a joke:

To mend the people's an absurdity,
A jargon, a mere philanthropic din,
Unless you make their betters better: – Fy!
I thought you had more religion, Mrs. Fry.

> (st. 75)

Among other things, she is to tell the great ones of the earth

>   that youth once gone returns no more,
> That hired huzzas redeem no land's distresses;
> Tell them Sir William Curtis is a bore, . . .

> Tell them, though it may be perhaps too late
> On life's worn confine, jaded, bloated, sated,
> To set up vain pretence of being great,
> 'Tis not so to be good; and be it stated,
> The worthiest kings have ever loved least state;
> And tell them – But you won't, and I have prated
> Just now enough; . . .
>
> (st. 76–77)

The mixture of the serious and the trivial here is disconcerting: Sir William Curtis and his tedium get in the way of the more important matters. The remainder of the passage is Hogarthian in its severity. There is an awareness of life itself, of the inevitable progress towards old age and death, which is complemented by the sharp-edged account of political and personal failures – the wealthy 'jaded, bloated, sated', the hired huzzas, the distress of the poor, the pomp of monarchy. Throughout *Don Juan* these things are assumed, and sometimes stated: high life 'is oft a dreary void' (XIV. st. 79); the poor are distressed, and driven to crime; the shopkeepers and hoteliers are making money, hand over fist; everywhere established figures (Lambro, Wellington) dominate others. It is this society which creates madhouses for those who do not conform; and Byron anticipates R. D. Laing and others in questioning the whole relationship between 'sanity' and 'madness':

> Shut up the world at large, let *Bedlam* out;
> And you will be perhaps surprised to find
> All things pursue exactly the same route,
> As now with those of *soi-disant* sound mind.
>
> (XIV. st. 84)

Byron's broad and humane judgement here is the foundation of his satire, whether personal or general. He is seeking some kind of profound revolution of moral and spiritual thought, a voyage of discovery which will change all our ideas:

> for truth is always strange;
> Stranger than fiction: if it could be told,
> How much would novels gain by the exchange!
> How differently the world would men behold!
> How oft would vice and virtue places change!
> The new world would be nothing to the old,
> If some Columbus of the moral seas
> Would show mankind their souls' antipodes.
>
> (XIV. st. 101)

Don Juan endeavours to alter our moral geography on many occasions: it is particularly concerned to identify and condemn cant and hypocrisy, but it is also prepared to question accepted values of all kinds. The principal example of this is the description of the siege of Ismail in Cantos VII and VIII. Byron's eye for detail is its guarantee of truth and seriousness: this is no long-distance view of war, but a close-up description which makes it look very different from the glory assumed by much patriotic verse. Byron may have had in mind Wordsworth's poem of thanksgiving after the defeat of Napoleon in 1814: he disliked both Wordsworth and Wellington, and the former's celebration of 'England' and his praise to the 'Just God of christianized Humanity' would have repelled him. The quotation (VIII. st. 9) '"Carnage" (so Wordsworth tells you) "is God's daughter:"' confirms this. Byron undertakes to show that warfare is no longer heroic. It begins with an artillery barrage, which is indiscriminate in its effect and kills soldiers and civilians alike; it goes on through every stage of the conflict, so that the reader is made to face

> the infinities of agony
> Which meet the gaze, whate'er it may regard –
> The groan, the roll in dust, the all-white eye
> Turn'd back within its socket –
>
> (VIII. st. 13)

and yet the condemnation is never allowed to become solemn or portentous, and if we think of a later generation it has more in common with the sharp and sardonic eye of Sasscon than with the compassionate grandeur of Owen. Byron has an eye for the absurd, as well as for the horrible:

Thrice happy he whose name has been well spelt
In the despatch: I knew a man whose loss
Was printed *Grove*, although his name was Grose.

(VIII. st. 18)

The tone of equanimity with which Byron describes some of the siege
must not be mistaken for callousness. He is quite capable of arousing
our pity and fear when he needs to, as he does when two Cossacks try
to kill a little girl of ten (who is rescued by Juan). For much of the time,
however, the dead-pan tone is pleasantly grim, almost as if the poet is
holding the reader's head and forcing him to look. The whole episode
becomes a fearful indictment of the state of society: this is the point of
the lyrical digression on Daniel Boone, after which we are pulled back
to the horrors of war with redoubled effect:

So much for Nature: – by way of variety,
Now back to thy great joys, Civilisation!

(VIII. st. 68)

The great joys turn out to be the entry into the town and its
consequences, and the heavy irony here is only one of many methods
used by Byron in the poem.

Don Juan uses these different methods because it is the work of an
opportunist: Byron will see an opening and dart through it, and part of
the excitement of the poem is its unexpected use of flashes of insight.
Its effect is at times not unlike that of *Gulliver's Travels* or *A Tale of a
Tub*, for Swift, like Byron, exploits every situation and turn of phrase
with dazzling versatility. To read Swift is to be invigorated by the
sheer intellectual and emotional excitement of keeping up with him,
and something of the same pleasure is found in reading *Don Juan*. Byron
is more self indulgent than Swift, more inclined to favour us with his
views and his spleen, but he is also deeply moving in his awareness of
the transience of human life.

Don Juan is the finest example of Byron's satire because of this
undercurrent of melancholy. *The Vision of Judgment* (1822) is more
perfect in its completeness, and it pleases the form-critics better, but
its very effectiveness and control mean that there is less room for the
sheer humanity which is found in the digressive untidiness of *Don Juan*.
It is another example of Byron making use of an opportunity; and
if the episodes of *Don Juan* are chosen to allow Byron's imagination
to get to work on pretentiousness and folly, a single combination of
circumstances has now presented itself. The poem, literally, is a gift.

The death of George III in January 1820 was, for Byron, unremarkable; except for the possibility that, as a peer of the realm, he

might return to England and attend the coronation of George IV. He saw the old King, who had reigned for sixty years, presided over the loss of the American colonies, and finally become incapable, as pathetic rather than offensive. But Southey's *A Vision of Judgement*, published in 1821, altered the whole picture. It was a heavy and overemphatic poem, which described George III being received into heaven with acclamation, while his radical opponents (with the exception of George Washington, whom not even Southey could condemn) were banished to hell.

The idea is absurd in itself. It depends on the obviously false theory that royalty will be recognized as such in heaven and be as pre-eminent there as on earth. It also perpetuates the crude idea of heaven as a reward for goodness (however that is defined) and of hell as punishment for wickedness. In Southey's case the foolishness of his original conception was only part of the trouble: in its execution the poem was lumbering and obvious, and Southey chose to add a sneaking preface which attacked Byron (though not by name) as an immoralist in his poetry and in his private life.

Byron's response was swift and deadly, but because of Southey's egregious folly he was able to use ridicule rather than venom. The poem begins and ends in laughter. As it opens, St Peter is a sleepy old porter with nothing to do; and as it ends, during the scuffle between St Peter and Southey, King George slips unnoticed into heaven:

> And when the tumult dwindled to a calm
> I left him practising the hundredth psalm.
>
> (st. 106)

The picture is comic, and even affectionate: Byron can afford to end on a magnanimous gesture, because the poem has amply demonstrated the limitations of the King's reign. In spite of his incompetence and of all the things which happened between 1760 and 1820 he can still, Byron suggests, be the object of an accidental generosity; he has slipped into heaven, so let him stay there. It is a ludicrous ending for one whose funeral was a conspicuous example of false pomp and ceremony:

> It seem'd the mockery of hell to fold
> The rottenness of eighty years in gold.
>
> (st. 10)

The poem is quite explicit about the abuses that flourished under George III. Satan, who is prosecuting, reminds us that

> 'He ever warr'd with freedom and the free:
> Nations as men, home subjects, foreign foes,

So that they utter'd the word "Liberty!"
Found George the Third their first opponent. Whose
History was ever stain'd as his will be
With national and individual woes?'

(st. 45)

Satan's witnesses for the prosecution are too many to be called; of the
individuals who do get a hearing John Wilkes is cheerfully generous,
but the author of the Junius letters is uncompromising: 'I loved my
country, and I hated him.' (st. 84) The antithesis is bare and allows no
escape.

The hearing of any further witnesses is prevented by the arrival of
Asmodeus bearing Southey, a figure whom Byron makes both ludicrous
and contemptible:

He said – (I only give the heads) – he said,
He meant no harm in scribbling; 'twas his way
Upon all topics; 'twas, besides, his bread,
Of which he butter'd both sides; 'twould delay
Too long the assembly (he was pleased to dread),
And take up rather more time than a day,
To name his works – he would but cite a few –
'Wat Tyler' – 'Rhymes on Blenheim' – 'Waterloo'.

He had written praises of a regicide;
He had written praises of all kings whatever;
He had written for republics far and wide,
And then against them bitterer than ever; . . .

(st. 96–97)

The control of tone here is masterly: Southey begins by whining,
and gradually gains confidence, finally condemning himself out of his
own mouth. This portrait is the key to the laughter of *The Vision of
Judgment*: by writing his ludicrous poem Southey has delivered himself
into Byron's hands, and the assured conduct of the poem is the result.
Byron has him by the throat: he can afford to give him a good shaking
and let him crawl away. All that happens to Southey is that he gets a
ducking in Derwentwater.

The danger of such a total demolition is that the reader will recoil
from the triumphant victor. Byron avoids this by the comic device of
letting people off: Southey goes on writing, and the King finds a place
in the choir stalls. Moreover, the poet himself is deeply conscious of
his own shortcomings, as well as those of others. He hopes, indeed, that
no one will ever be damned, realizing that the church takes a different

and much more severe view. Byron puts his generosity into the scale
against orthodox belief:

> I know this is unpopular; I know
> 'Tis blasphemous; I know one may be damn'd
> For hoping no one else may e'er be so;
>
> (st. 14)

and this has a bearing on his own state:

> God help us all! God help me too! I am,
> God knows, as helpless as the devil can wish,
> And not a whit more difficult to damn,
> Than is to bring to land a late-hook'd fish, . . .
>
> (st. 15)

The poet's humility and self-awareness contrast powerfully with Southey's
bland self-confidence. Southey's speech, rich 'with all the attitudes of
self-applause' (st. 95), turns into salesmanship of the worst kind, replete
with patter and special offers. By the side of it, Byron's statement of
his own inadequacy is carefully calculated to impress the reader as being
properly modest.

If Byron's careful placing of himself as a spiritual *ingénu* is important
for the success of the poem, the other major quality which contributes
to that success is the poet's humour. Once again, Southey unwittingly
provides the spark: his account of the King's reception into heaven
is turned by Byron into one of those funny stories about the pearly
gates in which the angels and archangels behave like human beings.
St Peter is a sleepy porter; Michael and Satan observe the formalities
like ambassadors:

> though they did not kiss,
> Yet still between his Darkness and his Brightness
> There pass'd a mutual glance of great politeness.
>
> (st. 35)

Throughout the poem Byron has fun with the angels, who resemble
comic types; and the poem provides opportunities, again and again,
for comic and ridiculous moments, brief cartoon sketches: St Peter
asleep, John Wilkes affably asking St Michael for his vote, Southey
arriving tucked under Asmodeus's left wing. The supreme example of
this opportunistic comedy is the moment which crucially undermines
all the assumptions of Southey's poem. St Peter hears a clatter, and is
about to nod off again, when a cherub rouses him:

'Saint porter,' said the angel, 'prithee rise!'
Waving a goodly wing, which glow'd, as glows
An earthly peacock's tail, with heavenly dyes;
To which the saint replied, 'Well, what's the matter?
Is Lucifer come back with all this clatter?'
'No,' quoth the cherub; 'George the Third is dead.'
'And who *is* George the Third?' replied the apostle:
'*What George? what Third?*'

(st. 17–18)

In four words, Byron has blown the assumptions of Southey's poem to pieces, and he has done so with a laugh.

The laughter of Byron's satire is one of its most distinguishing features. If Hobhouse always remembered Byron's laugh, the reader can find his own evidence for it everywhere. The danger is that it will turn everything into a joke (the shipwreck in Canto II of *Don Juan* is open to this criticism), but on the whole the laughter is cleverly justified; and, of course, it is a part of Byron himself, that strange personality who is so powerfully present in all the poems, penetrating, savage, tender, melancholy. With the possible exception of Coleridge, no other Romantic poet is as open and daring in his use of his own sensibility. We can admire him for this or condemn him, according to our sympathies; what we cannot dispute is the energy and opportunism of his poetry. The great pleasure of reading Byron comes from his ability to use the happy accident, to seize upon an invigorating idea, to exploit a situation, to admire, to love, to condemn, to ridicule: in other words, to make the most of life.

Notes

1. *Byron's Letters and Journals*, edited by Leslie A. Marchand, 12 vols (London, 1973–82), III, 225. All references are to this edition.

2. *Letters and Journals*, IX, 22.

3. *Letters and Journals*, VI, 10–11.

4. *Letters and Journals*, III, 220–21.

5. *Letters and Journals*, III, 220.

6. Leslie A. Marchand, *Byron, A Portrait* (London, 1971), p. 466.

7. *Byron, The Critical Heritage*, edited by Andrew Rutherford (London, 1970), p. 109.

8. *Letters and Journals* [n. 1 above], VIII, 19.

9. Andrew Rutherford, *Byron, A Critical Study* (Edinburgh and London, 1961), p. 15.

10. For a defence of the Highland poems see Bernard Blackstone, *Byron, A Survey* (London, 1975), pp. 16–18.

11. See Rutherford, p. 22: 'one finds in *English Bards* a coarsening of the traditional techniques – clumsy attempts at bathos, for example, commonplace antitheses, crude ridicule, lame epigrams, and heavy-handed irony: . . .'

12. *Blackstone*, p. 45.

13. *Rutherford*, p. 23.

14. *Letters and Journals*, II, 210.

15. Rutherford, p. 31.

16. *Byron, The Critical Heritage*, p. 37.

17. *Byron, The Critical Heritage*, p. 40.

18. *Letters and Journals*, V, 135.

19. Rutherford, p. 55.

20. *Letters and Journals*, IV, 76.

21. *Letters and Journals*, V, 175.

22. *Byron, The Critical Heritage*, p. 119.

23. *Letters and Journals*, IV, 152.

24. Anne K. Mellor, *English Romantic Irony* (Cambridge, Mass., and London, 1980), p. 33.

25. Jerome J. McGann, *Don Juan in Context* (London, 1976), p. 3.

26. *Letters and Journals*, VI, 67.

27. *Letters and Journals*, VI, 208.

28. *Letters and Journals*, VI, 99.

Chapter 9
Shelley

Shelley's poetry is exciting and demanding, for a number of reasons. In the first place, it contains a very considerable amount of Shelley's voluminous reading – philosophical, scientific, mythological, religious, and political. Secondly, it frequently attempts to describe that which is beyond description – a depth beyond depth, a height beyond height, a timelessness beyond time, a boundless space, all the features of a universe which we can stretch to imagine but cannot satisfactorily find words to compass. Thirdly, it is a poetry which moves with great speed; its characteristic effects are not those of logic or fixed clarity, but of a changing sensibility confronting an ever-changing world. It is a fitting poetry for an age of relativity: poet, reader, subject, engage in an endless process of interaction which is at the opposite extreme from the lapidary symbols of Wordsworth or Keats. And if the processes of interaction are relative, so that the verse seems constantly changing, this difficulty is compounded by the sheer vitality of the linguistic technique of Shelley's poetry, the way in which his words are, in Coleridge's phrase, 'living words' in a vital and metaphorical relationship with one another. The result is a breathless and often heady excitement, a sense of movement which has been well described by C. S. Lewis: he speaks of 'the air and fire of Shelley, the very antithesis of Miltonic solidity, the untrammelled, reckless speed through pellucid spaces which makes us imagine while we are reading him that we have somehow left our bodies behind'.[1] The result of this effect is a little like the feeling of looking at a Turner painting, where the light of the sky is reflected in the water, with the water itself shifting and moving, so that nothing is fixed, everything is in motion. It is not surprising that both Shelley and Turner loved Venice:

> Lo! the sun upsprings behind,
> Broad, red, radiant, half-reclined
> On the level quivering line
> Of the waters crystalline;
> And before that chasm of light,

As within a furnace bright,
Column, tower, and dome, and spire,
Shine like obelisks of fire,
Pointing with inconstant motion
From the altar of dark ocean
To the sapphire-tinted skies, . . .

('Lines written among the Euganean Hills', ll. 100–10)

And yet to say that Shelley is perpetually evanescent is to over-simplify his poetry dangerously. On another occasion he wrote of Venice in a spare, taut, athletic manner:

I rode one evening with Count Maddalo
Upon the bank of land which breaks the flow
Of Adria towards Venice; a bare strand
Of hillocks, heaped from ever-shifting sand,
Matted with thistles and amphibious weeds,
Such as from earth's embrace the salt ooze breeds
Is this; an uninhabited sea-side,
Which the lone fisher, when his nets are dried,
Abandons; and no other object breaks
The waste, but one dwarf tree and some few stakes
Broken and unrepaired, and the tide makes
A narrow space of level sand thereon, . . .

('Julian and Maddalo', ll. 1–12)

Here the effect is not that of Turner but of Caspar David Friedrich: the only moving things are the poet himself and Count Maddalo. The verse uses the heroic couplet but moves against it, making continual pauses as each part of the scene is individually identified: the dwarf tree, the broken stakes, the seaside from which even the lone fisherman has gone away; all these are precise elements in the landscape. It is important to realize that Shelley can do this, for it helps to counter the suggestion made by F. R. Leavis that he has a weak grasp of the actual, and the general idea that Shelley is some kind of ethereal poet, described by Matthew Arnold as 'a beautiful *and ineffectual* angel, beating in the void his luminous wings in vain'.[2] In fact, Shelley has many registers, and many tones: his poetry can be airy and evanescent, but it can also be precisely revolutionary and practical, as the Chartists who used it later in the nineteenth century knew. Frequently the far-seeing passions of an idealist are integrated with a precise understanding of the needs of his time. As Timothy Webb points out, the energetic opening of the 'Ode to the West Wind' is concerned with the landscape, but with the phrase 'pestilence-stricken multitudes' Shelley's imagination darts back 'from the woods by the Arno to the huddled and disease-ridden population of the cities'.[3] Sometimes Shelley is simple, as in the 'Song to the Men of England'; but more often, his political thought is linked to his philosophical idealism. The most powerful influences on his thinking were the New Testament and Plato. Although he was a good hater of churches and priests and was sent down from Oxford for publishing a pamphlet entitled *The Necessity of Atheism*, he found in the life of Jesus Christ an example of love and of suffering at the hands of tyrants; and in Plato he found (in the *Symposium*) a similar emphasis on love and (in the *Republic*) a belief in a greater reality than that which is present to our senses.

The result of all this is that Shelley's poetry is rarely simple. It exists in many different forms, from the luminous and ethereal *Epipsychidion* to the practical and topical 'Song to the Men of England'; more characteristically, the visionary and the practical are blended, as they are in Blake. Shelley is a revolutionary because he is a visionary, and his finest poems underpin the anti-tyrannical stance with an idealism which continually emphasizes the importance of making a new world of love. In the communication of this, the finest poems are those in which Shelley can find the classical or mythological framework which can control his complex, teeming connections between the ultimate aspirations and the immediate duty: the greatest example is *Prometheus Unbound*.

Shelley's antipathy to the political establishment of his own day was inspired by a profound distrust of monarchy, the church, and the law. Mary Shelley described how this began in childhood:

> Inspired with ardour for the acquisition of knowledge,
> endowed with the keenest sensibility and with the fortitude
> of a martyr, Shelley came among his fellow-creatures,
> congregated for the purposes of education, like a spirit
> from another sphere; . . . To a devoted attachment to those
> he loved he added a determined resistance to oppression.
> Refusing to fag at Eton, he was treated with revolting
> cruelty by masters and boys: this roused instead of taming
> his spirit, and he rejected the duty of obedience when it
> was enforced by menaces and punishment.[4]

Shelley's independent spirit, and his discontent with the values of traditional education and a land-owning family were revealed in 1811 in two self-defining acts of great significance: in February he and his friend

T. J. Hogg were sent down from Oxford, and in August he eloped with
Harriet Westbrook, the school-friend of one of his sisters. Thereafter
Shelley rejected his family and the English political conservatism of
his time, working for various causes such as Irish reform, freedom of
the press, and land reclamation in Wales. It was during this period
that he began a correspondence with William Godwin: *Political Justice*
had natural affinities with Shelley's own thinking, as *Queen Mab* (1812)
demonstrates.[5] In the third section Shelley mounts a sustained attack
on monarchical government and on those who support it or exist
upon it:

> The drones of the community; they feed
> On the mechanic's labour: the starved hind
> For them compels the stubborn glebe to yield
> Its unshared harvests; and yon squalid form,
> Leaner than fleshless misery, that wastes
> A sunless life in the unwholesome mine,
> Drags out in labour a protracted death,
> To glut their grandeur; many faint with toil,
> That few may know the cares and woe of sloth.
>
> (III. 108–17)

The force of these lines is characteristically Shelleyan in its directness:
the juxtaposition of the slothful courtier with the agricultural labourer
and the toiling miner is given even more point by the two verbs, 'they
feed' and 'to glut', which suggest one life swallowing another even
to satiety: meanwhile the miner is 'leaner than fleshless misery', an
image which typically (for Shelley) combines two things: an emblem
of misery, a fleshless starved creature, and an attempt to go beyond
that, to portray a figure who is thinner than fleshless, thinner even than
skeletal, more miserable than misery. Just as the image is getting lost in
depth upon depth of famine, Shelley pulls it back to the factual world
with the reference to the unwholesome mine; as he does so another
image comes to mind, that of the underground worker (often a woman
or a child) dragging a heavy tub of coal. For them, this is their only life:
they are dragging out their lives load by load in misery and labour to
glut the rich and slothful.

The influence of Paine and Godwin is obvious in the section which
follows, which traces the origin of kings and their parasites (they
are the products of vices) and predicts their overthrow under the
awakening influence of reason. When reason's voice is heard, the
thrones, falsehoods, and wars will become as hateful as truth seems to
be now. Also from Godwin is the condemnation of war which follows
in Section IV, in which the evils of wars are unequivocally ascribed to

the work of monarchs. They are supported by 'bullies' and 'hired bravos' who drive the poor to desperation and keep them in ignorance. So in a touching and precise paragraph of Section v Shelley develops Gray's line from the 'Elegy', 'Some mute inglorious Milton here may rest'. In Gray this is a matter for some wonder at what might have been, and for some sadness, a brooding melancholy over the different opportunities of human life; in Shelley it becomes something much stronger, as he allows the reader momentarily to perceive the bitterness and frustration of the talented but impoverished victim of tyranny:

> How many a rustic Milton has passed by,
> Stifling the speechless longings of his heart,
> In unremitting drudgery and care!
> How many a vulgar Cato has compelled
> His energies, no longer tameless then,
> To mould a pin, or fabricate a nail!
>
> (v. 137–42)

The last line focuses exactly on the trivial and mechanical work of nail-making or pin-making as opposed to the tameless energies of the great censor (or perhaps his grandson). Its precision, as the would-be Cato has to confine his energies to such work, gives force to the indignation, and transforms Gray's apparent acceptance and regret into something much more enlivening.

Queen Mab is an impressive early poem.[6] It overstates its case, and the dream-form means that it tends to be undisciplined, but its energy and sympathy are undoubted. It is not strange, as Mary Shelley pointed out, that Shelley

> should, even while so young, have believed that his written
> thoughts would tend to disseminate opinions which he
> believed conducive to the happiness of the human race[7].

This is not strange: what is unusual is the extent of Shelley's poetic enthusiasm, his ability to versify the themes which were to become major preoccupations of his later poetry: the hatred of tyranny, the hope for the future, and the techniques of vision. The last of these is central: Shelley employs the device of the Fairy's taking Ianthe's spirit into a world of vision in order to perceive a reality which is beyond the normal earthly sense-impressions. Ianthe is taken beyond the veil, which is the recurrent symbol in Shelley's poetry for the way in which the reality is hidden from mankind by a world of natural appearances, transitory and misleading. Its dominance in Shelley's work is due to the influence of Plato.

Plato was not taught at Oxford in Shelley's day: his admiration was a private enthusiasm. It began at Eton, when he read the *Symposium* (which he later translated): there he read of the soul's desire for the beautiful and the ideal, its search for 'the supreme beauty itself, simple, pure, uncontaminated with the intermixture of human flesh and colours and all other idle and unreal shapes attendant on mortality'.[8] The attempt to find such beauty leads from beautiful forms on this side of the veil to the ideal beyond: Shelley is continually striving for the beautiful which is beyond beauty as humankind can know it, the essential ideal beauty and love which are suggested by the beautiful things on this earth such as nature and women, but which lie behind them.

The symbol of the veil is closely associated with the symbol of the cave, taken from Plato's *Republic*. Within the cave are prisoners, chained so that they cannot turn and see the entrance: on the wall at the back of the cave are thrown the shadows of those who pass behind the prisoners, and these passing shadows are all that they can perceive. If they were unchained and turned to face the entrance to the cave they would be dazzled. Human beings are like the prisoners: they think that the world which they behold is the reality.

Plato, like Shelley, was a natural myth-maker, inventing such poetic myths as the description of the prisoners in the cave to explain the human condition. Shelley was clearly attracted by this quality, and by Plato's reforming zeal in the *Republic*; but above all, Plato's suggestions of the ideal found a natural affinity in Shelley's thought. The two things coalesce in *Prometheus Unbound*, as James A. Notopoulos has pointed out. 'The *Republic*', he writes, 'appealed to Shelley the reformer, whereas the *Symposium* appealed to Shelley the poet and lover.'[9]

Shelley's yearning for the ideal was balanced by a strong scientific and political curiosity. He was, for instance, extremely interested in electricity; and one notebook, described by Timothy Webb, contains nearly twenty pages of notes on Davy's *Elements of Agricultural Chemistry*. As Webb observes, 'it is instructive to discover the beautiful and ineffectual angel taking notes on the chemical action of manure'.[10] The result is extraordinary: Shelley has an amazing ability to enter into the lives of living creatures, of plants, the earth, the wind, the sky, clouds. They may be a part of the veil which hides the reality, but they also point the way towards something beyond themselves; and yet they are themselves, precious in their own beauty.

Alastor, or The Spirit of Solitude (1816), reflects this difficulty. It is a surprising work, a description of a powerful and impulsive progress of a nameless young poet through various forms of nature, followed by his untimely death. The poem was written after reading Wordsworth's *The Excursion*, and Shelley's Preface to *Alastor* ends with a quotation from it:

> 'The good die first,
> And those whose hearts are dry as summer's dust,
> Burn to the socket!'
>
> (I. 500–2)

The words are spoken by the Wanderer about Margaret, whose tragedy is recounted in Book I of the poem. She lives a good and virtuous life, loving and welcoming all to her cottage, but then dying slowly of neglect and despair. Like her, Shelley's poet is also one of those who seems too good for the world; like her he dies. One of the functions of the poem may have been to undermine the optimism of *The Excursion*; in which case, Shelley does so in more than one way. Not only is the poet a tragic figure; he is also more idealistic than Wordsworth's Wanderer. Set beside him in *Alastor* is the narrator, who speaks in lines that are clearly Wordsworthian in feeling and tone, hoping

> that my strain
> May modulate with murmurs of the air,
> And motions of the forests and the sea,
> And voice of living beings, and woven hymns
> Of night and day, and the deep heart of man.
>
> (ll. 45–50)

The narrator goes on to describe the dead young poet; like the Wanderer, he has been brought up from infancy under the influence of nature, although he is much more adventurous than the Wanderer (which may be a further implied criticism). In the vale of Cashmire he has a dream of a veiled maiden, telling him of 'knowledge of truth and virtue'

> And lofty hopes of divine liberty,
> Thoughts the most dear to him, and poesy.
>
> (ll. 159–60)

so that when he awakes from this vision he becomes desperately restless, travelling hectically by land and by small boat through sublime and beautiful landscapes, until his death. The ending of the poem quotes Wordsworth again:

> It is a woe too 'deep for tears,' when all
> Is reft at once, when some surpassing Spirit,
> Whose light adorned the world around it, leaves
> Those who remained behind, not sobs or groans,
> The passionate tumult of a clinging hope;
> But pale despair and cold tranquillity,

Nature's vast frame, the web of human things,
Birth and the grave, that are not as they were.

(ll. 714–20)

he Wordsworthian tone is intended to reflect upon the distance
tween Shelley and the older poet: if Wordsworth's Wanderer acquires
s own kind of equanimity and serenity, Shelley's idealist dies for his
liefs and aspirations. He also is a wanderer, but his travels take
m across the world, and his vision of beauty is so commanding
d powerful that it destroys his peace of mind. Moreover, it points
something even more ideal, for the maiden whom he sees is
iled. Wordsworth's Wanderer lives on, prosing away to the Solitary
out Despondency Corrected; Shelley's poet dies, unsatisfied with his
ngings and with the incompleteness of the view of the world. This,
elley implies, is what the real cause of grief is made of: the inability
the world, beautiful though it is, to satisfy the deepest longings of the
man heart. To accommodate oneself to this world is, as Blake saw, to
ny space to the imagination: and Shelley, like Byron, is commenting
what he saw as the limitations and parochialism of Wordsworth's
etry. The strongly worded Preface contrasts figures such as the poet
Alastor with 'meaner spirits' who abjure idealism and passion:

Their destiny is more abject and inglorious as their
delinquency is more contemptible and pernicious. They
who, deluded by no generous error, instigated by no sacred
thirst of doubtful knowledge, duped by no illustrious
superstition, loving nothing on this earth, and cherishing
no hopes beyond, yet keeping aloof from sympathies with
their kind, rejoicing neither in human joy nor mourning
with human grief; these, and such as they, have their
apportioned curse. They languish, because none feel with
them their common nature.

ere are enough echoes of Wordsworth's own prose and poetry in
s passage to suggest that Shelley, as a young idealist, was here
ng openly critical of the poet of *The Excursion*. It is a travesty of
ordsworth's beliefs, but a travesty which has its roots in a passionate
alism.

Alastor, therefore, is a poem of pure idealism, and this is pointed up
oughout by the implied criticism of Wordsworth. The word 'alastor'
ans 'evil spirit', and was suggested to Shelley as a title by his friend
cock: it has led some critics, notably Donald H. Reiman,[11] to see the
t as deluded, and the poem as a warning to mankind not to abandon
ial concerns. This is certainly a possible reading, consistent with

Shelley's known beliefs; but it ignores the very real excitement of the poet's voyage, his profound attachment to beauty, and the sympathy shown by the narrator at his death. If the alastor is an evil spirit, it is so in a sense which can be taken somewhat ironically, in that the poet's failure is a kind of divine discontent, a love of beauty which is never satisfied, and which leads him to seek for a beauty and love which are beyond the veil. There, says Shelley to the spirit of Wordsworth, is matter for grief: in the human condition itself, seen at its most essential and crucial in the poet, who cannot be content to accept the world as he finds it.

The remarks in the Preface to *The Revolt of Islam* concerning the education of a poet would seem to confirm this. Again Shelley contrasts the poet with those who are 'dull and unobservant', and expresses his aspirations openly. As in *Alastor*, the poem is brimming over with enthusiasm: the second paragraph of the Preface, setting out the nature of the work, is an enormous manifesto of evils and remedies. Shelley argues that the excesses of the French Revolution produced a loss of faith in reform, and a panic among those who had hoped for great things from it; it is now his task to chronicle a change, a gradual emergence into a more reasonable and hopeful view of mankind as capable of creating a a better world. Above all, the poem celebrates the need for love, 'the sole law which should govern the moral world', as the Preface puts it.

The poem itself is written in Spenserian stanzas, and in twelve cantos in imitation of *The Faerie Queene*. It is thus an expansive work, and a self-indulgent one, unquestioningly lengthy in its enthusiasm. Its dedication to Mary Shelley (Mary Wollstonecraft Godwin) describes her as 'thou Child of love and light', and sees her as his companion in a war against evil: she springs from two great parents, Mary Wollstonecraft and William Godwin, carrying within herself something of their qualities. She becomes the poet's beloved companion and kindred spirit:

> Thou Friend, whose presence on my wintry heart
> Fell, like bright Spring upon some herbless plain;
> How beautiful and calm and free thou wert
> In thy young wisdom, when the mortal chain
> Of Custom thou didst burst and rend in twain,
> And walked as free as light the clouds among, . . .
>
> (ll. 55–60)

As a piece of self-justification this is almost intolerable, but it foreshadows the relationship in the poem between Laon and Cythna, joint fighters in the war against tyrants and priests. The poem becomes a projection of himself and Mary as together and right, in a way which seems complacent. As usual, however, the poem finds strength in its portrayal of evil: the two idealists are burned by the King Othman at the insistence of the evil Iberian priest, who

> loathed all faith beside his own, and pined
> To wreak his fear of Heaven in vengeance on mankind.
> But more he loathed and hated the clear light
> Of wisdom and free thought, and more did fear,
> Lest, kindled once, its beams might pierce the night,
> Even where his Idol stood;
>
> (ll. 4079–84)

The priest and King are two of the human embodiments of evil, which is symbolized in the first Canto by the eagle, which fights with the serpent and is victorious; the terrific struggle is clearly intended as a reference to the failure of the French Revolution. At the end of it the serpent drops exhausted into the sea, and the triumphant eagle flies on its way; but the serpent emerges from the sea and takes refuge with the beautiful woman on the shore, who explains to the poet the conflict on earth between the two opposing forces of good and evil. The story of Laon and Cythna then unfolds: its ultimate message is that mankind must act to reform the world through love, but there is an uneasy feeling throughout that Shelley sees himself and Mary as prototypes of the good life, martyrs to a cruel world.

What is described insistently, laboriously, and self-centredly in *The Revolt of Islam*, the resistance to tyranny, is triumphantly and classically portrayed in *Prometheus Unbound*. If there is a reason for this, it lies in Shelley's choice of model. Instead of a Spenserian poem, with its freedom of action and vision, he now chose Aeschylean tragedy, with its spare action and high simplicity; instead of a loose and sprawling form, he chose the exacting form of lyric drama; and instead of a projection of himself and Mary as hero and heroine, he chose Prometheus. The legend of the fire-stealer, who defied the tyranny of Jupiter and intervened on behalf of mankind, had a natural appeal to Shelley; while the endless suffering which Prometheus endured when chained to the rock on Mount Caucasus was a type of fortitude in adversity which he greatly admired. If we add to this Prometheus' refusal to disclose the secret of Jupiter's downfall (his marriage to Thetis, and the son who would supersede him), and Prometheus' traditional association with the useful arts, it can be seen that for Shelley he was a very attractive hero; in Shelley's imagination he took the place of Satan, whom Shelley had admired for his defiance of God: but Shelley found the Greek myth superior to the Christian in that Prometheus embodied a range of noble and positive qualities which were not destroyed even during his suffering.

Shelley's drama is a very individual reworking of Aeschylus' *Prometheus Bound* and the fragments of *Prometheus Unbound*. The former shows Might and Violence enforcing the will of Zeus and overseeing Hephaestus, whose job it is to chain Prometheus to the rock. The pity which this evokes from Hephaestus and the Chorus is balanced by the temporizing of Oceanus, who urges Prometheus to change and make peace with Zeus. The play is therefore concerned with different reactions to tyranny, even to the end, when Prometheus refuses to reveal the secret of the fatal consequences of the love between Zeus and Thetis. Fragments of *Prometheus Unbound* suggest that the mother of Prometheus, Ge (mother of the earth, a figure to whom Shelley also appeals at the beginning of Alastor) urges him to swallow his pride and reveal the secret: he does so, and Prometheus is released by Heracles. This development was disagreeable to Shelley: 'I was averse', he wrote, 'from a catastrophe so feeble as that of reconciling the Champion with the Oppressor of mankind.'[12] Therefore his drama restores the original opposition between Prometheus and Jupiter; Prometheus is 'the type of the highest perfection of moral and intellectual nature, impelled by the purest and the truest motives to the best and noblest ends'.[13] In the course of the drama, Prometheus reveals what is for Shelley his true superiority over Jupiter, his refusal to hate. Jupiter's rule comes to an end because his tyranny, like everything else except the spirit of nobility and love in mankind, is subject to time; Prometheus is then released by Hercules, and united with Asia, the spirit of beauty and love.

Much of the splendid effect of Shelley's drama depends upon its combination of an Aeschylean simplicity with a lyric impulse, especially in the second half of the work. As Mary Shelley pointed out in her note to the poem, Shelley was fascinated by the grandeur of Aeschylus' tragedy, its austere concentration on 'the mighty passions and throes of gods and demi-gods'.[14] The abundant life of his poetic enthusiasm is thus contained within a mythological framework, until, in the extraordinary fourth act, Prometheus and Asia disappear, together with the whole tyrannical mechanism of Jupiter; Prometheus' parent, Mother Earth, is replaced by the Spirit of the Earth which holds dialogue with the Spirit of the Moon. Here Shelley idealizes the forms of creation: in Mary Shelley's words, he 'loved to idealize the real':

> to gift the mechanism of the material universe with a soul
> and a voice, and to bestow such also on the most delicate
> and abstract emotions and thoughts of the mind.[15]

The fourth act of *Prometheus Unbound* is an extraordinary example of such idealizing of the real: it is as though Shelley has succeeded, for once, in capturing the essence of some spirit that lies in all living things. Romantic poetry, as Coleridge saw, was always struggling to idealize and unify, and in this act it comes near to a kind of ballet, in words which make a celebratory music to hymn the joys of the newly restored world, free of tyranny and despair. If all living things were free to sing for joy, this is how they would sound.

The sustained lyricism of Act IV is the more effective by contrast with the controlled activity of Act I, and the whole process of the drama is from the static fixedness of Prometheus' defiance and Jupiter's tyranny to a free-moving delight and joy. So Jupiter is addressed in Prometheus' opening words in a language which is severe, commanding. The two figures, oppressor and victim, confront one another across a wasted world:

> *Prometheus*. Monarch of Gods and Daemons, and all Spirits
> But One, who throng those bright and rolling worlds
> Which Thou and I alone of living things
> Behold with sleepless eyes! regard this Earth
> Made multitudinous with thy slaves, whom thou
> Requitest for knee-worship, prayer, and praise,
> And toil, and hecatombs of broken hearts,
> With fear and self-contempt and barren hope.
>
> (I. 1. 1–8)

By contrast in Act IV the Spirit of the Earth is crying out for joy, celebrating an unconfined, overflowing delight. The image of a cloud borne by its own wind is characteristic of Shelley's sense of a self-energizing force.

> THE EARTH
> The joy, the triumph, the delight, the madness!
> The boundless, overflowing, bursting gladness,
> The vaporous exultation not to be confined!
>   Ha! ha! the animation of delight
> Which wraps me, like an atmosphere of light,
> And bears me as a cloud is borne by its own wind.
>
> (IV. 319–24)

Prometheus Unbound was written in Rome, and the delight in Italian warmth and the new life of spring provides an important, even dominating, series of images. In the Preface, Shelley describes the Italian spring as 'the inspiration of this drama': we can hardly accept this exclusively, because the central action of love overthrowing tyranny was a burning passion of Shelley's; but it does account for the particular effect of *Prometheus Unbound*, its combination of a classical simplicity with a romantic exuberance. It has a truly extraordinary energy, together with what Carlos Baker has called a 'clean exactness with which the whole is seen, as soon as its purpose is grasped, to fit together'.[16]

The crucial step in Act I is Prometheus' recantation of his original curse of Jupiter. The curse is spoken by the Phantasm of Jupiter, called up for the purpose by Prometheus; the curse itself (I. 1. 262–301) is a magnificent denunciation of tyranny, but when faced with his own words Prometheus repudiates them:

> It doth repent me: words are quick and vain;
> Grief for awhile is blind, and so was mine.
> I wish no living thing to suffer pain.
>
> (I. 1. 303–50)

Prometheus, the child of earth, is a Titan, immortal and God-like: symbolically he unites heaven and earth, the divine and the human, and in a statement such as the one above he shows the working of his own divine nature in preserving love in the face of his oppression. Shelley was at this point still thinking his way past the French Revolution: the excesses of the Reign of Terror, and the subsequent failure of the revolution, had been due to the hatred which had been engendered in the hearts of the French people. Prometheus demonstrates another way: by his renunciation of the curse, he presents an alternative way of love which Shelley believes will finally conquer. It is significant that Earth, at the moment of Prometheus' repentance, thinks that he has been vanquished; but Prometheus' empire is of the spirit.

The pattern of the sufferer who forgives the tyrant, and who is thought to be vanquished only to triumph in due course, brings Prometheus close to the figure of Jesus Christ; Shelley, although an atheist and priest-hater, was a dedicated reader of the New Testament. So when Mercury comes down to ask Prometheus to reveal the secret (that if Jupiter marries Thetis, he will be overthrown) and offers Prometheus the chance of living among the gods, 'lapped in voluptuous joy' (I. 1. 426), the scene resembles the temptation in the wilderness. In his love and steadfastness Prometheus resembles Jesus; in his defiance he is close to Milton's Satan, whom Shelley also admired.

The Furies, who arrive in consequence of Prometheus' refusal to tell the secret to Mercury, speak individually and in chorus. One cries 'Tear the veil', and it is torn to reveal the reality, the coming of Jesus Christ and the subsequent corruption of his message:

> One came forth of gentle worth
> Smiling on the sanguine earth;
> His words outlived him, like swift poison
> Withering up truth, peace and pity.
> Look! where round the wide horizon
> Many a million-peopled city
> Vomits smoke in the bright air.
>
> (I. 11. 546–52)

The juxtaposition is reminiscent of Blake, and the message is similar. Panthea sees 'a youth/With patient looks nailed to a crucifix' but then

> The heaven around, the earth below
> Was peopled with thick shapes of human death,
> All horrible, and wrought by human hands, . . .
>
> (ll. 584–88)

Among these deaths, described by the Furies, are those in France, where 'a disenchanted nation/Springs like day from desolation' (ll. 567–68), but where, in due course

>   kindred murder kin:
> 'Tis the vintage-time for death and sin:
> Blood, like new wine, bubbles within:
>
> (ll. 573–75)

The French are 'disenchanted' in a Spenserian sense, freed from a malevolent spell of influence; and the image of blood, bubbling like new wine within a cask, is a macabre image of a nation in some corporate act of harvesting blood. Prometheus, confronted as the others are in the midst of this carnage by the vision of Christ on the cross as a symbol of suffering and oppressed humanity, cries out for remission. The Fury replies that worse things remain than the outward manifestations of cruelty; these are the evils within, the terrors of the human heart. The Fury takes delight in perceiving that

> The good want power, but to weep barren tears.
> The powerful goodness want: worse need for them.
> The wise want love; and those who love want wisdom;
> And all best things are thus confused to ill.
>
> (ll. 625–28)

The strong and the rich live among suffering humanity as if it did not exist, says the Fury, whose apparent satisfaction with this state of things gives an ironic twist to its use of Jesus' words 'they know not what they do' (l. 631). Prometheus, instead of being angry with the callous and indifferent, pities those who are untouched by such words, that his compassion should reach so far astonishes the Fury, who vanishes. In its place, in relief, comes the chorus of Spirits, guardians 'of heaven oppressed mortality' (l. 674). One hears the cry of love, battling against tyranny; another the sigh of a man giving his life for another; a third, the dream of goodness in the mind of a sage; a fourth, the beauty of poetry:

> On a poet's lips I slept
> Dreaming like a love-adept
> In the sound his breathing kept;
> Nor seeks nor finds he mortal blisses,
> But feeds on the aereal kisses
> Of shapes that haunt thought's wildernesses.
> He will watch from dawn to gloom
> The lake-reflected sun illume
> The yellow bees in the ivy-bloom,
> Nor heed nor see, what things they be,
> But from these create he can
> Forms more real than living man,
> Nurslings of immortality!
> (ll. 736–49)

Shelley is here asserting the poet's freedom from material constraints, and his ability to transform the natural world, because at this point in the drama that is the most important human function which the poet represents: the ability of the imagination to continue to function in spite of oppression and tyranny. In his perception of that which lies beyond mortal beauty, the poet asserts the permanent heroism of the imagination; it may seem as if Shelley is here denying the actual world, but at this stage in the drama he is anxious to point to the superiority of the human spirit over evil and violence. Prometheus, meanwhile, demonstrates the real power of that evil: in his immobility on the rock he gathers into himself the victimization of mankind. He beholds the lot of humanity, and experiences the suffering; and although he hears of the hopeful signs indicate by the Spirits he cannot participate in them, chained as he is to the rock. Shelley is thus producing a direct opposition between the material and the spiritual, between the chained Prometheus and the free-moving spirits; Prometheus is a symbolic victim, enduring his torture and separated from the exiled figure of Asia, who (as we learn at the end of Act I) is waiting in the Indian vale which she has transformed by her presence.

As Act I is dominated by Prometheus, so Act II belongs to Asia, who opens the action by celebrating the creative power of spring. She and Panthea believe that a time will come when Asia and Prometheus will be united in a fertile world, and Asia, the child of Ocean, will be united with Prometheus, the child of earth. They follow the voices of this vision through a scene of natural benevolence and beauty to the pinnacle among the mountains which is the throne of Demogorgon. Demogorgon is the power beyond all powers, beyond both the tyranny of Jupiter and the defiance of Prometheus, the power at the centre of the world: Asia and Panthea go 'Down, down' into a depth beyond depth, to the centre of the world where the fate of the world lies coiled like a great snake beneath Demogorgon's throne. The spirit guides them:

> We have bound thee, we guide thee;
>   Down, down!
> With the bright form beside thee;
> Resist not the weakness,
> Such strength is in meekness
> That the Eternal, the Immortal,
> Must unloose through life's portal
> The snake-like Doom coiled underneath his throne
>   By that alone.
>   (II. 3. 90–98)

It is meekness which loosens power, just as it is love which is superior to all things: such paradoxes are part of the reality of Demogorgon's power. In scene 4 Asia and Panthea meet the reality of Demogorgon, as the veil falls. To Asia's questions, he answers that the world was made by God, but when Asia presses him about the nature of God ('Whom calledst thou God?', l. 112) he replies 'I spoke but as ye speak/For Jove is the supreme of living things' (ll. 112–13). Asia replies 'Who is the master of the slave?'; implying, who rules Jupiter, who is the slave of time, and his passions, and his hates? At which Demogorgon replies:

>   If the abysm
> Could vomit forth its secrets . . . But a voice
> Is wanting, the deep truth is imageless;
> For what would it avail to bid thee gaze
> On the revolving world? What to bid speak
> Fate, Time, Occasion, Chance, and Change? To these
> All things are subject but eternal Love.
>   (II. 4. 114–20)

There is, therefore, a power beyond all the powers of living things, an inconceivable power whose nature is imageless and hidden, so that for Demogorgon to describe it would falsify its nature. It is beyond the veil of all living and material things, which can themselves only be aware of Jupiter and Prometheus, tyranny and goodness, and their associated Furies and Spirits. In Asia's long speech before this exchange, we are given an account of one level of understanding, the mythological; by placing this where it is, Shelley suggests that there is a truth even beyond myth, a depth beyond depth, and one of the major achievements of *Prometheus Unbound* is its ability to point beyond the veil to something wonderful and imageless (though not, of course, anything like the Christian God).

Asia, meanwhile, gives the mythological account: there was a time of perfection, Heaven and Earth, and light and love; then came Saturn, who kept men under subjection, unfree (a period which corresponds to the Garden of Eden in the Judaeo-Christian tradition); then came the overthrow of Saturn by Jupiter, given power by Prometheus on condition that man should be free; disaster followed, until Prometheus gave to man hope, and love, and science, speech and thought, music and art, ships and cities. Such alleviations he gave to mankind, for which he was punished by Jupiter. This is Shelley's rewriting of the old myth of Prometheus the fire-stealer: but in this scene it is placed within the context of the greater myth, that of the imageless God who is not part of any sequential mythological process, who is beyond time, and who therefore stands apart from all other created things, including Jupiter. So one of the 'immortal Hours' (a precise oxymoron, which conveys exactly the deeper level of thought and myth behind the veil) waits for Asia and Panthea:

> My coursers are fed with the lightning,
>   They drink of the whirlwind's stream,
> And when the red morning is bright'ning
>   They bathe in the fresh sunbeam;
>   They have strength for their swiftness I deem,
> Then ascend with me, daughter of Ocean.
>
> (II. 4. 163–68)

The chariot pauses, in scene 5, within a cloud on the top of a snowy mountain, where there is a perceptible holding of breath, a marvellous and daring pause in the action before the destruction of Jupiter in Act III. During this scene there is an astonishing series of transformations: Asia is transfigured, so that even Panthea can scarcely endure the radiance of her beauty. Voices in the air then sing the lyric 'Life of Life! thy lips enkindle', and Asia replies:

> My soul is an enchanted boat,
> Which, like a sleeping swan, doth float
> Upon the silver waves of thy sweet singing;
>
> (II. 5. 72–74)

The music of these lyrics ends Act II in a mood of harmony and lightness, which looks forward to the lyricism of Act IV: *Prometheus Unbound* resembles an extended musical work in the way in which its thematic and tonal qualities alternate and interact. At this moment in the drama the melodious chant of Act II gives way to the tyrannical presence of Jupiter in Act III. His language is totally unlyrical: he uses blank verse like a sledgehammer, both in his vocabulary and in the assurance of the syntax:

> *Jupiter.* Ye congregated powers of heaven, who share
> The glory and the strength of him ye serve,
> Rejoice! henceforth I am omnipotent.
>
> (III. 1. 1–3)

But the car of the hour arrives. Demogorgon descends and takes the now powerless Jupiter with him to dwell in darkness. The world rejoices (symbolized by Ocean, the sea and parent of Asia, and Apollo, the sun god and god of poetry), and Hercules releases Prometheus to be united with Asia and his mother Earth, who feels the touch of his lips through her whole being:

> Thy lips are on me, and their touch runs down
> Even to the adamantine central gloom
> Along these marble nerves; 'tis life, 'tis joy,
> And through my withered, old, and icy frame
> The warmth of an immortal youth shoots down
> Circling. Henceforth the many children fair
> Folded in my sustaining arms; all plants,
> And creeping forms, and insects rainbow-winged,
> And birds, and beasts, and fish, and human shapes,
> Which drew disease and pain from my wan bosom,
> Draining the poison of despair, shall take
> And interchange sweet nutriment; to me
> Shall they become like sister-antelopes
> By one fair dam, snow-white and swift as wind,
> Nursed among lilies near a brimming stream.
>
> (III. 3. 85–99)

This passage conveys, as Shelley's poetry often does, the sense of life and movement in nature, and its very lack of precision helps to suggest the way that energy and life interpenetrate all things, so that all things participate in the stirring breathing life. All things begin to awake, move and live in the newly-born earth, which nourishes its created life with a love that is unhindered by Jupiter's tyranny and Prometheus' bondage. All things now are free until they die; and death becomes a process of two kinds, as it is in the New Testament. It is the death of the body, in which, in Asia's words, men and women cease 'to love, and move, and breathe, and speak'; they are gathered back into the earth from whence they came, as a mother gathers her children back into her arms. This is death seen from the point of view of a time-dominated world, a world of Saturn and Jupiter in which life succeeds life and tyrant succeeds tyrant. Mother Earth partakes of this life, but can also perceive the life beyond this, which is the life of the immortal Hours under which Jupiter's tyranny has been overthrown, a life of the spirit which transcends the rule of tyranny and overcomes it both in time and out of time. In this reading, death becomes a rending of the veil and a uniting with the immortal, a release of the spirit. Death then becomes, paradoxically, life: when Asia asks Earth about death, the reply is that

> Thou art immortal, and this tongue is known
> But to the uncommunicating dead.
>
> (III. 3. 111–12)

Asia, being immortal, cannot understand what death is: the phrase 'the uncommunicating dead' is used of those who are alive, and who find in death the lifting of the veil. This life beyond death is part of the Platonic substructure of *Prometheus Unbound*, in which the drama is continually placing its events against a background of a non-material reality. Beyond time, tyranny, and Jupiter, are the forces which Asia and Panthea discover in Act II, the immortal Hours which contain love, energy, and beauty, and which preside over Jupiter's downfall. The phrase 'immortal Hours' is oxymoronic, as we have seen; it suggests something 'in and out of time', and the paradox is taken up and given a ringing line at this point in Act III:

> Death is the veil which those who live call life:
> They sleep, and it is lifted: . . .
>
> (III. 3. 113–14)

The dead are those who are immersed in the materialism of this life, like the prisoners in Plato's cave: when they sleep, or die (as the opening of *Queen Mab* shows, Shelley was fascinated by the consanguinity of death and sleep) the veil of materialism is lifted. Prometheus' place in this pattern is central, because, Christ-like, he is both immortal and mortal. He is chained to the rock and suffers agonies of torture in a human body; but his torture is likely to be 'pain, pain ever, for ever' (I. 1. 3), because he is a Titan. His intervention on behalf of human kind is prompted by his love for them, and by his joy in the beauty and freedom which is embodied in Asia. The Spirit of the Earth, a benevolent nature spirit, reports (III. 4) a transformation of the world in which all creatures become beautiful; and just as the Spirit of the Earth finds a change in nature since the overthrow of Jupiter, so the Spirit of the Hour sees a new world of political systems, and a radical change of human behaviour. Thrones become kingless, and mankind walks without deceit and fear: thrones, altars, judgement-seats, and prisons lie in ruins, relics of the Jupiterian age. In this way mankind becomes free: the power that is greater than all tyranny is invoked by Asia and Panthea, and now man becomes almost unrecognizable in his freedom, yet still himself, or rather himself seen properly for the first time:

> The loathsome mask has fallen, the man remains
> Sceptreless, free, uncircumscribed, but man
> Equal, unclassed, tribeless, and nationless
> Exempt from awe, worship, degree, the king
> Over himself;
> (III. 4. 193–97)

He is still man in that he is not exempt from 'chance, and death, and mutability'; were it not for this, he would have infinite possibilities, since these human qualities are

> The clogs of that which else might oversoar
> The loftiest star of unascended heaven,
> Pinnacled dim in the intense inane.
>
> (III. 4. 202–4)

This last image, with its sense of some power to oversoar the stars, which themselves are 'pinnacled', yet 'dim' since they are so far away in the great nothingness of space, the 'unascended heaven' which is (in a breathtaking paradox) an 'intense inane', this illustrates very well the power of *Prometheus Unbound* to combine the human and earthly with the superhuman and the infinite. As Asia and Panthea went down to depth beyond depth, so now the vision is of the human spirit which could (were it not for the body) rise to height beyond height.

At the end of the third act, Prometheus and Asia disappear from the drama. This is not an anti-climax so much as a brilliantly-calculated measure which allows the freedom of action to be complete. Prometheus has achieved his end, and Jupiter has been overthrown; now the whole earth rejoices, and the narrative and human elements are left behind. Ione and Panthea waken to the voices of the past hours, giving way to a new gladness: Chorus and Semichoruses sing of the new earth in 'the mystic measure/Of music, and dance, and shapes of light' (ll. 77–78). They are free to dance, to dive, to soar, to run, and much of the joy of this section derives from the way in which these images of movement combine with the lyric rhythms of the choruses to make a musical effect. It is a sublime allegretto, a rapid, joyful, singing and moving pattern of sound and sense. In its turn this gives way to the conversation between Ione and Panthea, an equally beautiful adagio which describes the beauty and harmony of the awakened earth, and the ruin and destruction of ancient cities and warlike kings (Shelley's sonnet on Ozymandias is a further treatment of this theme). Into this serenity bursts the Earth herself, whose gladness is not so much reflective as exuberant:

> The joy, the triumph, the delight, the madness!
> The boundless, overflowing, bursting gladness,
> The vaporous exultation not to be confined!
>
> (ll. 319–21)

The extraordinary cluster of images here is about as far as Shelley can go in attempting to confine the unconfinable. Throughout *Prometheus Unbound* he has been faced with this problem of trying to express that which is almost beyond expression. Now he does so in language of warmth and spring. The barren frozen moon is thawed and becomes fertile; the earth feels love through all its frame, from the solidity of its granite to the most delicate of its plants:

> It interpenetrates my granite mass,
> Through tangled roots and trodden clay doth pass
> Into the utmost leaves and delicatest flowers;
>
> (ll. 370–72)

From allegretto to adagio, to the exchange between the Earth and the Moon, and now this light-hearted joy: the marvellous and extraordinary fourth act of *Prometheus Unbound* is a piece of writing that defies all normal categories and aspires to the condition of pure joy through words used as image and as music: the vision in these speeches (ll. 503–9) of the blue sky, the sparkling water, the bathing wood-nymph shaking her hair, all are emblematic of the joy of the whole earth as seen by Ione and Panthea. To their music comes the final grandeur of a last restatement, the symphonic conclusion by Demogorgon, who brings the work to an end with a triumphant finale. His return to the fundamental purpose of the drama is the equivalent of the final resolution to the major key:

> To suffer woes which Hope thinks infinite;
> To forgive wrongs darker than death or night;
> To defy Power, which seems omnipotent;
> To love, and bear; to hope till Hope creates
> From its own wreck the thing it contemplates;
> Neither to change, nor falter, nor repent;
> This, like thy glory, Titan, is to be
> Good, great and joyous, beautiful and free;
> This is alone Life, Joy, Empire, and Victory.
>
> (ll. 570–78)

In this final stanza Shelley not only sums up the major themes of the drama but also makes it clear that it is a continuing struggle of love and forbearance and hope. What he has done in *Prometheus Unbound* is to give poetic substance to that hope, and create a drama of what the world might become. Described in such a bald summary, it seems unreal and idealistic: read as a poetic drama, it is an inspiration. Above all, as Mary Shelley observed, 'through the whole poem there reigns a sort of calm and holy spirit of love';

> it soothes the tortured, and is hope to the expectant, till
> the prophecy is fulfilled, and Love, untainted by any evil,
> becomes the law of the World.[17]

The lyrical excellence of *Prometheus Unbound* leads naturally to a brief consideration of Shelley's lyrics. Asia's song from Act II, 'My soul is an enchanted boat', is one of a number of lyrical passages which celebrate music, water, and movement, sometimes all blended into one experience. In 'To Constantia, Singing', the poet finds a moment in which he is 'dissolved in these consuming ecstasies', and his soul is in flight, transcending the limitations of the body and of the material universe. The joy of such experiences lives on, even when the experience itself has ceased:

> Music, when soft voices die,
> Vibrates in the memory –
>
> (ll. 1–2)

The perfect placing of words here, in which the qualification 'when soft voices die' is succeeded by 'Vibrates', which is then itself located in the memory, is a consummate piece of lyric art. It is the placing of the crucial word 'Vibrates' which is so effective: it is an intensely physical word, yet one which describes the elusive movement of music in the air and in the mind, so that the lyric is a most beautiful combination of sense, memory, and feeling:

> Music, when soft voices die,
> Vibrates in the memory –
> Odours, when sweet violets sicken,
> Live within the sense they quicken.
>
> Rose leaves, when the rose is dead,
> Are heaped for the beloved's bed;
> And so thy thoughts, when thou art gone,
> Love itself shall slumber on.
>
> (ll. 1–8)

Similarly, 'With a guitar, to Jane' manages to produce a magic quality from its first line – 'Ariel to Miranda: – Take'. The rearrangement of the two names from *The Tempest* transforms them: they enter into relationship with one another in a way that the play allows but never achieves. Shelley sees it as a protective relationship in which he, as Ariel, the air spirit, watches over the journey through life of Jane, as a new Miranda. Just as Ariel was imprisoned in a tree, so Shelley is imprisoned in the body: both Ariel, as spirit, and Shelley, as poet, have powers beyond the ordinary, exist in a finer form, while Miranda exists as love. Through the spirit of its players, the guitar has learned something of the beauty of the earth:

> The clearest echoes of the hills,
> And softest notes of falling rills,
> The melodies of birds and bees,
> The murmuring of summer seas,
> And pattering rain, and breathing dew,
> And airs of evening;
>
> (ll. 69–74)

The music which the guitar plays is a result, as music is for Shelley, of the conjunction between player and instrument, of spirit and physical object. The guitar came from a tree, which was cut down and now lives 'in happier form again' (l. 56). So too, in 'To Jane: "the keen stars were twinkling"'

the notes were not sweet till you sung them
Again.
                    (ll. 5–6)

The voice gives a soul to the strings, even as the moon gives splendour
to the starlit heaven. The joy of such a moment which the lyrics
celebrate is a joy of the unexpected joining of spirit and non-spirit,
as it is found in the poet himself, in the way in which he inhabits a
body but is also capable of seeing beyond material things. The same
combination occurs in the lyrics of nature, in which flowers, trees,
water, and clouds embody their own spiritual beauty. They are the
expression of themselves, the earthly expression of the beauty that is
theirs: and a poem such as 'The Cloud' provides a perfect expression
of the kind of life which they represent. The cloud is life-giving and
sublime, carrying water, shade, dew, hail, and thunder; it is piloted by
lightning, joined by sunrise and sunset, a tent that parts to allow the
moon to shine upon the water. In all Shelley's animation of the cloud
we recognize the truth and beauty of the effects which he describes; but
by giving the cloud its own monologue, it is reconstituted as a speaking
force itself, a spirit which is behind all the physical effects and which
is present even when there are no clouds in the sky. When the clouds
disappear, the 'spirit-cloud', the essential cloud, is still in existence: it
arises and unbuilds its cenotaph, the blue dome of the sky. It is always
in existence on the earth, but not always seen; when it is seen, it is
being itself, but physically:

> I am the daughter of Earth and Water,
>   And the nursling of the Sky;
> I pass through the pores of the ocean and shores;
>   I change, but I cannot die.
>   (ll. 73–76)

The cloud is one of Shelley's greatest emblems of a Platonically
conceived nature. Another is the skylark. The cloud rejoices in its
cosmic adaptability, while the skylark has a vertical movement; both
are ever present, yet sometimes seem absent. The skylark, for instance,
is spirit:

> Hail to thee, blithe Spirit!
> Bird thou never wert,

These lines are so familiar that it is easy to forget that Shelley means
what he says, that he wants us to take them literally. In the imagination,
and in the reality, the skylark is not its physical form, the bird a few

inches long, but the spirit which is demonstrated in its flight and its singing:

> Higher still and higher
>   From the earth thou springest
> Like a cloud of fire;
>   The blue deep thou wingest,
> And singing still dost soar, and soaring ever singest.
>
> (ll. 6–10)

This is why some of the verses of 'To a Skylark' have been thought of as imprecise and difficult; Shelley is indulging in his favourite trick of describing a beauty almost beyond beauty. In this case we stop at a point which the skylark perfectly embodies, the moment at which something physical almost ceases to be physical and becomes spirit, essence. As the moon fades in the dawn, so we watch the skylark as it fades into the sky in an exquisite eye-and-ear-straining moment.

> Keen as are the arrows
>   Of that silver sphere,
> Whose intense lamp narrows
>   In the white dawn clear
> Until we hardly see – we feel that it is there.
>
> (ll. 21–25)

Nor surprisingly, perhaps, the skylark is likened to a poet; but the poet is hidden, not in darkness as we would expect, but in light:

> Like a Poet hidden
>   In the light of thought,
>
> (ll. 36–37)

To be hidden in the light, the poet and the bird must themselves be radiant: they are caught at the point of intersection between appearance and disappearance, between physical and spiritual. And, as the poem continues, we should observe the modesty which impels Shelley to plead to be taught by the skylark, instructed by the bird which flies so effortlessly into the sky while singing.

In such moments of music, and of natural beauty, the lyrics of Shelley consistently endeavour to connect the world of the sense with the world beyond. This can happen with moments of great beauty, and also with terror. Shelley courts terror, fascinated by the way in which dreams and imaginative conceptions can give substance to an emotion.

'To Night', for instance, begins with an enchanting line, but there is a sinister possibility in the dreams which accompany darkness:

> Swiftly walk o'er the western wave,
> Spirit of Night!
> Out of the misty Eastern cave,
> Where, all the long and lone daylight,
> Thou wovest dreams of joy and fear,
> Which make thee terrible and dear, –
> > > Swift be thy flight!

The combination of terror and beauty is found most plainly in the poem 'On the Medusa of Leonardo da Vinci in the Florentine Gallery'. Describing the painting in detail, Shelley asserts that 'its horror and its beauty are divine': and it is not the Medusan horror that turns the beholder to stone, but the arresting beauty of the dreadful face, 'the tempestuous loveliness of terror':

> Yet it is less the horror than the grace
> > Which turns the gazer's spirit into stone,
> Whereon the lineaments of that dead face
> > Are graven, till the characters be grown
> Into itself, and thought no more can trace;
> > 'Tis the melodious hue of beauty thrown
> Athwart the darkness and the glare of pain,
> Which humanize and harmonize the strain.
> > > > (ll. 9–16)

As Mario Praz points out, such lines are a development of aesthetic theories of the horribly beautiful in the later eighteenth century, but they mark an extraordinary development of the cultivation of feeling in the Romantic period.[18] In Shelley's poetry they return in his final poem, 'The Triumph of Life', in the figure of Rousseau with holes for eyes and grass for thin discoloured hair. Shelley's feeling for such imagery is connected with his stance as poet, his insistent cultivation of the imaginative life of feeling; his admiration for the Leonardo painting is part of his sense of the reality of the emotional life. This prophetic and emotional stance places the poet in an awkward relationship with the world, because life (as 'The Triumph of Life' indicates) is a destroyer of ideals and feelings. Thus, in the best known of his poems, the 'Ode to the West Wind', he cries to the wind

> Oh, lift me as a wave, a leaf, a cloud!
> I fall upon the thorns of life! I bleed!

A heavy weight of hours has chained and bowed
One too like thee: tameless, and swift, and proud.

(ll. 53–56)

Like 'To a Skylark', the Ode is so familiar that it is difficult to realize
how extraordinary these lines are: how Shelley has become engaged
with his own thoughts so that he becomes almost a part of moving
nature, of wave, leaf, cloud. The force of 'I fall' is tremendous, because
it indicates an attempt at flight, even though the first two lines of the
section begin with 'If':

If I were a dead leaf thou mightest bear;
If I were a swift cloud to fly with thee;

(ll. 43–44)

The verse gathers speed and strength as it crosses the lines:

A wave to pant beneath thy power, and share
The impulse of thy strength, only less free
Than thou, O uncontrollable!

(ll. 44–46)

Here the vital words, 'pant', 'power', and 'strength', lead up to the
actual vision of the wave as free and the wind as even more free, so
free that it is, in the pivotal and climatic word, 'uncontrollable'. The
five syllables of that word occupy the centre of the line with immense
presence and energy: not for the first time Shelley is here controlling the
uncontrollable but allowing the verse to enter into the very movement
of wind and wave, rolling and sweeping. Yet the wave, being part of
the sea, is free, and the wind is even freer; as a child is free, or thinks
himself to be so. Shelley turns to childhood here with an extraordinary
simplicity, almost as if the storm had lulled for a moment and the
imagination can afford to be less intense and more playful:

If even
I were as in my boyhood, and could be

The comrade of thy wanderings over Heaven,
As then, when to outstrip thy skiey speed
Scarce seemed a vision; . . .

(ll. 47–51)

and the whole section comes to a point of sudden stillness in the line
and a half which follows:

I would ne'er have striven
As thus with thee in prayer in my sore need.
(ll. 51–52)

The implication is that, being human, the poet has to pray: throughout
the poem he has been celebrating the wind in praise and prayer. As
Judith Chernaik has written. 'The remarkable achievement of "Ode
to the West Wind" is the adequacy of the secular image for divinity
– power and freedom – in its effortless fusion of nature and myth.
The very inclusiveness of the natural scene contributes to the religious
character of the invocation.'[19] Shelley's prayer is thus not to the Holy
Spirit but to the 'Wild Spirit', the destroyer and preserver, the sister
wind of the azure breeze of the spring: and the first three sections
of the Ode all end with the invocation 'oh, hear!' Shelley cries to
be heard by the wind which is the breath of autumn, the charioteer
of dead leaves, the stream-sky with cloud-leaves, the dirge-sound of
the dying year, the awakener from summer dreams: the third section,
when the Mediterranean's summer sleep is awakened to autumn storms,
is perhaps the most extraordinary in terms of movement even in this
astonishing poem of activity, in which the verse so accurately captures
the changes of the natural world. This third section is divided into
two long sentences, carrying the movement across the lines with a
gentle rocking, caused by the enjambments and the brilliant use of a
trochaic foot at the beginning of the third line 'Lulled by the coil of
his crystalline streams', and the dactylic 'Quivering within the wave's
intenser day' in the sixth line. Then, after the exclamation mark, the
verse gathers strength: the lines still run on, but now the suspension
of the clause throws tremendous emphasis on to the verbs:

                              Thou
    For whose path the Atlantic's level powers
    Cleave themselves into chasms, . . .
                        (ll. 36–38)

The idea is fearsomely strong, and the sound matches the sense; and
then the poet envisages the strange life at the bottom of the sea, the
sea-vegetation moving as the waves above make levels into chasms, so
powerfully that even the sea-bed itself trembles with fear:

                    While far below
    The sea-blooms and the oozy woods which wear
    The sapless foliage of the ocean, know

Thy voice, and suddenly grow gray with fear,
And tremble and despoil themselves: . . .

(ll. 38–42)

The imaginative entering into this strange and remote life of the sea-
bed, this life 'far below' the surface (which itself is strange enough) is
part of Shelley's ability, which has already been evident in *Prometheus
Unbound*, to enter into the life of vegetable nature. In the 'Ode to the
West Wind' the process is two-fold: as the poet identifies the activity
and feelings of natural objects with an instinctive sympathy, so in the
final section of the poem he longs to be invaded by the fierce spirit of
the wind:

> Be thou, Spirit fierce,
> My spirit! Be thou me, impetuous one!
>
> Drive my dead thoughts over the universe
> Like withered leaves to quicken a new birth!
> And, by the incantation of this verse,
>
> Scatter, as from an unextinguished hearth
> Ashes and sparks, my words among mankind!
> Be through my lips to unawakened earth
>
> The trumpet of a prophecy!

(ll. 61–69)

After the earlier sections it seems almost impossible to produce yet
another fortissimo, and yet this is precisely what Shelley does. The wind
is alive, capable of taking the dead human thoughts and awakening the
earth, even as the summer sea had been wakened; the words are capable
of setting fire to the cold and lifeless world, of becoming a trumpet-call,
and (in the climactic word) a 'prophecy'. Shelley's belief in the poet's
role as prophet, which he argues so powerfully in 'A Defence of Poetry'
is nowhere more unequivocally stated in verse than it is here: it is a cry
to the world to be renewed, awakened, reinvigorated. For this purpose,
Shelley bravely disregards the archetype: it is usually spring that awakens
the world, but by choosing the wind of the autumn storm he does two
things. He makes it abundantly clear that he is not forcing the natural
world into his own mould, but that the poem is occasioned by a specific
moment (on a day of tempestuous wind in a wood that skirts the Arno,
as the note says) and not the other way round; secondly he is seeing the
process of rebirth as being naturally preceded by the destruction of the
old unregenerate world. So the wind is 'Destroyer and preserver', and
the poem ends with the prophecy of a future which is the inevitable
consequence:

> O, Wind,
> If Winter comes, can Spring be far behind?
>
> (ll. 69–70)

Together with the first section of the Ode, this conclusion raises an interesting question: how far is the 'Ode to the West Wind' a political poem? The answer is that it is political in the sense that all Shelley's poems are seeking a better world, a new life to replace the old systems and old corruptions. The wind of autumn is a perfect symbol of a moving and cleansing power, evidence in the natural world of what was so poignantly missing in the human.

Shelley's poetry is greatly enriched by this awareness, by the tension between the ideal and the actual state of political affairs in his own day. He was encouraged by all manifestations of revolution, however brief, in Europe; and outraged by fresh evidence of brutality and tyranny, in particular by the news of the 'Peterloo massacre' in Manchester on 16 August 1819. This event caused the writing of 'The Mask of Anarchy', with its powerful stabbing denunciation:

> I met Murder on the way
> He had a mask like Castlereagh –
>
> (ll. 5–6)

The title has a double meaning: the whole process of government is a mask, or pretence, in which anarchy carries on his brow the words 'I am God, and King, and Law!' and the poem itself is a masque, or a masquerade, in which anarchy rides in triumph through London, feared by the citizens but welcomed by the slaves of money and the hired murderers. Against this rises the spirit of England, the true England of liberty and justice, urging the people to

> 'Rise like Lions after slumber
> In unvanquishable number,
> Shake your chains to earth like dew
> Which in sleep had fallen on you –
> Ye are many – they are few.'
>
> (ll. 368–72)

This poem, like some of the others written in 1819, is (in Mary Shelley's words) 'written for the people' and 'in a more popular tone than usual': in 'Song to the Men of England', for example, Shelley produces a direct incitement to rebellion:

> Men of England, wherefore plough
> For the lords who lay ye low?
> Wherefore weave with toil and care
> The rich robes your tyrants wear?
>
> (ll. 1–4)

Shelley's crusading spirit, which is so evident in these short-stanza poems, as part of the wider pattern of his *œuvre* in which all his poetry is infused with the ardent spirit of an idealist. This idealism led him to protest against all injustice, but also (as we have seen in connection with his lyrics) to rejoice in all manifestations of love and beauty. There are two conspicuous examples of this in his poetry, the 'Hymn to Intellectual Beauty' and *Epipsychidion*. The Hymn is a particularly clear example of what James A. Notopoulos calls Shelley's 'natural Platonism',[20] describing Beauty as the unseen power which visits the world, and which appears in evanescent forms:

> Like hues and harmonies of evening, –
>   Like clouds in starlight widely spread, –
>   Like memory of music fled, –
>
> (ll. 8–10)

The poet has dedicated his powers to Beauty, which he believes will eventually 'free/This world from its dark slavery', and he ends with a Wordsworthian dedication:

> Then let thy power, which like the truth
> Of nature on my passive youth
> Descended, to my onward life supply
> Its calm – to one who worships thee,
> And every form containing thee,
> Whom, Spirit fair, thy spells did bind
> To fear himself, and love all human kind.
>
> (ll. 78–84)

The antithesis is neat in the final line, depending as it does on the recognition of human selfishness as the opposite of the poet's dedication; usually the line would be 'To love himself, and fear all human kind' (as threats to that self-love), but Shelley's unobtrusive change indicates an entirely different view of the self.

If this seems elusive, not governed by a central symbol as the 'Ode to the West Wind' is, *Epipsychidion* is even more so. The girl who is ostensibly the love-object of the poem, Emilia Viviani, is described as a manifestation of the quintessential love of the kind discussed by Plato in the *Symposium*. She stands, as Earl Wasserman has pointed out, in relation to the poet as the infinite to the finite,[21] and this makes for some considerable difficulty. The title, which literally means 'about a little soul', also contains the suggestion of 'epicycle', the movement of a large wheel by means of a small one within. The idea that our own natures are epicyclically propelled by our best selves is an attractive one, and is connected with the whole Platonic conception of the ideal. Just as our mortal natures are liable to hamper the purity of the best self, so human beauty is only a rough expression of the exquisite soul, and poetry an attempt to embody in words the deep truths of the imagination. So Shelley addresses Emily as follows:

> I pray thee that thou blot from this sad song
> All of its much mortality and wrong,
> With those clear drops, which start like sacred dew
> From the twin lights thy sweet soul darkens through,
> Weeping, till sorrow becomes ecstasy:
> Then smile on it, so that it may not die.
>
> (ll. 35–40)

Just as the best self is surrounded by the remainder, and poetry is mortal and impure, so Emily is (in the words of the title) 'Imprisoned in the Convent . . .'. The imprisonment in a convent of a young girl would have been likely to have distressed Shelley on anti-religious grounds anyway: but it also becomes here a symbol of the imprisonment of the ideal on earth. It is to this spirit, this ideal, that Shelley longs to be united: he wishes to be as like Emily as possible, wishing that he and she were twins. He goes on to describe his first attraction to ideal beauty, his pursuit of the twin soul to his own, and his failure to find it: he comes across many mortal forms, but all are ultimately unsatisfactory. Then comes a figure like the moon, under whose spell he falls; and finally the sun, giving light and life:

> I stood, and felt the dawn of my long night
> Was penetrating me with living light:
> I knew it was the Vision veiled from me
> So many years – that it was Emily.
>
> (ll. 341–44)

With the removal of the veil, as always in Shelley, comes the moment of reality; and in *Epipsychidion* the use of the veil image comes with extraordinary force after the many failures of love that Shelley has previously described. This is why he uses the word 'Emily', which at first sight seems bathetic: Emily is herself, uniquely, the reality, the soul for which the poet's soul has been searching.

The final part of the poem is a fantasy in which the two souls fly together to a paradise island. They are supposed to be 'One passion in twin hearts', with a flame 'ever still/Burning, yet ever unconsumable':

> One hope within two wills, one will beneath
> Two overshadowing minds, one life, one death,
> One Heaven, one Hell, one immortality,
> And one annihilation.
> (ll. 584–87)

But then, as if exhausted at the climax of his passion, Shelley reflects that words, like all other mortal things, are inadequate:

> Woe is me!
> The winged words on which my soul would pierce
> Into the height of Love's rare Universe,
> Are chains of lead around its flight of fire –
> I pant, I sink, I tremble, I expire!
> (ll. 587–91)

These lines point to a very real difficulty of *Epipsychidion*: it is a characteristic Shelleyan poem of idealism and enthusiasm, described with a rare radiance, but it also has what seems to be (from the rhythms and images) a sexual element, and the mixture is uncomfortable. If Shelley was sexually attracted to Emilia Viviani, why does he indulge in all this rigmarole about twin souls? It is difficult, too, to see the island paradise 'twixt Heaven, Air, Earth, and Sea' (l. 457) as anything but an immature fantasy retreat. What is irritating about *Epipsychidion*, radiant and beautiful as it may be, is that its brilliant imagery seems to be pressed into the service of a dubious relationship, and then enlarged upon with a kind of uncritical egotistical enthusiasm.

Prometheus Unbound, as we have seen, is a rewriting of Aeschylus, rejecting the idea of a reconciliation between tyrant and victim. *Hellas* is closer to its original, *The Persians*. This was written by Aeschylus to celebrate the Athenian victory at Salamis in 480 B.C., which was a crucial step in the establishment of Greek liberty. In *Hellas*, Shelley sees the process as about to be repeated: the drama was written in the autumn of 1821, at the very beginning of the Greek uprising, but it looks forwards to the triumph of freedom and love as inevitable. The Turkish ruler, Mahmud, is seen as uneasy and time-bound, whereas the Greek ideal is seen as timeless:

> Greece and her foundations are
> Built below the tide of war,
> Based on the crystalline sea
> Of thought and its eternity:
>
> (ll. 696–99)

The empire of Greece is that of the spirit. In a reference to St Paul's preaching at Athens, Shelley sees it as embodying love and not hate:

> In sacred Athens, near the fane
> Of Wisdom, Pity's altar stood:
> Serve not the unknown God in vain,
> But pay that broken shrine again,
> Love for hate and tear for blood.
>
> (ll. 733–37)

The antithesis of love and hate is further emphasized when the shade of Mahomet the Second is summoned up (in Shelley's parallel with Aeschylus' Darius). Mahomet the Second had conquered Constantinople in 1453; he now prophesies the end of the Islamic empire, and underlines Mahmud's subjection to time and earthly fears, which lead to hate. In a fine piece of irony, Mahmud's hopes are given a boost when the great powers stand by and see Greece defeated (reversing the course of Aeschylus' play); but this is done only to emphasize the fragility of such a victory. The Turkish voices shouting 'Kill! crush! despoil!' (l. 1022) are succeeded by the magnificent final chorus, which (as Shelley himself pointed out) is a prophecy like those of Isaiah and Virgil (in the *Fourth Eclogue*):

> The world's great age begins anew,
>   The golden years return,
> The earth doth like a snake renew
>   Her winter weeds outworn:
> Heaven smiles, and faiths and empires gleam
> Like wrecks of a dissolving dream.
>
> (ll. 1060–65)

Adonais was inspired not only by Keats's death, but by the supposed cause of his death: Shelley was one of those who believed that the reviewers had killed Keats, and to Shelley this was one more example of a corruption that had to be fought. And, as he had done in *Prometheus Unbound*, Shelley once again found the right myth for his purposes; the story of the young man, loved by the goddess of love, slain by a wild beast and universally mourned. In this poem Adonis is changed to Adonais, a name which is both euphonious and suggestive of the Hebrew *Adonai* or Lord (Wasserman suggests that this removes the limited classical frame from the poem and makes Adonais into a season god)[22]; the goddess becomes not Venus but Urania, the muse of astronomy who had been invoked by Milton at the opening of *Paradise Lost* to preside over the most sublime poetry (referred to in st. 3 of *Adonais*). The astronomical references are significant when we remember that Adonais, like Milton's Lycidas, becomes a star; and the poem's final symbol is of an eternally shining star, an immortal spirit giving light to the mortal earth.

Adonais is concerned with a young poet and his untimely death. From that circumstance, Shelley writes a poem which contains many of his most cherished ideas. The lament for Keats's death becomes an affirmation of all that Shelley most admired, in the power of the human mind, in the beauty of nature, and in the benediction of human love. The reviewers, who stand in this poem for the evil forces of hate and prejudice which Shelley had been fighting all his life, are consumed and destroyed, not only by Byron's attack on them (st. 28) but by the sheer power of goodness, poetry, and love. The force of *Adonais* is overwhelming: it begins in weeping and ends in triumph, in the assurance of Keats's immortality and of the reality of the world of the spirit in which he now lives:

> Peace, peace! he is not dead, he doth not sleep –
> He hath awakened from the dream of life –
>
> (ll. 343–44)

These are the pivotal lines of the poem. Up to this point there has been the very proper mourning for Adonais, the due ceremonies which need to be observed. The mourners are not only Keats's fellow-poets, but the spirit-subjects of his poetry,

> The quick Dreams,
> The passion-winged Ministers of thought,
> Who were his flocks, whom near the living streams
> Of his young spirit he fed, and whom he taught
> The love which was its music. . . .
>
> (ll. 73–77)

Everything that he loved mourned Adonais: the poem celebrates this mourning in considerable detail, and this part of the poem has the same kind of necessary display of grief that is found in funeral services. But Shelley marks the turning-point of the poem with great clarity ('Peace,

peace!') where he contrasts the life of the eternal spirit with the decaying life on earth:

> *We* decay
> Like corpses in a charnel; fear and grief
> Convulse us and consume us day by day,
> And cold hopes swarm like worms within our living clay.
>
> (ll. 348–51)

Paradoxically it is we who are the corpses, and we who are eaten up by the worms of the cold thoughts; and after this extraordinary daring, Shelley sails into his great assertion of life:

> He has outsoared the shadow of our night;
> Envy and calumny and hate and pain,
> And that unrest which men miscall delight,
> Can touch him not and torture not again;
>
> (ll. 352–55)

The remarkable security of that first line is based upon Shelley's Platonism, but its power here is also due to the perfect placing of the words within the line. In verse after verse of this section of *Adonais*, especially the first lines, the sublimity is unerringly achieved:

> He is made one with Nature: there is heard
> His voice in all her music, . . .
>
> (ll. 370–71)

> He is a portion of the loveliness
> Which once he made more lovely: . . .
>
> (ll. 378–79)

> The splendours of the firmament of time
> May be eclipsed, but are extinguished not;
>
> (ll. 388–89)

The last verse refers to the figures, like Keats, who appear on earth with a transforming spirit: they include 'the inheritors of unfulfilled renown', such as Chatterton, Sidney, and Lucan, who welcome the spirit of Keats to his place among the stars. Then, just as the poem seems to be disappearing into a radiance of its own, Shelley anchors it in the touching atmosphere of the Protestant cemetery in Rome. It is here that the poet himself finally confronts the possibility of death:

> From the world's bitter wind
> Seek shelter in the shadow of the tomb.
> What Adonais is, why fear we to become?
>
> (ll. 457–59)

The poet is faced with the fact that his celebration of Keats has left him disenchanted with the earth on which he lives: the logic which he has to confront is that Keats's transcendent magnificence is the reality beyond the veil. So his own death would rend that veil, as he has always desired to do:

> The One remains, the many change and pass;
> Heaven's light forever shines, Earth's shadows fly;
> Life, like a dome of many-coloured glass,
> Stains the white radiance of Eternity,
> Until Death tramples it to fragments. – Die,
> If thou wouldst be with that which thou dost seek!
>
> (ll. 460–65)

The final three verses of *Adonais* are almost frightening in their sublimity: they press forward to a point at which the poet strives to be united with his fellow-poet, a point at which he loses his mortality and becomes himself a part of 'That Light whose smile kindles the Universe'. His mortality is consumed, and he travels in his spirit-bark guided by the soul of Adonais, which

> like a star,
> Beacons from the abode where the Eternal are.
>
> (ll. 494–95)

I have chosen to end with *Adonais* because its conclusion shows Shelley at his most successful in the treatment of the sublime. And Shelley's sublime is not an eighteenth-century aesthetic mode: it is a passionately-held belief in qualities of nobility, and love, and beauty, and the poetic imagination. In the world these are encumbered by time, and physicality, and the material world, and attacked by greed, tyranny, and corruption. Shelley's awareness of this, and his intense straining after an ideal, become almost terrifying in the final stanzas of *Adonais*: and in his unfinished 'The Triumph of Life', as we have seen, he grieves

> to think how power and will
> In opposition rule our mortal day,

And why God made irreconcilable
Good and the means of good;

(ll. 228–31)

and 'The Triumph of Life' ends with a last, unanswered question: 'Then, what is life? I cried.' – The answer, however, has been implied in *Adonais* and in much of the earlier poetry. At the end of *Adonais*, too, we may feel with A. Alvarez that 'Poetry of this order is a murderous art.'[23] Alvarez was writing about the last poems of Sylvia Plath, about the element of risk involved in writing them. 'The achievement of her final style is to make poetry and death inseparable',[24] he wrote. The same could be said of the last poems of Shelley, and we shall see Shelley clearly only if we realize that his intensity and excitement are evidence of the same kind of courage that inspired Sylvia Plath.

Notes

1. C. S. Lewis, 'Shelley, Dryden and Mr. Eliot', in *Selected Literary Essays*, edited by W. Hooper (Cambridge, 1969), p. 204.

2. Matthew Arnold, *Essays in Criticism*, Second Series (London, 1888), p. 252.

3. Timothy Webb, *Shelley: A Voice Not Understood* (Manchester, 1977), p. 82.

4. Shelley, *Poetical Works*, edited by Thomas Hutchinson, revised by G. M. Matthews (London, 1970), p. 835. I have used this Oxford Standard Authors edition for all quotations from the poetry and from Mary Shelley's notes.

5. Shelley had probably read *Political Justice* at school. See A. M. D. Hughes, *The Nascent Mind of Shelley* (Oxford, 1947), p. 38.

6. Although Carlos Baker described Queen Mab as 'a Titania in two-penny muslin who talks like an eighteenth-century bluestocking'; *Shelley's Major Poetry: The Fabric of a Vision* (London, 1948), p. 92.

7. *Poetical Works*, p. 836.

8. From Shelley's translation of the *Symposium*; quoted in Neville Rogers, *Shelley at Work* (Oxford, 1956), p. 141.

9. James A. Notopoulos, *The Platonism of Shelley* (Durham, N. C., 1949), p. 238.

10. Webb, *Shelley: A Voice Not Understood*, p. 236.

11. Donald H. Reiman, *Percy Bysshe Shelley* (London, 1976), pp. 35–41.

12. *Poetical Works*, p. 205.

13. *Poetical Works*, p. 205.

14. *Poetical Works*, p. 271.

15. *Poetical Works*, p. 272.

16. Baker, p. 118.

17. *Poetical Works*, p. 273.

18. Mario Praz, *The Romantic Agony* (London, 1933), pp. 41–43.

19. Judith Chernaik, *The Lyrics of Shelley* (Cleveland and London, 1972), p. 93.

20. Notopoulos, *The Platonism of Shelley*, pp. 14–17.

21. Earl R. Wasserman, *Shelley, A Critical Reading* (Baltimore and London, 1971). p. 429.

22. Wasserman, p. 465.

23. A. Alvarez, *Beyond All This Fiddle* (London, 1968), p. 57.

24. Alvarez, p. 57.

Chapter 10
Keats

In July 1816, Keats passed his examinations at Apothecaries' Hall, and
was thenceforth eligible to practise as a medical man. His guardian,
Richard Abbey, had plans for him to do so:

> He communicated his plans to his Ward, but his surprise
> was not moderate, to hear in Reply, that he did not intend
> to be a Surgeon – Not intend to be a Surgeon! why what
> do you mean to be? I mean to rely on my Abilities as a
> Poet – John, you are either Mad or a Fool, to talk in so
> absurd a Manner. My mind is made up, said the youngster
> very quietly. I know that I possess Abilities greater than
> most Men, and therefore I am determined to gain my
> living by exercising them. – Seeing nothing could be
> done Abby called him a Silly Boy, & prophesied a speedy
> Termination to his inconsiderate Enterprise.[1]

This confrontation brings out several things which are important for
an understanding of Keats and his poetry. In the first place, he is the
major Romantic poet who most obviously gives up an honourable
and satisfying career in order to devote his life to poetry. There are
signs that he had been distressed by some of the scenes which he
had witnessed as a medical student and as a 'dresser' (or surgeon's
assistant); but his progress from student to dresser in a good London
hospital shows that he was intending to take the full examination for
the MRCS.[2] By the time of the conversation with Abbey he had made
up his mind with a quiet certainty; and the assurance of his own
abilities, his faith in himself as a poet, is another revealing feature
of this encounter. Keats, like Wordsworth, knew that he possessed
'Abilities greater than most Men', and he was determined to exercise
them. He had a strong sense of his high calling, and an inner need to
give himself time to write. 'O for ten years', he wrote in 'Sleep and
Poetry',

> that I may overwhelm
> Myself in poetry; so I may do the deed
> That my own soul has to itself decreed.
>
> (ll. 96–98)

The decree of the soul to itself was – be a poet; and of all the Romantic poets, Keats is the one who seems most consciously to be working to fulfil that destiny. He studied other poets, and read classical legends, with an intense delight; he cut himself off from his friends in order to write, and set himself arduous poetic tasks, such as the writing of *Endymion*; he set off on a tour, in 1818, not just for pleasure but in pursuit of the sublime, which he thought he lacked experience of; and in every way he tried to prepare himself for the role of great poet with a single-minded and self-conscious determination.

The result is not, as might have been expected, a selfish and self-centred poetry which takes itself too seriously. Throughout his short life Keats's innate warmth and friendliness, his sensitive and robust humanity (which comes through so pulsingly in the letters) alleviates the high seriousness, and blends with the young man's intense idealism and his passionate scholarship. The last of these qualities is often under-estimated in discussions of Keats: he is traditionally thought of as the poet of the senses, because of his ability to write verse which captures the 'feel' of things, but a great deal of his poetry is affected by other poetry, by painting, and by other works of art. The poetry of Keats contains a library of references and an art gallery of images.

Many of these influences came Keats's way during his years as a medical student. He was well educated at school in Enfield, but left at fourteen; thereafter his interests in literature were encouraged by his former schoolmaster, Charles Cowden Clarke, who, among many other books, first lent Keats *The Faerie Queene*. Keats went through it, Clarke remembered, like a young horse turned into a spring meadow.[3] Later, at Guy's Hospital, he became friendly with Leigh Hunt, whose house at Hampstead, filled with books and paintings, was a continual source of excitement and delight for the student escaped from the hospital. The Hunts and their friends, and Charles Cowden Clarke, were like tutors to Keats, and the village of Hampstead, so refreshing after the centre of London, was his university. His enthusiasm and their encouragement were complementary, and no doubt played a part in the abandoning of his medical career. The life at Hampstead certainly played a big part in the early poems: the subjects and their treatment – friendship, literature, history, mythology, are those which Keats had absorbed with delight, and he was now adding his voice to the conversation of friends. Some early poems, therefore, to Haydon, Hunt, Clarke, George Felton Mathew, are those of plain friendship; others commemorate moments of particular significance experienced with friends, such as 'On Seeing the Elgin Marbles' (seen with Haydon) and 'On First Looking into Chapman's Homer' (with Clarke).

These and others were published in *Poems*, in 1817 (dedicated to Leigh Hunt). It is a young man's book, full of joy and delight in the world around him, with an epigraph on the title page from Spenser:

> 'What more felicity can fall to creature,
> Than to enjoy delight with liberty.'
>
> ('Muiopotomos', ll. 209–10)

The poems celebrate the pleasures of delight and freedom: they are not concerned with Keats's more painful experiences (his father's death in 1804, his mother's remarriage two months later, and her death in 1810) or with his encounters with death and suffering in the hospital. The world of the sick and dying has been left behind in the exuberant celebration of youth and hope:

> Life is the rose's hope while yet unblown;
> The reading of an ever-changing tale;
> The light uplifting of a maiden's veil;
> A pigeon tumbling in clear summer air;
> A laughing school-boy, without grief or care,
> Riding the springy branches of an elm.
>
> ('Sleep and Poetry', ll. 90–95)

The images tumble over one another in the poet's impatience to put down all the sources of his enjoyment; he delights in the ever-changing moments of beauty, the maiden at the moment of lifting her veil, the pigeon tumbling, the schoolboy. Later in the poem he recalls the image from Titian's *Bacchus and Ariadne*:

> the swift bound
> Of Bacchus from his chariot, when his eye
> Made Ariadne's cheek look blushingly.
>
> (ll. 334–36)

and the image is an apt one for the young Keats, leaping into experience with an energy which is beautifully caught by the image in Titian's painting and reworked here in the poem. Keats's placing of the word 'bound' is a foretaste of things to come: it cleverly holds the moment at the end of the line before going on to describe it in full, suspending the motion in the space at the end of the line just as Titian catches Bacchus springing from the chariot. The word 'bound', like the image in the painting, contains its own coiled energy, although the effect is dissipated in the lines which follow:

> Thus I remember all the pleasant flow
> Of words at opening a portfolio.
>
> (ll. 337–38)

Often in 'Sleep and Poetry', and in the 1817 volume in general, Keats's enthusiasm topples over into a kind of naivety, an ingenuous joy which is gauche and unsatisfying. The 'Imitation of Spenser', for instance, luxuriates in description but completely lacks the high and serious morality which gives backbone to the descriptions in *The Faerie Queene*.

Keats, the most self-conscious of young artists, was aware of this. In the poem 'To Charles Cowden Clarke' he excuses himself for not having addressed Clarke before by admitting that his 'wine was of too poor a savour' to one who had known Spenser, Shakespeare, and Milton:

> Small good to one who had by Mulla's stream
> Fondled the maidens with the breasts of cream;
> Who had beheld Belphoebe in a brook,
> And lovely Una in a leafy nook,
> And Archimago leaning o'er his book:
> Who had of all that's sweet tasted, and seen,
> From silvery ripple, up to beauty's queen;
> From the sequestered haunts of gay Titania,
> To the blue dwelling of divine Urania . . .
>
> (ll. 33–41)

Keats is being modest here, but in a determinedly immodest way. I too am a poet, he is claiming, I too can write of these things, and not at second hand either: the long description of the swan at the beginning of the poem is a demonstration of my powers, evidence of promise. And although in 'Sleep and Poetry' Keats realizes that there is another world waiting to be explored, he pushes it aside for the time being. This is something that will have to faced sooner or later, but at the moment Keats only gestures towards it before losing himself again in the image of the chariot:

> And can I ever bid these joys farewell?
> Yes, I must pass them for a nobler life,
> Where I may find the agonies, the strife
> Of human hearts – for lo! I see afar,

> O'er-sailing the blue cragginess, a car
> And steeds with streamy manes –
>
> (ll. 122–27)

These lines are sometimes taken as being of great portent for Keats's later poetry. In fact, they are remarkable in their refusal to do more than make a curt acknowledgement of future concerns. For the moment the charioteer drives on through the landscape of trees and mountains, past shapes of delight, and mystery, and fear:

> O that I might know
> All that he writes with such a hurrying glow
>
> (ll. 153–54)

The urgency is clear. The poet is desperate to see more of this extraordinary world of the imagination that is waiting to be explored, the accumulated riches of ancient and modern civilization. How much Spenser, Shakespeare, or Milton must have known! And how much there is still waiting to be discovered! The world of everyday concerns must not be allowed to get in the way of this:

> A sense of real things comes doubly strong,
> And, like a muddy stream, would bear along
> My soul to nothingness: but I will strive
> Against all doubtings, and will keep alive
> The thought of that same chariot, and the strange
> Journey it went.
>
> (ll. 157–62)

Keats sees the imaginative preservation of the vision as vital. This is what Wordsworth, Leigh Hunt, and Haydon have done (in 'Great Spirits now on earth are sojourning') and this is what the eighteenth-century poets failed to do. They swayed about on their heroic couplets like children on a rocking-horse, and Apollo must have been ashamed of them. In his enthusiasm, Keats misread Dryden and Pope: his open-eyed wonder at the poets of his own age or of a particular kind of Romantic sublimity leaves no room for proper discrimination. The images which express this wonder most effectively are those of the astronomer and the explorer in the finest poem of the 1817 volume, 'On First Looking into Chapman's Homer'. In the octave the geography is established as Apollo's own, for the poet is travelling in the realms of gold, the states, kingdoms, and islands of poetry. Finally he comes across Homer in Chapman's translation:

Then felt I like some watcher of the skies
When a new planet swims into his ken;
Or like stout Cortez when with eagle eyes
He stared at the Pacific – and all his men
Looked at each other with a wild surmise –
Silent, upon a peak in Darien.

(ll. 9–14)

The first image is that of the astronomer Herschel discovering the planet Uranus: he says nothing (in contrast with Chapman, who 'speaks out loud and bold'), and the reaction of Cortez and his men is silence. The two images, fashioned from such disparate experiences, are beautifully complementary. The sharp, precise simplicity of 'watcher of the skies', and the brilliant image of a planet moving through the darkness of the night sky into the orbit of a telescope as a swimmer moves through water, give way to another picture, that of men staring at an unknown ocean for the first time. Keats is stretching our imaginations through time and space, from the travelling poet, to the astronomer, and then to the explorer in Central America. Each is filled with amazement, and here the word 'Silent' performs its function so powerfully, summing up the wonder of the whole poem. Its placing at the beginning of the last line is crucial: the preceding two lines carry on the sense and are continuous in rhythm, so that the sentence is ready to fall heavily on the word 'Silent' at the beginning of the last line. In turn, this is qualified by the simple remoteness of the 'peak in Darien'.

The placing of 'Silent' is absolutely precise, and, because of that, thrilling. It is a crucial word, *the* crucial word of Keats's early poetry, because that poetry has been written in a continual battle to overcome silence. All Romantic poets face the problem that their deepest feelings often lie (as Wordsworth put it) 'far hidden from the reach of words', buried in a deep part of the questing self: Keats faces it with particular acuteness because he is concerned principally with wonder, the joy that comes from freedom and delight. He has chosen to celebrate the things he loves, the variety and beauty and friendship in the created world; he has to do so in words, and the words interpose themselves between the poet and the pure feeling. The proper reaction to delight and liberty is enjoyment and wonder, the silence of someone who is totally overwhelmed or immersed in the experience. Cortez and his men had it; Herschel had it; the poet has it too, but he has to use words in order to express it.

The overcoming of silence is the great problem of *Endymion* (1818). The story only takes a paragraph in the telling, and Keats was to write a poem which would 'make 4000 lines of one bare circumstances and fill them with poetry'.[4] He has to fill in the spaces that are left by the narrative, the imagination's wonder at the beauty of each episode and at the meaning of the legend. He found the story in one of his favourite quarries, Lemprière's *Classical Dictionary:*

> Endymion, a shepherd . . . Diana saw him naked as he slept on mount Latmos, and was so struck with his beauty that she came down every night from heaven to enjoy his company . . . The fable of Endymion's amours with Diana, or the moon, arises from his knowledge of astronomy, and as he passed the night on some high mountain, to observe the heavenly bodies, it has been reported that he was courted by the moon.

Keats saw the project of writing a long poem on this legend as a test of his abilities, and as a necessary further step after the short poems of the 1817 volume. He took himself off to the Isle of Wight in April 1817 to make a start on it: he hoped, as the early paragraphs tell us, to begin the poem in the spring and finish it in the autumn (it was actually finished in November).

Yet it was not all duty and apprentice-work. It was a poem which, like those of the 1817 volume, expressed Keats's love of enchantment and delight and his joy in the created world. The very word 'Endymion' was itself an example: like Coleridge, Keats was in love with the music of words, and its beautiful and mysterious four syllables thrilled him:

> The very music of the name has gone
> Into my being, and each pleasant scene
> Is growing fresh before me as the green
> Of our own valleys.
>   (I. 36–39)

The sound of the word, the beauty of the landscape, poetry itself, all these are part of Keats's love and hope, expressed in the apparently effortless (but in reality not so[5]) and magnificent first line:

> A thing of beauty is a joy for ever.

It is significant that in Lemprière's account Diana woos Endymion, a goddess loving a mortal, as if to signify the attractions of earth. Keats has deliberately chosen a legend about the interaction between earth and heaven, and this is a two-way process. The alliance of a beautiful shepherd and a goddess involves a love on both sides: the poem can be seen as an allegory (which might be expected from a lover of Spenser) of the soul's search for ideal beauty, but it should also be seen as the goddess's search for an earthly love.

And yet, if the poem is an allegory, it seems to have its own life outside the pattern of meaning. Keats wrote about the long poem in a letter of 1817:

> Do not the lovers of Poetry like to have a little region to wander in where they may pick and choose, and in which the images are so numerous that many are forgotten and found new in a second reading – which may be food for a week's stroll in the Summer?[6]

and *Endymion* certainly has room for strolling, for picking and choosing, so much so that the forward movement of the poem is often impeded by the cornucopia effect of its imagery. Nevertheless, this must be part of the poem's process as well: the poem is about Cynthia (Lemprière's Diana) and her love for a beautiful mortal, and because of this the poem necessarily celebrates the created world. Book 1 is a good example. The opening action is a gathering of the people of Latmos, the shepherds with their lord Endymion, and the singing of the hymn to Pan, the god of shepherds and of universal nature. The hymn to Pan is a gorgeous recital of the processes of life, creation, and harvest, a poem in itself; it was read by the young Keats to Wordsworth when the latter visited London in December 1817, and Wordsworth's verdict was 'a very pretty piece of Paganism', which disappointed the aspiring author. The odd thing is that Wordsworth was right (though we have no way of knowing the tone in which these words were spoken): it is a fine piece of paganism, wonderfully sensuous and rich. The full implications of the poem's pagan elements are not revealed until Book IV.

The subsequent action of Book I concerns the mortal's love for the immortal. Endymion is taken by his sister Peona to her bower, where he tells her of his love for the moon in words which indicate how difficult it is to find words which will properly express the feelings of love:

> Whence that completed form of all completeness?
> Whence came that high perfection of all sweetness?
> Speak, stubborn earth, and tell me where, O where
> Hast thou a symbol of her golden hair?
>
> (I. 606–9)

After his first encounter with Cynthia, Endymion is lovesick, in that the world has lost all its attraction for him; although he recognizes

that through our love for earthly things we move towards something
higher, he longs to be free:

> Wherein lies happiness? In that which becks
> Our ready minds to fellowship divine,
> A fellowship with essence; till we shine,
> Full alchemized, and free of space. Behold
> The clear religion of heaven!
>
> (I. 777–81)

The path to such a state is through the magic of earthly things, the
feelings which they evoke in us of wonder, so that we step

> Into a sort of oneness, and our state
> Is like a floating spirit's.
>
> (I. 796–97)

If love for earthly things can raise us above our mortal natures, how
much higher shall our love for immortal beauty raise us? and how does
it relate to the immortal's love for mortal things? The answer is that
in both cases it leads to a longing for wonder and enchantment. When
Endymion meets the Naiad in Book II, she tells him that he

> must wander far
> In other regions, past the scanty bar
> To mortal steps, before thou canst be ta'en
> From every wasting sigh, from every pain,
> Into the gentle bosom of thy love.
>
> (II. 123–27)

This seems to indicate that Endymion must pass beyond the regions
of sense; this is confirmed by the Naiad, who knows that her own
beautiful world of water and sea-floor is not enough. His proper course
is towards a deeper experience, suggested by the voice which tells him
to follow the airy voices

> through the hollow,
> The silent mysteries of earth, descend! (II. 213–14)

After many marvellous wanderings beneath the earth he meets Adonis,
who is in his winter sleep, and hears the story of Venus and Adonis (a
story, like his own, of a love between mortal and immortal). He then
meets Cynthia, in a section which is the most erotic and sensuous in

the poem; through her kiss she gives him 'an immortality of passion' (II. 808) and then leaves him asleep. When he awakes, Endymion is in a love-trance; he emerges from it on hearing the complaint of Alpheus for Arethusa, and her reply. The encounter reminds us of the unhappiness of love, and at one point Keats addresses the reader as

> Ye who have yearned
> With too much passion
> (II. 828–29)

which suggests that one of the processes which has to be undergone in the pursuit of love is an experiencing of the quenchless fires of longing. That these can be dangerous is shown in Book III, where Endymion has to rescue Glaucus and the enchanted knights who have fallen under the spell of Circe. The poem seems to be exploring the need to feel the power of love without being rendered ineffectual – in love or in anything else – by it. By the opening of Book IV, however, Endymion is perplexed, not only by the labyrinthine processes through which he has passed but also by the distressed figure of the Indian Maid. Her song to sorrow, however, gives way to the triumphant arrival of Bacchus; and Endymion's perplexity gives way to love, whereupon the Indian Maid is revealed as Cynthia herself. By choosing to love an earthly creature (as he thinks) Endymion has united himself with a higher order of reality in the figure of an immortal; just as the immortal has found her own satisfaction in an earthly form and in the love of a shepherd.

This interpretation is certainly in accord with the astonishing fertility and energy of the poem. Keats's ardent spirit seems unable to be content with anything less than a complete and overwhelming attempt to render in verse the power of love and passion for all earthly things. *Endymion* is a poem which affirms at all points the vitality of a healthy and passionate love; it is grounded in the experience of life as Keats then saw it. Writing to his friend Benjamin Bailey in November 1817, just as he was finishing the poem, Keats said that he was 'certain of nothing but of the holiness of the heart's affections and the truth of Imagination'[7]. In the same way the poem is about the truth of imagination in the Endymion story and its realization; it is also about the holiness of the heart's affections, which dwell on beauty, and on love, and are linked (as they are in the letter) with the poet's imagination. In the letter he goes on:

> What the imagination seizes as beauty must be Truth – whether it existed before or not – for I have the same idea of all our passions as of love – they are all in their sublime, creative of essential beauty.

It is this sublime vision of the great imagination playing on the created world that we find in *Endymion*. The nobleness of Keats's character, and his willingness to open his heart in poetry, makes it a rich poem of natural description, adolescent affections, idealisms, and sexual fantasies. Keats's delight in the created world is found in many places, notably in the Hymn to Pan from Book I:

> O thou, to whom
> Broad-leaved fig trees even now foredoom
> Their ripened fruitage – yellow-girted bees
> Their golden honeycombs; our village leas
> Their fairest-blossomed beans and poppied corn;
> The chuckling linnet its five young unborn
> To sing for thee; low creeping strawberries
> Their summer coolness; pent up butterflies
> Their freckled wings; yea, the fresh budding year
> All its completions –
>
> (I. 251–60)

We notice here the extraordinary use of adjectives, and especially of compound adjectives, together with the sense of abundance which comes from the piling up of one image upon another. Keats is trying out the skills which he later used to such effect in the *Odes*. Here its overwhelming richness can be cloying: the imagery becomes an obstacle to the narrative, and it is sometimes difficult to see the wood for the trees. This is another endearing fault: it is part of the poem's youthful enthusiasm, acknowledged in the dedication to Thomas Chatterton. Chatterton was an example of a type dear to the Romantic poets, 'the marvellous boy' of Wordsworth's 'Resolution and Independence', the youth who died before his promise could be fulfilled. That Keats was thinking deeply about Chatterton is suggested by an earlier and fuller version of the poem's dedication:

> Inscribed, with every feeling of pride and regret, and with a 'bowed mind', to the memory of the most English of poets except Shakespeare, Thomas Chatterton.

Chatterton's association with England, and his youthful genius, suggested to Keats the ideal combination which he hoped to find in himself. He was deeply aware of his own shortcomings at this time, conscious that he was not yet the youthful English genius that he hoped to be, aware that he had not matured sufficiently to fulfil his ambition. In the preface to *Endymion* he wrote:

> The imagination of a boy is healthy, and the mature
> imagination of a man is healthy; but there is a space
> of life between, in which the soul is in a ferment, the
> character undecided, the way of life uncertain, the
> ambition thicksighted: thence proceeds mawkishness, and
> all the thousand bitters which those men I speak of [the
> readers of English literature] must necessarily taste in
> going over the following pages.

It is touching to see Keats looking back on *Endymion* and thinking about the honour of English literature. His aspiring self is already rejecting the Keats who had written the poem and is looking ahead to the next stage in the climb upwards:

> I hope I have not in too late a day touched the beautiful
> mythology of Greece, and dulled its brightness: for I wish
> to try once more, before I bid it farewell.

The second try was *Hyperion*, begun in the autumn of 1818. Between *Endymion* and *Hyperion* there was a very significant episode of Keats's life, and that was his tour of the Lake District and Scotland with his friend Charles Brown. They started from Liverpool on 24 June, and Keats returned to Hampstead on 18 August. At first sight it may seem like an ordinary holiday, but like everything else it was seen by Keats as a necessary step forward in his poetical apprenticeship. His admiration of Wordsworth, and his experience with the writing of *Endymion*, had come together to suggest that something was lacking in his equipment: he had had no experience of the sublime, never seen a mountain, never known the kinds of moment described by Wordsworth in *The Excursion*. So he set off to remedy the deficiency, writing to his brother Tom from the Lake District:

> I shall learn poetry here and shall henceforth write more
> than ever, for the abstract endeavor of being able to add a
> mite to that mass of beauty which is harvested from these
> grand materials, by the finest spirits, and put into etherial
> existence for the relish of one's fellows.[8]

The excitement in these letters is palpable. 'I felt', he wrote on climbing Skiddaw, 'as if I were going to a Tournament.'[9] In the end, however, this enthusiasm gave way to a sense of strain: it is seen in the way in which the poetry written on the tour divides into attempts at the heroic on the one hand and comic verse on the other. Ben Nevis, for instance, overwhelmed Keats. He found himself on the summit in 'sullen mist' and took that mist as an appropriate symbol, so that

> all my eye doth meet
> Is mist and crag, not only on this height,
> But in the world of thought and mental might.
>
> ('Read me a lesson, Muse', ll. 12–14)

The difficulty was compounded by physical illness, as Keats was suffering from a bad sore throat and had to be shipped back to London; but the whole experience had important repercussions for his ideas about poetry. As he thought through the experiences of the summer tour, he came to the conclusion that it was not possible and not necessary to be like Wordsworth; that there were two kinds of poet and that he belonged to the other kind. In October 1818 he wrote to Richard Woodhouse:

> As to the poetical Character itself, (I mean that sort
> of which, if I am any thing, I am a Member; that sort
> distinguished from the wordsworthian or egotistical
> sublime; which is a thing per se and stands alone) it is
> not itself – it has no self – it is every thing and nothing –
> It has no character – it enjoys light and shade; it lives in
> gusto, be it foul or fair, high or low, rich or poor, mean or
> elevated – It has as much delight in conceiving an Iago as
> an Imogen. What shocks the virtuous philosopher, delights
> the camelion Poet. [10]

The reference to Shakespeare indicates a new-found confidence, an ability to engage in some kind of self-surrender in which 'A Poet is the most unpoetical of any thing in existence; because he has no Identity.'[11] *Hyperion* shows the effect of this. It is a much more sublime poem than *Endymion*, and much more powerful. It depends in part upon the influence of Milton, Dante, and Shakespeare, but it also shows Keats's growing ability to transcend the personal or lyrical and work in the sublime and epic mode. The story of the overthrow of the older Titans, led by Saturn, by the younger Gods, led by Jupiter (and, in particular, the replacing of Hyperion by the new sun god – and god of poetry – Apollo) was a story which was bound to attract Keats: it was a study of change and decay, but also one of new life and hope. The treatment of Saturn shows Keats's sympathy with passing greatness, and with powerless suffering; while the coming of Hyperion is overwhelming in its celebration of natural beauty, warmth, and poetic creativity.

The language of *Hyperion* is quite unlike the rich and sensuous couplets of *Endymion*. Now, like Milton, Keats uses blank verse, and writes in what he called 'a more naked and Grecian manner'.[12] A good example of the difference is found in the first four lines:

> Deep in the shady sadness of a vale
> Far sunken from the healthy breath of morn,
> Far from the fiery noon, and eve's one star,
> Sat grey-haired Saturn, quiet as a stone.

Keats commented on the word 'vale' that 'There is a cool pleasure in the very sound of vale',[13] and that remark itself shows how far he had come since he was enchanted with the word 'Endymion'. Now he sees beauty in something much simpler, something more natural: he is moving towards a classical simplicity. Instead of the abundance of *Endymion*, there is now a more restrained use of imagery. Thea's voice, for instance, is compared to the sighing of the wind among oak trees:

> As when, upon a trancèd summer night,
> Those green-robed senators of mighty woods,
> Tall oaks, branch-charmèd by the earnest stars,
> Dream, and so dream all night without a stir,
> Save from one gradual solitary gust
> Which comes upon the silence, and dies off,
> As if the ebbing air had but one wave;
> So came these words and went;
> > (*Hyperion*, I. 72–79)

The image seems at first to move away from the natural with the comparison of oaks to senators; yet by the image Keats seems to animate the tree-scape, since they are conferring together (or so it seems, as their branches stretch towards one another). And then the natural properties of the scene are beautifully reasserted, with the 'gradual solitary gust' which itself is like an ebbing air (an air like a gentle sea). The apparent simplicity disguises a most complex interaction of natural description and figurative language.

The landscape of *Hyperion* is important in establishing the appropriate background to the compassionate description of Saturn and Hyperion:

> Scarce images of life, one here, one there,
> Lay vast and edgeways; like a dismal cirque
> Of Druid stones, upon a forlorn moor,
> When the chill rain begins at shut of eve,
> In dull November, . . .
> > (II. 33–37)

Keats had seen the Castlerigg stone circle near Keswick at the end of June, but on a dark evening; he is now transferring his memory of it to November. The crags and cliffs and streams are all gloomy and dark, until with a clever stroke Keats lights up the whole scene with the arrival of Hyperion, the only one of the older gods who is still ruling. All the features of the sublime and terrifying scenery 'now saw the light and made it terrible' (II. 366); and by holding back this moment to the end of Book II, Keats provides a magnificent retrospect on the speeches of the fallen Titans which have gone before. At one extreme, these include the rage of Enceladus, rebelling against his fate like Milton's Moloch:

> Speak! Roar! Shout! Yell! ye sleepy Titans all.
> Do ye forget the blows, the buffets vile?
> (II. 317–18)

and at the other, Oceanus' pacific acceptance:

> We fall by course of Nature's law, not force
> Of thunder, or of Jove.
> (II. 181–82)

We have to recognize, says Oceanus, that we are but a stage in the progress of the world, and that our time is finished:

> So on our heels a fresh perfection treads,
> A power more strong in beauty, born of us
> And fated to excel us, as we pass
> In glory that old Darkness:
> (II. 212–15)

Oceanus' speech is almost unnatural in its restraint, and Enceladus reminds the reader that change is painful even when it is necessary. Keats allows his sympathy for the superseded Titans to be expressed in the superbly measured blank verse of their speeches, especially those of Oceanus and Clymene, whose simplicity of language is a wonderful use of the ten-syllable line:

> Yet let me tell my sorrow, let me tell
> Of what I heard, and how it made me weep,
> And know that we had parted from all hope.
> (II. 259–61)

It is Clymene, at this point of despair, who hears the voice crying
'Apollo!', which prepares the reader for the astonishing change to the
poem in Book III. With a flick of the wrist Keats turns from the Titans
and their woes ('O leave them Muse! O leave them to their woes', III.
3) and urges the Muse to indulge herself, in lines which are reminiscent
of *Endymion* but more effective because of what has gone before:

> Let the rose glow intense and warm the air,
> And let the clouds of even and of morn
> Float in voluptuous fleeces o'er the hills;
> Let the red wine within the goblet boil
> Cold as a bubbling well; let faint-lipped shells,
> On sands, or in great deeps, vermilion turn
> Through all their labyrinths; and let the maid
> Blush keenly, as with some warm kiss surprised.
>
> (III. 15–22)

Everything in this section has its own glow: the rose warms the air,
the shell turns vermilion, the maiden blushes. In his book, *Keats and
Embarrassment*, Christopher Ricks has pointed out how important and
significant blushing is as a human quality; now Keats turns from the
landscape of chasms and Druid stones to a glowing and rosy scene. On
the Isle of Delos, his birthplace, Apollo is visited by the great goddess
Mnemosyne (goddess of memory and mother of the Muses): she had
previously given him his lyre, and he now feels the young man's desire
to use this gift. He wishes, too, to dispel the melancholy which he feels
because of the gap between his gifts and his opportunities; if this is like
Keats himself, then so is his feeling for words, and as Keats fell in love
with the word 'Endymion' so Apollo shouts 'Mnemosyne', his throat
throbbing with the syllables. On Delos he feels unused and untried; yet
even as he voices his complaint, human experience comes to him in all
its complexity:

> Names, deeds, grey legends, dire events, rebellions,
> Majesties, sovran voices, agonies,
> Creations and destroyings, all at once
> Pour into the wide hollows of my brain,
> And deify me, as if some blithe wine
> Or bright elixir peerless I had drunk,
> And so become immortal.
>
> (III. 114–20)

It is through 'knowledge enormous' that he becomes a god, a god
who understands human experience but who is not overwhelmed by

it. As John Barnard puts it in his note to the Penguin edition of the poems, 'Apollo attains godhead through knowledge of suffering, and the relationship between poetic power and this knowledge is central to the meaning of *Hyperion*.'[14]

The truth of this summary is made clear by the later reworking of some of the material into 'The Fall of Hyperion' (1819). *Hyperion* itself breaks off in the middle of Book III and was published in 1820 as 'A Fragment' (that is, a fragment of an epic poem). 'The Fall of Hyperion' is also a fragment, but it is the fragment of a dream. The story of Saturn and Hyperion is no longer described directly, but it is placed within a framework of a dream which considers some of the fundamental problems of the poet's life and work. The poet now appears within the poem, describing the effect of the action on himself, and the interpretation of it by the shade Moneta: he is concerned not so much with change as with the effect of change, the tragic implications of the story. The influence of Dante is seen not only in the division of the poem into cantos, but in its deepening seriousness of tone: Keats is exploring the way in which beauty and pain coexist in the world. As he put it a letter of 10 June 1818, 'were it in my choice I would reject a Petrarchal coronation – on account of my dying day, and because women have Cancers'.[15] In this stark and shocking opposition we can see Keats the former medical student, and sense the contrast between the poet's happiness and the sufferer's pain. What is the connection between these two, and what connections should there be?

In the dream landscape of 'The Fall of Hyperion' the poet passes from a delightful landscape into a much sterner one. He struggles to the steps, where he finds strength coming to him, and so climbs upwards to the veiled shadow; he has been saved, he learns, because those who climb are

> those to whom the miseries of the world
> Are misery, and will not let them rest.
> ('The Fall of Hyperion', I. 148–49)

although he is not a reformer but a poet, and therefore (in the shadow's view) less commendable. The poet replies that not all poets are useless ('sure a poet is a sage,/A humanist, physician to all men', I. 189–90), but the shade continues to see him as a member of the dreamer-tribe, and therefore useless. True poets, according to the shade, are not dreamers but those who disturb the world:

> 'Art not thou of the dreamer tribe?
> The poet and the dreamer are distinct,
> Diverse, sheer opposite, antipodes.

> The one pours out a balm upon the world,
> The other vexes it.'
>
> (I. 198–202)

The poet's response is that he has been mistaken for one more of the ineffective and foolish poets of that generation. He shouts his reply past the shade towards the god of poetry himself:

> 'Apollo! faded, far-flown Apollo!
> Where is thy misty pestilence to creep
> Into the dwellings, through the door crannies,
> Of all mock lyrists, large self-worshippers
> And careless hectorers in proud bad verse.'
>
> (I. 204–8)

Poetry, it would seem, has been given a bad name through the ineffective poets, who are called by the shade 'dreamers'. Yet 'The Fall of Hyperion' itself is a dream, and so we have the paradox that an attack on dreams takes place within one. Yet we are meant to see the speaker here as dreamer *and* good poet, as the narrative goes on to demonstrate. The shade unveils herself (as Beatrice did to Dante) and is revealed as Moneta, another word for Mnemosyne. She engages to show the poet wonders through her power, and side by side she and the poet see Saturn, as he was at the beginning of *Hyperion*. From this point, Keats begins the reworking of the earlier poem, although dealing only with Saturn, Thea, and Hyperion, as presented by Moneta. As she says, she 'humanizes' things:

> I humanize my sayings to thine ear
> Making comparisons of earthly things;
>
> (II. 2–3)

She does what other figures in dream-poems do, conducting the poet through an imaginary world. In the process he is questioned about himself and his art in ways which illuminate his position and his ideas about poetry. In thus distancing the action behind his reflections and doubts, Keats is attempting, not very successfully, to follow Dante. His progress is towards a full awareness of human suffering, which is prefigured in the sadness of Saturn and Thea. It is introduced by the movement of the poem from the initial dream garden to the darker and more strenuous world of Moneta's temple; and as John Barnard has pointed out, this has a parallel in the letter written to John Hamilton Reynolds on 3 May 1818:[16]

I compare human life to a large Mansion of Many
Apartments, two of which I can only describe, the doors
of the rest being as yet shut upon me – The first we
step into we call the infant or thoughtless Chamber,
in which we remain as long as we do not think – We
remain there a long while, and notwithstanding the doors
of the second Chamber remain wide open, showing a
bright appearance, we care not to hasten to it; but are at
length imperceptibly impelled by the awakening of the
thinking principle – within us – we no sooner get into
the second Chamber, which I shall call the Chamber of
Maiden-Thought, than we become intoxicated with the
light and the atmosphere, we see nothing but pleasant
wonders, and think of delaying there for ever in delight:
However among the effects this breathing is father of
is that tremendous one of sharpening one's vision into
the heart head and nature of Man – of convincing one's
nerves that the World is full of Misery and Heartbreak,
Pain, Sickness and oppression – whereby This Chamber
of Maiden Thought becomes gradually darken'd . . .[17]

In 'The Fall of Hyperion' the relationship between this growing
consciousness and the function of the poet is explored through the
interchange between the poet and the goddess. Characteristically, Keats
is turning the sublime mode towards a resolution of his own problems,
or at least a statement of them. The story of Saturn is now 'distanced'
behind a strange dream-scape of doubt and emotional disturbance. Yet
that disturbance is the price that has to be paid: it is both a trouble and
a privilege. The poet's dreaming – that of the true poet – requires an
arduous devotion to the craft and an emotional courage, the kind of
courage which is found only in the poet and the fanatic. The fanatic's
dreams weave only 'a paradise for a sect'; the poet's dreams lead him, if
he perseveres, to a point where he can ask the shade to unveil. It is then
through her eyes as well as his own that he sees the figure of Saturn; it
is as though between the mythological subject and himself he has now
discovered the presence of a great and mysterious power.

I have taken 'The Fall of Hyperion' (July–September 1819) out of
chronological order because it is a reworking of *Hyperion*. It is now
necessary to return to the beginning of what Robert Gittings has
memorably described as 'the living year' of September 1818–September
1819. It began with the struggle of the first two books of *Hyperion* and
the nursing of his brother Tom, who died on 1 December; to this must
be added the love for Fanny Brawne, whom he had met in October. The
coexistence of love and death intensified Keats's already sharp awareness

of the possibilities and the frustrations of life. The first major poem of 1819, *The Eve of St Agnes*, exemplifies this, celebrating as it does the fragile and beautiful love of Madeline and Porphyro, surrounded by inimical forces of war and hate, and lost in the distant past (so that it seems threatened by time as well in the final stanza). In this contrast, the brilliant descriptions have their own part to play: it is as though they are not present for their own sakes, but because they make a constitutive symbol – that is, they describe the life and love itself that is so easily destroyed, and the more that life is described the worse the destruction seems to be. There is an intense contrast, for instance, between the cold of the two opening stanzas, and the warmth of Madeline's chamber; the more the senses are called to appreciate this, the stronger the poem.

The poem was begun in January 1819, and it shows the influence of a visit which Keats made during that month to Chichester. The town helped to establish the setting and atmosphere of the poem, which blended with the legend of St Agnes' Eve to provide Keats with a subject that was exactly fitted to the current temper of his mind. The conception of a young lover slipping into the castle and stealing his love from her violent and boorish relations is attractive in itself, especially when joined to the legend of St Agnes' Eve, when

> Young virgins might have visions of delight,
> And soft adorings from their loves receive
> Upon the honey'd middle of the night, . . .
> (ll. 47–49)

Keats adapts this to make the soft adorings more definite, as the lover enters his mistress's bedroom to make love to her. Anything else would have been namby-pamby, and quite unsuited to Keats's own ardent temperament: he said that he would despise a man 'who would be such an eunuch in sentiment as to leave a maid, with that Character about her, in such a situation'.[18] In this step he was probably influenced also by Shakespeare's *Romeo and Juliet*, which has obvious anticipations of the family hostility to Porphyro and the encouraging behaviour of old Angela.

The fusion of all these elements produces something which is quite different from any of them, and entirely Keats's own. The reader's attention is immediately captured and held by the richness of description, the brilliant use of line and stanza to convey the cold and the warmth, the youth and age – for this is a poem which works very effectively by using contrasts. Keats returns to his first love, the Spenserian stanza, and uses it triumphantly, from the moment of the first atmospheric opening onwards; the bitter chill and the frozen Beadsman with his numb fingers are described with extraordinary empathy. In particular, the alexandrine at the end of each stanza is used to great effect:

> and his weak spirit fails
> To think how they may ache in icy hoods and mails . . .
>
> (ll. 17–18)

> A shielded scutcheon blushed with blood of queens and kings.
>
> (l. 216)

In both of these cases there is crucial verb, which gathers up the weight of the line with its force; in the first example the whole line sharpens to a point at the word 'ache', which is the centre of what went before and what is to come after, both grammatically and in its place within the line.

The Beadsman is an old man, celibate, lonely, praying; he has a weak spirit, and is old ('The joys of all his life were said and sung') and dying. He has nothing to do with the music and the revelry of St Agnes' Eve: instead, 'His was harsh penance.' He acts as a contrast to what is to come, and from the opening onwards the action is very cleverly narrowed down to Madeline's room: it moves from the cold of the chapel, through the dancing (with Porphyro watching from the shadow of a pillar), through the conversation in Angela's room, and then up the stairs. There is a very powerful sense of moving towards the centre of everything, the reality beside which all the rest seems superficial. The moments which turn in the other direction, such as the charming gesture when Madeline helps Angela down the stairs, only serve to emphasize the general forward movement towards the bedchamber, where Madeline says her prayers and undresses for bed. As she unclasps her jewels, we can observe a characteristic example of Keats's observation and sympathy, for she

> Unclasps her warmèd jewels one by one
>
> (l. 228)

where the word 'warmèd' not only captures the tactile sense of the normally cold jewels but suggests the warm life that is a part of Madeline herself. Keats is, literally, putting flesh on an old legend: and Porphyro plays his part by turning the dream into reality:

> 'Tis dark: quick pattereth the flaw-blown sleet.
> 'This is no dream, my bride, my Madeline!'
>
> (ll. 325–26)

And in spite of her fears Porphyro does not leave her among her brutal kinsfolk; they escape, and her wishes on St Agnes' Eve come true as

> These lovers fled away into the storm.
>
> (l. 371)

At this point Keats suddenly changes tense, and turns the present into the past. We are suddenly aware of what we have subconsciously known all along, ever since the magic of the first line of the poem: that this is an old story, that in listening to it we have been transported imaginatively to another period. Our surrender to the story is like Madeline's fascination with the legend, and her determination to act it out:

> She closed the door, she panted, all akin
> To spirits of the air, and visions wide –
> No uttered syllable, or, woe betide!
>
> (ll. 221–23)

Her entry into the room, filled as it is with mystery and magic, is like the reader's entry into the poem. And as the lovers flee away into the storm, Keats sharply and neatly reminds us that it was then, not now: that for Madeline the legend may have come true, but that we exist in another time and another place. It is a marvellous lesson in the creative power of the imagination: we have come to believe in the immediacy and reality of Madeline and Porphyro, when they are suddenly distanced from us so that we recognize them for what they are, creatures of the poet's fertile brain.

Thus Keats is able to do two things in *The Eve of St Agnes*: one is to celebrate the joys of young love, the contemplation of, and union with, a beautiful, pure, and kind girl; the other is to remind us, if we needed reminding, that this *is* romance, that we do live in another world, a world in which lovers do not escape from castles. And although we may catch something of the mystery of the Middle Ages in a place like Chichester, we actually live in an age which is quite different.

But which of these worlds is the 'real' world? Is it not true that the figure of Madeline, with her heart beating and catching her breath, has a 'reality' which is more vivid than our everyday existence? Is not our normal existence, with its awareness of sorrow and transience, somehow less exciting and life-enhancing than our existence in the world of the imagination? Which is more valuable? And which is more true, beautiful, essential, 'real'? This is the question of *Lamia* and of the *Odes*.

In *Lamia* Keats seems to have been striving for a new maturity in his verse, an absence of anything that could possibly be laughed at or thought of as undeveloped. The poem loses something of that touching openness of *The Eve of St Agnes*, but what replaces it is a remarkable energy in the couplets, what Keats himself described as 'that sort of fire in it which must take hold of people in some way'.[19] Yet if the atmosphere of *The Eve of St Agnes* is medieval, that of *Lamia* is classical. It deals, not with the realization of a legend, but with the dangers of enchanted love.

In this poem the opposition is between the enchantment of Lycius' love for Lamia and the cold philosophy of Apollonius. The happiness of the lovers is conveyed in a sensuous picture of great charm:

> they reposed
> Where use had made it sweet, with eyelids closed,
> Saving a tithe which love still open kept,
> That they might see each other while they almost slept;
>
> (II. 23–26)

but Lycius destroys this sensuous and unthinking bliss by conventionally suggesting that they should be married. This is presumably an attempt to make the relationship more stable and permanent; as so often in Keats, the sweet purity of the moment resists any attempt to prolong it, and the marriage ceremony attracts the philosopher Apollonius who destroys Lamia and thus kills Lycius. The contrast between marriage and death is poignant, and Keats clearly has sympathy with the lovers in spite of his recognition that the destruction of the enchantress is right and inevitable. He calls Lamia 'the tender-personed Lamia' (II. 238), and the celebrated commentary on the other things which philosophy has destroyed (II. 229–38) makes it clear that Keats has both a recognition of necessity and a regret that it should be so. The poem remains delicately balanced between approval of Lamia together with a recognition of her fundamental unreliability and dislike of Apollonius combined with a respect for his correctness.

Ideally, of course, the poet would wish to hold the truth of Apollonius and the beauty of Lamia in synthesis; it is this teasing possibility which is at the centre of the *Odes*. The *Odes* speak of desires and yearnings, of possibilities and impossibilities, of the joys of the imagination and the frustrations of the human state. As early as March 1818 Keats had been pondering these matters: in the verse epistle to John Hamilton Reynolds he lightly touches them with reference to Claude's painting *The Enchanted Castle*. He describes the painting (a castle by a lonely sea) and then adds his own dream-vision to it:

See! what is coming from the distance dim!
A golden galley all in silken trim!
Three rows of oars are lightening, moment-whiles
Into the verdurous bosoms of those isles.
Towards the shade, under the castle wall,
It comes in silence – now 'tis hidden all.

('To J. H. Reynolds, Esq.' ll. 55–60)

we are to imagine that there is a galley behind the castle, for of course
we cannot see it; the possibility that it might be there is evidence of
the glorious freedom of the imagination. The normal sight, of course,
is not free: there is no ship in the painting. We have to acknowledge
that our dreams and the reality are not the same, and that we live in
a world where the ideal has to give way to the actual, and

Things cannot to the will
Be settled, but they tease us out of thought.

(ll. 76–77)

This last phrase returns in the 'Ode on a Grecian Urn', while the
'Ode to a Nightingale' is anticipated in the lines which follow. Keats
is exploring the problems which the imagination raises. Is it, he asks

that imagination brought
Beyond its proper bound, yet still confined,
Lost in a sort of purgatory blind,
Cannot refer to any standard law
Of either earth or heaven? It is a flaw
In happiness, to see beyond our bourne –
It forces us in summer skies to mourn;
It spoils the singing of the nightingale.

(ll. 78–85)

In addition to these problems of the existence of the imagination in
some middle state – neither in heaven nor on earth – there is the further
difficulty of the coexistence on earth of beauty and pain. As he sits by
the seashore, the poet sees into the sea

where every maw
The greater on the less feeds evermore. –
But I saw too distinct into the core
Of an eternal fierce destruction, . . .

(ll. 94–97)

The *Odes* are explorations of these preoccupying conflicts, and it is important to realize that they are the mature expressions of a number of deep-seated anxieties; so that the occasions on which they were written come as unbidden yet appropriate moments, containing within themselves an essential presentation of the idea which the poet has the genius to perceive and make into great art. Charles Brown's story of Keats writing the 'Nightingale' Ode during one fine morning in the garden at Hampstead, and the immediate composition of 'To Autumn' after a Sunday walk near Winchester, both suggest a moment in which the external world spoke of an inner preoccupation. In both cases the idea may have been simmering in Keats's head during the spring and the autumn respectively, but there is an astonishing assurance and sense of 'fitness' about the *Odes* which comes from something more pressing than a perusal of Lemprière or a collection of legends.

The *Odes* are rich because they contain material from so many areas of Keats's sensibility. The pictorial and artistic inheritance, found in

> Away! away! for I will fly to thee
> Not charioted by Bacchus and his pards
> > ('Ode to a Nightingale', ll. 31–32)

(which is probably another reminiscence of Titian's *Bacchus and Ariadne*) or in the description of the Grecian Urn, is balanced by the sense-descriptions of actual states of physical feeling, such as 'My heart aches' and the image of taste in

> him whose strenuous tongue
> Can burst Joy's grape against his palate fine;
> > ('Ode on Melancholy', ll. 27–28)

The intellectual and the physical meet in the *Odes*: indeed the idea of transience is mediated and transformed through the senses, is given substance and emotional resonance by being associated with a sense-impression which is part of a mood. Thus a painting by Titian, or a figuring of Autumn, or a reference to the Muses' fountain of Hippocrene become part of a complicated world of thought and feeling, of a Coleridgean bringing of the whole soul of man into activity.

Such fullness of expression is held within the control of strong yet easy stanza forms. These have been fully studied by H. W. Garrod[20] and M. R. Ridley,[21] who have pointed out that each of the major *Odes* is a variation of a basic pattern, and that the pattern was developed by Keats out of his dissatisfaction with the two sonnet forms, Shakespearean and Petrarchan. The basic structure of the ode-stanza is a combination of these two forms: it begins usually with four lines rhyming ABAB, as in a Shakespearean sonnet, which gives a good regular beginning and then allows the reader to pause and take breath:

> Thou still unravished bride of quietness,
>   Thou foster-child of silence and slow time,
> Sylvan historian, who canst thus express
>   A flowery tale more sweetly than our rhyme:
>
> ('Ode on a Grecian Urn', ll. 1–4)

This is followed by an adaptation of the Petrarchan sestet, sometimes rhyming CDECDE but freely adapted by Keats into different combinations. By this union of Shakespearean quatrain and Petrarchan sestet, Keats avoided what he saw as the disadvantages of both forms, the thrice-repeated quatrain and 'pouncing' rhyme of the Shakespearean sonnet, and the overweighing of the sestet by the octave in the Petrarchan. He then varies the pattern: in the 'Nightingale' Ode by shortening a line to give a pause in the rhythm, and in 'To Autumn' by adding an extra line to give an eleven-line stanza which suggests in its very form a richness which is overflowing. In each case, there is an almost classical sense of decorum and correctness: as Keats wrote in the sonnet on the Sonnet (written just before the spring odes) entitled 'If by dull rhymes our English must be chained':

> Let us inspect the lyre, and weigh the stress
> Of every chord and see what may be gained
> By ear industrious, and attention meet; . . .
> So, if we may not let the Muse be free,
> She will be bound with garlands of her own.
>
> (ll. 7–9, 13–14)

He is going to turn the conditions of art, the exigencies of form, to his own advantage.

'Ode to a Nightingale' begins with the utmost directness and clarity: 'My heart aches'. Although the cause of the heartache is not yet clear, the feeling is immediately obvious: the first phrase makes the vital point about the human-centred subject of the *Odes*. The heart is the organ of feeling, of shared humanity, the part of the body in which sadness is translated into physical ache; and the *Odes* are about problems of behaviour which are consequent upon our very status as human beings, those of transient happiness, and illness, and the precarious life of the imagination. So we learn, later in this first stanza, that the drowsy numbness is not the result of any drug but 'being too happy in thine happiness', another piece of evidence of the poet's humanness. The heartache and numbness are due not to any poison but to the reverse, a kind of awareness which is able to recognize the happiness of the bird's song so deeply that it becomes painful. Again this is an awareness which we can recognize as common, and which is evidence of the human limitations of sense-enjoyment, pleasure so intense that it somehow becomes hard to bear.

If the first part of the stanza emphasizes the strength of the inner feelings, the second provides the cause:

> That thou, light-winged Dryad of the trees,
>   In some melodious plot
> Of beechen green, and shadows numberless,
> Singest of summer in full-throated ease.
>
> (ll. 7–10)

The switch from inner to outer is clearly signalled by 'thou': and from this point onwards the verse runs more freely, as if the poet had escaped from the imprisonment of his own feelings. From the heavy syllables of 'My heart aches', the stanza progresses to the last line, which moves with freedom and grace, anticipating the liberty, warmth, and music which are associated with the nightingale. It is the same contrast which is found in the third stanza, where Keats longs to

> Fade far away, dissolve, and quite forget
> What thou among the leaves hast never known,
> The weariness, the fever, and the fret
> Here, where men sit and hear each other groan;
> Where palsy shakes a few, sad, last grey hairs,
> Where youth grows pale, and spectre-thin, and dies; . . .
>
> (ll. 21–26)

Again the placing of 'thou' distances the nightingale from the immediate world of which the poet is so deeply and painfully conscious: the nightingale is 'among the leaves', a phrase whose studied vagueness is in direct contrast to the precision of the other images of old age and young illness. The three verbs in the first line, 'Fade', 'dissolve', 'forget', all indicate a blurring of the actual; yet the lines that follow suggest that the poet has a significantly precise knowledge of the actual from his own experience, so the desire to fade and forget is not just a desire to escape. It is a delicious indulgence, and the poet knows that it is: he is as aware as anyone (probably more, since he had been a doctor and had recently nursed his dying brother) of the conditions of living

> Where but to think is to be full of sorrow
> And leaden-eyed despairs;
> Where Beauty cannot keep her lustrous eyes,
> Or new Love pine at them beyond tomorrow.
>
> (ll. 27–30)

It is from this point of acute consciousness that the poet makes his defiant bid for liberty and beauty. The pattern of a going-out and return is common in Romantic poetry, and here Keats moves into the enchanted night, the sweet-scented darkness; as he listens to the bird's song, the whole process of fading becomes more serious, as the poet realizes that the ultimate form of fading is a gentle dissolving into annihilation, a death without pain at the moment of listening to the nightingale's song. This would certainly be an escape from the trouble and suffering of mortal life; and a death at the moment of such intense enjoyment of beauty would be a supreme conclusion. The bird's song would become a requiem, although the poet would not hear it.

Therein lies the difficulty: the ending which seems so beautiful would also be an ending of the ability to respond to that beauty. The poet is caught in a recognition of the complexity he has discovered:

> Still wouldst thou sing, and I have ears in vain –
> To thy high requiem become a sod.
>
> (ll. 59–60)

The poem is no longer about suffering and heartache, and the escape from these into beauty: it is about the fact that in order to appreciate great beauty you must be alive, which means being open to pain and misery. And, of course, all human beings must die, have ears in vain, become sods, while the nightingale's song will be heard, as it has been for centuries. The verse which follows is a marvellous example of the travelling imagination, as Keats goes back across the hungry generations of humanity to the classical world of emperor and clown and to the Old Testament world of Ruth, and then beyond these historical times into a world of the fairy landscape (magic, but forlorn, as Keats perhaps saw Claude's *The Enchanted Castle*).

The final stanza suddenly returns to the present, the here-and-now; as though the imagination had been so stretched that it springs back to rest across the word 'Forlorn'. The lines which follow seem to me to be a mock lament, as the poet contemplates his return to the self: it is a kind of death, he wryly suggests, signalled by the tolling bell of 'Forlorn'. Moreover, the fancy has cheated him again: all this talk of escape is eyewash, he remarks, with the affectionate dismissal of fancy as a 'deceiving elf'. He is left with the local landscape, himself under the tree in the Hampstead garden, the bird's song getting fainter – 'Adieu! adieu!' The syllables sound like bird song, and the surroundings are sketched with a beautiful economy – the meadows, the stream, the hillside, the next valley; now the poet is left with the teasing question, the concluding and enveloping lines which are both comic and serious:

> Was it a vision, or a waking dream?
> Fled is that music – Do I wake or sleep?
>
> (ll. 79–80)

On one level he knows perfectly well that he is awake, and therefore the question is funny; but in addition, Keats is asking a searching pair of questions: is my imagination awake now, as I enjoy all this beauty and am conscious of pain as well? Or was the imagination awake, truly awake, then? And which, in all the meanings of that much-maligned word, is *real*? Is it the world of the nightingale's song, the tender night beyond time and space; or is it this world, of sense-impressions and feelings, of old age and despair, of beauty and transience? The complications of the last two lines are endless, for they refer to the complications of life itself, and of the poem's rich expression of them; the poem ends, very properly, on a question mark. And beneath these articulated questions, there is another which is equally important but unexpressed: how should one behave in the face of these complex realizations of the different claims of joy and sorrow, escape and reality? This is the question which is explored and answered in the other *Odes*.

The 'Ode on a Grecian Urn' is significantly different. It is an indoor, not an outdoor poem, and it deals with art and not nature. It belongs to that part of Keats's mind which responded eagerly to the Elgin Marbles and to all other examples of Greek art: its style, in consequence, is subtly altered. Instead of the natural rhythms and pauses of the 'Ode to a Nightingale', the 'Ode on a Grecian Urn' has a network of sound-patterns, of assonance, of deliberate echoes, all of which suggest that the poet was aiming for a purposeful effect. The first line of the final stanza is the most obvious example:

> O Attic shape! Fair attitude!

and here Keats, who was such a dedicated craftsman, must have been conscious of the clash of sound and sense. It is as though he was attempting in verse to make something of an equivalent of the urn itself, a work of art which draws attention to itself *as* a work of art and not as some representation of reality. The Ode is drawing attention to itself as a poem, an artefact made with words; and so there are quatrains with an intricate pattern of sound and repetition:

> Heard melodies are sweet, but those unheard
> Are sweeter: therefore, ye soft pipes, play on:
> Not to the sensual ear, but, more endeared,
> Pipe to the spirit ditties of no tone: . . .
>
> (ll. 11–14)

Not only is there the obvious echo effect of 'Heard . . . unheard' and 'sweet . . . sweeter', but there is also the assonance of 'the sensual ear . . . endeared' and the daring 'spirit ditties', where the bitty sound contrasts with the longer 'pipes . . . pipe' and the final 'no tone'. The doubling and echoing is reminiscent of a poet brought up on the theory and practice of Renaissance rhetoric; it takes a different form in the figure of anaphora used in the questions of the first stanza:

> What men or gods are these? What maidens loth?
> What mad pursuit? What struggle to escape?
> What pipes and timbrels? What wild ecstasy?
>
> (ll. 8–10)

and we can discover the same artifice in the strange formality, the oblique address of the first two lines:

> Thou still unravished bride of quietness,
> Thou foster-child of silence and slow time,

where the chiming sounds of the long 'i's – bride, quietness, child, silence, time – all suggest something more shaped, deliberate, and organized than the 'My heart aches' of the Nightingale Ode. And this, above all, is why the poem ends with such a flourish: the celebrated last two lines are not just there to be puzzled over but they bring to a conclusion a poem which has throughout been dealing in intricate and subtle organizations of sound and sense. The gnomic utterance of the poem's ending is not tacked on, but is a piece of artistic panache which is totally in keeping with the previous self-consciousness with words that is one of the poem's most notable achievements.

By creating such a work of art, Keats himself re-poses the problem which is presented by the urn. Several Grecian vases went into the creation of the vase in the poem,[22] but they all share the same stillness, the same beauty that is held in the perfection of the work of art. By the side of such artistry and elegance, human life seems imperfect, messy, and transient. And yet, of course, for all its ideal perfection, the urn is only art: its great limiting defect is that it never changes, never moves, that its human beings never become alive with the breathing life of a living, enjoying, and suffering human creature. The perfection of the urn is a wonderful idea, an idea which teases us because of its very difference from life. It teases us out of thought 'as doth eternity'; it holds before us an ideal which is beyond us, inhuman, and therefore not an ideal, while yet remaining one, paradoxically – as D. H. Lawrence said, 'yet so it is, so it isn't'.[23] In Keats's poem, as in some of Lawrence's work, the reader is made to appreciate that matters of such sensitivity and complexity cannot be simplified to 'it is' and 'it isn't'.

It is in this respect that the Grecian urn forms the perfect symbol. It holds within itself such contrary suggestions of life and also of death that it can be viewed either as a representation of imaginative freedom and perfection:

> Heard melodies are sweet, but those unheard
> Are sweeter; . . .

or as a 'Cold Pastoral'. Its complex fullness of meaning is found in the first line, 'Thou still unravished bride of quietness', where the word 'still' means both 'motionless' and 'yet-': the urn is standing as still as a bride at the altar, perfect, virginal, yet also 'yet-unravished', as though it is like a bride whose marriage has never been consummated. The result is a wonderfully compressed double sense, a rich symbiosis, in which the urn seems both perfect and virginal, yet also uncreative and sterile.

The reader is led towards both of these interpretations during the course of the poem. There is the teasing perfection of the lover, poised always at the point of being about to kiss, his love happier (or is it?) than the feverish and panting human love; yet there is also the poignant desolation of the little town, whose streets 'for evermore/Will silent be'. It is clear that stillness, while it has its joy, has also its sorrow. It is into this state of uncertainty that the last stanza strikes its extraordinary pun, 'Attic . . . attitude', followed by other double meanings in 'brede' and 'overwrought'; it is as if Keats at this point is intent on entangling the reader yet further in the complexities which he has created. And the lines which follow appear to resolve the difficulties, but they do not:

> Thou, silent form, dost tease us out of thought
> As doth eternity: Cold Pastoral!

> When old age shall this generation waste,
> Thou shalt remain, in midst of other woe
> Than ours, a friend to man, to whom thou say'st,
> 'Beauty is truth, truth beauty, – that is all
> Ye know on earth, and all ye need to know.'
>
> (ll. 44–50)

At first we seem to see the urn as remote; the men and maidens on it are 'marble' and it is a 'shape' or an 'attitude'. This is confirmed by the 'silent form' and the impressively direct 'Cold Pastoral!' Yet in opposition to this we have the wasting power of old age, and the woe of future generations, against which the urn is seen as a friend, presumably as a permanent refreshment for the spirit in a world of change. It is in its role as friend to man that the urn speaks: for the first time in the poem this work of art which has been so profoundly and mysteriously associated with silence now gives voice to its secret.

One major difficulty of these lines is to decide where, if anywhere, the quotation marks should go. Full details of the arguments may be found in the editions of Keats's poetry by Miriam Allott and by John Barnard. Here there is only space to say that the quotation marks around 'Beauty is truth, truth beauty' appear in the 1820 volume which was seen through the press by Keats; yet the line and a half which follows seems to be a part of the message (it could, of course, be a rather sardonic comment by the poet on the urn's statement, but that would be out of keeping with the tone of the poem). If the urn does say this, however, it is surely making claims which are too strong, and the last line and a half undercuts 'Beauty is truth, truth beauty' whether it is read within quotation marks or not.

'Beauty is truth, truth beauty', I have suggested, is in one sense a final flourish, a grand claim on behalf of art. It is not using truth in the sense of factual truth, because (as Keats well knew) truth is often not beautiful. It refers to a truth of art, the unflinching presentation of life, the central excellence of art which Keats in a letter of 1817 described as 'its intensity',

> capable of making all disagreeables evaporate, from their being in close relationship with Beauty and Truth –
> Examine King Lear and you will find this exemplified throughout;[24]

The example of *King Lear* indicates that Keats was thinking of a quality in great art which transforms fact into truth, and it is this truth which he is concerned with in the 'Ode on a Grecian Urn'. In another letter of 1817, he wrote: 'What the imagination seizes as Beauty must be truth – whether it existed before or not – for I have the same Idea of all our Passions as of Love they are all in their sublime, creative of essential Beauty.'[25] In the light of these ideas, 'Beauty is truth, truth beauty' would seem to be not a logical statement so much as an apprehension of a creative and imaginative moment in which the two blend into one.

It is this statement which is commented on by the last line and a half of the poem. This could be taken in two ways, in directions which brilliantly correspond to the different directions which the poem has been taking. It could, for instance, be an outrageous statement. To claim that 'Beauty is truth, truth beauty' is all you know or need to know is, from one point of view, quite wrong. We need to know many other things, such as courage, endurance, hope, pity, and love; if the urn misses these out, it is being arrogant and exclusive. Yet there is another sense in which the idea is tenable, if it is seen as a statement of the kind of artistic perfection which is to be prized above all the lesser activities of life: at these supreme creative moments of perception and exaltation, the remainder of life ceases to matter.

As he confronts the urn, therefore, the poet considers two conflicting apprehensions and holds them together in his mind. One is the knowledge of its beauty, the still and permanent beauty that is so refreshing to contemplate, with its figures caught in timeless gestures and holding for ever moments which for mortals are all too fleeting. At the same time there is the awareness that such a beauty and such moments are not everything: that beyond the urn is a world of suffering and change, of joy and despair. What is so extraordinarily skilful about the last two lines is the way in which they hold together such radically different emotions, the understanding of the wonder of art and the simultaneous understanding of its limitations. If the Nightingale Ode shows the states of imagination and reality as separate, the 'Ode on a Grecian Urn' shows them as coexisting.

All the odes have their own 'feel' and character; and the 'Ode on Melancholy' is stranger and more exotic than the Nightingale Ode or the 'Ode on a Grecian Urn'. It moves through a Spenserian landscape of the mind, though with the details of each sense-impression most precisely and beautifully portrayed, to consider the nature of melancholy and the mind's reaction to it. The poet's argument is that sensitivity and melancholy are closely allied, and that it is important not to avoid melancholy. To seek oblivion through any of the means described in the first stanza is to 'drown the wakeful anguish of the soul', and it is this state of wakeful anguish which is so important. It comes from the contemplation of beauty, and is fed by that contemplation, so that the process becomes one of exquisite pain:

Then glut thy sorrow on a morning rose,
Or on the rainbow of the salt sand-wave,
Or on the wealth of globèd peonies;
Or if thy mistress some rich anger shows,
Emprison her soft hand, and let her rave,
And feed deep, deep, upon her peerless eyes.

(ll. 15–20)

Melancholy becomes associated with rare and precious moments, even if they are painful, like the anger of a loved one. The response is not to avoid it, but to 'glut thy sorrow'; the defiant 'glut', with its associations with eating, is vitally important in establishing the full-blooded gut reaction to the situation, the determination to devour experience whatever the cost. The cost is measured in terms of transience, of the passing of happiness:

She dwells with Beauty – Beauty that must die;
And Joy, whose hand is ever at his lips
Bidding adieu; and aching Pleasure nigh,
Turning to poison while the bee-mouth sips:

(ll. 21–24)

The image of the bee-mouth sipping takes up the image of eating from the previous stanza, and from the poison of the first lines; now it reaches a climax in the image of the grape bursting against the roof of the mouth, the bursting of joy in one delightful moment after which joy is but an empty grape-skin. So the last two lines suggest triumph and disaster, and a Spenserian enchantment:

His soul shall taste the sadness of her might,
And be among her cloudy trophies hung.

(ll. 29–30)

There is a promise and a privilege in 'His soul shall taste', but the taster is also a victim, whose soul is hung up like a battle trophy by the sovran melancholy. But the privilege outweighs the victimization: whatever the consequences, to have experienced the things of beauty is to have lived to the full. The 'Ode on Melancholy' is a defiant and courageous poem, which exhorts the reader to seek out beauty no matter what the accompanying consequence – the increased sense of sorrow at the transience of happiness – may be.

The same defiance, the refusal to prefer oblivion, is found in the question and answer in 'To Autumn':

> Where are the songs of Spring? Ay, where are they?
> Think not of them, thou hast thy music too –
>
> (ll. 23–24)

This is a command to concentrate on the fleeting beauty of autumn rather than the fertile promise of spring; and autumn is a perfect example for Keats of the beauty that is associated with heartache, because it is so fine and it passes away so soon. It makes its point so well that the poet does not have to introduce a moral, or ask more than the briefest of questions: the more the autumn season is described, the more it speaks for itself. It becomes a constitutive symbol, something which expresses more and more intensely what it is and means just by being itself. In its being is its meaning: and since Keats manages so remarkably to convey the sounds, sights, and images of autumn, the actual meaning of the poem deepens and increases with each accumulation of detail and felt life. The more powerfully that autumn is brought before the reader, the more powerful is the sense of the transience of earthly beauty. The final verse, in particular, is infused with a perceptible sadness, for the day is dying, the gnats mourning, and the swallows getting ready to depart. The progress of the poem from the golden harvest-time of the first verse to the evening clouds of the last is another way in which the poem subtly suggests the inevitable process of time and change.

The poem, then, makes its point by the power of its description, by the intense fidelity of its observation. It is very undemonstrative, even unassuming in its refusal to claim any apparent 'message'; and indeed it is easy to read it just as a word-picture of autumn, without realizing that the very word-picture is the meaning itself. From the first lines, which build up the idea of the earth and the sun conspiring together to bring ripeness and fertility to all things, to the last description of the redbreast whistling and the swallows gathering, the poem shows a wonderful combination of the sense of fullness to overflowing (helped by the eleven-line stanza, which has one more line than in the other odes, and so creates a kind of 'extra-line' feeling) with a delicate and precise observation.

'To Autumn' came to Keats quickly and naturally. He was at Winchester during September 1819, and described a Sunday scene to Reynolds:

> How beautiful the season is now – How fine the air. A
> temperate sharpness about it. Really, without joking, chaste
> weather – Dian skies – I never lik'd stubble-fields so much
> as now – Aye better than the chilly green of the Spring.
> Somehow a stubble-plain looks warm – in the same way

that some pictures look warm. This struck me so much in my sunday's walk that I composed upon it.[26]

By the following Tuesday the poem was included in a letter to Richard Woodhouse. It seems such a simple and immediate process of composition and rendering of the subject that it is easy to under-estimate the art that lies behind it and the spirit which is within it. It lends credence to the idea that Keats was the poet of the senses, too, because the poem's description of sense-impressions is so vivid. In reality, however, it is a poem which (like much of Keats) is more profound than it appears. It is the result of a sudden fusion between the poet and the moment, the internal and the external, the mind and the symbol; as such it is deceptive in its straight-forwardness. What is behind and within the poem is Keats himself, a man speaking to men: one who had thought deeply about poetry and the role of the poet, who had pondered and rejected the solutions of orthodox Christianity (he was out in the fields on that Sunday, not in Winchester Cathedral), and who had, above all, resolved to experience life in all its joy and all its disappointment.

Notes

1. Quoted in Robert Gittings, *John Keats* (London, 1968), pp. 152–53.

2. Gittings, p. 103.

3. Gittings, p. 68.

4. To Benjamin Bailey, 8 October 1817; *The Letters of John Keats, 1814–1821*, edited by Hyder E. Rollins, 2 vols (Cambridge, 1958), I, 170. All references to the letters are from this edition.

5. See Gittings, pp. 186–87.

6. To Benjamin Bailey, 8 October 1817; *Letters*, I, 170.

7. To Benjamin Bailey, 22 November 1817; *Letters*, I, 184.

8. To Tom Keats, 25–27 June 1818; *Letters*, I, 301.

9. To Tom Keats, 29 June, 1, 2 July 1818; *Letters* I, 307.

10. To Richard Woodhouse, 27 October 1818; *Letters*, I, 386–87.

11. To Richard Woodhouse, 27 October 1818; *Letters*, I, 387.

12. To B. R. Haydon, 23 January 1818; *Letters*, I, 207.

13. Marginal note to *Paradise Lost*, I 318–21; quoted in John Barnard, *John Keats, the Complete Poems* (Harmondsworth, 1973), p. 610.

14. Barnard, p. 616.

15. To Benjamin Bailey, 10 June 1818; *Letters*, I, 292.

16. Barnard, p. 677.

17. To J. H. Reynolds, 3 May 1818; *Letters*, I, 280–81.

18. Richard Woodhouse to John Taylor, 19, 20 September 1819; *Letters*, II, 163.

19. To George and Georgiana Keats, 17–27 September 1819; *Letters*, II, 189.

20. H. W. Garrod, *Keats* (Oxford, 1926), pp. 83–91.

21. M. R. Ridley, *Keats' Craftsmanship* (London, 1933), pp. 195–210.

22. See Ian Jack, *Keats and the Mirror of Art* (Oxford, 1967), Ch. 13, and James Dickie, 'The Grecian Urn: an Archaeological Approach', *Bulletin of the John Rylands Library*, 52 (1969), reprinted for the Keats-Shelley Memorial Association (Folkestone, 1973).

23. *The Letters of D. H. Lawrence*, edited by James T. Boulton (Cambridge, 1979), I, 129.

24. To George and Tom Keats, 21, 27 December 1817; *Letters*, I, 192.

25. To Benjamin Bailey, 22 November 1817; *Letters*, I, 184.

26. To J. H. Reynolds, 21 September 1819; *Letters*, II, 167.

Poetry and Prophecy:
A Final Word

Keats's 'To Autumn', the last poem to be studied in this book, points onwards, towards an awareness of beauty and a sense of strain or sadness in Victorian poetry. In 'The Princess', Tennyson's lyric poet feels the tears

> Rise in the heart, and gather to the eyes,
> In looking on the happy Autumn-fields,
> And thinking of the days that are no more.
>
> ('Tears, idle tears')

And one way of perceiving the legacy of the romantic poets to the Victorians is as some kind of heightened awareness of feeling and beauty, one which sharpened in poignancy as the nineteenth century went on. In *The Darkling Plain* (with its title taken from the bleak ending of Matthew Arnold's 'Dover Beach'), John Heath-Stubbs has argued that 'intuitive Romanticism, finding itself confronted by the bleak materialism of the industrial age, and an atmosphere of increasing doubt and spiritual intensity, maintained itself among certain poets who were, in one way or another, outcasts from their time'[1]. This is fair enough as far as it goes: Rossetti helped to rediscover Blake, and Yeats wrote of himself and his friends that

> We were the last romantics – chose for theme
> Traditional sanctity and loveliness;
>
> ('Coole Park and Ballylee, 1931', ll. 41–42)

but such a view of Romanticism as the forerunner of the aesthetic movement and of Yeats's myth-making is only one part of the story; Bloom's idea that Darley and Beddoes represent a waste of imagination is closer. The Romantic movement, and especially its six great poets together with John Clare, stand for freedom: Clare writes in 'A Vision':

I kept my spirit with the free

(l. 16)

and this is the tradition which was handed down through Ruskin to Morris. It is a tradition which is seen by E.P. Thompson as moralist and Utopian, an English tradition which is related to Marxism but which has its roots in the Romantic period. Romanticism, in other words, is 'tougher' (Thompson's word) than might have been thought: it affirms values of freedom, decency, equality of opportunity, of experience, of the good society. It lies behind the work of Ruskin, of Morris, and of the early Socialists, as well as that of Rossetti and Yeats. It is found in the assumptions of much nineteenth-and twentieth-century literature, and it governs our responses to the technological age of which we are all prisoners.

But if one important word in Clare's line is 'free', the other is 'spirit'. It is not an easy quality to define, but it exists in Romantic poetry in a particular energy, a special fire, a sense of pressure, in what Hazlitt called 'gusto'; this quality, whatever name is given to it, exists in the workings of the imagination rather than the fancy and makes the whole, as Coleridge saw, alive. It is with this elusive quality that I conclude this book, not only because it is fundamental to Romantic poetry but because at least one description of it returns to the passage in Ezekiel from which this study set out. 'The whole is instinct with spirit,' wrote Wordsworth of a seventeenth-century poem (Montrose on the death of Charles I):

> and every word has its separate life; like the Chariot of the
> Messiah, and the wheels of that Chariot, as they appeared
> to the imagination of Milton aided by that of the Prophet
> Ezekiel. It had power to move of itself but was conveyed
> by Cherubs,
>
>   as with stars their bodies all
> And wings were set with eyes, with eyes the wheels
> Of Beryl, and careering fires between.[2]

Wordsworth is calling up the spirits of two great imaginative powers among the cloud of witnesses: Milton, the most prophetic of modern poets, and Ezekiel, the most poetical of ancient prophets. Together they preside over a poetry which, in all its variety, abundance, and Romantic energy, is 'instinct with spirit', filled with a life that comes from the tenacious hold upon the individual vision.

Notes

1. John Heath-Stubbs, *The Darkling Plain* (London, 1950), p. xv.

2. Wordsworth, 'Essays upon Epitaphs' II; *The Prose Works of William Wordsworth*, edited by W. J. B. Owen and J. W. Smyser, 3 vols (Oxford, 1974), II, 71.

Chronology

Note: Dates refer to date of first publication unless otherwise stated.

DATE	WORKS OF POETRY	OTHER WORKS	HISTORICAL/CULTURAL EVENTS
1750	Gray *Elegy*	Rousseau *Discours sur les Sciences et les Arts* Johnson *The Rambler*	
1751–53			
1754			George Crabbe b.
1755		Rousseau *Discours sur l'origine et les fondements de l'inégalité parmi les hommes*	
1756			
1757	Gray *Odes* (including *The Bard*)	Burke *Enquiry into the Origin of our Ideas of the Sublime and Beautiful*	William Blake b.
1758			
1759	Johnson *Rasselas*		Wolfe takes Quebec
1760		Sterne *Tristram Shandy* I & II	Accession of George III
1761		Rousseau *Julie, ou la Nouvelle Héloïse*	

DATE	WORKS OF POETRY	OTHER WORKS	HISTORICAL/CULTURAL EVENTS
1762	Macpherson *Fingal, and other poems by Ossian*	Rousseau *Du Contrat Social* *Émile*	
1763–64			Hargreaves's Spinning Jenny
1765	Percy *Reliques of Ancient English Poetry*	Walpole *The Castle of Otranto*	
1766		Lessing *Laocoön*	
1767–69			
1770	Goldsmith *The Deserted Village*		William Wordsworth b. Thomas Chatterton d.
1771	Beattie *The Minstrel*, Book I		Walter Scott b. Thomas Gray d.
1772			S. T. Coleridge b.
1773			Darby's cast-iron bridge
1774	Beattie *The Minstrel*, Book II	Goethe *Werther*	Robert Southey b.
1775			J. M. W. Turner b. Jane Austen b. American War of Independence begins
1776	Paine *Common Sense*	Smith *The Wealth of Nations*	John Constable b. Declaration of American Independence
1777–79			Rousseau d. (1778) Voltaire d. (1778)
1780			Gordon riots

DATE	WORKS OF POETRY	OTHER WORKS	HISTORICAL/CULTURAL EVENTS
1781		Rousseau *Confessions* I	British surrender at Yorktown
		Kant *Critique of Pure Reason*	Lessing d. George Stephenson b.
1782	Cowper *Poems*	William Gilpin *Observations . . . on the River Wye*	
1783	Crabbe *The Village* Blake *Poetical Sketches*		Treaty of Paris (establishing American Independence) Pitt the Younger Prime Minister
1784			Dr Johnson d.
1785	Cowper *The Task*		Peacock b. de Quincey b.
1786	Burns *Poems*	William Gilpin *Observations . . . on Cumberland and Westmorland* Beckford *Vathek*	Goethe in Italy
1787			
1788			G. G. Byron b.
1789	Blake *Songs of Innocence Book of Thel*	Gilbert White *Natural History of Selborne*	Fall of Bastille
1790	Blake *Marriage of Heaven and Hell French Revolution* (latter not published)	Burke *Reflections on the Revolution in France*	Wordsworth and Robert Jones walk through Switzerland
1791		Paine *Rights of Man* I Boswell, *Life of Johnson*	Flight and recapture of Louis XVI Mozart d. John Wesley d.

DATE	WORKS OF POETRY	OTHER WORKS	HISTORICAL/CULTURAL EVENTS
1792	Samuel Rogers *The Pleasures of* *Memory*		P. B. Shelley b. Sir Joshua Reynolds d. September Massacres
1793	Blake *Visions of the* *Daughters of Albion* *America* Wordsworth *An Evening Walk* *Descriptive Sketches* (both published)	Godwin *Political Justice* Wordsworth *Letter to the Bishop of* *Llandaff* (unpublished)	John Clare b. Execution of Louis XVI The Terror War between Britain and France
1794	Blake *Songs of Innocence and* *of Experience* *Europe* *Book of Urizen*	Ann Radcliffe *The Mysteries of* *Udolpho* Godwin *Caleb Williams*	Fall of Robespierre Gibbon d.
1795	Blake *Book of Los* Coleridge *The Eolian Harp*		J. Keats b. G. Darley b.
1796	Coleridge *Poems*	M. Lewis *The Monk*	Napoleon's campaign in Italy
1797	Southey *Poems* Coleridge *The Rime of the* *Ancient Mariner* (written)	Ann Radcliffe *The Italian*	Treaty of Campo Formio (abolishing Venetian Republic) Burke d. Mary Shelley b. Mary Wollstonecraft d.

DATE	WORKS OF POETRY	OTHER WORKS	HISTORICAL/CULTURAL EVENTS
1798	Coleridge *Kubla Khan* (written) Wordsworth *Simon Lee, Tintern Abbey*, many of the others in *Lyrical Ballads* written Wordsworth and Coleridge *Lyrical Ballads*		Napoleon invades Switzerland
1799	Campbell *The Pleasures of Hope*		Napoleon becomes First Consul
1800	*Lyrical Ballads*, second edition, with Preface Bloomfield *The Farmer's Boy*		Cowper d.
1801	Southey *Thalaba*		
1802	Scott *Minstrelsy of the Scottish Border*, I and II Coleridge *Dejection: An Ode* (letter to Sara Hutchinson)		Peace of Amiens Wordsworth married
1803			Beddoes b.
1804	Blake *Milton*		Napoleon crowned Emperor
1805	Scott *Lay of the Last Minstrel*		Trafalgar Austerlitz
1806			

DATE	WORKS OF POETRY	OTHER WORKS	HISTORICAL/CULTURAL EVENTS
1807	Byron *Hours of Idleness* Wordsworth *Poems in Two Volumes* Crabbe *The Parish Register*	Charles and Mary Lamb *Tales from Shakespeare*	Abolition of slave trade
1808	Scott *Marmion*	Goethe *Faust* I (completed)	
1809	Byron *English Bards and Scotch Reviewers*	Coleridge *The Friend*	Convention of Cintra Tennyson b. Paine d.
1810	Crabbe *The Borough* Scott *The Lady of the Lake* Blake *Jerusalem* (begun 1804, printed 1820)	Wordsworth 'Topographical Description of the Country of the Lakes', in Joseph Wilkinson, *Select Views in Cumberland*	
1811		Jane Austen *Sense and Sensibility* Shelley and Hogg *The Necessity of Atheism*	Prince of Wales becomes Regent Shelley sent down from Oxford; marries Harriet Westbrook
1812	Byron *Childe Harold's Pilgrimage*, I and II Crabbe *Tales*		Napoleon invades Russia; retreat from Moscow Browning b. Dickens b.
1813	Byron *The Bride of Abydos* *The Giaour* Shelley *Queen Mab*	Jane Austen *Pride and Prejudice*	Southey becomes Poet Laureate

DATE	WORKS OF POETRY	OTHER WORKS	HISTORICAL/CULTURAL EVENTS
1814	Wordsworth *The Excursion*	Jane Austen *Mansfield Park* Scott (anon.) *Waverley*	Napoleon abdicates
1815	Byron *Hebrew Melodies* Scott *Lord of the Isles* Wordsworth *The White Doe of Rylstone*	Scott *Guy Mannering*	Waterloo Byron marries
1816	Coleridge *Christabel* *Kubla Khan* (published) Byron *Childe Harold's Pilgrimage*, III *Prisoner of Chillon* Shelley *Alastor*	Jane Austen *Emma* Thomas Love Peacock *Headlong Hall* Scott *The Antiquary*	Shelley marries Mary Wollstonecraft-Godwin Byron's separation; he leaves England
1817	Byron *Manfred* Keats *Poems* Shelley *Laon and Cythna* (became *The Revolt of Islam*, 1818) Crabbe *Tales of the Hall*	Coleridge *Biographia Literaria* Scott *Rob Roy*	Jane Austen d.
1818	Byron *Childe Harold's Pilgrimage*, IV *Beppo* Keats *Endymion*	Jane Austen *Northanger Abbey* *Persuasion* Mary Shelley *Frankenstein*	

DATE	WORKS OF POETRY	OTHER WORKS	HISTORICAL/CULTURAL EVENTS
1819	Crabbe *Tales of the Hall* Byron *Don Juan*, I and II Wordsworth *Peter Bell*		Massacre of Peterloo
1820	John Clare *Poems, Descriptive of Rural Life* Keats *Lamia, Isabella, The Eve of St. Agnes, Hyperion, and other Poems* Shelley *Prometheus Unbound* Blake *Jerusalem*	Scott *Ivanhoe* Lamb *Essays of Elia*	Accession of George IV
1821	Shelley *Epipsychidion* *Adonais* Byron *Don Juan*, III–IV Clare *The Village Minstrel*	Beddoes *The Improvisatore* John Galt *Annals of the Parish*	Keats d.
1822	Shelley *The Triumph of Life* Byron *The Vision of Judgment*	Beddoes *The Bride's Tragedy*	Shelley d.
1823	Byron *Don Juan*, VI–XIV		
1824			Byron d.
1825	Beddoes *Death's Jest-Book* (begun)	Coleridge *Aids to Reflection* Hazlitt *The Spirit of the Age*	

DATE	WORKS OF POETRY	OTHER WORKS	HISTORICAL/CULTURAL EVENTS
1826			
1827	Clare *The Shepherd's Calendar* *Poems by Two Brothers* (Alfred and Charles Tennyson)		Blake d. Battle of Navarino
1828–29			
1830	Tennyson *Poems, Chiefly Lyrical*	Coleridge *On the Constitution of the Church and State*	Hazlitt d.

General Bibliographies

(i)   Historical and social background
(ii)   Individual winters connected with the French and American Revolutions
(iii) The general background of Romanticism
(iv)   General books on Romantic poetry

The number of books, articles, editions, and anthologies on the Romantic period is enormous. Anyone wishing to establish a comprehensive list should consult *The New Cambridge Bibliography of English Literature*, vol. III, edited by G. Watson (Cambridge, 1969), and continue by examining, year by year, the relevant sections of *The Year's Work in English Studies*, the *Annual Bibliography of English Language and Literature*, and the *Modern Language Association International Bibliography*. The MLA has also published the helpful *The English Romantic Poets: A Review of Research and Criticism*, edited by F. Jordan (third edition, New York, 1972). A 'selective and critical bibliography' has appeared since 1965 as a supplement to *English Language Notes*, and is now (since 1980) published by the Garland Press, New York. A current bibliography of criticism on the second-generation Romantic poets appears annually in the *Keats–Shelley Journal*, and *The Wordsworth Circle* reviews books annually in its summer number.

The bibliography below lists those books which I have found most reliable and helpful; in the space available it can in no sense be a complete list. The place of publication is London, except where stated otherwise.

In the bibliographies of individual authors, I have indicated with an asterisk books which may be of particular use to undergraduates.

(i)   Historical and social background

Halevy, E.   *England in 1815* (1921).
The Liberal Awakening (1926). (A sequel to the above; detailed social history.)

Hammond, J. L. and B.   *The Village Labourer, 1760–1832* (1911).
The Town Labourer, 1760–1832 (1917).
The Skilled Labourer, 1760–1832 (1919).
(The first two have been re-issued with interesting critical introductions, 1978.)

Hobsbawm, E.   *The Age of Revolution: Europe 1789–1848* (1962).
(An economic and political study.)

Low, D. M.   *That Sunny Dome* (1977). (A readable, lively, and intelligent 'portrait of Regency Britain'.)

Marshall, D.   *Eighteenth Century England* (1962).

Perkin, H.   *Origins of Modern English Society, 1780–1880* (1969). (Useful complement to the Hammonds' work, mentioned above, since it deals with other classes.)

Slater, G.   *The English Peasantry and the Enclosure of Common Fields* (1907). (Useful background for Clare.)

Tate, W. E.   *The English Village Community and the Enclosure Movements* (1967). (More up to date than Slater; good on community life in villages.)

Watson, J. S.   *The Reign of George III* (Oxford, 1960). (Good straight history in the Oxford History series.)

White, R. J.   *From Waterloo to Peterloo* (1957). (Lively, beautifully written portrait of the years 1815–19.)

Woodward, Sir E. L.   *The Age of Reform*, second edition (Oxford, 1962). (Sequel to Watson; straight history.)

The American Revolution and after

Beloff, M.   *Thomas Jefferson and American Democracy* (1948).

Cunliffe, M.   *George Washington* (1959). (Short biography.)

Donoughue, B.   *British Politics and the American Revolution* (1964).

Jensen, M.   *The Founding of a Nation* (1968).

Trevelyan, Sir G. O.   *The American Revolution*, 4 vols (1917). (Now somewhat outdated, but a wonderful account.)
George the Third and Charles James Fox (1920).

Wright, E.   *Fabric of Freedom, 1763–1800* (1965).

The French Revolution and after

Carlyle, T.   *History of the French Revolution* (first published 1837; numerous editions thereafter.) (Still worth reading for its exciting, day-by-day account.)

Cobb, R.   *The Police and the People, French Popular Protest, 1789–1820* (Oxford, 1970). (Detailed research into provincial reactions to the revolution.)
Reactions to the French Revolution (Oxford, 1972).

Cobban, A.   *The Social Interpretation of the French Revolution*
                    (Cambridge, 1964).

Deane, S.   *The French Revolution and the Enlightenment in
                    England, 1789–1832* (Cambridge, Mass., 1989).

Goodwin, A.   *The Friends of Liberty: The English Democratic
                    Movement in the Age of the French Revolution* (1979).

Lefebvre, G.   *The French Revolution, from its origins to 1793*
                    (1962). (Detailed account.)
                    The French Revolution, from 1793 to 1799 (1964).
                    (Sequel to above.)
                    Napoleon, from 18 Brumaire to Tilsit (1969).

Markham, F.   *Napoleon* (1963).

Paulson, R.   *Representations of Revolution (1789–1820)* (New
                    Haven and London, 1983). (On pictorial and
                    literary representations of the Revolution.)

Prickett, S. (ed.) *England and the French Revolution (1989)*. (Selected
                    extracts from contemporary accounts, with
                    commentary.)

Sydenham, M. J.   *The First French Republic, 1792–1804* (1974).
                    The Girondins (1961). (Dramatic account of
                    moderate party.)

Thompson, J. M.   *The French Revolution* (Oxford, 1943). (In my
                    view, the best account for non-historians; readable,
                    informative.)

Watson, J. R. (ed.) *The French Revolution in English Literature and
                    Art (Yearbook of English Studies*, special number,
                    vol. 19, 1989).

The Industrial Revolution

Ashton, T. S.   *The Industrial Revolution, 1760–1830* (1947). (A
                    useful corrective to the Hammonds' view.)

Deane, P.   *The First Industrial Revolution* (Cambridge, 1965).

Klingender, F.   *Art and the Industrial Revolution* (1947, revised
                    1968).

Thompson, E. P.   *The Making of the English Working Class* (1963).

(ii)   Individual writers connected with the French and American Revolutions

Rousseau

Rousseau   *Oeuvres Complètes*, Pléiade edition (Paris, 1969)

The Social Contract and Discourses, trans. and ed. by G. D. H. Cole, rev. J. H. Brumfitt and John C. Hall (1973).

La Nouvelle Héloïse, trans. and abridged by J. H. McDowell (Philadelphia and London, 1968). (Has a good introduction and reads well.)

Confessions, trans. J. M. Cohen (Harmondsworth, 1964).

Émile, trans. B. Foxley, introduced by B. Jimack (1974).

Broome, J. H.   *Rousseau, A Study of his Thought* (1963).

Duffy, E.   *Rousseau in England* (Berkeley and Los Angeles, 1973).

Green, F. C.   *Jean-Jacques Rousseau* (Cambridge, 1955).

Hall, J. C.   *Rousseau* (1973).

Masters, R. D.   *The Political Philosophy of Rousseau* (1968).

Burke, Paine, Godwin

Burke   *Reflections on the Revolution in France*, ed. W.B. Todd (New York, 1968).

Boulton, J. T. (ed.)   *A Philosophical Inquiry into the Origin of our Ideas of the Sublime and Beautiful* (1958).

Boulton, J. T.   *The Language of Politics in the Age of Wilkes and Burke* (1963).

Brailsford, H. N.   *Shelley, Godwin and their Circle* (1913).

Butler, M. (ed.)   *Burke, Paine, Godwin, and the Revolution Controversy* (Cambridge, 1984). (Selection of contemporary writings, with introduction and notes.)

Fennessy, R. R.   *Burke, Paine, and the Rights of Man* (The Hague, 1963).

Earl Fitzwilliam and   *The Works and Correspondence of the Right*
Sir R. Bourke (eds).   *Honourable Edmund Burke*, 8 vols (1852).

Foner, P. S. (ed.)   *The Complete Writings of Thomas Paine* (New York, 1945).

Priestley, F. E. L. (ed.)   *William Godwin, Enquiry into Political Justice*, 3 vols, (Toronto, 1946).

St Clair, W.   *The Godwins and the Shelleys* (1989).

Smith, O.   *The Politics of Language, 1791–1819* (Oxford, 1984).

On the connections between these figures and the Romantic poets see:

Woodring, C.   *Politics and English Romantic Poetry* (Cambridge, Mass., 1970).

On the general effect of the age on poetry, see:

Butler, M.   *Romantics, Rebels and Reactionaries* (Oxford, 1981). (Locates the writers of the period firmly in the currents of the age; some superb insights, especially on the satire of the age, and generally a most valuable and different view from that of the present book.)

Rodway, A.   *The Romantic Conflict* (1963). (A sociological study which discusses the poetry in relation to the age.)

Whitehead, A. N.   *Science and the Modern World* (Cambridge, 1933). (Chapter 5, entitled 'The Romantic Reaction', is a brief but valuable study of 'the discord between the aesthetic intuitions of mankind and the mechanism of science' in the period.)

Williams, R.   *Culture and Society: 1780–1850* (1959). (Section on the Industrial Revolution.)

See also a most valuable essay on the effect of the French Revolution on English poetry:

Abrams, M. H.   'English Romanticism: the Spirit of the Age', in *Romanticism Reconsidered*, ed. by N. Frye (New York, 1963).

(iii)   The general background of Romanticism

Furst, L. R.   *Romanticism in Perspective* (1969). (A comparative study of Romantic movements in England, France, and Germany.)

Romanticism, second edition (1976). (A short book in the 'Critical Idiom' series; handy and brisk.)

(ed.) *European Romanticism, Self-Definition* (1980). (Extracts from documents of Romanticism in Europe.)

Halsted, J. B.   (ed.) *Romanticism* (1969). (A collection of contemporary writings, fewer than in Furst, but each longer.)

Morse, D.   *Perspectives in Romanticism* (1981). (Subtitled 'A Transformational Analysis'; deals with the development of certain Romantic characteristics – e.g. of languages and ways of seeing – as they are transformed from the eighteenth century and moving towards the twentieth.)

Romanticism (1982). (A companion volume to the above, entitled 'A Structural Analysis' and 'concerned to represent romanticism as a series of intellectual structures rather than as a climate of opinion'.)

Schenk, H. G.   *The Mind of the European Romantics* (1966). (Useful intellectual history.)

Wellek, R.   *A History of Modern Criticism, 1750–1950* (1955, in progress: vol. I deals with the later eighteenth century, vol. II with the Romantic period; each discusses a great deal of useful critical material.)

Concepts of Criticism (New Haven, 1963). (Contains valuable essays on 'The Concept of Romanticism in Literary Scholarship', and 'Romanticism Re-examined'.)

For more detailed studies of French, German, Spanish, and Italian Romanticism, see the bibliography in Furst (1976). See also the periodical *Studies in Romanticism*: there is an especially interesting number on Romanticism itself, Fall 1970, written in shock and horror after the student troubles of 1968. See also the catalogues of the two exhibitions arranged by the Arts Council of Great Britain:

The Romantic Movement (1959).

The Age of Neo-Classicism (1972).

In connection with the former, and the link between literature and the visual arts, see:

Heffernan, J. A. W.   *The Re-Creation of Landscape: A Study of Wordsworth, Coleridge, Constable and Turner* (Hanover, N. H., 1985).

In connection with the latter, see:

Buxton, J.   *The Grecian Taste* (1978). (A beautifully written book which is a timely reminder of the neo-classical elements in the period.)

For an understanding of the spirit of the age, and for contemporary insights into individual poets, see especially:

Howe, P. P. (ed.)   *The Complete Works of William Hazlitt*, 21 vols (1930–34).

Masson, D. (ed.)   *The Collected Writings of Thomas de Quincey*, 14 vols (1896).

Morley, E. J. (ed.)   *Henry Crabb Robinson on Books and their Writers*, 3 vols (1938).

(iv)   General books on Romantic poetry

For literary history, see:

Elton, O.   *A Survey of English Literature, 1780–1830* (1912). (Still a very good coverage.)

Jack, I.   *English Literature, 1815–1832* (Oxford, 1963). (Very good on second-generation Romantic poets and their contemporaries.)

Jackson, J. R. de J.   *Poetry of the Romantic Period* (1980). (Described by the author as 'a history of poems rather than poets'.)

Renwick, W. L.   *English Literature, 1789–1815* (Oxford, 1963). (In the same Oxford series as Jack, above; much thinner, but often sharp and pointed.)

For pre-Romantic and early Romantic poetry, see:

Deane, C. V.   *Aspects of Eighteenth-Century Nature Poetry* (Oxford, 1935).

Hussey, C.   *The Picturesque* (1927). (Classic account of an important pre-Romantic way of seeing nature).

Monk, S. H.   *The Sublime* (New York, 1935). (Another excellent account of an important pre-Romantic element).

Stone, P. W. K.   *The Art of Poetry, 1750–1820* (1967). (On poetic theories and the use of language.)

Watson, J. R.   *Picturesque Landscape and English Romantic Poetry* (1970). (Short account of the influence of the picturesque upon the major poets, except Blake.)

Willey, B.   *The Eighteenth-Century Background* (1940). (Lucid and helpful account of currents of thought, especially about nature.)

Williams, R.   *The Country and the City* (1973). (Challenges simple notions about nature and the countryside in English poetry.)

For general accounts of Romantic poetry and Romantic theory, see:

Abrams, M. H.   *The Mirror and the Lamp* (New York, 1953). (Erudite study of Romantic critical ideas in contrast to neo-Classical ones.)

Natural Supernaturalism (New York, 1971). (Superb on the 'natural religion' of the major Romantics; especially helpful on Wordsworth.)

Armstrong, I.   *Language as Literary Form in Nineteenth-Century Poetry* (Sussex, 1982). (Chapters on the language of Blake, Wordsworth, Shelley.)

Ball, P. M.   *The Central Self* (1968). (On identity and self-expression in Romantic poetry.)

General accounts of Romantic poetry additions

Bate, J.   *Shakespeare and the English Romantic Imagination* (Oxford, 1989).

Beach, J. W.   *The Concept of Nature in Nineteenth-Century English Poetry* (New York, 1956). (On science and on religion in relation to nature: on Wordsworth and Shelley.)

Blackstone, B.   *The Lost Travellers* (1962). (On movement and wandering in Romantic poetry.)

Bloom, H.   *The Visionary Company*, revised edition (Ithaca and London, 1971). (On passion, vision, inspiration, imagination.)

Bowra, C. M.   *The Romantic Imagination* (1950). (Good account of a central theme.)

Brisman, L.   *Romantic Origins* (Ithaca and London, 1978). (On Romantic myths of origins and creation.)

Bush, D.   *Mythology and the Romantic Tradition* (New York, 1937). (A sequel to a similar book on the Renaissance, dealing with poetic use of classical myth and legend.)

Chase, C.   *Decomposing Figures* (Baltimore, 1986).

Clubbe, J., and Lovell, E. Jr.   *English Romanticism, The Grounds of Belief* (1983). (Good on why the Romantic poets thought as they did.)

Cooke, M.   *The Romantic Will* (New Haven and London, 1976). ('Relates the romantic will to the art and consciousness of being'.)

Cooper, A. M.   *Doubt and Identity in Romantic Poetry* (New Haven, 1988).

Curran, S.   *Poetic Form and British Romanticism* (Oxford, 1986). (On the forms of Romantic poetry, including such neglected things as the hymn.)

Ellison, J.   *Romanticism, gender, and the ethics of understanding* (Ithaca, 1990).

Everest, K.   *English Romantic Poetry* (Milton Keynes, 1990). (A short 'Open University' survey, with emphasis on the historical background.)

Foakes, R. A.   *The Romantic Assertion* (1958). (A study of language, noting distinguishing features of Romantic poetry.)

Frye, N.   *A Study of English Romanticism* (Brighton, 1983.) (Deals with myth; the macabre; the revolutionary; the epiphanic.)

Gaull, M.   *English Romanticism, The Human Context* (New York, 1988).

Hough, G.   *The Romantic Poets* (1953). (A brief introduction.)

Keith, W. J.   *The Poetry of Nature: Rural Perspectives in Poetry from Wordsworth to the Present* (Toronto, 1980). (On Wordsworth and Clare, but of general significance also.)

Knight, G. W.   *The Starlit Dome* (1941). (Subtitled 'Studies in the Poetry of Vision'; deals with Wordsworth, Coleridge, Shelley, and Keats.)

Kroeber, K.   *Romantic Narrative Art* (Madison, Wis., 1960). (On narrative poems.)

Lockridge, L.   *The Ethics of Romanticism* (Cambridge, 1989).

McFarland, T.   *Romanticism and the Forms of Ruin* (Princeton, 1981). (On the use of the fragmentary.)

McGann, J. J.   *The Romantic Ideology* (Chicago, 1983).

Manning, P. J.   *Reading the Romantics: Text and Context* (Oxford, 1990).

Mellor, A. K.   *English Romantic Irony* (Cambridge, Mass., 1980). (An important discussion of F. Schlegel's theory of Romantic Irony.)

O'Flinn, P.   *How to Study Romantic Poetry* (Oxford, 1988).

Paulson, R.   *Breaking and Remaking: Aesthetic Practice in England 1700–1820* (New Brunswick, NJ, 1990).

Perkins, D.   *The Quest for Permanence* (Cambridge, Mass., (1959). (Subtitled 'The Symbolism of Wordsworth, Shelley and Keats'.)

Piper, H. W.   *The Active Universe* (1962). (A study of pantheism and the Romantic imagination.)

Punter, D.   *The Romantic Unconscious* (Hemel Hempstead, 1989). (Sub-titled 'a study in narcissism and patriarchy'.)

Rajan, T.   *Dark Interpreter: the Discourse of Romanticism* (Ithaca, 1980).

Rajan, T.   *The Supplement of Reading: Figures of Understanding in Romantic Theory and Practice* (Ithaca, 1990).

Read, H.   *The True Voice of Feeling* (1947). (Essays on a main theme – including 'organic form' – and related essays.)

Simpson, D.   *Irony and Authority in Romantic Poetry* (1979). (On the relationship between author and reader.)

Siskin, C.   *The Historicity of Romantic Discourse* (Oxford, 1988).

Stevenson, W.   *Poetic Friends: A Study of Literary Relationships during the English Romantic Period* (New York, 1990).

Swingle, L. J.   *The Obstinate Questionings of English Romanticism* (Baton Rouge, Louisiana, 1988). (On self-questioning in Romantic poetry.)

Weiskel, T.   *The Romantic Sublime* (Baltimore and London, 1976). (For advanced students: on 'the structure and psychology of transcendence', the relationship between subjective and objective.)

Wolfson, S.   *The Questioning Presence: Wordsworth, Keats, and the Interrogative Mode in Romantic Poetry* (Ithaca, 1987). (Very good on the indeterminacies and probings of Romantic poetry.)

In addition, two works by distinguished twentieth-century poets should be consulted:

Auden, W. H.   *The Enchafèd Flood* (1951). (An engaging and stimulating book about the use of the sea in Romantic poetry.)

Eliot, T. S.   *The Use of Poetry and the Use of Criticism* (1933). (Altogether more sober-sided; has chapters on Wordsworth and Coleridge, and Shelley and Keats.)

There are useful collections of essays, as follows:

Abrams, M. H. (ed.)   *English Romantic Poets, Modern Essays in Criticism* (New York, 1960).

Abrams, M. H.   *The Correspondent Breeze: Essays on English Romanticism* (New York, 1984).

Aers, D., Cook, J., and Punter, D.   *Romanticism and Ideology* (1981).

Behrendt, C. (ed.)   *History and Myth: Essays on English Romantic Literature* (Detroit, 1990).

Bloom, H. (ed.)   *Romanticism and Consciousness* (New York, 1970).

Cunningham, A., and Jardine, N. (eds)   *Romanticism and the Sciences* (Cambridge, 1990).

Eaves, M. and Fischer, M.   *Romanticism and Contemporary Criticism* (Ithaca, 1986).

Ford, B. (ed.)   *From Blake to Byron* (Harmondsworth, 1982). (The New Pelican Guide to English Literature, vol. 5.)

Ford, B. (ed.)   *Romantics to Early Victorians* (Cambridge, 1990). (A guide to the arts in Britain; vol. 6 of a series.)

Frye, N. (ed.)   *Romanticism Reconsidered* (New York, 1963). (Four long essays.)

Hanley, K., and Selden, R. (eds)   *Revolution and English Romanticism* (Hemel Hempstead, 1990). (Papers from a 1989 conference on Romanticism and Revolution.)

Hilles, F. W. and Bloom H. (eds)   *From Sensibility to Romanticism* (New York, 1965). (Chiefly useful for pre-Romanticism and early Romantics.)

Hoffmeister, G. (ed.)   *European Romanticism: Literary cross-currents, modes, and models* (Detroit, 1990).

Kitson, P. (ed.)   *Romantic Criticism, 1800–1825* (1989). (Selection of critical essays by the Romantics.)

Johnston, K. R., et al. (eds)   *Romantic Revaluations: Criticism and Theory* (Bloomington, Ind., 1990).

Jordan, J., Logan, J. and Frye N. (eds)   *Some British Romantics* (Dayton, Ohio, 1966).

Kroeber, K. and Walling, W. (eds)   *Images of Romanticism* (New Haven and London, 1978). (On literature and the visual art of the period.)

Kumar, S. K. (ed.)   *British Romantic Poets, Recent Revaluations* (1966).

Levinson, M., et al.   *Rethinking Historicism* (Oxford, 1989).

Lipking, L. (ed.)   *High Romantic Argument* (Ithaca, 1981).

McGann, J. J.   *The Beauty of Inflections* (Oxford, 1985). (On historicism and poetry, with essays on, among others, Coleridge, Crabbe, Byron, and Keats.)

Mellor, A. K. (ed.)   *Romanticism and Feminism* (Bloomington, Ind., 1988).

Porter, R., and Teich, M. (eds)   *Romanticism in National Context* (Cambridge, 1988).

Prickett, S. (ed.)   *The Romantics* (1981). (Essays on art, religion, and philosophy, as well as on literature.)

Reed, A.   *Romanticism and Language* (1984). ('Language-oriented perspectives on the period'.)

Ruoff, G. (ed.)   *The Romantics and Us: Essays on Literature and Culture* (New Brunswick, NJ, 1990).

Simpson, D. (ed.)   *Kant, Fichte, Schelling, Schopenhauer, Hegel* (Cambridge, 1984). (An anthology of essays by these writers.)

Wheeler, K. M. (ed.)   *German Aesthetic and Literary Criticism: the Romantic Ironists and Goethe* (Cambridge, 1984). (Part of the growing concern with Romantic Irony: contains a selection of essays by German writers.)

Thorpe, C. D., Baker, C., and Weaver, B. (eds)   *The Major English Romantic Poets* (Carbondale, Ill., 1957).

Watson, J. R. (ed.)   *An Infinite Complexity* (Edinburgh, 1983).

Romantic reviews and reviewers have been well studied. See:

Hayden, J. O.   *The Romantic Reviewers 1802–24* (Chicago, 1969). (Contains a good bibliography.)
Romantic Bards and British Reviewers (1971.)

Redpath, T. (ed.)   *The Young Romantics and Critical Opinion, 1807–1824* (1973). (On the critical reception given to Byron, Shelley, and Keats, with extracts).

In addition to these general collections, there are individual *Critical Heritage* volumes on all the major poets except Wordsworth, and on some of the others as well:

Blake (G. E. Bentley Jr)
Coleridge (J. R. de J. Jackson)
Byron (A. Rutherford)
Shelley (J. E. Barcus)
Keats (G. M. Matthews)
Scott (J. O. Hayden)
Southey (L. Madden)
Clare (M. Storey)
Crabbe (A. Pollard)

'Casebooks'

There are 'casebooks' on *The Romantic Imagination* (John Spencer Hill); on Blake's *Songs of Innocence and of Experience* (M. Bottrall); on Wordsworth, *Lyrical Ballads* (A. R. Jones and W. Tydeman) and *The Prelude* (W. J. Harvey and R. Gravil); on Coleridge, *'The Ancient Mariner' and Other Poems* (A. R. Jones and W. Tydeman); on Byron, *'Childe Harold's Pilgrimage' and 'Don Juan'* (J. Jump); on Keats's Odes (G. S. Fraser and on *Keats: Narrative Poems* (J. S. Hill); and on *Shelley: Shorter Poems and Lyrics* (P. Swinden).

Brief introductions to the major poets may be found in the excellent *Writers and their Work* series published under the auspices of the British Council, as follows:

Blake (K. Raine)
Wordsworth (J. R. Watson)
Coleridge (K. Raine)
Byron, I, II, III (B. Blackstone)
Shelley (G. M. Matthews)
Keats (M. Allott)

Individual Authors

Notes on biography, major works and criticism

BEDDOES, Thomas Lovell (1803–1849), born Bristol, the son of a scientist; educated at Charterhouse and Pembroke College, Oxford; studied at Göttingen, and lived abroad for much of the remainder of his life. His play *Death's Jest-Book* was written between 1825 and 1829, but not published until 1850; wrote poetry (including 'Dream-Pedlary') and became interested in radical and subversive politics, so much so that he was deported from Bavaria in 1833 and had to settle in Zurich. Later he became much obsessed with death, and committed suicide in January 1849.

> H. W. Donner, ed., *The Works of Thomas Lovell Beddoes* (1935). (Includes letters.)
>
> J. Higgens, ed., *Thomas Lovell Beddoes, Selected Poems* (Manchester, 1976). (Contains a valuable list of articles/chapters on Beddoes)
>
> Ricks, C. *The Force of Poetry* (Oxford, 1984). (Contains an essay on *Death's Jest Book*.)
>
> Thompson, J. R. *Thomas Lovell Beddoes* (New York, 1985).

BLAKE, William (1757–1827), born in London, third of seven children of James Blake, hosier; visionary in childhood. Attended Henry Pars's drawing school, 1768–72; apprenticed to an engraver, James Basire, 1772–79; student at the Royal Academy, 1779. Present at Gordon riots and burning of Newgate, 1780. Married Catherine Boucher, 1782: no children. *Poetical Sketches* printed by friends but not distributed, 1783. His brother Robert died aged 19, 1787, after which Blake believed that he continued to communicate with him. *Songs of Innocence* engraved, 1789; *The Marriage of Heaven and Hell* engraved 1790. Thereafter *The French Revolution* printed but not published (1791); *America: a Prophecy* (1793); *Europe* (1793); *The First Book of Urizen* (1794); *Songs of Innocence and of Experience* (1794). In 1796–97 Blake was at work on an extended series of illustrations to Young's *Night Thoughts* and Gray's *Poems*: in 1800 he moved to a cottage near Felpham, Sussex, returning to London in 1803. In 1804 the title pages of *Milton* and *Jerusalem* were engraved, but Blake continued to work on them for some years afterwards (*Milton* until about 1809, *Jerusalem* until about 1820). During these years Blake was very poor, making a living by engraving designs for Wedgwood's catalogue. In later life Blake gathered round him some devoted followers, including John Linnell, for whom he painted the illustrations to the *Book of Job*; died 12 August 1827.

G. Keynes, ed., *The Complete Writings of William Blake* (1966). (Contains prose, letters, and marginalia as well as poetry.)

W. H. Stevenson, ed., *The Poems of William Blake* (Longman's Annotated English Poets, 1971). (Contains a good modernized text and notes.)

G. E. Bentley Jr, ed., *William Blake's Writings*, 2 vols (Oxford, 1978). (Full bibliographical information.)

G. Keynes, ed., *The Letters of William Blake*, third edition (Oxford, 1980).

D. V. Erdman, ed., *The Illuminated Blake* (1975). (Monochrome illuminated versions.) There are inexpensive coloured editions of: *Songs of Innocence and of Experience*, ed. G. Keynes (1970); *The Marriage of Heaven and Hell*, ed. G. Keynes (1975); *The Book of Urizen* (1978).

There are expensive facsimiles of all the Prophetic Books produced by the Trianon Press for the Blake Trust, most of which are held in libraries. There is a neat and helpful selection in *William Blake, Selected Poems*, ed. P. H. Butter (1982).

There is an 'Oxford Authors' *William Blake*, ed. M. Mason (Oxford, 1988), and a selection by W. H. Stevenson (1988).

See: Adams, H., *Blake and Yeats, The Contrary Vision* (Ithaca and London, 1955).

Adams, H., *William Blake: A Reading of the Shorter Poems* (Washington UP, 1968). (Useful on 'seeing through the eye'.)

Alford. S. E., *Irony and the Logic of the Romantic Imagination* (1989). (On Romantic Irony in F. Schlegel and Blake.)

Beer, J. B., *Blake's Humanism* (Manchester, 1968). (Attempts to see Blake as a whole.)

Beer, J. B., *Blake's Visionary Universe* (Manchester, 1969).

Bentley, G. E. Jr, ed., *Blake Books* (Oxford, 1977). (Contains a massive amount of bibliographical information, including 250 pages on books and articles about Blake.)

Bentley, G. E. Jr, ed., *Blake Records* (Oxford, 1969). (Another massive book, containing all known references to Blake by his contemporaries; useful biographical evidence.)

Bentley, G. E. Jr., *Blake Records Supplement* (1988). (Containing all the items which have turned up since *Blake Records* was published.)

Bindman, D., *Blake as an Artist* (1977). (An art historian's view.)

*Blackstone, B., *English Blake* (1949). (On Blake and the tradition of English thought.)

Bloom, H., *Blake's Apocalypse* (1963). (On the 'argument' of Blake's poetry.)

Bronowski, J., *William Blake and the Age of Revolution* (1965). (On Blake and his age, and on his radicalism.)

Curran, S. and Wittreich, J. A. Jr, eds, *Blake's Sublime Allegory* (Madison, Wis., 1973).

*Damon, S. F., *A Blake Dictionary* (1973). (Indispensable for looking up Blake's symbols.)

Damrosch, L. Jr., *Symbol and Truth in Blake's Myth* (Princeton, 1981).

Eaves, M. *William Blake's Theory of Art* (Princeton, 1982). (On 'expressive' rather than 'mimetic' theory and practice.)

*Erdman, D. V., *Blake: Prophet against Empire*, second edition (Princeton, 1969). (Detailed study of Blake and contemporary history.)

Erdman, D. V. and Grant, J. E., eds, *Blake's Visionary Forms Dramatic* (Princeton, 1970).

Essick, R. N., *William Blake and the Language of Adam* (Oxford, 1989). (On Blake's language and techniques.)

*Frye, N., *Fearful Symmetry* (Princeton, 1947). (Important discussion of Blake's work, especially his imagination.)

Fuller, D., *Blake's Heroic Argument* (1987). (Good on the Prophetic Books.)

Gilchrist, A., *The Life of William Blake*, 2 vols (1863). (The standard life; there is a convenient edition with notes by R. Todd, 1945.)

*Gleckner, R. F., *The Piper & the Bard: A Study of William Blake* (Detroit, 1959). (On *Songs of Innocence and of Experience*.)

Gleckner, R. F., *Blake's Prelude: Poetical Sketches* (Baltimore and London, 1983). (On Blake's first book.)

*Gleckner, R. F. and Greenberg, M. L. (eds), *Approaches to Teaching Blake's 'Songs of Innocence and Experience'* (New York, 1989).

Glen, H., *Vision and Disenchantment: Blake's Songs and Wordsworth's Lyrical Ballads* (Cambridge, 1983). (A comparison between the two, in which Wordsworth comes off worse.)

*Hagstrum, J. H., *William Blake, Poet and Painter* (Chicago, 1964). (On Blake's illuminated books).

Hilton, N., *Literal Imagination: Blake's Vision of Words* (Los Angeles, 1983).

Hilton, N. (ed.), *Essential Articles for the Study of William Blake 1970–1984* (Hamden, Conn., 1986).

Hilton, N. and Vogler, T. A., *Unnam'd Forms: Blake and Textuality* (Berkeley and Los Angeles, 1986). (Essays by several hands.)

Holloway, J., *Blake, the Lyric Poetry* (1968). (A short book, neat and useful.)

Keynes, G., *Blake Studies* (Oxford, 1971). (Essays on various topics by Blake's greatest editor.)

*Leader, Z., *Reading Blake's 'Songs'* (1981). (Good on Blake's antecedents, especially Isaac Watts.)

Lindsay, D. W., *Blake: 'Songs of Innocence' and 'Experience'* (1989). (In the 'Critics Debate' series.)

Lindsay, J., *William Blake, His Life and Work* (1978).

Mellor, A. K. *Blake's Human Form Divine* (Berkeley and Los Angeles, 1974).

Mitchell, W. J. T., *Blake's Composite Art* (Princeton, 1978). (On the relationship between visual and verbal in Blake.)

Paley, M. D., *Energy and the Imagination* (Oxford, 1970). (On the interaction of two important features.)

Paley, M. D. *The Continuing City: William Blake's Jerusalem* (New York and London, 1983).

Paley, M. D. and Phillips, M., eds, *William Blake, essays in honour of Sir Geoffrey Keynes* (Oxford, 1973).

Phillips, M., ed., *Interpreting Blake* (Cambridge, 1978).

Raine, K., *Blake and Tradition*, 2 vols (Princeton, 1968). (Learned discussion of influences on Blake, especially those of hermetic philosophy and of the mystics.)

*Raine, K., *William Blake* (1974). (Short and well-illustrated introduction.)

Tannenbaum, L. *Biblical Tradition in Blake's Early Prophecies* (Princeton, 1982).

BYRON, George Gordon, Lord (1788–1824), born London, but lived as a child in Aberdeen; born with deformed foot. Inherited title, 1798, with a seat at Newstead, Nottinghamshire. Educated at Harrow and Trinity College, Cambridge; published *Hours of Idleness* (1807), followed by *English Bards and Scotch Reviewers* (1809); tour of Portugal, Spain, Greece, Turkey, and Albania, 1809–11. On his return Byron spoke in the House of Lords against a bill to punish frame-breaking by death; abandoned politics after spectacular success of *Childe Harold's Pilgrimage* Cantos I and II, March 1812; verse tales (*Lara, The Corsair,* etc.) written 1812–15, during which time Byron eclipsed Scott as the most famous poet of the age. Married Annabella Milbanke, January 1815; separated 1816, after which Byron left for the Continent (April 1816). Travelled to Switzerland; friendship with Shelley. Wrote *The Prisoner of Chillon, Childe Harold's Pilgrimage* Canto III (1816). To Italy (mainly Venice and Pisa), 1817: *Childe Harold's Pilgrimage* Canto IV (1818); *Beppo* (1818); *Don Juan* begun 1818. In 1819 began a long-lasting relationship with Teresa Guiccioli, whom Byron followed to Ravenna. *The Vision of Judgment* published in Leigh Hunt's *The Liberal* (1822). Inspired by the philhellenic movement and the uprisings of the Greeks in 1823, Byron set out to join the cause of Greek independence; he died of fever, badly treated by the doctors, at Missolonghi, 19 April 1824.

McGann, J. J., ed., *Lord Byron: The Complete Poetical Works*, 3 vols (Oxford, 1980–81).

F. Page, ed., *Poetical Works*, rev. J. Jump (1970).

Marchand, L. A., ed., *Byron's Letters and Journals*, 12 vols (1973–82). There is a one-volume 'Oxford Authors' selection, ed. J. J. McGann (1986); the letters and journals are used in a one-volume *Byron, a Self-Portrait*, ed. P. Quennell (Oxford, 1990).

See: Ashton, T. L., *Byron's Hebrew Melodies* (1972). (A pleasing study of a neglected topic.)

Beatty, B., *Byron's 'Don Juan'* (1985). (Unusual, and good on Aurora Raby and her part in the poem.)

*Beatty, B., *Byron: 'Don Juan' and Other Poems: A Critical Study* (1987). (A Penguin 'Masterstudy', useful as an introduction.)

*Beatty, B. and Newey, V., *Byron and the Limits of Fiction* (Liverpool, 1988). (Useful essays.)

*Blackstone, B., *Byron, A Survey* (1975). (A book which goes overboard at times, but which is also very enlivening and informative.)

Buxton, J., *Byron and Shelley* (1968). (On the literary relationships; not just biographical.)

Calvert, W. J. *Byron: Romantic Paradox* (1935). (On neo-Classical and Romantic elements.)

Cooke, M., *The Blind Man Traces the Circle* (Princeton, 1969). (Not so lively as its title implies: subtitled 'on the patterns and philosophy of Byron's poetry'.)

*Doherty, F. J., *Byron* (1969). (An intelligent introduction.)

Eliot, T. S., 'Byron', reprinted in *On Poetry and Poets* (1957).

Elledge, W. P., *Byron and the Dynamics of Metaphor* (Nashville, 1968). (On polarities of metaphor in Byron.)

Garber, F., *Self, Text, and Romantic Irony: the example of Byron* (Princeton, 1988). (Applying the theories of F. Schlegel to Byron.)

Gleckner, R., *Byron and the Ruins of Paradise* (Baltimore and London, 1967). (Emphasizes 'the Fall' in Byron's poetry.)

Graham, P. W., *'Don Juan' and Regency England* (Charlottesville, Va., 1990).

Joseph, M. K., *Byron the Poet* (1964). (Good on assessing criticism, judicious.)

*Jump, J., *Byron* (1972). (A safe but uninspiring introduction.)

Jump, J., *Byron, A Symposium* (1975). (A collection of essays.)

Kelsall, M., *Byron's Politics* (Brighton, 1986).

Lovell, E. J. Jr, ed., *Medwin's Conversations with Lord Byron* (Princeton, 1966).

McGann, J. J., *Fiery Dust* (Chicago, 1968). (Essays on various poems, especially on self-expression.)

McGann, J. J., *Don Juan in Context* (1976)

Marchand, L. A., *Byron*, 3 vols (1957). (The standard biography.)

*Marchand, L. A., *Byron, A Portrait* (1971). (A shorter, rewritten version of the above.)

Marchand, L. A., *Byron's Poetry: A Critical Introduction* (New York, 1965). (Well balanced and dependable.)

Marshall, W. H., *The Structure of Byron's Major Poems* (Philadelphia, 1962). (Concerned with structure and irony.)

Page, N., *A Byron Chronology* (1988).

*Rutherford, A., *Byron, A Critical Study* (Edinburgh, 1961). (A fine, serious book, perhaps over-critical at times, but a strong guide through the poems.)

Rutherford, A. (ed.), *Byron: Augustan and Romantic* (1990).

*Storey, M., *Byron and the Eye of Appetite* (1986). (On Byron and the material world.)

West, P., *Byron and the Spoiler's Art* (1960). (More eccentric than Rutherford, but stimulating.)

CLARE, John (1793–1864), born Helpstone, Northamptonshire, the son of a farm-labourer. He worked as a labourer and as a gardener, but rose from obscurity with *Poems Descriptive of Rural Life* (1820). This and *The Village Minstrel* (1821) made him acclaimed as a peasant poet, and patronized as such; his subsequent books, however, were less successful: they were *The Shepherd's Calendar* (1827) and *The Rural Muse* (1835). Pressures upon him such as the enclosure of his village and a failure at small farming, led to a breakdown in 1837, when he was treated in Essex at a private asylum. He escaped from there and walked back to Northamptonshire, but was certified insane and sent to St Andrew's Hospital, Northampton, where he lived for the remainder of his life. He died there 20 May 1864 and was buried at Helpstone.

The principal scholarly edition of Clare is in progress: E. Robinson and D. Powell, eds, *The Early Poems of John Clare* (Oxford, 1989) and *The Later Poems of John Clare* (Oxford, 1984). There is a good selection of *John Clare: Poems and Prose* by E. Robinson and D. Powell (Oxford, 1984), which has superseded the 1967 selection by E. Robinson and G. Summerfield. Other modern editions include:

Robinson, E., *The Parish* (1990).

Summerfield, G., *John Clare, Selected Poetry* (1990).

The Letters of John Clare have been edited by M. Storey (Oxford, 1985).

Before that, there were modern editions of Clare as follows:

Tibble, J. W. ed., *The Poems of John Clare*, 2 vols (1935). (The pioneering edition, now superseded.)

Grigson, G., ed., *Poems of John Clare's Madness* (1949).

Robinson, E. and Summerfield, G., eds, *The Later Poems of John Clare* (Manchester, 1964).

Robinson, E. and Summerfield, G., eds, *The Shepherd's Calendar* (1964).

Tibble, J. W. and A., eds., *John Clare, Selected Poems* (1965). (With modern spelling and punctuation)

Robinson, E. and Summerfield, G., eds, *Selected Poems and Prose of John Clare* (1967).

Tibble, A., ed., *The Midsummer Cushion* (Ashington/Manchester, 1978).

Thornton, R. K. R., ed., *The Rural Muse* (Ashington/Manchester, 1982).

Tibble, J. W. and A., eds, *The Prose of John Clare* (1951).

Grainger, M., ed., *The Natural History Prose Writings of John Clare* (Oxford, 1983).

See: Barrell, J., *The Idea of Landscape and the Sense of Place, 1730–1840* (Cambridge, 1972). (Good on landscape, enclosures.)

Blunden, E., ed., *Sketches in the Life of John Clare by Himself* (1931).

*Brownlow, T., *John Clare and Picturesque Landscape* (Oxford, 1983). (Bright and sharp.)

Chilcott, T., *'A Real World and Doubting Mind': A Critical Study of the Poetry of John Clare* (Hull, 1985).

Crossan, G., *A Relish for Eternity: The Process of Divinization in the Poetry of John Clare* (Salzburg, 1976).

Deacon, G., *John Clare and the Folk Tradition* (1983).

Howard, W., *John Clare* (New York, 1981).

*Storey, M., *The Poetry of John Clare: A Critical Introduction* (1974). (A very good, straightforward and helpful book.)

Tibble, J. W., and A., *John Clare: A Life*, revised edition (1972).

Todd, J. M., *In Adam's Garden: A Study of John Clare's Pre-Asylum Poetry* (Gainesville, Florida, 1973). (On Clare and the 'Fall'.)

COLERIDGE, Samuel Taylor (1772–1834), born Ottery St Mary, Devon, the youngest son of a clergyman. Educated Christ's Hospital, London, and Jesus College, Cambridge; Cambridge education interrupted when he got into debt and enlisted in the army. By 1794 he had become friendly with Southey, with whom he planned 'Pantisocracy' scheme; married Sara Fricker (whose sister had married Southey) 1795. Settled at Nether Stowey, north Somerset; joined by William and Dorothy Wordsworth, 1797–98, followed by their publication of *Lyrical Ballads* (1798). To Germany, 1798–99, to study at Göttingen; on his return settled at Keswick with his family. Periods of poor health and increasing dependence on opium followed; fell in love with Wordsworth's sister-in-law, Sara Hutchinson. He attempted a new start by journeying to Malta (where he worked as secretary to the Governor) and Italy, 1804–6. On his return he lived increasingly with the Wordsworths; published *The Friend* (periodical essay) 1809–10; quarrelled with Wordsworth 1810, patched up in 1812. Lectured in London on Shakespeare, 1812. Published *Biographia Literaria* (1817), *Sibylline Leaves* (poems) (1817). After 1816 he lived at Highgate, under the care of Dr Gillman, until his death, 25 July 1834.

The most convenient edition of Coleridge's *Poems* is that of J. B. Beer (1974). This Everyman edition contains the text of the 'Letter to Sara Hutchinson' which is not present in *The Complete Poetical Works of Coleridge*, ed. E. H. Coleridge, 2 vols (1912), or the one-volume edition by E. H. Coleridge (1921). Under the general editorship of Kathleen Coburn, *The Collected Works of Samuel Taylor Coleridge* (1969–, in progress) will contain an edition of the poems.

> For the student of Coleridge's poetry the most useful volumes in the new *Collected Works* are:
> White, R. J., ed., *Lay Sermons* (1972).
> Engell, J. and Bate, W. J., eds, *Biographia Literaria* (1983). (This supersedes the edition by J. W. Shawcross (Oxford, 1907).)
> There is a convenient Everyman edition by G. Watson (1956).
> There is a selection of Coleridge's Criticism of Shakespeare, edited by R. A. Foakes (1989).
> Griggs, E. L., ed., *Collected Letters of Samuel Taylor Coleridge*, 6 vols (1956–71).
> Coburn, K., ed., *The Notebooks of Samuel Taylor Coleridge*. (In progress: 1957–). (Four volumes to date, with four volumes of notes.)

See: Adair, P., *The Waking Dream* (1967). (Emphasizes day-dream and reverie in Coleridge.)
Barth, R., *The Symbolic Imagination: Coleridge and the Romantic Tradition* (Princeton, 1977)
Barth, R, *Coleridge and the Power of Love* (Columbia, Missouri, 1989).
*Beer, J. B., *Coleridge the Visionary* (1959). (Very good on Coleridge's reading.)
Beer, J. B., *Coleridge's Poetic Intelligence* (1977). (On the combination of poetical and intellectual interests.)
Beer, J. B., ed., *Coleridge's Variety* (1972). (Essays.)
Chambers, E. K., *Coleridge* (1938).
Christensen, J., *Coleridge's Blessed Machine of Language* (Ithaca and London, 1982).
Coleman, D., *Coleridge and 'The Friend'* (Oxford, 1988). (On Coleridge and his short-lived periodical.)
Cornwell, J., *Coleridge: Poet and Revolutionary, 1772–1804* (1973).
Crawford, W. B., *Reading Coleridge* (Ithaca and London, 1979). (Essays.)
Davidson, G., *Coleridge's Career* (1990).
*Dekker, G., *Coleridge and the Literature of Sensibility* (1978). (On 'Dejection', setting it in the context of eighteenth-century poetry.)
*Everest, K., *Coleridge's Secret Ministry* (Sussex, 1979). (On the early conversation poems.)
Fruman, N., *Coleridge, the Damaged Archangel* (1972). (On Coleridge as plagiarist.)
Gallant, C. (ed.), *Coleridge's Theory of Imagination Today* (New York, 1989).
Goodson, A. C., *Verbal Imagination: Coleridge and the Language of Modern Criticism* (Oxford, 1989).
Griggs, E. L. ed., *Wordsworth and Coleridge: Studies in Honor of G. M. Harper* (Princeton, 1939). (Essays.)
*Hamilton, P., *Coleridge's Poetics* (Oxford, 1983).

Harding, A. J., *Coleridge and the Inspired Word* (Montreal, 1985).

Hayter, A., *A Voyage in Vain* (1973). (On Coleridge's journey to Malta, 1804, what led up to it, and what followed.)

Hodgson, J. A., *Coleridge, Shelley, and Transcendental Inquiry* (Lincoln, Neb., 1989). (Subtitled 'Rhetoric, argument, and metapsychology'.)

House, H., *Coleridge* (1953). (Very good introduction.)

Jasper, D., *Coleridge as Poet and Religious Thinker* (1985) (Good on prose work and on Coleridge's religious ideas.)

*Lowes, J. L., *The Road to Xanadu*, second edition (1930). (Pioneer study of Coleridge's voluminous reading and its effect upon his poetry.)

Mc Kusick, J. C., *Coleridge's Philosophy of Language* (New Haven, 1986).

*McFarland, T., *Coleridge and the Pantheist Tradition* (Oxford, 1969). (On Coleridge's theory and practice, and on German influences.)

Magnuson, P., *Coleridge and Wordsworth: A lyrical dialogue* (Princeton, 1988).

Modiano, R., *Coleridge and the Concept of Nature* (1985).

Nethercot, A. H., *The Road to Tryermaine* (Chicago, 1939). (Tries to do for 'Christabel' what Lowes had done for the other major poems; not so successful, but still interesting.)

Newlyn, L., *Coleridge, Wordsworth, and the Language of Allusion* (Oxford, 1986). (Sensitive to poetic relationship between the two.)

Parker, R., *Coleridge's Meditative Art* (Ithaca and London, 1975). (On influences, especially seventeenth-century divines).

*Prickett, S., *Coleridge and Wordsworth: The Poetry of Growth* (1970). (Useful on both poets, especially on symbols and on language.)

Read, H., *Coleridge as Critic* (1949.) (A short book, on Coleridge's poetic theory.)

Richards, I. A., *Coleridge on Imagination* (1934). (Extended study of Coleridge's theory of poetry.)

*Watson, G., *Coleridge the Poet* (1966). (On 'how successful a poet he was'.)

Whalley, G., *Coleridge and Sara Hutchinson* (1955).

Wheeler, K. M., *Sources, Processes, and Methods in Coleridge's 'Biographia Literaria'* (Cambridge, 1980). (Argues that there is more coherence in the work than at first appears.)

Wheeler, K. M., *The Creative Mind in Coleridge's Poetry* (1981).

*Willey, B., *Nineteenth Century Studies* (1949). (Chapter on Coleridge.)

Yarlott, G., *Coleridge and the Abyssinian Maid* (1967). (On the major poetry.)

CRABBE, George (1754–1832), born Aldeburgh, Suffolk, son of a collector of sale tax. Apprenticed to an apothecary; in 1780 went to London, where he was befriended by Burke. Published *The Library* (1781), *The Village* (1783). Crabbe took Holy Orders, and became chaplain to the Duke of Rutland at Belvoir, Leicestershire; thereafter became a country clergyman, and published no more verse until the successful *The Parish Register* (1807). This was followed by *The Borough* (1810), *Tales* (1812), and *Tales of the Hall* (1819). In 1814 Crabbe became vicar of Trowbridge, Wiltshire, and died there 3 February 1832.

Ward, A. W., ed., *Poems by George Crabbe*, 3 vols (1905–7).
Pollard, A., ed., *New Poems by George Crabbe* (1960).
The *Life* of Crabbe was written by his son, and formed volume 1 of the eight-volume edition of *The Poetical Works of George Crabbe*. It has since been reissued separately (1932, 1947).

See: *Bareham, T., *George Crabbe* (1977). (Good on Crabbe in his time.)
Chamberlain, R. L., *George Crabbe* (New York, 1965).
*Haddakin, L., *The Poetry of Crabbe* (1955). (First modern study to take Crabbe seriously.)
Hatch, R. B., *Crabbe's Arabesque: Social Drama in the Poetry of George Crabbe* (Montreal, 1976). (Somewhat fanciful title, deals with conflict in Crabbe.)
*New, P., *George Crabbe's Poetry* (1976). (Excellent critical study.)
Sigworth, O. F. *Nature's Sternest Painter* (Tucson, Arizona, 1965). (Five essays on different aspects of Crabbe's poetry.)

DARLEY, George (1795–1846), born Dublin, educated privately and at Trinity College, Dublin; moved to London, and became a writer for the *London Magazine*, 1823; subsequently wrote for *The Athenaeum*. Published *Sylvia* (1829), and *Nepenthe* (1839); also wrote plays (*Thomas à Becket, Ethelstan, King of Wessex*); died 23 November 1846.

Ridler, A., ed., *Selected Poems of George Darley* (1979).

See: Abbott, C. C., *The Life and Letters of George Darley* (1928).
Brisman, L., *Romantic Origins* (Ithaca and London, 1978). (Contains a chapter on Darley.)

KEATS, John (1795–1821), born Finsbury, London, son of a livery-stable keeper. His father died in 1804, and his mother promptly married again; she died in 1810. Keats was at school at Enfield, 1803–10, followed by an apprenticeship to Thomas Hammond, surgeon, in Edmonton. He became a student at Guy's Hospital in 1815, and passed his medical examinations in 1816. In the same year he met Leigh Hunt, wrote his 'Chapman's Homer' sonnet and 'Sleep and Poetry', and abandoned medicine as a career. *Poems* (1817) published; during 1817 engaged in writing *Endymion* (published 1818). Walking tour of the Lake District and Scotland, 1818; returned to London to find his brother Tom very ill, and nursed him until his death, 1 December 1818. *Hyperion* begun; met Fanny Brawne, November 1818. *The Eve of St Agnes, La Belle Dame sans Merci*, the great *Odes* written 1819; became engaged to Fanny Brawne, December 1819. *Lamia, Isabella*, etc. published (1820); Keats recommended to go to Italy for his health, and set out with Joseph Severn, September 1820: died at Rome, 23 February 1821.

Garrod, H. W., ed., *The Poetical Works of John Keats* (1956).
Allott M., ed., *The Poems of John Keats* (1970). (Longman's Annotated English Poets, with good notes.)
Barnard, J., ed., *John Keats, the Complete Poems* (Harmondsworth, 1973). (Chronological, good notes.)
Stillinger, J., ed., *The Poems of John Keats* (1978). (In his book, *The Texts of Keats's Poems* (1974), Stillinger claims that other texts are inaccurate.)

Rollins, H. E., ed., *The Letters of John Keats*, 1814–21, 2 vols (Cambridge, Mass., 1958).
Rollins, H. E., ed., *The Keats Circle: Letters and Papers* (1816–1879), 2 vols (Cambridge, Mass., 1965).
There is an 'Oxford Authors' *John Keats*, ed. E. Cook, containing a good selection of letters as well as the majority of the poems. Keats's *Poems of 1820* are available in an annotated student text, ed. D. G. Gillham (Plymouth, 1988).

See: Aske, M., *Keats and Hellenism* (Cambridge, 1985).
Baker, J., *John Keats and Symbolism* (Brighton, 1986).
*Barnard, J., *John Keats* (Cambridge, 1987). (Good introduction.)
Bate, W. J., *The Stylistic Development of Keats* (1945). (On Keats's craftsmanship.)
*Bate, W. J., *John Keats* (Cambridge, Mass., 1963). (A superb biography.)
Bate, W. J., *Keats: A Collection of Critical Essays* (Englewood Cliffs, N. J., 1964).
Bayley, J., 'Keats and Reality', *Proceedings of the British Academy*, 48 (1962), 91–126.
*Blackstone, B., *The Consecrated Urn* (1959). (On growth and form; processes and patterns.)
Bush, D., *John Keats* (1966). (In the 'Masters of World Literature' series; a fine introduction.)
Dickstein, M., *Keats and his Poetry* (Chicago, 1971). (Well-balanced, careful study.)
Ende, S. A., *Keats and the Sublime* (New Haven and London, 1976).
Ford, N. F., *The Prefigurative Imagination of Keats* (Stanford, 1951). (On Keats and the imagination.)
*Gittings, R., *John Keats* (1968). (Detailed and moving life.)
*Jack, I., *Keats and the Mirror of Art* (Oxford, 1967). (On Keats's use of painting and sculpture.)
Jones, J., *John Keats's Dream of Truth* (1969). (Good on Keats's delicate perceptions.)
Levinson, M., *Keats' Life of Allegory: the Origins of a Style* (Oxford, 1988).
Patterson, C. I., *The Daemonic in the Poetry of Keats* (1970). (On the Greek daemonic in Keats.)
Muir, K., *John Keats: A Reassessment* (Liverpool, 1958).
Murry, J. M., *Keats and Shakespeare* (1925). (Influential and pioneer study that sees Keats in the tradition of Shakespeare.)
Pettet, E. C., *On the Poetry of Keats* (Cambridge, 1957). (One of the few books to discuss *Endymion* at length; otherwise unexciting.)
*Ricks, C., *Keats and Embarrassment* (Oxford, 1974). (Beautifully written and sensitive study of Keats's interest in blushing and in other signs of human feeling.)
*Ridley, M. R., *Keats's Craftsmanship* (Oxford, 1933). (Good on verse forms of the *Odes*.)
Sperry, S., *Keats the Poet* (Princeton, 1973).
*Stillinger, J., *The Hoodwinking of Madeline* (Urbana, Ill., 1971). (Lively, anti-Romantic view of 'The Eve of St Agnes'; Provocative throughout.)

Stillinger, J., *Twentieth Century Interpretations of Keats's Odes* (Englewood Cliffs, N. J., 1968).
Van Ghent, D., (rev. Robinson, J. C.) *Keats: the Myth of the Hero* (Princeton, 1983).
Vendler, H., *The Odes of John Keats* (Cambridge, Mass., 1983).
Walsh, W., *Introduction to Keats* (1981). (A short and useful book.)
*Ward, A., *John Keats; the Making of a Poet* (1963). (Good on life and works.)
Wasserman, E. R., *The Finer Tone: Keats's Major Poems* (Baltimore and London, 1953, revised 1967).
White, R. S., *Keats as a Reader of Shakespeare* (Norman, Oklahoma, 1987).

ROGERS, Samuel (1763–1855), born in London, the son of a banker. He was a rich man, and renowned for his hospitality, especially his famous breakfasts. *The Pleasures of Memory* published 1792; *Italy*, 1822; at the age of eighty-seven he declined the Laureateship on the death of Wordsworth; died 1855.

Bishop, M., ed., *Recollections of the Table Talk of Samuel Rogers by A. Dyce* (1952).
Clayden, P. W., *The Early Life of Samuel Rogers* (1887).
Clayden, P. W., *Rogers and his Contemporaries* (1889).
Hale, J. R., ed., *The Italian Journal of Samuel Rogers* (1956).
Watson, J. R., 'Samuel Rogers: The Last Augustan', in *Augustan Worlds*, ed. by J. C. Hilson, M. M. B. Jones and J. R. Watson (Leicester, 1976).

SCOTT, Sir Walter (1771–1832), born Edinburgh, son of a lawyer; educated Royal High School and Edinburgh University. He became a lawyer, and was called to the Scottish Bar in 1792; during vacations he made expeditions into the Borders collecting folk-songs and ballads, publishing *Ministrelsy of the Scottish Border* in three volumes (1802–3). Scott's great period as a poet was from 1805 to 1812, after which he was eclipsed by the rising star of Byron: *The Lay of the Last Minstrel* (1805), *Marmion* (1808), and *The Lady of the Lake* (1810) are his most notable poems. In 1812 he purchased Abbotsford, and began building a house there; he began writing novels, publishing *Waverley* in 1814, and a series of other masterpieces thereafter. In 1826 the publishing house of which he was a partner went bankrupt, and Scott worked heroically to pay off the debts; his health gave way under the strain, and he died 21 September 1832.

Robertson, J. L., ed., *The Poetical Works of Scott* (Oxford, 1894). (Standard one-volume edition.)
Crawford, T., ed., *Sir Walter Scott, Selected Poems* (Oxford, 1972). (Annotated.)

Scott is the subject of one of the great biographies of the language, by J. G. Lockhart (first published 1838, subsequently reprinted many times). See also:
Buchan, J., *Sir Walter Scott* (1932).
Crawford, T., *Scott* (Edinburgh, 1963). (Chapter 3 on Scott as poet.)
Johnson, E., *Sir Walter Scott, the Great Unknown* (1970).

See: Alexander, J. H., '*The Lay of the Last Minstrel*': *Three Essays*
        (Salzburg, 1978).
        Davie, D., 'The Poetry of Sir Walter Scott', *Proceedings of the British
        Academy*, 47 (1961), 60–75.

See also the essays by William Ruddick, J. H. Alexander, and
Kathryn Sutherland in:
        J. H. Alexander and David Hewitt, eds, *Scott and His Influence*
        (Aberdeen, 1983).
        Wilson, A. N., *The Laird of Abbotsford* (1980).

SHELLEY, Percy Bysshe (1792–1822), born Sussex, the son of Sir Timothy
    Shelley, Baronet. Educated at Eton and University College Oxford; sent
    down from Oxford after two terms (March 1811) for publishing (with T.
    J. Hogg) *The Necessity of Atheism*. Married Harriet Westbrook, August
    1811: lived in various parts of Great Britain; wrote *Queen Mab* (1812). Left
    Harriet for Mary Wollstonecraft Godwin, 1814; married Mary after Harriet's
    suicide, 1816. *Alastor* written near Windsor, published 1816; in that year met
    Byron in Switzerland. *Laon and Cythna* (later retitled *The Revolt of Islam*)
    written back in England, 1816–17. In 1818 left England: visited Byron at
    Venice ('Lines written among the Euganean Hills', 'Julian and Maddalo');
    thence to Naples, Rome, and Pisa (*Prometheus Unbound* 1818–19, published
    1820). Moved to Lerici, April 1821; drowned at sea, 8 July 1822.

        Ingpen, R. and Peck, W. E., eds, *The Complete Works of Percy Bysshe
        Shelley*, 10 vols (1965).
        Hutchinson, T., revised Matthews, G. M., *The Complete Poetical
        Works of Percy Bysshe Shelley* (1970). (A revision of the useful
        one-volume edition.)
        Matthews, G. and Everest, K. (eds), The Poems of Shelley (1989–).
        (Longman's English Poets edition, with full headnotes and
        annotated explanatory notes to each poem.)
        Rogers, N., ed., *The Complete Poetical Works of Shelley* (Oxford,
        1972–; in progress, two volumes published). (Criticized by some
        textual scholars for not using earliest text.)
        Jones, F. L., ed., *The Letters of Percy Bysshe Shelley*, 2 vols (Oxford,
        1964).

        If there has been a spectacular revival of Wordsworth criticism since
        the early 1950s, there has been a similar reassessment of Shelley in
        the 1970s. This took time to emerge after the criticism of Shelley in
        the 1930s by two most influential figures:

        Eliot, T. S., *The Use of Poetry and the Use of Criticism* (1933).
        Leavis, F. R., *Revaluation* (1936). (Hostile chapter on Shelley.)

Thereafter see:
        *Allott, M., ed., *Essays on Shelley* (Liverpool, 1982).
        *Arnold, M., *Essays in Criticism*, Second Series (1888).
        Baker, C., *Shelley's Major Poetry: The Fabric of a Vision* (Princeton,
        1948).
        Bloom, H., *Shelley's Mythmaking* (New Haven and London, 1959).

Blunden, E., *Shelley, A Life Story* (1946). (Now largely superseded, it stills reads well.)

Bradley, A. C., 'Shelley's View of Poetry', *Oxford Lectures On Poetry* (1909).

*Butter, P., *Shelley's Idols of the Cave* (Edinburgh, 1954). (Good on symbols.)

Cameron, K. N., *The Young Shelley* (1950). (Subtitled 'The Genesis of a Radical'.)

Cameron, K. N., *Shelley, The Golden Years* (1974). (A sober and reliable account.)

Chernaik, J., *The Lyrics of Shelley* (Cleveland and London, 1972).

Clark, T., *Embodying Revolution: The Figure of the Poet in Shelley* (1989).

Cronin, R., *Shelley's Poetic Thought* (1981). (Good on the relationship between thought and expression.)

Curran, S., *Shelley's Cenci: Scorpions Ringed with Fire* (Princeton, 1970).

Curran, S., *Shelley's Annus Mirabilis* (San Marino, California, 1975). (Shelley from autumn 1818 to January 1820; very good on Eastern philosophy.)

*Dawson, P. M. S., *The Unacknowledged Legislator: Shelley and Politics* (1980).

Duerksen, R. A., *Shelley's Poetry of Involvement* (1989).

Grabo, C., *A Newton among Poets* (Chapel Hill, N. C., 1930). (On the use of science in *Prometheus Unbound*.)

Hall, S. (ed.), *Approaches to Teaching Shelley's Poetry* (New York, 1990).

Holmes, R., *Shelley: The Pursuit* (1974). (Almost too determined to debunk myths, but a lively account.)

Hughes, A. M. D., *The Nascent Mind of Shelley* (Oxford, 1947).

King-Hele, D., *Shelley: His Thought and Work* (1960). (Useful on Shelley and science.)

*Leighton, A., *Shelley and the Sublime* (1984). (Good on such poems as 'Mont Blanc.')

Lewis, C. S., 'Shelley, Dryden, and Mr Eliot' in *Selected Literary Essays*, ed. Hooper, W. (Cambridge, 1969).

McNiece, G., *Shelley and the Revolutionary Idea* (Cambridge, Mass., (1969).

Murphy, J. V., *The Dark Angel* (1975). (On Shelley and the Gothic tradition.)

*Notopoulos, J. A., *The Platonism of Shelley* (Durham, N. C., 1949). (Fine study of the influence of Plato, and of Shelley's 'natural Platonism'.)

O'Neill, M., *The Human Mind's Imaginings: Conflict and achievement in Shelley's poetry* (Oxford, 1989). (Sensitive to the qualities of the verse in the individual poems.)

*O'Neill, M., *Percy Bysshe Shelley: A Literary Life* (1989). (Sets Shelley's poetry in context; an excellent book for students.)

*Pirie, D., *Shelley* (Milton Keynes, 1988). (Useful Open University introduction.)

Pulos, C. E., *The Deep Truth: A Study of Shelley's Scepticism* (Lincoln, Nebraska, 1954).

*Raine, K., Introduction to *Shelley* (Harmondsworth, 1973). (Penguin 'Poet to Poet' series.)

Reiman, D. H., *Percy Bysshe Shelley* (Revised edition, New York, 1989).

Ridenour, G. M., ed., *Shelley: A Collection of Critical Essays* (Englewood Cliffs, N. J., 1965).

Robinson, C. E., *Shelley and Byron: The Snake and Eagle wreathed in Fight* (Baltimore and London, 1976). (Principally on Shelley.)

Rogers, N., *Shelley at Work* (Oxford, 1956).

Wasserman, E. R., *Shelley, a Critical Reading* (Baltimore and London, 1971).

Webb, T., *The Violet in the Crucible* (Oxford, 1976). (On Shelley as translator.)

*Webb, T., *Shelley: A Voice not Understood* (Manchester, 1977). (An excellent introduction.)

Welburn, A. J., *Power and Self-Consciousness in the Poetry of Shelley* (1986).

White, N. I., *Shelley*, revised edition (1947).

Wilson, M., *Shelley's Later Poetry* (New York, 1959). (Subtitled 'A Study of his Prophetic Imagination').

Woodings, R. B., ed., *Shelley* (1968). (Essays.)

SOUTHEY, Robert (1774–1843), born Bristol, son of a shopkeeper, Educated Westminster School and Balliol College, Oxford, but left without taking a degree, 1974; friendship with Coleridge and others, and forming of the 'Pantisocracy' scheme; married Edith Fricker, 1795. Wrote revolutionary plays (*The Fall of Robespierre*, with Coleridge; *Wat Tyler, Joan of Arc*). Travelled to Portugal, 1795–96; legal studies in London, 1796–97; wrote *Madoc*, 1798–99; *Thalaba*, 1799–1800. Settled in Lake District at Greta Hall, Keswick, 1803; Poet Laureate, 1813. Became a prolific prose writer and an industrious book-collector, especially on Spain and Portugal; wrote *A Vision of Judgement*, a monumentally insensitive poem with a Preface attacking Byron. After 1839 Southey's mind gave way; he died 21 March 1843.

Southey, C. C., ed., *The Life and Correspondence of the Late Robert Southey*, 6 vols (1849–50).

Curry, K., ed., *New Letters of Robert Southey*, 2 vols (New York, 1965).

Simmons, J., ed., *Southey* (1945). (Standard biography.)

See: Carnall, G., *Robert Southey and His Age* (Oxford, 1969). (Major study of Southey and the politics of his time.)

Curry, K., *Southey* (1975). (A short introduction.)

Raimond, J., *Robert Southey, l'homme et son temps, son œuvre, son rôle* (Paris, 1968). (The best book on Southey as a poet; in French.)

WORDSWORTH, William (1770–1850), born at Cockermouth, Cumberland, second of five children of John Wordsworth, attorney and land-agent; in 1778 his mother died, and the boys were sent to school at Hawkshead, Westmorland, lodging with Ann Tyson; in 1783 his father died, leaving the children in guardianship of uncles in Penrith, whom the young Wordsworth disliked. In 1787, matriculated at St John's College, Cambridge: spent his first long vacation back at Hawkshead, his second with his beloved sister Dorothy, and his third (just before Final Examinations, 1790) on a walking tour of Switzerland with Robert Jones. To France, November 1791: important and formative friendship with Michel Beaupuy, and met Annette

Vallon; their child, Caroline, born December 1792. Wordsworth returned to England, late 1792: shocked by declaration of war between England and France, February/March 1793; published *An Evening Walk* and *Descriptive Sketches* (1793). Wrote unpublished 'Letter to the Bishop of Llandaff' supporting revolution, but disturbed by its course under Robespierre; wrote 'Salisbury Plain' poems, 1793–95; *The Borderers*, 1796. Friendship with Coleridge (whom he probably first met in 1795) led to residence near him in north Somerset and to composition of *Lyrical Ballads* (1798). To Germany, 1798–99, where he began work on poem about his own childhood, later *The Prelude* (finished 1805, revised and published 1850). Returned to England, and took up residence at Grasmere, December 1799; published second edition of *Lyrical Ballads* (1800), with Preface; married Mary Hutchinson from Sockburn, Co. Durham, 1802. Wordsworth was greatly distressed by the death of his brother John at sea, February 1805, and turned for consolation to a new friend, Sir George Beaumont (Coleridge in Malta and Italy); published *Poems in Two Volumes* (1807); contributed to Coleridge's periodical *The Friend* (1809–10), and produced Tract *On the Convention of Cintra* (1809); estrangement from Coleridge, 1810–12, following malicious tale-bearing of Basil Montagu. Appointed Distributor of Stamps for Westmorland, and moved to Rydal Mount, 1813; published *The Excursion* (1814); *The River Duddon* (1820), and various collected editions of the *Poems* (1827, 1832, 1836–37, 1849). Hon. DCL, University of Durham, 1838; Poet Laureate, 1843; died 23 April 1850.

The most recent and comprehensive edition of the poems is the series of volumes entitled *The Cornell Wordsworth* (1975–, in progress). This edition contains photographs of the original manuscripts, in addition to the usual texts, variants, and notes: it is in process of replacing the edition by E. de Selincourt and H. Darbishire, *The Poetical Works of William Wordsworth*,, 5 vols (Oxford, 1940–49).

The one-volume *Poetical Works of Wordsworth*, ed. Thomas Hutchinson, revised by E. de Selincourt (1936), is convenient, but it prints the 1850 text of *The Prelude* and does not contain 'Home at Grasmere', 'The Ruined Cottage', and 'The Pedlar' (except in so far as these are found incorporated in Book I of *The Excursion*). J. O. Hayden's two-volume Penguin edition (1977) prints the poems chronologically, rather than in Wordsworth's own idiosyncratic arrangement.

The Prelude, ed. E. de Selincourt, second edition revised by H. Darbishire (Oxford, 1959) prints the 1805 and 1850 texts. There is a convenient three-text edition (1798–99, 1805, 1850) edited by Jonathan Wordsworth, M. H. Abrams, and S. Gill (1979), which has added to J. C. Maxwell's two-text edition (Harmondsworth, 1971).

Lyrical Ballads has been edited by R. L. Brett and A. R. Jones (1963; second edition, 1991) which gives the poems printed in 1798 and 1800, with later variants. *Lyrical Ballads, 1798*, has been edited by W. J. B. Owen (1967, 1969). The 1805 edition has been edited by Derek Roper (Plymouth, 1987).

The 'Oxford Authors' *William Wordsworth*, ed. S. Gill (Oxford, 1984), contains a selection of the major poems in chronological order.
Wordsworth: the 1807 Poems (1990) has been edited by A. Jones.
de Selincourt, E., ed., *Journals of Dorothy Wordsworth*, 2 vols (1941).
Owen, W. J. B., and Smyser, J. W., eds, *The Prose Works of William Wordsworth*, 3 vols (Oxford, 1974).

Shaver, C. L., Moorman, M., and Hill, A. G., eds, *The Letters of William and Dorothy Wordsworth*, second edition (Oxford, 1967–82).

The early criticism of Wordsworth is very valuable, and the essays by Hazlitt and the chapters of Coleridge's *Biographia Literaria* are essential reading:

Hazlitt, W., 'My First Acquaintance with Poets' in *Complete Works*, ed. Howe, P. P., 21 vols (London, 1930–34), vol, XVII.
Hazlitt, W., 'Mr Wordsworth' in *Complete Works*, vol. XI.
Coleridge, S. T., *Biographia Literaria*, Chs 4, 14, 17–22.

See: *Arnold, M., 'Wordsworth', *Essays in Criticism*, second series (1888).
        *Bradley, A. C., 'Wordsworth', *Oxford Lectures on Poetry* (1909).
        *Legouis, E., *The Early Life of Wordsworth* (1897).

A reader of G. T. Dunklin, ed., *Wordsworth: Centenary Studies* (Princeton, 1951) could be forgiven for thinking that Wordsworth was no longer a 'living' author. Since then there has been a remarkable resurgence of interest in his work, and a new discovery of his greatness as a poet.

See: Abrams, M. H., ed., *Wordsworth* (Englewood Cliffs, N.J., 1972). ('Twentieth–century views' collection).
        Austin, F., *The Language of Wordsworth and Coleridge* (1989).
        Baker, J., *Time and Mind in Wordsworth's Poetry* (Detroit, 1980). (Good on time and mortality in Wordsworth.)
        Bate, J., *Romantic Ecology: Wordsworth and the Environmental Tradition* (1991).
        Bateson, F. W., *Wordsworth: A Re-interpretation* (1954, revised edition 1956). (Good readings of individual poems, intelligent, controversial in its emphasis on the William-Dorothy relationship.)
        *Beer, J. B., *Wordsworth and the Human Heart* (1978). (On his humanity.)
        *Beer, J. B., *Wordsworth in Time* (1979). (On 'the human consciousness within the time-process'.)
        Bewell, A., *Wordsworth and the Enlightenment* (New Haven, 1989). (Good on Wordsworth and anthropology.)
        Byatt, A. S., *Unruly Times: Wordsworth and Coleridge in their Time* (1970).
        Curtis, J. R., *Wordsworth's Experiments with Tradition* (Ithaca and London, 1971). (On the poems written in 1802; texts printed.)
        *Danby, J. F., *The Simple Wordsworth* (1960). (A most humane, generous, and moving account, especially of *Lyrical Ballads*.)
        Davies, H. S., *Wordsworth and the Worth of Words* (Cambridge, 1987). (Good on word-patterns in Wordsworth.)
        Devlin, D. D., *Wordsworth and the Poetry of Epitaphs* (1980). (Begins, like Ferguson, from Wordsworth's 'Essays on Epitaphs'; helpful.)
        Durrant, G., *William Wordsworth* (Cambridge, 1969). (Introductory.)
        Durrant, G., *Wordsworth and the Great System* (Cambridge, 1970). (Good on Wordsworth and science.)
        Ferguson, F., *Wordsworth: Language as Counter-Spirit* (New Haven and London, 1977).
        Galperin, W. H., *Revision and Authority in Wordsworth: The Interpretation of a Career* (Philadelphia, 1989).

Garber, F., *Wordsworth and the Poetry of Encounter* (Urbana, Ill., and London, 1971).

*Gill, S., *William Wordsworth: A Life* (Oxford, 1989).

Gilpin, G. H. (ed.), *Critical Essays on William Wordsworth* (Boston, Mass., 1990).

*Hamilton, P., *Wordsworth* (Brighton, 1986).

*Hartman, G., *Wordsworth's Poetry, 1787–1814* (New Haven and London, 1964). (A massive, impressive study on the self and the external world, challenging many received notions about man and nature; good bibliography. See also Hartman's essay on 'Tintern Abbey' in *The Unmediated Vision* (New Haven and London, 1954.)

Hartman, G. H., *The Unremarkable Wordsworth* (Minneapolis, 1987). (A collection of Professor Hartman's essays on Wordsworth.)

Hodgson, J. A., *Wordsworth's Philosophical Poetry. 1997–1814* (Lincoln, Nebraska, 1980).

*Jacobus, M., *Tradition and Experiment in Wordsworth's Lyrical Ballads (1978)* (Oxford, 1976). (Sharp, incisive, sets *Lyrical Ballads* in the context of earlier poetry.)

Jacobus, M., *Romanticism, Writing, and Sexual Difference: Essays on 'The Prelude'* (Oxford, 1989).

Johnston, K., *Wordsworth and The Recluse* (Ithaca and London, 1984). (On Wordsworth's unfinished 'The Recluse', including *The Excursion.*)

*Jones, J., *The Egotistical Sublime: A History of Wordsworth's Imagination* (1954). (A seminal account of the workings of Wordsworth's imagination.)

Kelley, T. M., *Wordsworth's Revisionary Aesthetics* (Cambridge, 1988).

Kneale, J. D., *Monumental Writing: Aspects of rhetoric in Wordsworth's Poetry* (Lincoln, Neb., 1989).

Leavis, F. R., *Revaluation* (1963). (Essay on Wordsworth.)

Levinson, M., *Wordsworth's Great Period Poems: Four Essays* (Cambridge, 1986). (On 'Tintern Abbey', 'Michael', the 'Immortality Ode', and 'Peele Castle'.)

Lindenberger, H., *On Wordsworth's Prelude* (Princeton, 1963). (Fine detailed study of the poem, especially its use of time.)

Liu, A., *Wordsworth: the sense of history* (Stanford, 1989).

*Moorman, M., *William Wordsworth, The Early Years, 1770–1799* (Oxford, 1958).

Moorman, M., *William Wordsworth, The Later Years, 1800–1850* (Oxford, 1965).

*Parrish, S. M., *The Art of the Lyrical Ballads* (Cambridge, Mass., 1973). (Good on the dramatic element.)

Perkins, D., *Wordsworth and the Poetry of Sincerity* (Cambridge, Mass., 1964).

Pinion, F. B., *A Wordsworth Chronology* (1988).

*Pirie, D. B., *William Wordsworth: The Poetry of Grandeur and of Tenderness* (1982). (Refreshing, sensitive to two central features of Wordsworth's poetry.)

*Prickett, S., *Wordsworth and Coleridge, The Lyrical Ballads* (1975). (Very short, to the point.)

Reed, M. L., *Wordsworth: The Chronology of the Early Years 1770–1799* (Cambridge, Mass., 1967).

Reed, M. L., *Wordsworth, The Chronology of the Middle Years 1800–1815* (Cambridge, Mass, 1975).

*Ricks, C., *The Force of Poetry* (Oxford, 1984). (Reprints two of Ricks's essays on Wordsworth.)

Roe, N., *Wordsworth and Coleridge: The Radical Years* (Oxford, 1988). (On the two poets and the French Revolution.)

Ruoff, G. W., *Wordsworth and Coleridge: the making of the major lyrics, 1802–1804* (Hemel Hempstead, 1989).

Salvesen, G., *The Landscape of Memory* (1965). (Places Wordsworth in the tradition of confessional literature.)

Sheats, P. D., *The Making of Wordsworth's Poetry, 1785–1798* (Cambridge, Mass., 1973). (Straightforward work on the early poems.)

Sherry, C., *Wordsworth's Poetry of the Imagination* (1980). (On the childhood vision.)

Simpson, D., *Wordsworth and the Figurings of the Real* (1982). (On the mind and its environment.)

Simpson, D., *Wordsworth's Historical Imagination: The Poetry of Displacement* (1987). (On Wordsworth as related to his social and historical circumstances.)

Stein, E. *Wordsworth's Art of Allusion* (Pennsylvania, 1988).

Thomas, W. K., and Ober, W. U., *A Mind For Ever Voyaging: Wordsworth at work portraying Newton and Science* (Edmonton, 1989).

Todd, F. M., *Politics and the Poet* (1957). (On Wordsworth and politics.)

Trilling, L., *The Liberal Imagination* (1951). (Essay on 'The Immortality Ode'.)

Turner, J., *Wordsworth: Play and Politics: A study of Wordsworth's Poetry, 1787–1800* (1986). (Good on the idea of 'Play' as used by D. W. Winnicott, applied to Wordsworth's poetry.)

Ward, J. P., *Wordsworth's Language of Men* (Brighton, 1984). (Includes interesting material on sentence structure and length.)

Watson, J. R., *Wordsworth's Vital Soul* (1983). (On the sacred and profane in Wordsworth's poetry, using religious and anthropological ideas.)

Wesling, D., *Wordsworth and the Adequacy of Landscape* (1970). (Short, intelligent book on Wordsworth's use of landscape.)

Williams, J., *Wordsworth: Romantic poetry and revolution politics* (Manchester, 1989).

Wordsworth, J., *William Wordsworth: the Borders of Vision* (1983).

Wordsworth, J., ed., *Bicentenary Wordsworth Studies* (Ithaca and London, 1970). (Much more buoyant than Dunklin's 1951 *Centenary Studies*, indicating the renewed interest in Wordsworth.)

Wordsworth, J., Jaye, M. C., and Woof, R., *William Wordsworth and the Age of English Romanticism* (New Brunswick, NJ, 1987).

Index